독해력 UP

펀펀 리딩
플러스 100

펀펀 리딩 플러스 100

초판 1쇄 인쇄 2025년 2월 27일
초판 1쇄 발행 2025년 3월 18일

지은이   전은지
발행인   임충배
홍보/마케팅   양경자
편집   김인숙, 왕혜영
디자인   이경자, 김혜원
펴낸곳   도서출판 삼육오(Pub.365)
제작   (주)피앤엠123

출판신고 2014년 4월 3일
등록번호 제406-2014-000035호

경기도 파주시 산남로 183-25
TEL 031-946-3196 / FAX 050-4244-9979
홈페이지 www.pub365.co.kr

ISBN 979-11-94543-09-1 13740
© 2025 전은지 & PUB.365

독해력 UP

펀펀 리딩 플러스 100

저자 **전은지**

PUB윤오

All-In-One Reading Book
독해 + 문법 + 어휘 + 듣기

흔히 한국인의 영어는 읽기 능력에 비해 말하기, 듣기 능력이 상대적으로 떨어진다고 합니다.

실제로 오랫동안 영어를 공부한 사람들 중에 문자로 된 글은 잘 읽고 이해하는데, 외국인과 대면했을 때 자신의 의사를 제대로 전달하지 못하는 경우가 많습니다. 말하지 못하는 영어는 죽은 영어라는 인식과 함께, 요즘은 말하기 능력을 짧은 시간에, 가장 쉽고 효과적으로 향상시킬 수 있는 교재가 영어 교육 시장에서 큰 인기를 얻고 있습니다.

그러나 영어를 포함한 외국어 학습을 논할 때, 읽기, 말하기, 듣기는 사실상 분리된 학습이라 볼 수 없습니다. 단어를 모르는 사람은 문장의 뜻을 이해할 수 없고, 단어 각각의 뜻은 알지만 문법을 알지 못하는 사람 역시 문장의 의미를 정확히 파악할 수 없습니다. 문자로 된 영문을 읽고 이해하지 못하는 사람은 영어로 잘 말할 수 없고, 발음을 제대로 알아듣지 못하는 사람은 제대로 된 발음으로 말할 수 없습니다. 이렇듯 외국어 학습에서 독해, 문법, 어휘, 듣기, 말하기는 서로 밀접하게 관련되어 있어서 이 중 일부분에만 치우친 학습은 올바른 외국어 학습이라 볼 수 없습니다.

이 책은 이러한 사실을 고려하여 독해를 기본으로 문법, 어휘, 듣기 학습이 동시에 효과적으로 이루어질 수 있도록 구성하였습니다. 여러 분야의 학습을 동시에 도모하는데 독해를 기본으로 한 데에는 이유가 있습니다. 어떤 글을 읽고 그 의미를 파악하고 이해하는 능력을 독해력이라고 하는데, 외국어 학습에서 독해력은 대단히 중요한 능력입니다. 외국어 학습의 목적과 목표는 개인마다 차이가 있겠지만, 독해력 향상은 누구에게나 외국어 학습의 중요한 목표 중 하나 꼽힙니다. 대다수 외국어 관련 시험에서 독해 문항이 주를 이루는 것도 이 때문입니다.

독해력을 향상시키려면, 일단 어휘력이 기본이 되어야 합니다. 그러나 어휘 하나만으로 독해력을 높일 수 없고, 기본적인 문법, 구문에 대한 학습이 병행되어야 합니다. 그래서 독해력 향상을 위한 학습은 어휘, 문법, 구문 학습이 반드시 함께 이루어져야 합니다. 이렇게 읽기 능력을 키울 때 듣기와 말하기까지 병행된다면 가장 이상적인 외국어 학습이라 할 수 있습니다.

이 책에 원어민의 MP3 파일을 제공하는 이유도 여기에 있습니다. 단순히 눈으로 읽고 의미를 파악하는 데서 끝나지 않고, 귀로 듣고 이를 따라서 소리 내어 반복적으로 읽는다면, 이 책 한 권으로 읽기, 듣기, 말하기까지 향상시킬 수 있을 것입니다.

Interesting Stories
재밌는 상식 + 다양한 분야별 지문

재미가 없으면 공부할 의욕이 생기질 않는 점을 고려하여 이 책에서 다루는 100편의 지문은 흥미롭고 유익한 주제 위주로 선별하였습니다. 또한, 아무리 재미있는 콘텐츠를 담고 있는 책이라도 실질적인 영어 학습에 별 도움이 되지 못한다면 쓸모없는 책이 되기 때문에, 선생님이 칠판에 판서하면서 수업하듯이 설명해 주는 학습의 하이라이트(Learning Spotlight)라는 코너를 마련하여 지문을 분석하고, 문장구조와 문법, 그리고 어휘의 첨삭 설명을 통해 혼자서 공부하는 데에도 큰 어려움이 없도록 배려하였습니다. 한 권의 독해책을 통해 재미와 공부라는 두 마리 토끼를 모두 잡을 수 있도록 노력하였습니다.

영어가 어렵게만 와닿고 흥미가 없어 영어 학습에 어려움을 겪고 있는 모든 분들에게 이 책이 사막의 '오아시스'이자 영어의 바른 길잡이가 되길 바라며, 재미있게 읽으면서 문법, 어휘뿐 아니라 독해력, 청취력, 말하기 능력까지 향상되는 기회가 될 수 있기를 바랍니다.

저자 전은지

01 Did You Know **Household Dust Is A Bunch Of Dead Skin Cells?**

Dust in your house is mostly made of dead skin cells. It is estimated that 30,000-40,000 dead skin cells are flaked off from your body per minute. Given the fact that the human body sheds dead skin cells constantly, we can say that common house dust is practically a bunch of dead skin cells.

Of course there are other things in household dust, such as the dried-up dead bodies of dust mites. Dust mites eat humans' dead skin cells and live in bedding, carpets and soft furnishings. When they are alive, they are the cause of allergies. After they die, they become part of household dust. It's not surprising that they are hated by everyone.

Another component is tiny fibers fallen from clothing, furniture fabrics and bedding. Furthermore, if you have pets in your house, your cute little pets will highly contribute to dust production since they drop all kinds of things. Pets drop dead skin cells and dried-up dead bodies of pet mites as well as hair. And if they wear dog clothing, they will also drop tiny bits of fiber.

STEP 01 독해지문

독해지문은 총 100편으로, 크게 10개의 일상 생활에서 흔히 만날 수 있는 주제들이며, 1개의 주제에 각 10편의 지문이 들어 있습니다. 일반적인 상식, 그리고 재미와 흥미를 느낄 수 있는 내용으로 구성되어 있습니다. 재미있게 읽으며 영어 실력은 물론 다양한 배경 지식도 쌓을 수 있는 기회가 될 것입니다

STEP 02 어휘

본문의 내용을 이해하는데 핵심적인 단어와 숙어, 관용어 표현 등을 정리하여 제공합니다. 해석을 보지않고 내용을 이해하도록 도전해 보세요!

Words & Expressions

dust 먼지 be made of …로 만들어지다 cell 세포, 감방, 전지 skin cell 피부세포 it is estimated that … 라고 추정되다 flake 벗어져 나온 얇은 조각, 벗겨지다, 벗어져 나오다(off) per minute 1분당 shed 헛간, (피, 눈물, 잎)흘리다, (허물)벗다 constantly 끊임없이 practically 실질적으로, 사실상 a bunch of 다수의(+복수명사) dust mite 먼지 진드기 bedding 침구 soft furnishing 가정용 직물 the cause of allergy 알레르기 원인 component 구성요소 tiny 작은 fiber 섬유 fabric 직물, 천 furniture fabric 가구용 직물 pet 애완동물 contribute 공헌하다, 기여하다 highly contribute to …에 대단히 기여하다 dog clothing 애완견용 옷 tiny bits of fibers 작은 섬유 조각들

01 Did You Know **Household Dust Is A Bunch Of Dead Skin Cells?**

1. (정답 : c) 이 글의 요지를 고르세요.
  a. 인간의 몸은 일 분만에 3만개 이상의 죽은 피부 세포를 떨어뜨린다.
  b. 먼지 진드기가 나쁜 이유는 인간의 죽은 피부 세포를 먹기 때문이다.
  c. 집 먼지는 대부분 죽은 피부 세포로 이루어졌다.
  d. 집 안에서 애완동물을 키우는 건 건강에 해롭다.

2. (정답 : b) 집안의 먼지는 _____ 로 이루어져 있다.
  a. 먼지 진드기와 애완동물의 털
  b. 죽은 피부 세포, 죽은 먼지 진드기의 마른 사체와 작은 섬유 조각
  c. 옷, 가구용 직물과 침구
  d. 애완동물 진드기와 애견용 옷

🐜 **Understanding Checkpoint**

1. What is the main idea of the story?
  a. Human body sheds over 30,000 dead skin cells per minute.
  b. Dust mites are bad because they eat humans' dead skin cells.
  c. Household dust mainly consists of dead skin cells.
  d. Raising pets inside the house is bad for your health.

2. Dust in your house is made of _____.
  a. Dust mites and pets' hair
  b. Dead skin cells, dried dead bodies of dust mites and tiny fibers
  c. Clothing, furniture fabrics and bedding
  d. Pet mites and dog clothing

3. Choose the correct words for each sentence.
  a. Due to the civil war, an estimated / estimate / estimation 3 million people were forced to live in unhealthy and dangerous places.
  b. I like cake as far as / as well as / as long as doughnuts, but sandwich is my most favorite.
  c. When I went into the shed, I shed tears of fear because there was a snake shedded / shedding / shed its skin.

Answer: 1. c 3. b 3. estimated / as well as / shedding

STEP 03 독해 체크

독해 내용에 대한 세 가지 형식의 문제를 풉니다. 문제는 1) 지문의 내용을 제대로 이해했는지 요지 또는 제목을 찾는 문제, 2) 세부적인 내용을 이해하였는지를 묻는 문제, 3) 지문에 나온 단어와 문법, 문장 구문을 응용하여 맞는 표현을 고르는 문제로 구성되어 있습니다.

▶ 해설은 홈페이지(www.pub365.co.kr) 무료로 다운로드

MP3 제공

STEP 04 리스닝 드릴

지문의 이해를 바탕으로 정확한 발음 확인과 듣기 실력 향상을 위해 받아쓰기를 합니다. Dictation은 독해지문과 동일한 지문으로, 발음, 청취 측면에서 훈련이 필요한 단어나 표현, 또는 본문의 주요 내용 위주로 빈칸 처리가 되어 있습니다. 처음은 그냥 들어보고, 다음은 빈칸을 채워보고, 마지막으로 소리 내어 지문을 다시 읽을 것을 추천합니다. MP3 파일을 듣고, 따라 읽는 과정에서 듣기와 말하기, 발음 훈련뿐 아니라 본문 내용을 복습하는 효과까지 얻을 수 있습니다.

STEP 05
학습 하이라이트

마치 선생님이 칠판에 판서하며 수업하듯 문장 구조와 문법, 어휘를 천천히 파헤쳐 봅니다. 혼자서도 어렵지 않게 공부할 수 있으며, 특히 초급 단계에서는 반드시 알고 있어야 할 필수 어휘는 형광색으로 표시해두었습니다.

STEP 06 부록

1) **단어장** : Words & Expressions에서 다룬 모든 단어를 알파벳순으로 정리하였습니다. 단어의 위치도 표시되어 있으므로, 복습용으로 활용할 수 있습니다. 굳이 외우지 않아도 되는 수준 높은 어휘는 회색처리 되어 있습니다.

2) **구두점의 쓰임** : 콤마, 하이픈, 세미콜론 등 지문에 자주 등장하는 구두점의 정의와 용례를 정리하여 부록으로 담았습니다.

 목차

Chapter 06 Myth Or Fact

Chapter 07 The Supernatural

Chapter 08 Interesting Stories

Chapter 09 The Amazing Records

Chapter 01

Health

MP3

Dust in your house is mostly made of dead skin cells. It is estimated that 30,000-40,000 dead skin cells are flaked off from your body per minute. Given the fact that the human body sheds dead skin cells constantly, we can say that common house dust is practically a bunch of dead skin cells.

Of course there are other things in household dust, such as the dried-up dead bodies of dust mites. Dust mites eat humans' dead skin cells and live in bedding, carpets and soft furnishings. When they are alive, they are the cause of allergies. After they die, they become part of household dust. It's not surprising that they are hated by everyone.

Another component is tiny fibers fallen from clothing, furniture fabrics and bedding. Furthermore, if you have pets in your house, your cute little pets will highly contribute to dust production since they drop all kinds of things. Pets drop dead skin cells and dried-up dead bodies of pet mites as well as hair. And if they wear dog clothing, they will also drop tiny bits of fiber.

Words & Expressions

dust 먼지 be made of …로 만들어지다 cell 세포, 감방, 전지 skin cell 피부세포 It is estimated that … 라고 추정되다 flake 떨어져 나온 얇은 조각, 벗겨지다, 떨어져 나오다(off) per minute 1분당 shed 헌간, (피, 눈물, 땀)흘리다, (허물을)벗다 constantly 끊임없이 practically 실질적으로, 사실상 a bunch of 다수의(+ 복수명사) dust mite 먼지 진드기 bedding 침구 soft furnishing 가정용 직물 the cause of allergy 알레르기 원인 component 구성요소 tiny 작은 fiber 섬유 fabric 직물, 천 furniture fabric 가구용 직물 pet 애완동물 contribute 공헌하다, 기여하다 highly contribute to …에 대단히 기여하다 dog clothing 애완견용 옷 tiny bits of fibers 작은 섬유 조각들

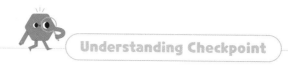

1. What is the main idea of the story?

    a. Human body sheds over 30,000 dead skin cells per minutes.

    b. Dust mites are bad because they eat humans' dead skin cells.

    c. Household dust mainly consists of dead skin cells.

    d. Raising pets inside the house is bad for your health.

2. Dust in your house is made of _____ .

    a. Dust mites and pets' hair

    b. Dead skin cells, dried dead bodies of dust mites and tiny fibers

    c. Clothing, furniture fabrics and bedding

    d. Pet mites and dog clothing

3. Choose the correct words for each sentence.

    a. Due to the civil war, an <u>estimated</u> / <u>estimate</u> / <u>estimation</u> 3 million people were forced to live in unhealthy and dangerous places.

    b. I like cake <u>as far as</u> / <u>as well as</u> / <u>as long as</u> doughnuts, but sandwich is my most favorite.

    c. When I went into the shed, I shed tears of fear because there was a snake <u>shedded</u> / <u>shedding</u> / <u>shed</u> its skin.

Answer 1. c 2. b 3. estimated ǀ as well as ǀ shedding

Listening Drill – Dictation

Dust in your house is mostly made of dead skin cells. _____ 30,000-40,000 dead skin cells are _____ your body per minute. ____ the fact that the human body _____ constantly, we can say that common house dust is _____ a bunch of dead skin cells.

Of course there are other things in household dust, such as the dried-up dead bodies of dust mites. Dust mites eat humans' dead skin cells and live in bedding, carpets and soft furnishings. When they are alive, they are _____. After they die, they become part of household dust. It's not surprising that they are hated by everyone.

Another component is tiny fibers fallen from clothing, furniture fabrics and bedding. Furthermore, if you have pets in your house, your cute little pets will _____ dust production since they drop _____ of things. Pets drop dead skin cells and dried-up dead bodies of pet mites _____ hair. And if they wear dog clothing, they will also drop _____ fiber.

Did You Know Household Dust Is A Bunch Of Dead Skin Cells?

① Dust in your house is mostly made of dead skin **cells**.

= household dust (단수) + is   be made of …로 구성되다   cell 세포, 작은 방 (감방)

② It is **estimated** that 30,000-40,000 dead skin cells are flaked off from

that…로 추청되다   (수동태) …에서 벗겨져 나오다

your body per minute.

1분당, 1분마다

③ Given the fact that the human body **sheds** dead skin cells **constantly**,

that 이하를 감안할 때   shed v. 벗다, 벗어내다, 흘리다   끊임없이
= Considering the fact that

we can say that common house dust is **practically a bunch of** dead skin cells.

that 이하라고 말할 수 있다   실질적으로   뭉치, 다발, 묶음
                                                    (a bunch of 한 다발, two bunches of 두 다발)

④ Of course there are other things in household dust,

= dust in the house (household 가정)

(such as the dried-up dead bodies of dust **mites**).

a. 바싹 마른   dust 먼지 + mite 진드기
dried-up (a. 마른) + dead bodies (n. 시체)

⑤ Dust mites [1] eat humans' dead skin cells and [2] live in bedding, carpets

(圉) 주어 dust mites 동사 [1] eat [2] live   침구 (bed 침대)   카펫

and soft furnishings.

소프트 퍼니싱 (커튼, 침대 의자 등에 쓰이는 직물, 천)

⑥ When they are alive, they are (the cause of allergies).

dust mites   알레르기의 원인

⑦ After they die, they become part of household dust.

⑧ It's not surprising that they are hated by everyone.

= It's no wonder that (놀랍지 않다)   미움을 받다(수동태)

⑨ Another **component** is **tiny** fibers (fallen from clothing,

another + 단수명사 (component) + 단수동사 is   수식   tiny fibers (which are) fallen from…
                                                     …에서 떨어진 작음 섬유조각들 (수동)

furniture **fabrics** and bedding).

fabric n. 직물, 천 (fabricate v. 만들다, 꾸며내다)

⑩ Furthermore, if you have pets in your house, your cute little pets

가정법 현재 : if + 주어 you + 현재 동사 have, 주어 pets + will + 동사원형 contribute

will highly **contribute** to dust production since they drop all kinds of things.

…에(to) 상당히(highly) 기여하다(contribute)　　　　　　because they = your cute little pets

⑪ Pets drop ¹⁾ dead skin cells and ²⁾ dried-up dead bodies of pet mites

등 Pets drop ¹⁾ and ²⁾ as well as ³⁾

as well as ³⁾ hair.

…또한, 마찬가지로

⑫ And if they wear dog clothing, they will also drop tiny bits of fiber.

가정법 현재 : if + 주어 they + 현재 동사 wear, 주어 they + will + 동사원형 drop

---

집 먼지가 죽은 피부 세포 뭉치라는 거 아세요?

❶ 집 안 먼지는 대부분 죽은 피부 세포로 이루어져 있습니다.

❷ 일분마다 우리 몸에서 떨어지는 죽은 피부 세포가 대략 3-4만개 정도 됩니다.

❸ 우리 몸이 끊임없이 죽은 피부 세포를 흘린다는 걸 감안할 때, 일반적인 집 먼지는 실질적으로 죽은 피부 세포 뭉치라고 할 수 있습니다.

❹ 물론 집 먼지 중에는 다른 것들도 있는데, 이를 테면 죽은 먼지 진드기의 마른 시체를 들 수 있습니다.

❺ 먼지 진드기는 인간의 죽은 피부 세포를 먹으며 침구, 카펫, 직물 등에서 삽니다.

❻ 살아있을 때는 알레르기의 원인이 됩니다.

❼ 그리고 죽은 후에는 집 먼지가 됩니다.

❽ 먼지 진드기가 모두에게 미움을 받는 것도 당연합니다.

❾ 또 다른 성분은 옷, 천 가구, 침구에서 떨어진 작은 섬유입니다.

❿ 그래서 집 안에 애완동물이 있는 경우, 작고 귀여운 애완동물이 집안 먼지 생산에 큰 공을 세운다고 보면 되는데, 애완동물은 온갖 종류의 것들을 다 떨어뜨리기 때문입니다.

⓫ 애완동물은 죽은 피부 세포, 말라버린 애완동물 진드기 시체 뿐 아니라 털도 떨어뜨립니다.

⓬ 애완동물이 개 옷을 입고 있다면, 작은 섬유 조각도 떨어뜨릴 겁니다.

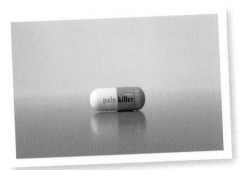

Painkillers are supposed to kill pain. But unfortunately sometimes and in some cases, painkillers can cause you pain because they carry side effects like any type of drug. They can be dangerous even under normal use, so be careful not to misuse or abuse them.

Many people know that painkillers commonly cause constipation. So painkiller users should drink lots of water when taking them. Also painkillers can have an effect on both your heart and lungs. Some painkillers not only cause a feeling of sedation but also slow down the functioning of the heart and lungs. So if you have a problem with your cardiovascular or respiratory systems, you have to be extra careful. And some people complain of a feeling of sleepiness after taking them. That's because certain kinds of painkillers numb the receptors in the body that sense pain.

Aside from these, there are other side effects of painkillers such as addiction, difficulty sleeping and hallucinations. The best way to prevent possible side effects is to consult your doctor before use.

Words & Expressions

painkiller 진통제 side effect 부작용 under normal use 정상적인 사용으로도 misuse 오용, 남용, 학대 constipation 변비 have an effect on …에 영향을 미치다 heart 심장 lung 폐 slow down 느리게 하다 functioning 기능, 작용 sedation 진정제가 투여된 상태 cardiovascular 심혈관의 respiratory 호흡기의 numb 마비시키다 receptor 수용기 sense 느끼다, 감각 addiction 중독 difficulty sleeping 불면증, 수면장애 (= insomnia) hallucination 환각 consult 상담하다

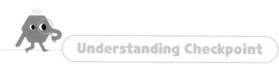

1. What is the main idea of this story?

    a. Painkillers may have unexpected side effects and cause pains.

    b. You should drink lots of water when taking painkillers.

    c. Painkillers are supposed to cause addiction and difficulty sleeping.

    d. Painkillers are evil so shouldn't be taken by anyone.

2. According to the article, almost every drug _____ .

    a. slows down the function of many organs

    b. can kill all kinds of pains

    c. causes hallucinations

    d. carries side effects

3. Choose the correct words for each sentence.

    a. Government officials who <u>misuse</u> / <u>mistreat</u> / <u>mistake</u> power for their own benefits must be punished.

    b. Are there any <u>the other</u> / <u>another</u> / <u>other</u> students who want to try these pants on?

    c. Please tell me if you have a problem <u>as</u> / <u>with</u> / <u>into</u> the cardiovascular system.

Answer **1.** a   **2.** d   **3.** misuse ǀ other ǀ with

Listening Drill ~ Dictation

Painkillers are supposed to kill pain. But unfortunately sometimes and in some cases, painkillers can cause you pain because they _____ like any type of drug. They can be dangerous even _____ , so be careful not to misuse or abuse them.

Many people know that pain killers _____ . So painkiller users should drink lots of water _____ . Also painkillers can have an effect on both your heart and lungs. Some painkillers not only cause _____ but also slow down the functioning of the heart and lungs. So if you have a problem with your _____ or _____ systems, you have to be extra careful. And some people _____ a feeling of sleepiness after taking them. That's because certain kinds of painkillers _____ the receptors in the body that sense pain.

Aside from these, there are other side effects of painkillers such as addiction, difficulty sleeping and _____ . The best way to prevent possible side effects is to consult your doctor before use.

Did You Know Painkillers Can Cause You A Wide Variety Of Pains?

① **Painkillers** are supposed to kill pain.
진통제　　　　…하기로 되어 있다

② But **unfortunately** (sometimes and in some cases), painkillers can cause you pain
불행히도, 안타깝게도　　　　가끔 그리고 몇몇(어떤) 경우　　　cause A B : A에게 B를 야기하다
ex) cause him problems 그에게 문제를 야기하다

because they carry **side effects** (like any type of drug).
carry (동반, 수반하다) + side effects (부작용) = have side effects 부작용이 있다

③ They can be dangerous even under normal use, so be careful not to
= painkillers　　　심지어(even) 정상적인 사용으로도　　　…하지 않도록 주의하다

(**misuse** or **abuse**) them.
misuse v. 남용하다, 학대하다, 욕하다　disuse n. 사용하지 않음, 폐기
abuse v. 남용/오용/학대하다　overuse v. 남용하다

④ Many people know that painkillers **commonly** cause constipation.
일반적으로, 흔히　　　변비 (설사 diarrhea, loose bowels)

⑤ So painkiller users should drink lots of water when taking them.
when painkiller users take them (painkillers)
주절의 주어users와 일치, 생략 / 능동 taking

⑥ Also painkillers can **have an effect on** (both your heart and lungs).
영향을 미치다 = affect　both A and B : A와 B 둘 다

⑦ Some painkillers not only [1] cause a feeling of sedation but also [2] slow down
🔁 주어 painkillers + 동사 (not only) [1] cause… (but also) [2] slow down…

the **functioning** of the heart and lungs.
기능, 작용　　　폐는 양쪽에 있어서 복수 lungs

⑧ So if you have a problem with your cardiovascular or **respiratory** systems,
가정법 현재 if　…에(with) 문제가 있다　cardiovascular systems 심혈기관 또는 respiratory systems 호흡기관

you have to be extra careful.
be careful 조심하다, be extra careful 특별히 더 조심하다

⑨ And some people **complain** of a feeling of sleepiness after taking them.
v. 항의하다, 불평하다　　　주절의 주어 people과 일치해서 생략, 능동 taking
I complained of this problem. 이 문제를 항의했다.　= after they take painkillers
I complained to him about this problem. 이 문제에 대해 그에게 항의했다.

⑩ That's because certain kinds of painkillers **numb**
because이하 절의 주어 kinds (복수 : 진통제의 어떤 종류들)   마비시키다 (b 묵음)

the **receptors** (in the body) (that **sense** pain).
　　　　　　└─ 수식 ─┘   (통증을 감지하는) (신체 내의) 수용기들
* 관계대명사 that의 선행사는 body가 아니라 receptors, 복수이므로 동사 sense에 –s가 붙지 않는다.

⑪ Aside from these, there are other side effects of painkillers such as
…외에도 (= apart from)   유도부사 there + 복수동사 are + other + 복수 명사 effects   ( )와 같은 것들

(**addiction**, difficulty sleeping and **hallucinations**).
　중독　　　　수면장애　　　　　　　　환각

⑫ The best way to (prevent possible side effects) is to **consult**
　　　　　　└─ 수식 ─┘   명사적 용법의 to부정사 (상담하는 것)
주어 The best way to ( ) …하는 가장 좋은 방법 + 동사 is

your doctor before use.

---

❶ 진통제는 통증을 없애야 합니다.

❷ 하지만 안타깝게도 가끔 그리고 어떤 경우 진통제가 통증을 유발하기도 하는데 다른 약이 그렇듯 진통제에도 부작용이 있기 때문입니다.

❸ 정상적인 사용으로도 위험할 수 있기 때문에 남용, 오용하지 않도록 조심해야 합니다.

❹ 진통제가 일반적으로 변비를 일으킨다는 건 많이 알고 있습니다.

❺ 그러니 진통제 사용자들은 복용 시 물을 많이 마셔야 합니다.

❻ 그리고 진통제는 심장과 폐 모두에 영향을 미칠 수 있습니다.

❼ 어떤 진통제는 진정되는 느낌만 드는 게 아니라 심장과 폐 기능을 느리게 만들기도 합니다.

❽ 그래서 심혈관계나 호흡기에 문제가 있다면 각별히 더 조심해야 합니다.

❾ 그리고 진통제를 복용한 후 졸음을 호소하는 사람들이 있습니다.

❿ 그건 진통제 중 어떤 종류는 통증을 감지하는 신체의 수용기를 마비시키기 때문입니다.

⓫ 이 외에도 진통제의 다른 부작용들이 있는데, 중독, 불면증, 환각을 들 수 있습니다.

⓬ 이런 가능한 부작용을 예방하는 최선의 방법은 사용하기 전에 의사와 상의하는 것입니다.

03 Cracking Your Knuckles Has Nothing To Do With Arthritis?

Knuckle cracking is an annoying bad habit. Its sound is unpleasant to hear, and the person who cracks his or her knuckles looks a little bit scary and bad. Moreover, there is a myth that knuckle cracking leads to arthritis. But that is not true for knuckle cracking does not cause arthritis. Maybe the cracking sound misleads us because people believe that if something cracks, it must be being damaged. But the truth is that nothing is cracked or damaged.

There were a few studies about this and the results indicated that knuckle cracking was not associated with arthritis. However, those studies also discovered that it would be better for knuckle crackers to stop it because it is associated with several hand problems. According to those studies, knuckle crackers are more likely to have weaker grip strength, hand swelling, or damage to the ligaments surrounding the joints than people who don't crack their knuckles.

Words & Expressions

have nothing to do with ...와 관련이 없다 (have something to do with ..와 관련이 있다.) crack 갈라지다, 깨지다 knuckle 관절 knuckle cracking 손가락 관절 꺾기 annoying 짜증나는 habit 습관 unpleasant 불쾌한, 불편한 scary 무서운 myth 신화, 낭설 lead to ...로 인도하다 mislead 잘못 인도하다, 오해하게 만들다 damage 손상을 주다, 손상, 피해, 손해배상금 arthritis 관절염 be associated with ...와 관련이 있다 indicate 나타내다 grip 꽉 붙잡음, 이해, 통제 strength 힘, 장점 swell 붓다, 불룩해지다 (swelling 부은 곳, 붓기 hand swelling 손이 붓는 것) ligament 인대 joint 관절

1. What can be the best title of this story?

    a. The Reason Why We Should Crack Our Knuckles

    b. Start Cracking Your Knuckles For Your Hands

    c. Hand Swelling VS. Joint Damage

    d. Knuckle Cracking : Not Related To Arthritis

2. According to the experts, knuckle crackers _____ .

    a. tend to have weaker grip strength than who don't crack their knuckles

    b. are likely to be hospitalized because of arthritis

    c. have no choice but to have at least three hand problems

    d. must stop cracking their knuckles since knuckle cracking is annoying

3. Choose the correct words for each sentence.

    a. I think we have to wait a few / a little / much more minutes for them.

    b. The little boy looked scared because his teacher looked scared / scary / scare.

    c. I just don't want to be associated / association / associate with those barbaric people.

Answer   **1.** d   **2.** a   **3.** a few | scary | associated

Listening Drill – Dictation

Knuckle cracking is an   bad habit. Its sound is   , and the person who cracks his or her knuckles looks a little bit scary and bad. Moreover, there is a myth that knuckle cracking   . But that is not true for knuckle cracking does not cause arthritis. Maybe the cracking sound   us because people believe that if something cracks, it   damaged. But the truth is that nothing is cracked or damaged.

There were a few studies about this   knuckle cracking   arthritis. However, those studies also discovered that it   knuckle crackers to stop it because it is associated with several hand problems. According to those studies, knuckle crackers   have weaker grip strength, hand swelling, or   the ligaments surrounding the joints than people who don't crack their knuckles.

Did You Know Cracking Your Knuckles Has Nothing To Do With Arthritis?

1 Knuckle cracking is an **annoying** bad habit.

비인칭주어 + be annoying (주어가) 짜증나는 것이다
인칭 주어 + be annoyed (주어가) 짜증나다

2 Its sound is **unpleasant** to hear, and the person (who cracks his or her knuckles)

주어 = the sound of knuckle cracking

수식

the person looks scary and (looks) bad

looks a little bit **scary** and bad.

scary 무서운 / scare 겁주다 / scared 겁먹은

3 Moreover, there is a myth that knuckle cracking leads to arthritis.

there + is (단수동사) + a myth (실제 주어-단수)   …로 이어지다, …가 되다

4 But that is not true for knuckle cracking does not cause arthritis.

= because, since

5 Maybe the cracking sound **misleads** us because people believe that

mis + lead 호도하다, 오해하게 만들다
mislead us 우리가 오해하도록 (잘못 알게) 만들다

if something cracks, it must be being **damaged**.

가정법 현재 if + 동사 현재형, it must 동사원형   be + being 현재진행형 / being + damaged 수동태 – 현재진행형 수동태
                                                    (현재 손상을 입고 있는 중)

6 But the truth is that nothing is cracked or damaged.

사실은 that 절 이하이다   is cracked or (is) damaged 수동태

7 There were a few studies about this and the results indicated that

유도부사 there + 복수동사 were + 복수명사 a few studies   결과는 that 절 이하이다

knuckle cracking was not **associated with** arthritis.

…와 관련이 없다 (관련이 있다 be associated with = be related with/to)

8 However, those studies also discovered that it would be better for knuckle

앞 문장의 a few studies (복수)   it would be better for A to 동사 : A가 …하는 게 더 낫다

crackers to stop it because it is associated with several hand problems.

9 According to those studies, knuckle crackers are more likely

🔁 be more likely to have [1], [2], [3] than …보다 [1], [2], [3]을 가질 가능성이 더 크다

to have weaker [1] **grip strength**, [2] **hand swelling**, or [3] **damage** to

hand 손 + swelling 붓기, 붓다   damage to ( ) : ( )에 대한 손상, 손해
                                  ( ) = 관절을 둘러싼 인대

26

(the ligaments surrounding the **joints**) than people who don't crack

joint 관절, 이음　　　　　수식　　　　　joint 관절, 이음

their knuckles.

손가락 관절 꺾기와 관절염은 아무 상관이 없다는 거 아세요?

1 손가락 관절 꺾기는 짜증나는 나쁜 버릇입니다.

2 소리도 듣기에 좋지 않고, 손가락 관절을 꺾는 사람은 좀 무섭고 불량해 보입니다.

3 게다가 손가락 관절 꺾기를 하면 관절염에 걸린다는 설도 있습니다.

4 그러나 그건 낭설이며, 손가락 관절 꺾기가 관절염을 일으키지는 않습니다.

5 아마 꺾는 소리 때문에 잘못 생각하게 된 것 같은데, 사람들은 무언가 꺾이는 소리가 나면 손상되는 것이라 믿기 때문입니다.

6 하지만 사실 꺾이거나 손상되는 건 없습니다.

7 이에 관해 연구한 몇 가지 조사 결과를 보면, 손가락 관절 꺾기는 관절염과 아무 상관이 없습니다.

8 하지만 그 연구에서는 손가락 관절을 꺾는 사람들은 그 버릇을 그만 두는 게 좋다는 사실도 발견했는데 몇 가지 손 문제와 관련이 있기 때문입니다.

9 앞의 연구 결과에 의하면, 손가락 관절을 꺾는 사람들은 그렇지 않은 사람들보다 잡는 힘이 약해지고 손이 붓고, 관절 주변을 감싼 인대가 손상될 가능성이 더 높다고 합니다.

04 Did You Know **Doctors Don't Know Exactly Why We Have Earwax?**

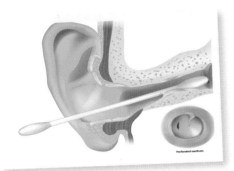

Interestingly, it is said that doctors don't know exactly why we have earwax. However, there are several theories as to why. Doctors think that earwax might have something to do with the ear's self-cleaning process. They also think it could have antibacterial properties. Wax is generally believed to protect the ears by preventing dirts or small bugs from entering our inner ears. Additionally, no one knows for sure why the amount of earwax differs depending on the individuals. Some people make lots of wax, while on the other hand, some don't make any wax. Of course, we don't know why that is.

Fortunately, doctors do know the safest way to remove extra earwax. Although many of us use cotton swabs to remove earwax, doctors recommend that we should not put any cotton swab or small object inside our ear canal. That's because you could push earwax in further or damage the inside of your ear canal or eardrum inadvertently. The best way is to use a moist washcloth. Just wrap it around your finger and clean your earlobes. If you want to remove excess earwax, let some warm water go in your ear, then tip your head to the side to dump it out. Then clean your inner ear with a soft, dry washcloth.

Words & Expressions

interestingly 흥미롭게도 earwax 귀지 (또는 wax) theory 이론 as to why 이유, 원인에 관해 self-cleaning 자가 청소 process 과정 antibacterial 항균성의 property 성질, 특성 dirt 먼지 depending on the individual 개인에 따라 prevent from -ing ...하지 못하게 막다, 방해하다 inner ears 내이 (outer ears 외이) no one knows for sure 아무도 확실하게 모른다 differ 다르다 remove 제거하다 (get rid of) cotton swab 면봉 canal 운하, 수로, 관 (ear canal 이도) recommend 권하다, 추천하다 eardrum 고막 inadvertently 본의 아니게 moist 촉촉한 washcloth 수건 wrap 싸다, 포장하다 tip 기울이다 tip one's head to the side 한쪽으로 머리를 기울이다 dump out 갖다 버리다

Understanding Checkpoint

1. What is the main idea of the story?

    a. Doctors don't know beans about earwax so we should not listen to them.

    b. Earwax must be removed by small objects such as cotton swabs.

    c. The exact reason why we have ear wax is not known yet, but the best way to remove it is known.

    d. It is absolutely critical to remove excess earwax with a washcloth.

2. According to the passage, which sentence is <u>wrong</u>?

    a. Doctors managed to discover why we have earwax.

    b. Using a cotton swab might not be the safest way to remove extra earwax.

    c. Not everyone has the same amount of earwax.

    d. There are more than one theory as to why we have earwax.

3. Choose the correct words for each sentence.

    a. The apple pie you made was too sweet, <u>moreover</u> / <u>in addition</u> / <u>while</u> the strawberry pie your sis made was very tasty.

    b. Ask Max. He <u>has</u> / <u>gets</u> / <u>does</u> know the right answer and he is right over there.

    c. I want his explanation <u>as to why</u> / <u>as why</u> / <u>as of why</u> he left so soon yesterday.

                                         Answer   **1.** c   **2.** a   **3.** while ǀ does ǀ as to why

Listening Drill – Dictation

Interestingly, it is said that doctors don't know exactly why we have earwax. However, there are several theories   . Doctors think that earwax   the ear's self-cleaning process. They also think it could have antibacterial properties. Wax   protect the ears by preventing dirts or small bugs from entering our inner ears. Additionally, no one knows for sure why the amount of earwax differs   . Some people make lots of wax, while on the other hand, some don't make any wax. Of course, we don't know why that is.
Fortunately, doctors do know   to remove extra earwax. Although many of us use   to remove earwax, doctors recommend that we should not put any cotton swab or small object inside our ear canal. That's because you could push earwax   or damage the inside of your ear canal or eardrum   . The best way is to use   . Just wrap it around your finger and clean your earlobes. If you want to remove excess earwax, let some warm water go in your ear, then tip your head to the side to   . Then clean your inner ear with a soft, dry washcloth.

Did You Know Doctors Don't Know Exactly Why We Have Earwax?

1 Interestingly, it is said that doctors don't know exactly why we have earwax.

that 절 이하라고 한다   = wax 귀지 (beewax 밀납)

2 However, there are several theories as to why.

There 복수동사 are + 복수명사 theories   as to (about) + why 이유에 관해

3 Doctors think that earwax might **have something to do with**

might 추측   관련이 있다
…일지도 모른다 (have nothing to do with = don't have anything to do with 관련이 없다)

the ear's self-cleaning process.

self 스스로 - cleaning 청소

4 They also think it could have **antibacterial properties**.

doctors   earwax   anti 반(反), 항(抗) + bacterial 박테리아의
                                              antibiotic 항생제 / antiseptic 소독제, 방부제 / antiviral 항바이러스의

5 Wax is generally believed to protect the ears by **preventing** (dirts or small bugs)

주어 be believed to 동사원형 …라고 (하다고) 믿어지다, 다들 …라고 생각하다   prevent ( ) from –ing ( )이 …하지 못하게 막다, 방해하다

from entering our **inner** ears.

안쪽의, 내부의 (outer 바깥의) (innerwear 속옷 inner peace 마음의 평화)

6 Additionally, no one knows (for sure) why the amount of earwax **differs**

no one knows why … why 이하 절을 아무도 모른다   why절 주어 the amount (3인칭 단수현재) + 동사 differs

depending on the individuals.

개인에 따라 = the amount of earwax is different from person to person 귀지의 양이 사람마다 다르다

7 Some people make lots of wax, while on the other hand, some don't make any wax.

반면 (on the other hand 생략 가능)   some = some people

8 Of course, we don't know why that is.

why 의문문이 아닌 명사절 (왜 그런 것인지를) – 주어/동사 위치가 바뀌지 않는다 why that is

9 **Fortunately**, doctors do know the safest way (to **remove** extra earwax).

다행히도   본동사 know를 강조하는 강조의 조동사 do   ↑   수식   way to ( ) …하는 방법

10 Although many of us use cotton swabs to remove earwax, doctors **recommend** that

면봉 (= swab)   recommend that 주어 + should + 동사원형 : that …를 추천/권고하다

we should not put (any cotton swab or small object) inside our ear canal.

ear 귀 + canal 수로, 관 - 이도

⑪ That's because you could ¹⁾ push earwax in further or ²⁾ damage

이유는 … 때문이다   further, farther : 둘 다 far의 비교급. 보통 '거리'는 farther, '정도, 시간, 수량'은 further를 쓰는데
구어에서는 이를 구분하지 않고 farther보다 further를 쓰는 경우가 많다.

(the inside of your ear canal or eardrum) **inadvertently**.

본의 아니게, 무심코 (purposedly 일부러)

⑫ The best way is to use a **moist** washcloth.

way to 동사원형 …하는 방법   moist a. 촉촉한 moisture n. 습기
the safe way to eat ( ) ( )를 먹는 안전한 방법 / the fast way to get there 거기 가는 빠른 방법

⑬ Just ¹⁾ wrap it around your finger and ²⁾ clean your earlobes.

            it = moist washcloth   = lobes 귓볼

⑭ If you want to remove **excess** earwax, ¹⁾ let (some warm water) go in your ear,

                여분의, 과도한   let ( ) 동사원형 go
                (access 입장, 접속하다)   사역동사 let - ( )이 귀에 들어가게 하다

then ²⁾ **tip** your head to the side to dump it out.

       tip v. 기울이다, n. 끝, 조언   dump out 버리다 / it = excess earwax

⑮ Then clean your inner ear (with a soft, dry washcloth).

〔 의사도 귀지가 생기는 정확한 이유를 잘 모른다는 거 아세요? 〕

❶ 흥미롭게도 의사들은 귀지가 생기는 정확한 이유는 잘 모른다고 합니다.

❷ 하지만 그 이유에 대한 몇 가지 이론은 있습니다.

❸ 의사들은 귀지가 귀의 자가 청소 과정과 관련이 있으리라 생각합니다.

❹ 또 귀지에 항바이러스 성질이 있다고 생각합니다.

❺ 일반적으로 귀지가 먼지나 작은 벌레가 귀 안쪽으로 들어오지 못하게 막아 귀를 보호한다고 합니다.

❻ 그리고 개인에 따라 귀지의 양이 차이 나는 확실한 이유 역시 아무도 모릅니다.

❼ 어떤 사람은 귀지가 많이 생기는데 반해, 어떤 사람은 전혀 생기지 않기도 합니다.

❽ 물론 이유는 모릅니다.   ❾ 다행히 의사들은 너무 많이 생긴 귀지를 제거하는 가장 안전한 방법을 알고 있습니다.

❿ 많은 사람들이 귀지를 제거하려고 면봉을 사용하지만, 의사들은 면봉이나 다른 작은 물건을 이도에 넣지 말 것을 권고합니다.

⑪ 그러다 귀지를 더 안쪽으로 밀어 넣을 수도 있고 또는 본의 아니게 이도나 고막 안쪽에 손상을 입힐 수도 있기 때문입니다.

⑫ 가장 좋은 방법은 젖은 수건을 사용하는 것입니다.   ⑬ 손가락에 수건을 감고 귀 볼을 닦으세요.

⑭ 여분의 귀지를 제거하고 싶다면 따뜻한 물을 귀 안으로 흘려 보낸 후 머리를 한 쪽으로 기울여 귀지를 내버리세요.

⑮ 그리고 부드럽고 마른 수건으로 귀 안 쪽을 닦습니다.

31

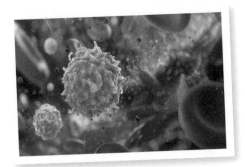

Amazingly there are about 5,000,000 red blood cells in just one drop of blood other than 7,000 white blood cells and 450,000 platelet cells. And of course there are water, salt, fat, vitamins, sugar, and so on. No wonder blood is thicker than water. In fact, blood feels like warm soup. Blood is a little bit soupy and gooey because it is a mixture of liquid and lots and lots of cells. Many people think that the three main ingredients of blood are red blood cells, white blood cells and platelets. But actually, plasma, a yellow liquid material in the blood, makes up more than half of the blood.

Red blood cells carry oxygen around our body, white blood cells find and kill harmful germs, and platelets make blood clot to stop bleeding when we get injured. Here are some interesting facts about blood. Red blood cells live for about four months. White blood cells eat up not only bacteria and germs but also dead cells. And the factory that makes new red and white blood cells is bone marrow.

Words & Expressions

amazingly 놀랍게도 **red blood cell** 적혈구 **other than** ...외에, ...말고 **white blood cell** 백혈구 **platelet** 혈소판 **no wonder** 놀랄 일도 아니다, 당연하다 **thick** 두꺼운, 짙은, 굵은 (thin 연한, 얇은) **soupy** 수프같은, 걸쭉한 **gooey** 끈끈한 (sticky) **mixture** 혼합물 (v. mix 혼합하다) **plasma** 혈 장, 플라즈마 **liquid** 액체, 액체의 **material** 물질 **make up** 이루다 **more than half of...** ...의 반 이상 **oxygen** 산소 **harmful** 해로운 **germ** 세균 **bleed** 피가 나다 **injure** 부상 **get injured** 부상당하다 **clot** 엉기게 하다 (blood clot 혈전) **eat up** 먹어 치우다 **factory** 공장 **bone marrow** 골수

32

1. What is the main idea of the story?

    a. The color of blood is red because of the platelets.

    b. Blood is a mixture of lots of ingredients.

    c. The platelet is the most important among blood ingredients.

    d. The most essential ingredient in blood is bone marrow.

2. According to the article, you can guess _____ .

    a. red blood cells make up most of the blood

    b. bone marrow plays an important role in making oxygen

    c. without blood platelets, you could bleed to death

    d. blood is useful due to its red color

3. Choose the correct words for each sentence.

    a. White blood cells not only find <u>because</u> / <u>but also</u> / <u>however</u> kill harmful germs.

    b. There <u>is</u> / <u>are</u> / <u>were</u> tons of cells in blood.

    c. Plasma makes <u>up</u> / <u>off</u> / <u>over</u> more than half of the blood.

Answer **1.** b **2.** c **3.** but also ǀ are ǀ up

Amazingly there are about 5,000,000 red blood cells in just one drop of blood 7,000 white blood cells and 450,000   . And of course there are water, salt, fat, vitamins, sugar, and so on. No wonder   . In fact, blood   warm soup. Blood is a little bit soupy and gooey because it is a mixture of liquid and lots and lots of cells. Many people think that the three main ingredients of blood are red blood cells, white blood cells and   . But actually, plasma, a yellow   in the blood, makes up   the blood.

Red blood cells carry oxygen around our body, white blood cells find and kill harmful germs, and platelets   to stop bleeding when we get injured. Here are some interesting facts about blood. Red blood cells live for about four months. White blood cells   not only bacteria and germs but also dead cells. And the factory that makes new red and white blood cells is   .

Did You Know There Are 5,000,000 Red Blood Cells In One Drop Of Blood?

1 **Amazingly** there are about 5,000,000 red blood **cells** in just one drop of **blood**
놀랍게도   적혈구   세포   단 한 방울의 피
blood n. 피, 혈액 bleed v. 피를 흘리다
피 두 방울 two drops of blood (O)
two bloods (X) two drops of bloods (X)

other than the 7,000 white blood cells and 450,000 platelet cells.
…외에   백혈구 세포   혈소판 세포

2 And (of course) there are water, salt, fat, vitamins, sugar, and so on.
물론   n. 지방 a. 뚱뚱한   기타 등등

3 No wonder blood is **thicker** than water.
(It is) no wonder (that)   피는 물보다 진하다 (속담)
당연하다, 놀랍지 않다   thick 진한, 두꺼운 (↔ thin 연한, 얇은)

4 In fact, blood feels like warm soup.
…같은 느낌이다 (seem like …처럼 보이다)

5 Blood is a little bit soupy and gooey because it is a **mixture** of **liquid**
약간, 어느 정도   soup n. 수프   goo n. 찐득찐득한 것   …의 혼합
soupy a. 수프 같은   gooey a. 끈적거리는

and lots and lots of cells.

6 Many people think that (the three main ingredients of blood) are ¹⁾ red blood cells,
that 이하 문장 주어 ( ) blood가 아니라 ingredients + 동사 are

²⁾ white blood cells and ³⁾ platelets.

7 But actually, plasma, (a yellow liquid material in the blood), **makes up**
= 동격   이루다, 형성하다
주어 plasma (3인칭 단수 현재) + 동사 makes up

more than half of the blood.
…의 반 이상   half of ..의 반 / less than half of ..의 절반 미만

8 ¹⁾ Red blood cells carry **oxygen** around our body,
산소를 운반하다 (oxygen 산소 oxidant 산화제 oxide 산화물)

²⁾ white blood cells find and kill **harmful germs**,
백혈구 (주어) + 찾고 + 죽이다   해로운   세균

and ³⁾ platelets make blood **clot** to stop **bleeding** when we get **injured**.

사역동사 make + 목적어 blood + 동사원형 clot   get + pp (수동) 상처를 입다

피를 엉기게 만들다   clot v. 엉기다, 굳다

stop -ing ...하는 것을 멈추게 하다 / stop to 동사 ...를 하려고 멈추다

⑨ Here are some interesting facts about blood.

여기에 ...가 있다 (실제 주어 facts가 복수이므로 복수 동사 are)

⑩ Red blood cells live for about four months.

for + 기간 : 얼마 동안 약 4개월 동안

⑪ White blood cells eat up (not only) bacteria and germs (but also) dead cells.

백혈구가 먹어 치우는 것 : bacteria, germs, dead cells   bacterium (단수) bacteria (복수) / datum (단수) data (복수)

not only A but also B : A뿐 아니라 B도

⑫ And the factory (that makes new red and white blood cells) is bone marrow.

수식

주어 the factory + 동사 is   bone marrow = marrow 골수

피 한 방울에 5백만 개의 적혈구가 있다는 거 아세요?

❶ 놀랍게도 단 한 방울의 피 안에 5백만 개의 적혈구 외에 7천개의 백혈구, 45만개의 혈소판이 들어 있습니다.

❷ 물론 물, 소금, 지방, 비타민, 설탕 등도 들어 있습니다.

❸ 물이 피보다 진할 만도 하지요.

❹ 사실 피는 따뜻한 수프 같은 느낌이 납니다.

❺ 피는 약간 질척하고 끈적거리는데, 이는 피가 액체와 엄청나게 많은 세포의 혼합물이기 때문입니다.

❻ 많은 사람들이 피의 세 가지 주요 성분이 적혈구, 백혈구, 혈소판으로 알고 있습니다.

❼ 하지만 실제 피의 노란색 액체 물질인 혈장(플라즈마)이 피의 반 이상을 차지합니다.

❽ 적혈구는 온 몸에 산소를 운반하고, 백혈구는 해로운 세균을 찾아 죽이며 혈소판은 상처가 났을 때 피가 멎도록 피를 엉기게 만듭니다.

❾ 피에 관한 재미있는 사실이 있습니다.

❿ 적혈구는 약 4달 정도 삽니다.

⑪ 백혈구는 박테리아와 세균 뿐 아니라 죽은 세포도 먹어 치웁니다.

⑫ 그리고 새 적혈구와 백혈구를 만드는 공장은 골수입니다.

06 Did You Know **Your Hands Can Tell You About Your Health?**

If your fingers get swollen, hypothyroidism may be the cause, which means the thyroid gland is not producing enough of its hormone. Swollen fingers may also happen when you sleep right after eating salty ramen late at night, but in this case, your fingers will return to normal in a few hours or days.

If your palms are redder than normal, you may have one of the following three problems. If you feel an itchy or burning pain, it's possible that you have eczema. Or you may be allergic to something being worn or applied on your hands. Lastly, red palms could indicate that you have a problem with your liver. Not all people with red palms have a liver disease, but it's not a bad idea to get a checkup.

Generally, nails turn white when you press on them, then return to a pinkish color when you stop pressing. But if your nails stay white for a few minutes, you may have anemia or low iron. How about blue fingertips? Of course, this is not a good sign either. Although this symptom is common in women when it's cold, if it lasts more than an hour, you must go to the hospital right away.

Words & Expressions

get swollen 붓다 hypothyroidism 갑상선 기능 저하증 hormone 호르몬 thyroid 갑상선의 gland (내분비)선, 샘 thyroid gland 갑상선 right after 직후 late at night 밤늦게 in a few hours to days 몇 시간에서 며칠 이내에 redder than normal 정상보다 붉은 (redder = more red) palm 손바닥 itchy 가려운 eczema 습진 be allergic to ...에 알러지가 있다 it's not a bad idea to ...하는 것이 나쁘지 않다 get a checkup (병원에서) 검사를 받다 turn white 희게 변하다 pinkish 분홍빛의 anemia 빈혈 low iron 철분 부족 fingertip 손가락 끝 be not a good sign 좋은 징조가 아니다 symptom 징후 be in common in ..에게 흔하다 last 지속하다 right away 즉시

1. What is the main idea of the story?

    a. Eating salty ramen late at night is not a good thing to do for your health.

    b. Hands as well as feet reveal various information about your health.

    c. If you see your hands, you will get lots of information about your health.

    d. People whose fingertips are blue must go to the hospital ASAP.

2. According to the passage, which sentence is <u>wrong</u>?

    a. The lack of thyroid hormone is the main cause of hypothyroidism.

    b. If you sleep right after eating salty ramen late at night, your fingers may be swollen.

    c. It is possible for people who have red palms to have a liver problem.

    d. During the winter, women's fingertips originally turn blue.

3. Choose the correct words for each sentence.

    a. If you feel faint again, please check your health <u>diagnosis</u> / <u>syndromes</u> / <u>symptoms</u> and signs with your doctor.

    b. After applying this ointment <u>on</u> / <u>in</u> / <u>to</u> my skin, I feel all itchy.

    c. Stop <u>talking</u> / <u>to talk</u> / <u>talked</u>, please. You have to be quiet because you are in a library.

Answer **1.** c **2.** d **3.** symptoms ⏐ on ⏐ talking

Listening Drill - Dictation

If your   , hypothyroidism may be the cause, which means   is not producing enough of its hormone. Swollen fingers may also happen when you sleep right after eating salty ramen late at night, but in this case, your fingers will return to normal in a few hours or days.

If your palms are redder than normal, you may have one of the following three problems. If you   or burning pain, it's possible that you have   . Or you may be allergic to something being worn or   your hands. Lastly, red palms could   that you have a problem with your liver. Not all people with red palms have a liver disease, but   get a checkup.

Generally, nails turn white when you press on them, then return to a pinkish color when you stop pressing. But if your nails stay white for a few minutes, you may have   . How about blue fingertips? Of course, this is not a good sign   . Although this symptom   women when it's cold, if it lasts more than an hour, you must go to the hospital right away.

Did You Know Your Hands Can Tell You About Your Health?

❶ If your fingers get **swollen**, hypothyroidism may be the cause,

get pp 수동태   hypo (감소, 부족) + thyroid (갑상선) + ism – 갑상선 기능저하증
(swell – swelled – swollen)   (hyper (과도, 흥분) + thyroid (갑상선) + ism – 갑상선 기능항진증)

which means the thyroid gland is not **producing** enough of its hormone.

(which 앞의) 콤마 + which   thyroid 갑상선+gland 샘
: 계속적 용법   갑상샘, 갑상선 샘

❷ Swollen fingers may also happen when you sleep

부은 손가락 swelling finger (X)

(right after eating **salty** ramen) late at night, but in this case,

짠 라면을 먹은 직후   salt n. 소금 salty a. 짠

your fingers will return to normal (in a few hours or days).

정상으로 돌아오다   몇 시간 또는 며칠 안에

❸ If your **palms** are redder than normal,

palm 손바닥   redder = more red 비교급
가정법 현재 : if 주어 your palm + 동사 현재형 are, 주어 you + may + 동사원형 (have)

you may have one of the following three problems.

one of the 복수명사 : …중 하나

❹ If you feel an (**itchy** or burning pain), it's possible that you have eczema.

feel an itchy pain or feel a burning pain   that절 이하일 가능성이 있다
가렵거나 (feel itchy) 화끈거린다면 (have a burning sensation)

❺ Or you may be allergic to something (being **worn** or **applied on** your hands).

…에(to) 알레르기가 있다   수식   something which is worn or applied on your hands
손에 끼우거나 (be worn) 바른 (be applied) 무언가

❻ Lastly, red palms could indicate that you have a problem with your **liver**.

마지막으로   = have an issue with …에 문제가 있다   간
three problems 중 마지막 세 번째라서 lastly

❼ Not all people (with red palms) have a liver **disease**,

부분 부정   수식   손바닥이 붉은 사람들   질병
손바닥이 붉은 사람들 모두가 그런 건 아니다 (그런 사람도 있고 아닌 사람도 있다)

but it's not a bad idea to get a **checkup**.

…하는 게 나쁘지 않다 (가주어 it, 진주어 to동사)   get a checkup 건강검진 받다

❽ Generally, nails turn white when you press on them, then return to a pinkish color

(흰색이 아니었다가) 희게 되다   nails   …로 되돌아가다

when you stop pressing.

stop –ing …를 그만두다 (stop singing 노래를 멈추다 / stop to sing 노래하려고 하던 걸 멈추다)

⑨ But if your nails stay white for a few minutes, you may have **anemia** or low iron.

가정법현재 if 주어 your nails + 현재 동사 stay, 주어 you + may + 동사원형 have　　　빈혈

철분이 부족하면 (low iron) 빈혈이 생기기 때문에 anemia와 low iron은 유의처럼 쓰인다.
(iron deficiency 철 결핍증, iron deficiency anemia 철 결핍성 빈혈)

⑩ How about blue fingertips?

finger 손가락 + tip 끝부분

⑪ Of course, this is not a good sign either.

not either 역시(…도) 아니다

⑫ Although this **symptom** is common in women when it's cold,

증상, 징후　　　…사이에 흔하다　　　　날씨를 나타낼 때 비인칭 주어 it

if it lasts (more than an hour), you must go to the hospital **right away**.

한 시간 이상　　　　　　　　　　　　　　　　즉시 (= immediately, in no time)

가정법 현재 if 주어 it (3인칭 단수 현재) + 현재 동사 lasts, 주어 you + must + 동사원형 go

---

손이 당신의 건강에 관해 말해준다는 거 아세요?

❶ 손가락이 부었다면, 갑상선이 생산하는 호르몬이 부족한 갑상선기능저하 때문일 수 있습니다.

❷ 밤늦게 짠 라면을 먹은 직후 잠이 들어도 손가락이 부을 수 있지만 이런 경우는 몇 시간 혹은 며칠 내에 손가락이 정상으로 돌아옵니다.

❸ 손바닥이 정상보다 더 붉다면 다음 세 가지 문제 중 하나일 수 있습니다.

❹ 가려움이나 후끈한 통증이 느껴지면 습진일 가능성이 있습니다.

❺ 또는 손에 끼고 있거나 손에 바른 무언가에 알레르기가 있을 수도 있습니다.

❻ 마지막으로 붉은 손바닥은 간에 문제가 있을 수도 있다는 뜻입니다.

❼ 손바닥이 붉은 사람은 모두 간에 질병이 있다는 건 아니지만, 그래도 한 번 검사를 받는 게 나쁘지 않을 겁니다.

❽ 일반적으로 손톱을 누르면 희게 변했다가 누르지 않으면 손톱은 다시 분홍빛으로 돌아옵니다.

❾ 하지만 희게 변한 손톱이 몇 분 간 계속된다면 빈혈이나 철분 부족일 수 있습니다.

❿ 손톱 끝이 푸른색인 건 어떨까요?

⓫ 당연히 좋은 징조가 아닙니다.

⓬ 추울 때 여성들에게 흔한 징후이긴 하지만, 이것이 한 시간 이상 지속될 경우에는 즉시 병원에 가야 합니다.

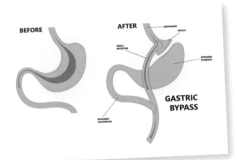

Researches conducted by U.S. doctors said that more than half of diabetes patients who underwent gastric bypass surgery were cured thanks to its effect on improving blood sugar control. Researchers at Imperial College London also recognized its effect, saying, "it's clear that gastric bypass surgery has a significant beneficial effect on glucose control." It seems that gastric bypass surgery will become more and more popular since obese patients with type 2 diabetes can lose weight and be cured at the same time. It's like 'killing two birds with one stone.'

Many obese patients with diabetes quitted taking medication after this surgery. Naturally people are under the impression that this surgery is an easy way out of obesity and the risk of type 2 diabetes by just one operation. It sounds so easy and tempting. Yet the reality is not so easy and tempting. If you undergo this surgery, you will have a smaller stomach which is connected to the small intestine, which means your cute little stomach can hold a very limited amount of food. If you eat more than a quarter of a cup of solid food, or eat some solid food with a cup of water, you may be sick because your small stomach can't handle that much food.

1. What can be the best title of this story?

a. Gastric Bypass Surgery : A Breakthrough For Obese Patients With Diabetes

b. Eating A Small Amount Of Food Can Be Dangerous

c. The Increase In Obese People With Type 2 Diabetes In The US

d. Type 2 Diabetes Patients Take The Easy Way Out

2. According to the passage, which sentence is right?

a. Obese people with type 2 diabetes must undergo gastric bypass surgery.

b. Gastric bypass surgery can improve blood sugar control.

c. Doctors only in the US admit the awesome effect of gastric bypass surgery.

d. Gastric bypass surgery doesn't have any positive effect on glucose control.

3. Choose the correct words for each sentence.

a. You are supposed to <u>make</u> / <u>conduct</u> / <u>exam</u> scientific researches on this matter.

b. I hate my nose. I want to <u>undergo</u> / <u>be undergone</u> / <u>underwent</u> plastic surgery.

c. Mr. Witt has had an effect <u>to</u> / <u>on</u> / <u>for</u> me since I was 12 years old.

d. You are under the impression <u>during</u> / <u>while</u> / <u>that</u> I am rich, but I'm not.

Answer **1.** a **2.** b **3.** conduct ㅣ undergo ㅣ on ㅣ that

Researches   U.S. doctors said that more than half of diabetes patients who underwent gastric bypass surgery were cured thanks to its effect on improving
            . Researchers at Imperial College London also recognized its effect, saying, "it's clear that gastric bypass surgery   glucose control." It seems that gastric bypass surgery will become more and more popular since   type 2 diabetes can lose weight and be cured at the same time.
    'killing two birds with one stone.'
Many obese patients with diabetes   after this surgery. Naturally people   this surgery is an easy way out of obesity and the risk of type 2 diabetes by just one operation. It sounds so easy and tempting. Yet the reality is not so easy and tempting. If you   , you will have a smaller stomach which is connected to the small intestine, which means your cute little stomach can hold   food. If you eat more than   a cup of solid food, or eat some solid food with a cup of water, you may be sick because your small stomach can't handle that much food.

Did You Know How Much Food You Can Eat After Gastric Bypass Surgery?

1 Researches (conducted by U.S. doctors) said that more than half of diabetes
Researches (which were) conducted by …에 의해 실시된 조사 (수동) · · · 의 반 이상 · · · 당뇨병
이 문장의 주어는 doctors가 아니라 researchers + 동사 said · · · that이하 절 주어 surgery가 아니라 diabetes patients 동사 were

patients (who underwent gastric bypass surgery) were cured thanks to
수술받다 undergo - underwent - undergone · · · cure 치료하다
(주어가 수술을 받을 때 undergo를 수동태로 쓰지 않는다) · · · be cured 치료되다

its effect on improving blood sugar control.
= the effect of gastric bypass surgery · · · blood sugar 혈당 + control 조절

2 Researchers (at Imperial College London) also recognized its effect, saying,
수식 · · · 효과를 인정하면서 다음과 같이 언급하다
주어 researchers 동사 recognized

"it's clear that gastric bypass surgery has a significant beneficial effect on
가주어 it, 진주어 that 절 · · · have an effect on …에 영향을 미치다
It's clear that … that 이하는 명확하다

glucose control."

3 It seems that gastric bypass surgery will become (more and more) popular
that 절 이하로 보이다 · · · (점점 더) 인기가 있다

since obese patients (with type 2 diabetes) can [1] lose weight
수식 · · · 2형 당뇨병을 가진 비만 환자들
obese a. 비만한 (overweight, corpulent) obesity n. 비만
patient with 병명 : 어떤 병을 앓는 환자

and [2] be cured at the same time.
동시에 (= simultaneously)

4 It's like 'killing two birds with one stone.'
돌 하나로 새 두 마리 잡다 (일석이조 一石二鳥)

5 (Many obese patients with diabetes) quitted taking medication after this surgery.
주어 ( ) 동사 quitted · · · quit + -ing …하는 것을 끊다 · · · take medication 약을 복용하다
(약 복용은 항상 take를 쓰고, drink, have 등은 쓰지 않는다.)

6 Naturally people are under the impression that this surgery is an easy way out of
be under the impression that : that 이하라는 생각을 갖다 (think)

[1] obesity and [2] the risk of type 2 diabetes by just one operation.
an easy way out of [1] and [2] by … : …함으로서 [1]과 [2]에서 쉽게 벗어나는 · · · operation = surgery 수술

7 It sounds so easy and tempting.
…로 들리다 (it seems …처럼 보이다) · · · tempt v. 유혹하다 temptation n. 유혹 tempting a. 귀가 솔깃한, 유혹적인

8 Yet the reality is not so easy and tempting.

9 If you undergo this surgery, you will have a smaller stomach (which is connected

are undergone (X)

수식

( ) – smaller stomach 수식 : 작은 창자에 연결된 더 작은 위장

to the small **intestine**), which means your cute little **stomach**

콤마 + which means – 앞 문장에 이어 순서대로 해석

can hold a very limited amount of food.

매우 제한적인 양의
a large amount of food / a small amount of food
많은 양의 음식 / 적은 양의 음식

10 If you eat more than a quarter of a cup of **solid** food, or eat some solid food

…의 1/4 (half a cup of solid food 단단한 음식 반 컵)
가정법 현재 if 주어 you + 현재 동사 eat, 주어 you + may + 동사 원형 be

with a cup of water, you may be sick because your small stomach can't **handle**

물 한 컵과   다루다, 처리하다

that much food.

그렇게 많은 (much를 강조하는 that) 음식

위장우회수술 후 얼마나 먹을 수 있는지 아세요?

1 미국의 의사들이 실시한 연구조사에서 위장우회수술을 받은 당뇨병 환자들 중 반 이상이 혈당 조절을 개선시키는 이 수술의 효과 덕분에 병이 치료되었다고 합니다.

2 임페리얼 칼리지 런던의 연구원들 역시 이 효과를 확인하면서 '위장우회수술이 포도당 조절에 대단히 유익한 효과를 낸다'고 말했습니다.

3 위장우회수술의 인기가 점점 더 높아질 것 같은데, 2형 당뇨병을 가진 비만한 환자들이 살도 빼고 동시에 치료도 받을 수 있기 때문입니다.

4 일석이조라 할 수 있습니다.

5 당뇨병을 가진 많은 비만한 환자들은 이 수술 후 약 복용도 끊었습니다.

6 사람들이 이는 단 한 번의 수술로 비만과 2형 당뇨병의 위험에서 쉽게 벗어날 수 있는 방법이라 생각하는 것도 당연합니다.

7 너무 쉽고 유혹적으로 들리니까요.

8 하지만 현실은 그다지 쉽지도, 유혹적이지도 않습니다.

9 이 수술을 받으면, 작은창자에 연결된 더 작은 위장을 갖게 되는데, 이 말은 작고 귀여운 위장에 대단히 제한적인 양의 음식만 들어갈 수 있다는 뜻입니다.

10 단단한 음식을 1/4컵 이상 먹거나 단단한 음식을 물 한 컵과 함께 먹는다면 병이 날지도 모르는데, 작은 위장이 그렇게 많은 음식을 처리할 수 없기 때문입니다.

Even today, not a few doctors are said to use leeches when practicing medicine, especially in Southeast Asia. Mostly, they use leeches to stimulate patients' blood circulation by draining excess blood to reduce the chance of blood congestion. It's called 'leech therapy.' In some cases, this unorthodox therapy has saved limbs by helping patients return the blood to normal circulation. In fact, if normal blood flow isn't restored within 48 hours after surgery, there will be a risk of amputation.

Leeches are also used to let blood out. Leeches have been used in medicine for centuries around the world since they are good at sucking blood. In the past, people just put this thankful bloodsucker on the bite when assaulted by a venomous snake. Once the leeches had sucked enough blood to feel full, they voluntarily fell off. Then, they died from ingesting the venom and the patients survived.

These days, leech therapy continues to be practiced in the same way. That's why animal rights activists are upset about leech therapy because once the leeches have filled up on blood and fallen off, the practitioners just throw them away to be destroyed.

Words & Expressions

upset v. 속상하게(화나게) 만들다 a. 화가 난 n. 배탈, 언짢음, 곤경 (be upset about ...에 대해 화가 나다, 언짢아 하다) leech 거머리 therapy 치료법 stimulate 자극하다 blood circulation 혈액 순환 drain (물, 액체) 빼내다, 비우다 congestion 혼잡, 막힘 blood congestion 울혈 unorthodox 비정통적인 limb 사지 (팔, 다리) restore (이전 상태로) 회복시키다 normal blood flow 정상적인 혈액 흐름 amputate (수술로 팔이나 다리를) 절단하다 (n. amputation) a risk of amputation 사지절단의 위험 be good at ...를 잘 하다 suck 빨다 bloodsucker 흡혈귀, 피를 빠는 것 assault 공격하다 venom 뱀 독 venomous snake 독사 (viper) voluntarily 스스로, 자발적으로 feel full 배부름을 느끼다 fall off 떨어지다 survive 살아남다 in the same way 같은 방식으로 animal (rights) activist 동물 (권익) 보호론자 fill up (가득) 채우다 practitioner 의술을 행하는 사람, 의사

1. What is the main idea of the story?

    a. The normal blood circulation is absolutely important.

    b. Leeches have been used to treat patients for many years.

    c. Thankfully, all kinds of bloodsuckers are useful to humans.

    d. Leeches and mosquitoes are creepy bloodsuckers.

2. According to the passage, which sentence is right?

    a. These days, it's hard to find doctors who use leeches to treat patients.

    b. The leech therapy is unorthodox, but it can save limbs of all patients bitten by venomous snakes.

    c. Leeches had been used in medicine for many years only in Southeast Asia.

    d. No need to worry about how to tear off leeches because they will fall off by themselves once they feel full.

3. Choose the correct words for each sentence.

    a. Please do not waste wastes. We can save the Earth <u>from</u> / <u>by</u> / <u>of</u> recycling.

    b. Demi Moore is said to use leeches to cleanse her body because she believes leeches help her <u>stay</u> / <u>stayed</u> / <u>staying</u> healthy.

    c. Not <u>a few</u> / <u>a little</u> / <u>much</u> medical practitioners around the world have been using leeches.

Answer 1. b 2. d 3. by ǀ stay ǀ a few

Listening Drill – Dictation

Even today,   are said to use leeches when practicing medicine, especially in Southeast Asia. Mostly, they use leeches to stimulate patients'   by draining excess blood to reduce the chance of blood congestion. It's called 'leech therapy.' In some cases, this   has saved limbs by helping patients return the blood to normal circulation. In fact, if normal blood flow isn't restored   after surgery, there will be   .

Leeches are also used to let blood out. Leeches have been used in medicine for centuries around the world since they are good at sucking blood. In the past, people just put this thankful bloodsucker   when assaulted by a venomous snake. Once the leeches had sucked enough blood to feel full, they   fell off. Then, they died from ingesting the venom and the   .

These days, leech therapy continues to be practiced in the same way. That's why animal rights activists   leech therapy because once the leeches have filled up on blood and fallen off, the   just throw them away to be destroyed.

Did You Know Why Animal Activists Are Upset About Leech Therapy?

❶ Even today, not a few doctors are said to use leeches when **practicing medicine**,

not a few = many　　…라고 한다　　주절의 주어 doctors와 주어가 일치해서 주어 생략

not a few doctors (복수명사) are (복수동사)　　when they practice medicine 그들이 진료를 할 때

especially in Southeast Asia.

❷ Mostly, they use leeches to **stimulate** patients' blood **circulation**

환자의 혈액순환을 자극하기 위해 (거머리를 사용한다)　　순환, 유통, 배포

by **draining** excess blood to **reduce** the chance of blood **congestion**.

drain (액체) 빼내다, 배수관　　혈액응고의 가능성을 줄이기 위해 (여분의 피를 빼낸다)　　혼잡, 정체, 울혈

blood congestion 울혈, traffic congestion 교통정체, nasal congestion 코막힘

❸ It's called 'leech therapy.'

❹ In some cases, this **unorthodox** therapy has saved **limbs**

이 비정통적인 치료법 = leech therapy　　limbs = arms and legs 사지 (팔과 다리)

b 묶음

by helping patients return the blood to normal **circulation**.

help + 목적어 patients + 동사원형 return　　normal blood circulation 정상적인 혈액 순환

❺ In fact, if normal blood **flow** isn't restored within 48 hours after surgery,

정상적인 혈액 흐름 (순환)　　be restored within …이내에 회복되다 (수동)

= normal blood circulation

there will be a risk of **amputation**.

…의 위험이 있다　　amputate v. 사지를 절단하다 amputation n. 사지절단

(dismember v. (사지를 잘라) 시신을 훼손하다, 동물 시체를 자르다)

❻ Leeches are also used to **let** blood **out**.

let ( ) out ( )을 내보내다

❼ Leeches have been used in medicine for centuries around the world

현재완료 for 기간 : …동안 현재까지 사용되어 왔다　　for centuries 수 세기 동안　for years 수년 동안

since they **are good at** sucking blood.

= because　　be good at -ing …를 잘 하다 (be bad at -ing …를 못하다)

❽ In the past, people just put this thankful bloodsucker on the bite

put ( ) on the bite ( )를 물린데 올려놓다　　bloodsucker : 이 문장에서는 leech를 가리킴.

when **assaulted** by a **venomous** snake.

주절의 주어 people와 일치해서 주어 생략　　venom n. 뱀의 독 venomous a. 맹독의 venomous snake = viper 독사

when people were assaulted by… = when being assaulted by

⑨ Once the leeches had sucked enough blood to feel full, they **voluntarily** fell off.

voluntarily ad. 자발적으로 voluntary a. 자발적인
volunteer n. 자원봉사자, 자원하는 사람 v. 자원하다

⑩ Then, they died from **ingesting** the venom and the patients survived.

die from -ing …로 사망하다   살아남다 (수동태 be survived로 쓰지 않는다.)

⑪ These days, leech therapy continues to be practiced in the same way.

continue to 동사원형 + be + pp 수동태

⑫ That's why animal rights activists are upset about leech therapy

이것이 바로 that 이하 절의 이유이다   …에 대해 화를 내다

because once the leeches have ¹⁾ filled up on blood and ²⁾ fallen off,

have filled up 배를 다 채우고 and have fallen off 떨어져나가다

the practitioners just throw them away to be destroyed.

거머리들(them)이 죽도록(be destroyed 수동) 내다 버리다(throw away)

동물 보호론자들이 왜 거머리 치료를 못 마땅하게 여기는지 아세요?

❶ 심지어 오늘날에도, 특히 동남아시아의 적지 않은 의사들이 의료 시술 때 거머리를 사용한다고 합니다.

❷ 대부분의 경우 이들은 추가적인 혈액을 뽑아내 환자의 혈액 순환을 촉진하고 혈액 응고의 가능성을 줄이기 위해 거머리를 사용합니다.

❸ 이를 '거머리 치료'라고 부릅니다.

❹ 어떤 경우, 비정통적인 이 치료법이 환자의 혈액 순환이 정상으로 돌아오는데 도움을 주어 실제 사지절단을 막아주기도 합니다.

❺ 사실 수술 후 48시간 이내 혈액 순환이 정상으로 돌아오지 않으면 사지절단의 위험이 있습니다.

❻ 또한 거머리는 피를 빼내는데도 사용됩니다.

❼ 거머리들은 수 백 년 간 전 세계에서 의학에 사용되었는데, 거머리들이 피를 아주 잘 빨기 때문입니다.

❽ 과거에는 사람들이 독사의 공격을 받으면 고마운 이 흡혈 동물을 물린 부위에 올려놓았습니다.

❾ 거머리들은 일단 배부를 정도로 피를 빤 후에는 스스로 떨어집니다.

❿ 그러면 거머리들은 뱀독으로 죽고, 환자는 뱀독에서 살아남았습니다.

⑪ 요즘 거머리 치료도 이와 같은 방식으로 이루어집니다.

⑫ 그래서 동물 권익 보호론자들이 거머리 치료법에 광분하는 것인데, 더러운 피로 배를 채운 거머리가 떨어져 나가면 시술자들이 거머리가 죽게 갖다 버리기 때문입니다.

We have heard a lot about the benefits of eating fish instead of meat. Fish oil completely differs from meat fat. It helps cardiovascular system, joints, brain and so on. Although there is a multitude of benefits, you should think again before eating fish because nearly 40% of the fish available to us nowadays comes from fish farms.

Commonly, farmed fish are carnivorous such as salmon, tuna and shrimp. These farmed fish live in overcrowded and unclean conditions where there is a high risk of infection, contagion and contamination. According to a study, farmed salmon carry higher levels of contaminants like dioxins than wild salmon do. That means farmed salmon can be dangerous to humans since their polluted flesh can pollute our body when we eat it. And there are also several other problems such as antibiotics and residues from chemicals used to clean fish farming nets.

But farmed fish are more widely available and cheaper than wild fish because farmed fish can be harvested all year round. So when shopping at the supermarket, choose wisely and carefully for the sake of your health.

Words & Expressions

benefit 이득, 혜택 instead of 대신 completely 완전히(absolutely) differ from …와 다르다 (be different from) joint 관절 and so on 기타 등등 a multitude of 수많은 (+ 복수 명사) nearly 거의 available 입수 가능한 nowadays 요즘 fish farm 어류 양식장 commonly 보통, 일반적으로 carnivorous 육식의 salmon 연어 (단수, 복수 동일) tuna 참치 shrimp 새우 farmed fish 양식 어류 overcrowded 너무 붐비는 there is a high risk of …의 위험이 높다 infection 감염 contagion 전염, 전염병 contamination 오염 contaminant 오염물질 dioxin 다이옥신 pollute 오염시키다 polluted flesh 오염된 살(고기) antibiotics 항생제 residue 잔여물 chemical 화학물질 fish farming net 양식할 때 사용되는 어망 harvest 추수하다, 수확하다 all year round 일 년 내내

1. What is the main idea of the story?

    a. Carnivorous fish such as salmon is dangerous for its sharp teeth.

    b. It would be better not to eat salmon or tuna due to its oil.

    c. Farmed fish may not be a good choice for your health.

    d. Farmed fish has to be cheaper than wild fish.

2. According to the passage, which sentence is right?

    a. Fish oil is totally different from meat fat.

    b. Fish is helpful for health, while on the other hand, fish oil is not helpful at all.

    c. Wild fish is more vulnerable to infection than farmed fish.

    d. Farmed fish is cheaper than wild fish because it is carnivorous.

3. Choose the correct words for each sentence.

    a. Several medicines are <u>available</u> / <u>bearable</u> / <u>inexcusable</u> in any drugstore so you can easily buy them.

    b. This technique will open up a multitude of new <u>possible</u> / <u>possibility</u> / <u>possibilities</u>.

    c. You think you are ambitious but I think you are greedy. Ambition differs <u>with</u> / <u>from</u> / <u>as</u> greed, you know.

Answer **1.** c   **2.** a   **3.** available ǀ possibilities ǀ from

We have heard a lot about the benefits of eating fish   meat. Fish oil completely differs from meat fat. It helps cardiovascular system, joints, brain and so on. Although there is   , you should think again before eating fish because nearly 40% of the fish   nowadays comes from fish farms.

Commonly, farmed fish are   such as salmon, tuna and shrimp. These farmed fish live in   conditions where there is   infection, contagion and contamination. According to a study, farmed salmon carry higher levels of contaminants like dioxins than wild salmon do. That means farmed salmon can be dangerous to humans since their   can pollute our body when we eat it. And there are also several other problems such as   and residues from chemicals used to clean fish farming nets.

But farmed fish are more widely available and cheaper than wild fish because farmed fish can   . So when shopping at the supermarket, choose wisely and carefully   your health.

Did You Know Not All Fish Is Good For Our Health?

1 We have heard a lot (about the benefits of eating fish) instead of meat.

많이 듣다 　　　　어류를 섭취하는 것의 이로움에 대해 　　　　대신

2 Fish oil completely **differs from** meat fat.

다르다 be different from

보통 fish oil / meat fat으로 쓰고 fish fat / meat oil로는 잘 쓰지 않는다. 돼지의 fat은 lard, 소,양의 fat은 tallow

3 It helps cardiovascular system, joints, brain and so on.

= fish oil　　심혈관의

4 Although there is a **multitude** of benefits, you should think again before eating fish

there is a multitude of 복수명사 　　　　　　　　　　　　주절의 주어 you와 주어 일치, 생략
is 단수동사가 온 것은 benefits가 아닌 a multitude 때문 　　　　= before you eat fish
There is a couple of people. 커플 한 쌍(2명)이 있다. (is + a couple)
There are two couples. 커플 두 쌍(4명)이 있다. (are + two couples)

because nearly 40% of the fish (**available** to us nowadays) comes from fish farms.

　　　　　　　　　수식　　　　　　　　　　　　　양어장　　　　　fish farming 양어
　　　fish which is available to us 우리가 사용할 수 있는 생선　　fish farmer 양어민
　　　주어 fish (3인칭 단수현재) + 동사 comes　　　　　　　farmed fish 양식된 어류

5 Commonly, farmed fish are **carnivorous** (such as **salmon**, **tuna** and **shrimp**).

fish는 단수, 복수형이 동일　　carnivorous a. 육식의 herbivorous a. 초식의
복수 fishes로 쓰기도 하나, 이 문장의 fish는 복수 + are

6 These farmed fish live in (**overcrowded** and unclean) conditions (where there is

These (복수) + farmed fish (복수) + live 복수동사　　　　수식　　　　수식
　　　　　　　　　　　　　　　　　　　　　　　　　　　　　붐비고 더러운 상태인 곳
　　　　　　　　　　　　　　　　　　　　there is a high risk of ( ) : ( )의 위험이 있다

a high risk of **infection**, **contagion** and **contamination**).

infectious a. 감염되는　　　　contaminated a. 오염된
contagious a. 전염성의　　contaminant n. 오염물질

7 According to a study, farmed salmon carry higher levels of **contaminants**

salmon은 단수, 복수 형태 동일　　비교급 higher A than B
이 문장의 salmon은 복수 + carry/do (복수동사) (carries/does X)

like dioxins than wild salmon do.

– than wild salmon carry (carry 대신 쓰인 대동사 do)

8 That means farmed salmon can be dangerous to humans

…에게 위험하다

since their **polluted flesh** can pollute our body when we eat it.

= because　　　pollute v. 오염시키다 polluted a. 오염된 pollutant n. 오염물질

50

⑨ And there are also several other problems such as (antibiotics and residues

there are (복수) + 복수 명사 problems

from chemicals) (used to clean fish farming nets).

수식 | chemicals which are used… : …에 사용된 화학물질에서 온 잔여물

앞서 나온 other problems의 예 - antibiotics, residues

⑩ But farmed fish are more widely available and cheaper than wild fish

더 널리 구하기 쉽고 더 싼 (비교급) farmed fish와 wild fish 비교

because farmed fish can be harvested all year round.

일년 내내 = all year long, throughout the year

⑪ So when shopping at the supermarket, choose (wisely and carefully)

주절의 주어 you와 일치, 생략   명령형 (주어 you 생략)

When you shop at the supermarket, you choose…

for the sake of your health.

…를 위해서

모든 생선이 다 건강에 좋은 건 아니라는 거 아세요?

❶ 육류 대신 생선을 섭취할 때의 이점에 관해 우리는 많이 들어왔습니다.

❷ 생선 기름은 육류 지방과는 완전히 다릅니다.

❸ 생선 기름은 심장혈관계, 관절, 뇌 등에 도움이 됩니다.

❹ 이렇게 유익한 점이 많은데도 불구하고 생선을 먹기 전에 한 번 더 생각해야 하는 이유는, 오늘날 우리가 구할 수 있는 생선의 약 40%가 양어장에서 오기 때문입니다.

❺ 보통 양어장 생선은 연어, 참치, 새우처럼 육식성입니다.

❻ 이들 양식어는 너무 붐벼서 비좁고 더러운 환경에서 생활하는데, 그래서 감염, 전염, 오염의 위험이 높습니다.

❼ 한 연구에 의하면, 양식된 연어는 자연산 연어보다 다이옥신 같은 오염물질 함유율이 더 높다고 합니다.

❽ 이 말은 양식 연어의 오염된 살을 우리가 먹으면 우리 몸도 오염되기 때문에 양식 연어가 인간에게 위험할 수 있다는 뜻입니다.

❾ 또 항생제와 양식 어망 청소에 쓰인 화학품의 잔여물 같은 또 다른 문제도 있습니다.

❿ 하지만 양식어는 자연산 생선보다 구하기도 쉽고 값도 싼데, 이는 양식어가 일 년 내내 수확되기 때문입니다.

⓫ 그러니 슈퍼마켓에서 장을 볼 때 건강을 위해 지혜롭고 신중하게 선택하세요.

10 Did You Know Why Carrot Juice Is Called Miracle Juice?

Carrot juice is called miracle juice because its health-friendly effects are miraculous. As everybody already knows, drinking carrot juice, as well as eating carrots is good for eyes and prevents night blindness. And carrot juice is thought to reduce the risk of certain types of cancer including skin and breast cancer due to the high amount of beta carotene. Beta carotene changes to vitamin A in the body and there is a connection between vitamin A and cancer prevention.

Vitamin A is said to strengthen bones, teeth and nails, and enhance your hair condition. Drinking carrot juice is allegedly excellent for the liver since vitamin A reduces bile and fat in the liver. That's not all. Carrot juice aids in the resistance to infections. Thanks to these properties and vitamin A, carrot juice is recommended as the best drink for pregnant women. When choosing carrots, you should choose the darker ones because the darker the color, the more carotene it contains. And one more thing. Although carrot juice is a miracle juice, just remember, 'Too much is as bad as too little.'

Words & Expressions

miracle 기적 (miraculous 기적적인) effect 효과 night blindness 야맹증 be thought to ...라고 한다 (be said to) reduce the risk of ...의 위험을 줄여주다 breast cancer 유방암 the high amount of 상당한 양의 beta carotene 베타카로틴 connection 관계, 연관 cancer prevention 암 예방 strengthen 강하게 하다 nail 손톱, 발톱 (fingernail, toenail) enhance 향상시키다 allegedly 알려진 바에 의하면 bile 담즙 liver 간 That's not all. 이게 다가 아니다 aid 돕다 in the resistance to ...에 대해 저항하는 property 특성, 성질 pregnant woman 임산부 Too much is as bad as too little 과유불급 (너무 많은 것은 너무 적은 것 만큼 나쁘다)

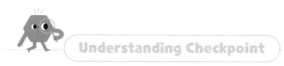

1. What can be the best title of this story?

  a. Amazing Benefits of Carrots
  b. Carrots VS. Carrot Juice : The Winner Is...
  c. The Richest Source of Vitamin A
  d. Too Much Is As Bad As Too Little

2. The reason why carrot juice is called miracle juice is because _____ .

  a. only magicians can make carrot juice
  b. its nutritional effects are that good
  c. it can prevent all kinds of cancer
  d. it can make blind men see

3. Choose the correct words for each sentence.

  a. My aunt said she had no choice but to divorce him <u>because</u> / <u>since</u> / <u>due to</u> his erratic behavior.
  b. The boss had a hard time when he had to deal with <u>persistence</u> / <u>resistance</u> / <u>assistance</u> to change in his office.
  c. Some people think the more money you have, <u>the worse</u> / <u>the more</u> / <u>the most</u> you can express your opinion.

Answer **1.** a **2.** b **3.** due to | resistance | the more

Carrot juice is called miracle juice because its _____ are miraculous. As everybody already knows, drinking carrot juice, as well as eating carrots is good for eyes and prevents _____. And carrot juice is thought to reduce the risk of certain types of cancer including skin and breast cancer due to the high amount of beta carotene. Beta carotene _____ vitamin A in the body and there is _____ vitamin A and cancer prevention.

Vitamin A is said to _____ bones, teeth and nails, and _____ your hair condition. Drinking carrot juice _____ the liver since vitamin A reduces bile and fat in the liver. That's not all. Carrot juice aids in _____ . Thanks to these properties and vitamin A, carrot juice is recommended as the best drink for pregnant women. When choosing carrots, you should choose the darker ones because the darker the color, the more carotene _____ . And one more thing. Although carrot juice is a miracle juice, just remember, '_____ '

Did You Know Why Carrot Juice Is Called Miracle Juice?

1 **Carrot** juice is called **miracle** juice because its **health-friendly**
당근   n. 기적   건강에 유익한
(environmental-friendly / eco-friendly 환경 친화적인, user-friendly 사용하기 편리한, child-friendly 아동 친화적인)

effects are **miraculous**.
                     a. 기적적인

2 As everybody already knows, drinking carrot juice, (as well as
everybody 단수 + knows 단수동사   as well as …뿐 아니라
이 문장의 주어 drinking (3인칭 현재 단수) + 동사 ¹⁾ is and ²⁾ prevents

eating carrots) ¹⁾ is good for eyes and ²⁾ **prevents** night blindness.
                                          v. 예방하다   night 밤 + blindness 보이지 않음 : 야맹증

3 And carrot juice is thought to reduce the risk of certain types of cancer (including
                     …라고들 한다 (be said to 동사, be thought to 동사)   수식
                              certain types of cancer의 예 : 피부암, 유방암을 포함한 특정 종류의 암
                          reduce the risk of ( ) : ( )의 위험을 줄이다

skin and breast cancer) due to the high amount of beta carotene.
     skin cancer 피부암 breast cancer 유방암   많은 양의 (↔ 적은 양의 the low amount of)
                              due to + 명사구 (주어+동사 절이 올 수 없다) = because of … 때문에

4 Beta carotene changes to vitamin A (in the body) and
               …로 (to) 변하다   체내에서

there is a connection between vitamin A and cancer **prevention**.
          …와 … 사이에 관련이 있다. (둘 사이 between, 둘 이상 among)   예방, 방지

5 Vitamin A is said to ¹⁾ **strengthen** (bones, teeth and nails),
Vitamin A is said to strengthen ( ) and enhance ( )
비타민 A는 ( )를 강화하고 ( )를 향상시킨다고 한다.
               strong a. 강한 strength n. 힘, 강도 strengthen v. 강하게 하다
               (long a. 긴 length n. 길이 lengthen v. 길게 하다 / wide a. 넓은 width n. 폭 widen v. 넓히다
               deep a. 깊은 depth n. 깊이 deepen v. 깊어지다)

and ²⁾ **enhance** your hair condition.
          v. 향상시키다

6 Drinking carrot juice is allegedly **excellent for** the liver
당근 주스를 마시는 것 (동명사 주어, 단수)   be good for …에 좋다 / be excellent for …에 아주 좋다

since vitamin A reduces (bile and fat) in the liver.
               bile n. 담즙, 분노, 증오심

7 That's not all.

54

❽ Carrot juice **aids** in the **resistance to** infections.

⋯에(in) 도움을 주다   ⋯에(to) 대산 저항력

❾ Thanks to these properties and vitamin A, carrot juice is **recommended** as

thanks to 덕분에 + 명사구 (절이 오지 않는되다)
due to / because of 때문에 + 명사구

⋯로 추천되다 (수동)

the best drink for **pregnant** women.

= expectant mother 임산부

❿ When choosing carrots, you should choose the darker ones

주절의 주어 you와 일치, 생략 when you choose carrots

because the darker the color, the more carotene it contains.

the 비교급 + the 비교급 : ⋯할수록 더 ⋯하다 (색이 진할수록/어두울수록 더 많이 함유하다)
The more, the better 많은 수록 좋다
The less sugar you consume, the healthier you will be. 설탕을 덜 섭취할수록 더 건강해질 것이다

⓫ And one more thing.

= And (there is) one more thing.

⓬ Although carrot juice is a miracle juice, just remember,

'Too much is as bad as too little.'

지나치게 많은 것 (being too much)은 너무 적은 것 (being too little) 만큼이나 좋지 않다 (as bad as) 과유불급 (過猶不及)

왜 당근 쥬스가 기적의 쥬스라고 불리는지 아세요?

❶ 당근 주스는 기적의 쥬스라고 불리는데, 왜냐하면 당근 쥬스가 지닌 건강에 유익한 효능이 기적적이기 때문입니다.

❷ 다들 이미 알고 있듯이 당근 주스를 마시거나 당근을 섭취하면 눈에 좋고 야맹증을 예방할 수 있습니다.

❸ 그리고 당근 주스가 피부암과 유방암 같은 암의 위험을 줄여준다고 알려진 건 베타카로틴 함량이 높기 때문입니다.

❹ 베타카로틴은 몸 안에서 비타민 A로 바뀌는데, 비타민 A와 암 예방은 관련이 있습니다.

❺ 비타민 A는 뼈, 치아, 손톱을 강화시켜 주고 머릿결도 좋아지게 한다고 합니다.

❻ 당근 주스를 마시면 비타민 A가 간의 담즙과 지방을 줄여주기 때문에 간에도 좋다고 알려져 있습니다.

❼ 이게 다가 아닙니다.

❽ 당근 주스는 감염에 저항하는데도 도움을 줍니다.

❾ 이러한 특성과 비타민 A 때문에 당근 주스는 임신한 여성에게 가장 좋은 음료로 추천 받고 있습니다.

❿ 당근을 고를 때 색이 더 진한 걸 고르는 게 좋은데, 색이 진할수록 카로틴 함량이 높기 때문입니다.

⓫ 그리고 한 가지 더.

⓬ 당근 주스가 기적의 주스인 건 맞지만, '과유불급'이란 말을 잊지 마세요.

Chapter 02

Food

MP3

11 Did You Know 'Sweetbread' Is Neither Sweet Nor Bread?

Surprisingly, 'sweetbreads' are not a kind of bread; they are a kind of meat. More specifically speaking, sweetbread is a gland from young animals, frequently from piglets, calves or lambs. People have used these glands as edible organ meats for a long time. You can make various sweetbreads depending on what ingredients are used. Sweetbread made from the thymus, an organ in the neck, is often called 'neck sweetbread', and sweetbread made from the pancreas, a belly organ near the stomach, is called 'belly sweetbread.' These are the two basic types of sweetbreads, but other glands are also eaten and also called 'sweetbreads.' For example, 'ear sweetbread' is made from one of the salivary glands in the mouth.

Mostly, sweetbreads are boiled first to remove a thin skin. While boiling, add salt, vinegar or lemon juice. In some cases, people soak them in milk or water for several hours to remove all the blood.

Words & Expressions

sweetbread 스위트브레드(어린 돼지, 양, 소의 췌장, 흉선) gland 분비선(샘) frequently 자주, 종종 piglet 아기 돼지 (pig 돼지) calf 송아지 (복수 calves) lamb 새끼 양 (sheep 양) edible 먹을 수 있는, 식용의 (eatable) organ 내장, 장기 depending on ...에 따라 ingredient 재료 thymus 흉선 pancreas 췌장 belly 배 stomach 위장 salivary 침을 분비하는 (saliva 침) boil 끓이다 vinegar 식초 soak 담그다

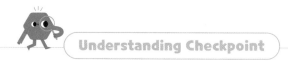

1. What is the main idea of the story?

    a. It is barbaric and unacceptable to eat internal organs of young animals.

    b. It sounds like sweet-tasting bread but sweetbread is a kind of meat.

    c. Sweetbread is supposed to taste like sweet bread, but it tastes bitter.

    d. Sweetbread is a kind of meat but you can buy it at a local bakery.

2. Two basic types of sweetbread are _____ .

    a. neck sweetbread and belly sweetbread

    b. ear sweetbread and neck sweetbread

    c. salivary sweetbread and throat sweetbread

    d. thymus sweetbread and piglet sweetbread

3. Choose the correct words for each sentence.

    a. The salary of the job I am applying for is between $5k and $6k <u>to say nothing of my experience</u> / <u>depending on experience</u> / <u>as far as my experience is concerned</u>.

    b. There are several fruits in the basket <u>in addition</u> / <u>for example</u> / <u>moreover</u> mango, watermelon, and kiwi.

    c. Several calves <u>is</u> / <u>are</u> / <u>was</u> eating grass on the ground peacefully.

Answer   **1.** b   **2.** a   **3.** depending on experience ⏐ for example ⏐ are

Listening Drill – Dictation

Surprisingly, 'sweetbreads' are not a kind of bread; they are a kind of meat.
_____ , sweetbread is a gland from young animals, _____ from piglets, calves or lambs. People have used these glands _____ for a long time.
You can make various sweetbreads _____ what ingredients are used. Sweetbread _____ , an organ in the neck, is often called 'neck sweetbread', and sweetbread made from _____ , a belly organ near the stomach, is called 'belly sweetbread.' These are the two basic types of sweetbreads, but other glands _____ and also called 'sweetbreads.' For example, 'ear sweetbread' is made from one of _____ in the mouth.
Mostly, sweetbreads are boiled first _____ . While boiling, add salt, vinegar or lemon juice. In some cases, people _____ them in milk or water for several hours to remove all the blood.

59

Did You Know 'Sweetbread' Is Neither Sweet Nor Bread?

❶ Surprisingly, 'sweetbreads' are not a **kind** of bread; they are a kind of **meat**.
놀랍게도 (문장 전체를 수식하는 부사)   …종류의, 일종의 (kind n. 종류 a. 친절한)   (식용) 고기
(문장 전체 수식하는 부사 예 : amazingly 놀랍게도, unexpectedly 예상 못하게도, generally 일반적으로)

❷ More **specifically** speaking, sweetbread is a gland (from young animals),
더 구체적으로 말하면   ↑ 수식
(exactly speaking 정확히 말하면 / more exactly speaking 더 정확히 말하면)   a gland from ( ), frequently (a gland) from ( )

frequently from (piglets, calves or lambs).
자주, 종종   pig 돼지 / piglet 아기돼지, cow 소 / calf 송아지, sheep 양 / lamb 아기 양, goat 염소 / kid 아기 염소
복수형 calf-calves, shelf-shelves, half-halves, scarf-scarves, knife-knives, wife-wives,
hankerchief-hankerchieves

❸ People have used these glands as **edible organ** meats **for a long time**.
현재완료 have used + for 기간   edible = eatable 먹을 수 있는   오랫동안
얼마 기간 동안 …해왔다   (potable a. 마실 수 있는)

❹ You can make **various** sweetbreads **depending on** (what **ingredients** are used).
a. 다양한, 여러 가지의   …에 따라 (어떤 재료가 사용되느냐에 따라)   (음식의) 재료, 성분

❺ Sweetbread (made from the thymus), (an organ in the neck), is often called
          ↑ 수식   = 동격
주어 sweetbread, 동사 is called

'neck sweetbread', and sweetbread (made from the pancreas), (a belly organ
                                   ↑ 수식   = 동격
                                          pancreas (췌장) - 복수라서 -s가 붙은 게 아님

near the stomach), is called 'belly sweetbread.'

❻ These are the two basic types of sweetbreads, but other glands are also [1] eaten
기본적인 두 가지 종류   ☺ other gland are [1] eaten and (other glands are) [2] called

and also [2] called 'sweetbreads.'

❼ For example, 'ear sweetbread' is made from one of the salivary glands in the mouth.
                    …로 만들어지다   one of the + 복수명사
          The table is made of wood. (물리적/외형적 변화) Cheese is made from milk. (전혀 다른 것으로의 변화)

❽ Mostly, sweetbreads are boiled first to remove a **thin** skin.
주로, 일반적으로   먼저 익히다 (boil v. 끓이다, 삶다 boiler n. 보일러 boiled egg 삶은 달걀)
                                              thin 얇은, 가는

60

⑨ While boiling, **add** (salt, vinegar or lemon juice).
주절의 주어 you와 일치, 생략 (주절은 명령문이라 주어 you 생략)
= While you boil, you add salt, vinegar or lemon juice.

⑩ In some cases, people **soak** them in (milk or water) for several hours
담그다   them = sweetbreads   기간의 for – 몇 시간 동안

to remove all the blood.

'스위트브레드'가 달콤하지도 않고 빵도 아니라는 거 아세요?

❶ 놀랍게도 스위트브레드는 빵 종류가 아니라 고기 종류입니다.

❷ 더 구체적으로 말하면, 스위트브레드는 새끼 돼지, 송아지, 새끼 양 같은 어린 동물의 분비선입니다.

❸ 사람들은 오랫동안 동물의 분비선을 식용 가능한 내장기관 고기로 사용해왔습니다.

❹ 사용하는 재료에 따라 다양한 스위트브레드를 만들 수 있습니다.

❺ 흉선(목구멍의 장기)으로 만든 스위트브레드는 종종 '목 스위트브레드'라 불리고, 췌장이나 위장과 가까운 복부 장기로 만든 스위트브레드는 '배 스위트브레드'라고 불립니다.

❻ 이는 스위트브레드의 기본적인 두 종류인데 다른 분비선들 역시 식용되고 있으며, 역시 '스위트브레드'라고 불립니다.

❼ 예를 들어 '귀 스위트브레드'는 입 속 침샘 중 하나로 만든 것입니다.

❽ 대부분의 경우 스위트브레드는 얇은 피막을 제거하기 위해 먼저 끓입니다.

❾ 끓일 때 소금, 식초 또는 레몬즙을 첨가합니다.

❿ 어떤 경우 사람들은 피를 모두 제거하기 위해 몇 시간 동안 우유나 물에 담그기도 합니다.

12 Did You Know Vegetarians Do Not Eat Marshmallow?

Have you heard that vegetarians don't eat marshmallow? Not all vegetarians turn it down, but some vegetarians do refuse to eat it because it contains ingredients from animals.

There are several types of vegetarians, depending on what kinds of foods they eat.

Ovo-lacto vegetarians, for example, are vegetarians who choose not to eat meat of any kind, but do eat eggs and dairy products. They think it's OK to eat eggs, milk products and honey because they can get those foods without killing animals.

On the other hand, vegans do not eat any kind of animal meat, eggs or animal fat, nor dairy products like ice cream or yogurt. Their diet mainly includes fruits, vegetables and grains. So, they won't eat bread with butter, a chocolate cake covered with whipped cream, food cooked with lard (pigs' fat), or honey. There is one more thing vegans refuse to eat : gelatin. Gelatin is a kind of protein derived from the tissues, bones and skins of animals, usually cows and pigs. That's why vegans refuse to eat desserts made with gelatin, such as jelly or marshmallow.

Words & Expressions

vegetarian 채식주의자 turn down 거절하다 refuse 거부, 거절하다 depending on ...에 따라 ovo-lacto vegetarian 유란 채식주의자 dairy 유제품의 (dairy product 유제품 = milk product) grain 곡물 whipped 매를 맞은, 거품이 인 lard 라드, 돼지기름 gelatin 젤라틴 protein 단백질 derive 비롯되다, ...에서 끌어내다 tissue 조직

Understanding Checkpoint

1. What can be the best title of this story?

   a. Shocking News : Marshmallow Is Meat?

   b. Three Types Of Vegetarians

   c. Desserts made of Animals

   d. Why Do Some Vegetarians Refuse To Eat Marshmallow?

2. According to the passage, which sentence is right?

   a. Some vegetarians refuse to eat marshmallow due to its disgusting taste.

   b. All vegetarians don't eat gelatin and marshmellow.

   c. Vegans will refuse to taste a small piece of milk chocolate.

   d. Ovo-lacto vegetarians think eggs and milk products are OK to eat since these foods taste too good to refuse.

3. Choose the correct words for each sentence.

   a. There is more than one way to skin a cat. Actually, there are <u>much</u> / <u>several</u> / <u>only one</u> ways of doing it.

   b. <u>Dairy</u> / <u>Diary</u> / <u>Daily</u> farms are farms where farmers raise cows to make milk or milk products.

   c. How much is a roasted potato <u>sprinkling</u> / <u>sprinkled</u> / <u>to sprinkle</u> lightly with cheese powder?

   d. I won't prepare food for you, <u>no</u> / <u>nor</u> / <u>not</u> for your family.

Answer 1. d 2. c 3. several ǀ Dairy ǀ sprinkled ǀ nor

Listening Drill – Dictation

                     vegetarians don't eat marshmallow? Not all vegetarians
         , but some vegetarians do refuse to eat it because it contains ingredients from animals.

There are several types of vegetarians, depending on   .

Ovo-lacto vegetarians, for example, are vegetarians who choose not to eat meat of any kind, but do eat eggs and   . They think   eggs, milk products and honey because they can get those foods   animals.

On the other hand, vegans do not eat any kind of animal meat, eggs or animal fat, dairy products like ice cream or yogurt. Their diet mainly includes fruits, vegetables and grains. So, they won't eat bread with butter, a chocolate cake covered with whipped cream,   (pigs' fat), or honey. There is one more thing vegans refuse to eat : gelatin. Gelatin is a kind of protein   the tissues, bones and   , usually cows and pigs. That's why vegans refuse to eat desserts made with gelatin, such as jelly or marshmallow.

Did You Know Vegetarians Do Not Eat Marshmallow?

1 Have you heard that **vegetarians** don't eat marshmallow?
that 이하를 들어본 적이 있는가　　채식주의자 (vegetable n. 채소 vegetation n. 초목)
(have pp 현재완료-경험)

2 Not all vegetarians **turn it down**, but some vegetarians do refuse to eat it
부분 부정　　　　　　　turn down = refuse 거절하다　　　　　동사 refuse를 강조하기 위한 강조의 조동사 do
　　　　　　　　　　 it = marshmallow

because it **contains ingredients** (from animals).
　　　　it = marshmallow　　　　　수식

3 There are several types of vegetarians, depending on (what kinds of foods they eat).
　　　　　　　　　　　　　　　　　　( )에 따라 (그들이 무슨 종류의 음식을 먹는지에 따라)

4 Ovo-lacto vegetarians, for example, are vegetarians (who choose not to eat
ovo : egg (란 卵) / lacto : milk (유 乳)　　　( )인 채식주의자　수식　　　to부정사의 부정 - not to 동사
계란, 우유는 먹는 채식주의자　　　　　　 choose to eat 먹기로 선택하다 (↔ choose not to eat 먹지 않기로 선택하다)

meat of any kind), but do eat eggs and **dairy** products.
　　동사 eat을 강조하기 위한 강조의 조동사 do　　　dairy 유제품의, 유제품 회사 ('diary 일기'와 철자 혼동 주의)

5 They think it's OK to eat (eggs, milk products and **honey**)
　　　　　　　　먹어도 된다 (it's not OK to eat 먹으면 안 된다)　milk products = dairy products 유제품
　　　　　　　　It 가주어, to eat 진주어

because they can get those foods (without killing animals).
　　　　　　= eggs, milk products, honey　동물을 죽이지 않고도 (전치사 without + 동명사)

6 On the other hand, vegans do not eat (any kind of animal meat,
　　　　　　　　　　do not eat A nor B : A도 안 먹고 B도 안 먹다

eggs or animal fat), nor (dairy products like ice cream or yogurt).
　　　　　　　dairy products의 예 - ice cream, ypgurt

7 Their **diet** mainly includes (fruits, **vegetables** and **grains**).
주어 (vegans의 식사-3인칭 단수현재) 동사 includes
　　diet 식사, 식습관, 다이어트(체중감량)

8 So, they won't eat ¹⁾ bread with butter, ²⁾ a chocolate cake (covered with
그들이 먹지 않는 것 네 가지 ¹⁾, ²⁾, ³⁾, ⁴⁾　　　　　　　　　　수식
　　　　　　　　　　　　　　　　　　　cake (which is) covered with …로 덮인 케이크

whipped cream), ³⁾ food (cooked with lard (pigs' fat)), or ⁴⁾ honey.
　　　　수식
food (which is) cooked with …로 조리한 음식

⑨ There is one more thing vegans refuse to eat : gelatin.

유도부사 주어는 실제 주어에 따라 동사가 결정된다.
단수 주어 <u>There is one thing</u> that vegans refuse to eat. 비건이 먹기를 거절하는 한 가지가 있다.
복수 주어 <u>There are</u> several <u>types</u> of vegetarians. 채식주의자에 몇 가지 종류가 있다.

⑩ Gelatin is a kind of **protein derived from** (the tissues, bones and skins)

↑ 수식
protein (which is) derived from ( ) of animals 동물의 ( )에서 나온 단백질

of animals, usually cows and pigs.

(animals 중에서도) 보통 usually 소와 돼지

⑪ That's why vegans refuse to eat desserts (made with gelatin), such as jelly

↑ 수식
desserts (which are) made with 젤라틴으로 만든 디저트의 예 : 젤리, 마시멜로우

or marshmallow.

채식주의자들이 마시멜로우를 먹지 않는다는 거 아세요?

① 채식주의자들이 마시멜로우를 먹지 않는다는 거 들어보셨나요?

② 모든 채식주의자들이 이를 거부하는 건 아니지만 일부 채식주의자들은 이것이 동물에서 나왔다는 이유로 먹기를 정말 거부합니다.

③ 채식주의자에는 그들이 어떤 음식을 먹느냐에 따라 몇 가지 종류가 있습니다.

④ 예를 들어 유란 채식주의자는 모든 종류의 고기는 먹지 않지만 계란과 유제품은 먹는 채식주의자들입니다.

⑤ 이들은 계란, 유제품, 그리고 꿀은 동물을 죽이지 않고 얻을 수 있는 음식이기 때문에 먹어도 괜찮다고 생각합니다.

⑥ 반면 비건은 모든 종류의 동물 고기, 계란, 동물 지방은 물론이요 아이스크림, 요구르트 같은 유제품도 먹지 않습니다.

⑦ 그래서 이들의 식단은 과일, 야채, 곡물이 들어갑니다.

⑧ 그래서 버터 바른 빵, 휘핑크림이 덮인 초콜릿 케이크, 라드(돼지기름)로 요리한 음식과 꿀은 먹지 않습니다.

⑨ 비건이 먹기를 거부하는 게 한 가지 더 있는데, 바로 젤라틴입니다.

⑩ 젤라틴은 일종의 단백질로 동물 특히 소와 돼지의 조질, 뼈, 가죽에서 나옵니다.

⑪ 그래서 비건은 젤리, 마시멜로우 같은 젤라틴으로 만든 디저트 먹기를 거부하는 겁니다.

Shark Fin Soup Is As Dangerous As Sharks?

Shark fin soup is dangerous not because of shark's sharp teeth, but because of its mercury content.

In China and Hong Kong, the popularity of shark fin soup has been rising among people. Many Chinese people think that shark fin soup is good for their health because it is highly nutritious. They believe that shark fin soup is rich in various vitamins and minerals, especially Vitamin A. But, lots of scientists and nutritionists disagree with their opinion. According to their research, it contains no Vitamin A at all, and the amount of minerals found in shark fin soup is not very high.

It is also widely believed that shark fin soup can prevent cancer. But scientifically, it is not proven that shark fin soup has cancer fighting abilities.

On the contrary, shark fin soup is said to be bad for our health due to its high mercury content. So, doctors recommend that pregnant women and young children avoid eating shark fins. Actually, dolphin meat and tuna are also considered to be dangerous because they also contain high levels of mercury.

Words & Expressions

fin 지느러미 teeth 이빨들 (단수 - tooth) mercury 수은 content 내용물 popularity 인기 highly nutritious 영양가가 높은 be rich in ...이 풍부한 nutritionist 영양학자 contain 함유하다 prevent 예방하다 scientifically 과학적으로 cancer fighting abilities 항암효과(능력) on the contrary 오히려, 반대로 recommend 권고하다, 추천하다 pregnant 임신한 (n. pregnancy) tuna 다랑어, 참치

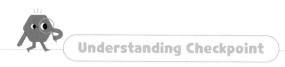

1. What is the main idea of the story?

a. Sharks are dangerous so never eat or touch them if you don't want to die.

b. Doctors said shark fin soup is not healthful but dangerous for your health.

c. Shark fin soup is expensive because of its mercury content.

d. No wonder the popularity of shark fin soup has been rising.

2. Many scientists and nutritionists think _____ .

a. shark fin soup has cancer fighting abilities

b. Chinese people must eat nutritious shark fin soup as often as possible

c. shark fin soup is not rich in vitamins and minerals

d. people who enjoy shark fin soup will die due to Vitamin A

3. Choose the correct words for each sentence.

a. I am going to reveal top 10 reasons for fast food's <u>popular</u> / <u>popularly</u> / <u>popularity</u>.

b. I don't want my two wobbly <u>teeth</u> / <u>tooth</u> / <u>tooths</u> to fall out. I just want them to stay as they are.

c. The soil of this region is <u>higher</u> / <u>high</u> / <u>highly</u> rich in nitrogen and phosphorus.

Answer **1.** b **2.** c **3.** popularity ∣ teeth ∣ highly

Listening Drill - Dictation

Shark fin soup is dangerous not because of shark's sharp teeth, but because of its mercury content.

In China and Hong Kong, the popularity of shark fin soup _____ among people. Many Chinese people think that shark fin soup _____ because it is _____ . They believe that shark fin soup _____ various vitamins and minerals, especially Vitamin A. But, lots of scientists and nutritionists disagree with their opinion. According to their research, _____ at all, and the amount of minerals found in shark fin soup is not very high.

_____ that shark fin soup can prevent cancer. But scientifically, it is not proven that shark fin soup has cancer fighting abilities.

On the contrary, shark fin soup is said to be bad for our health _____ . So, doctors recommend that pregnant women and young children avoid eating shark fins. Actually, dolphin meat and tuna _____ dangerous because they also contain high levels of mercury.

Did You Know Shark Fin Soup Is As Dangerous As Sharks?

❶ Shark fin soup is dangerous not because of shark's sharp teeth, but because of its

shark 상어 fin 지느러미 soup 수프   not because of A (명사구), but because B (명사구) A 때문이 아니라 B 때문
= 샥스핀   (not because A (절), but because B (절) A때문이 아니라 B 때문 not A but B A가 아니라 B)

mercury **content**.

content n. 내용물, 목차 a. 만족하는 v. 만족하다

❷ In China and Hong Kong, the **popularity** of shark fin soup has been rising

주어 the popularity, 동사 has been rising (현재 완료has pp 진행be -ing)

among people.

❸ Many Chinese people think that shark fin soup is good for their health

…에 좋다, 유익하다 (be bad for ..에 나쁘다)

because it is highly **nutritious**.

매우   nutritious a. 영양가 높은 nutrition n. 영양 nutritionist n. 영양사

❹ They believe that shark fin soup **is rich in** various (vitamins and minerals),

be rich in 풍부하다 (↔ be poor in, be low in 부족하다)

especially Vitamin A.

❺ But, (lots of scientists and **nutritionists**) **disagree with** their opinion.

주어 ( ), 동사 disagree with (agree with …에 동의하다)

❻ According to their research, [1] it contains no Vitamin A at all,

their research의 내용 [1]과 [2]   no/not .. at all 전혀 없다, 전혀 아니다

and [2] the amount of (minerals found in shark fin soup) is not very high.

수식

the amount of ( ) is not high   minerals (which are) found in …에서 발견되는 미네랄

❼ It is also widely believed that shark fin soup can **prevent** cancer.

또한 (also) that 이하라고 널리 (widely) 믿어지다   예방하다, 막다
(It is believed that …라고 한다)

❽ But scientifically, it is not proven that shark fin soup has cancer fighting abilities.

that 이하는 증명된 바 없다   cancer 암 fighting 싸우는 abilities 능력 – 항암효능

❾ On the contrary, shark fin soup is said to be bad for our health due to

오히려, 그와는 반대로   …라고 한다 (is thought to, is believed)   = because of

its high **mercury** content.

수은, 수성

⑩ So, doctors recommend that (pregnant women and young children) **avoid** eating shark fins.

avoid -ing …하는 걸 피하다

⑪ Actually, (**dolphin** meat and **tuna**) are also considered to be dangerous

돌고래 고기와 참치 (다랑어)　　　　　　be (also) considered to 동사원형 : (또한) …로 여겨지다, 간주되다

because they also contain high levels of mercury.

dolphin meat and tuna

상어 지느러미 수프(샥스핀)가 상어만큼이나 위험하다는 거 아세요?

① 상어 지느러미 수프가 위험한 이유는 상어의 날카로운 이빨 때문이 아니라 수은 함량 때문입니다.

② 중국과 홍콩에서 상어 지느러미 수프의 인기가 사람들 사이에서 높아지고 있습니다.

③ 많은 중국인들은 상어 지느러미가 영양가가 높기 때문에 건강에 유익하다고 생각합니다.

④ 이들은 상어 지느러미 수프에 다양한 비타민과 미네랄, 특히 비타민 A가 풍부하다고 믿고 있습니다.

⑤ 하지만 많은 과학자들과 영양학자들은 이들의 의견에 동의하지 않습니다.

⑥ 이들의 연구에 따르면 상어 지느러미에는 비타민 A가 전혀 없고 상어 지느러미 수프에 든 미네랄의 양은 높지 않다고 합니다.

⑦ 또한 상어 지느러미 수프가 암을 예방한다고 널리 믿고 있습니다.

⑧ 그러나 과학적으로 상어 지느러미 수프에 항암 효능이 있다고 밝혀진 바 없습니다.

⑨ 반대로 상어 지느러미 수프는 수은 함량 때문에 건강에 해롭습니다.

⑩ 그래서 의사들은 임산부와 어린이들은 상어 지느러미 수프 섭취를 피하라고 권합니다.

⑪ 실제 돌고래 고기와 참치 역시 높은 수은 함량 때문에 위험하다고 간주되고 있습니다.

Eating spiders? It sounds dangerous, but some people do it. Surprisingly, quite a few Cambodians think spiders are tasty. In Cambodia, many people eat spiders almost everyday. They find them similar to fried chicken. They are said to eat fried spiders as an everyday snack. This may seem unbelievable, but it's true. It is easy to find edible spiders in Cambodia. There are spiders everywhere, especially in Skuon, the small town in Cambodia.

This town is famous for fried spiders. The villagers breed spiders in holes in the ground and hunt them in the forest as well. Usually, they cook spiders with oil. Not all people are willing to eat deep-fried spiders. Some people like them, but some people don't. In fact, they don't look very appetizing. These spiders are as big as fists and look crisp on the outside.

Nobody knows for sure how they started eating spiders, but some scholars suggest that they might have been forced to eat them because they didn't have enough food to eat in the 1970s.

Words & Expressions

fry 튀기다 tasty 맛있는 (delicious, inviting, yummy) edible 식용의, 먹을 수 있는 similar to ...와 비슷한 unbelievable 믿기 힘든 villager 마을 사람, 주민 breed 키우다, 사육하다 deep-fried 뜨거운 기름에 튀긴 fist 주먹 crisp 바삭바삭한 (= crispy) scholar 학자

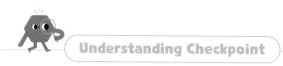

1. What is the main idea of the story?

    a. The taste of fried spiders is similar to fried chicken.

    b. Cambodians are strong because they have enough food to eat such as spiders.

    c. It is a poor decision to eat fried spiders because steamed spiders are much more delicious.

    d. It is not difficult to find people who eat fried spiders in Cambodia.

2. According the passage, which sentence is right?

    a. Maybe Cambodians started eating spiders reluctantly for they didn't have much food.

    b. Fried chicken is the second most popular snack in Cambodia.

    c. Skuon, the capital city of Cambodia, has been raising spiders as a food resource.

    d. Deep-fried spiders are popular but not good for health.

3. Choose the correct words for each sentence.

    a. People think dogs bite strangers but the truth is not all dogs <u>bite</u> / <u>bites</u> / <u>biting</u> strangers.

    b. I cannot stand the idea of eating snail, but my friend Judy <u>found</u> / <u>made</u> / <u>have</u> it delicious.

    c. I told you to check his credit card first thing in the morning but you <u>don't</u> / <u>didn't</u> / <u>doesn't</u>.

Answer 1. d   2. a   3. bite ǀ found ǀ didn't

Eating spiders? It sounds dangerous, but some people do it. Surprisingly, quite a few Cambodians think spiders are tasty. In Cambodia, many people eat spiders almost everyday. They find them   fried chicken. They are said to eat fried spiders as an everyday snack. This may   , but it's true. It is easy to find   in Cambodia. There are spiders everywhere, especially in Skuon, the small town in Cambodia.

This town is famous for fried spiders. The villagers   spiders in holes in the ground and hunt them in the forest   . Usually, they cook spiders with oil. Not all people   deep-fried spiders. Some people like them, but some people don't. In fact, they don't   . These spiders are   and look crisp on the outside.

Nobody knows for sure how they started eating spiders, but some scholars suggest that they   eat them because they   in the 1970s.

Did You Know Cambodians Like To Eat Fried Spiders?

① Eating spiders?

② It sounds dangerous, but some people do it.

It sounds + 형용사 : ⋯처럼 들리다　　　　　　　　　eating spiders

③ Surprisingly, **quite a few** Cambodians think spiders are **tasty**.

quite a few + 가산 명사의 복수 = many　　　　　　taste v. (어떤) 맛이 나다 n. 맛, 입맛
quite a little + 불가산 명사 = much　　　　　　　tasty a. 맛있는 (delicious)

④ In Cambodia, many people eat spiders almost everyday.

⑤ They find them **similar to** fried chicken.

　　　　　　　　　　⋯와 비슷한, 유사한
주어 (They) + find + 목적어 (them=spiders) + 형용사 (similar) : 주어는 (목적어)가 (형용사)라고 생각하다, 여기서 find는 think의 의미

⑥ They are said to eat fried spiders as an everyday snack.

They=Cambodians // are said to ⋯라고 한다　　　매일 먹는 간식으로

⑦ This may seem **unbelievable**, but it's true.

This (그들이 매일 간식으로 거미를 먹는 것) 믿기 힘들게 보일 수 있다.

⑧ It is easy to find edible spiders in Cambodia.

가주어 it 진주어 to find　　　= eatable 식용의

⑨ There **are** spiders **everywhere**, especially in Skuon, (the small town in Cambodia).

There + are (복수동사) + spiders (복수명사)　　　　　　　= 동격
　　　be everywhere 사방천지에 ⋯이 있다, 어디에 가도 있다

⑩ This town **is famous for** fried spiders.

be famous for (긍정적으로) 유명하다 (be well-known for, be renowned for)
be notorious for (부정적으로) 악명 높다

⑪ The villagers ¹⁾ **breed** spiders in holes in the ground and ²⁾ hunt them

　　　　　　v. 키우다, 사육하다 (breed-bred-bred)　　　　　　　= spiders
주어 villagers + 동사 breed, hunt (주민들은 키우고 사냥한다)

in the forest as well.

　　　또한, 역시

⑫ Usually, they cook spiders with oil.

⑬ Not all people **are willing to** eat deep-fried spiders.
부분 부정 (모든 사람이 다 …인 건 아니다)   be willing to 동사 : 기꺼이 …하다

⑭ Some people like them, but some people don't.
don't like them

⑮ In fact, they don't look very appetizing.
deep fried spiders   look appetizing 맛있어 보이다 (appetite n. 입맛 appetizer n. 입맛 돋우는 전체요리)
look boring 지루해 보이다 look crisp 바삭해 보이다

⑯ These spiders ¹⁾ are as big as fists and ²⁾ look **crisp** on the outside.
as big as …만큼 큰   바삭해 보이다 crisp 바삭바삭한(= crispy)

⑰ Nobody knows for sure (how they started eating spiders),
아무도 확실히 모른다   의문문이 아니라 명사절 (how + 주어 + 동사)
God only knows. = Nobody knows.   (어쩌다 그들이 거미를 먹게 되었는지를)

but some **scholars** suggest that they might have **been forced to** eat them
n. 학자 (a. scholary 학자의, 학구적인)   might have pp 과거 추측 (…일지도 모른다)
be forced to 어쩔 수 없이 to…하다

because they didn't have enough food (to eat) in the 1970s.
수식 ↑ ↑ 수식   먹을 충분한 음식 (food to eat)
a shirt to wear 입을 셔츠, a place to live 살 곳, books to read 읽을 책들

┌─ 캄보디아인들이 튀긴 거미 먹기를 좋아한다는 거 아세요? ─┐

❶ 거미를 먹는다?   ❷ 위험한 것 같지만 어떤 사람들은 먹습니다.

❸ 놀랍게도 상당히 많은 캄보디아인들이 거미를 맛있다고 생각합니다.

❹ 캄보디아에서는 많은 사람들이 거의 매일 거미를 먹습니다.   ❺ 이들은 거미 맛이 튀긴 닭고기와 비슷하다고 생각합니다.

❻ 이들은 매일 먹는 간식으 로 튀긴 거미를 먹는다고 합니다.   ❼ 믿기 힘들지만 사실입니다.

❽ 캄보디아에서 식용 거미는 쉽게 찾을 수 있습니다.

❾ 사실 사방 어디에서나 거미를 찾을 수 있는데 특히 캄보디아의 한 작은 마을 스쿠온이 그렇습니다.

❿ 이 마을은 튀긴 거미로 유명합니다.

⑪ 마을 사람들은 땅의 구멍에 거미를 키우기도 하고 숲에서 거미를 사냥하기도 합니다.

⑫ 일반적으로 이들은 기름으로 거미를 요리합니다.   ⑬ 모든 사람들이 튀긴 거미를 기꺼이 먹는 건 아닙니다.

⑭ 어떤 이들은 좋아하지만 어떤 이들은 그렇지 않습니다.   ⑮ 사실 거미는 그다지 맛있어 보이지 않습니다.

⑯ 이 거미는 주먹 크기만 하고 겉이 바삭해 보입니다.

⑰ 어떻게 해서 이들이 거미를 먹게 되었는지 확실하게 아는 사람은 없지만, 일부 학자들은 1970년대에 먹을 게 부족해서 어쩔 수 없이 먹게 된 게 아닌가 생각합니다.

You can shed 9 pounds in a month by eating African Mango. Thankfully, this special mango reduces bad cholesterol and burns average 2 inches of belly fat within a month. More thankfully, it is cheap compared to other diet foods, supplements or diet pills. Of course it's a whole lot cheaper than gym membership fees. It costs less than a dollar per serving, so it's cheaper than a can of soda.

Dr. Oz was the person who made it famous in America. He called it a "breakthrough supplement" and a "miracle in your medicine cabinet" on his The Dr. Oz Show on September 13, 2010. Ever since then, many people have experienced its awesome effect.

For instance, Dr. Tanya Edwards, M.D. called African Mango extract a "miracle pill" because she lost 7 pounds in a month with the help of it. She said she didn't make any changes to her eating habits or exercise routine.

With the recent popularity of African Mango, there are dozens of African Mango products being sold online. Be careful when you select one of these products, however, because not all of them are effective or trustworthy.

Words & Expressions

shed (피, 눈물) 흘리다, 없애다, (옷, 허물) 벗다, (나뭇잎) 떨어뜨리다, (빛) 비추다 thankfully 고맙게도 reduce 줄이다 burn fat 지방을 태우다, 연소시키다 average 평균 supplement 보조제, 보충제 a whole lot 대단히 gym 체육관 fee 요금 per one serving 1회 먹는 분량에, 일인분에 approximately 대략 annually 매년 lose weight 체중을 감량하다 breakthrough 돌파구, 획기적 성공 medicine cabinet 약품 보관 찬장 awesome 굉장한, 대단한 extract n. 추출, 발췌 v. 뽑아내다, 추출하다 eating habit 식습관 exercise routine 평소에 하는 운동 trustworthy 신뢰할 만한

Understanding Checkpoint

1. What is the main idea of the story?

    a. Dr. Oz must be the salesperson who wants to sell African Mango.

    b. Diet pills are better than African Mango.

    c. African Mango can be a good solution to the obesity problem.

    d. As far as African Mango is concerned, the cheaper, the better.

2. Dr. Oz is the person who _____ .

    a. spent millions of dollars annually trying to lose weight

    b. called African Mango extract a "miracle pill"

    c. experienced African Mango's miraculous effects

    d. was the host of The Dr. Oz Show

3. Choose the correct words for each sentence.

    a. As terrorists appeared <u>at</u> / <u>in</u> / <u>on</u> TV screen, passers-by stopped walking and watched the news.

    b. Why are some methods so much more effective <u>that</u> / <u>than</u> / <u>then</u> others?

    c. A myriad of bones and skeletons found near the crime scene have <u>sheded</u> / <u>shed</u> / <u>shedding</u> light on this murder case.

    d. Can you believe this is her third <u>served</u> / <u>serving</u> / <u>serves</u> of macaroni and cheese?

Answer **1.** c **2.** d **3.** on ∣ than ∣ shed ∣ serving

Listening Drill – Dictation

You can _____ 9 pounds in a month by eating African Mango. Thankfully, this special mango _____ and burns average 2 inches of belly fat _____ .
More thankfully, it is cheap compared to other diet foods, supplements or diet pills. Of course it's _____ gym membership fees. It costs less than a dollar per serving, so it's cheaper than a can of soda.
Dr. Oz _____ . In America He called it a "breakthrough supplement" and a "miracle in your medicine cabinet" _____ his The Dr. Oz Show on September 13, 2010. Ever since then, many people have experienced its awesome effect.
For instance, Dr. Tanya Edwards, M.D. called African Mango extract a "miracle pill" because she lost 7 pounds in a month with the help of it. She said she _____ her eating habits or exercise routine.
With _____ of African Mango, there are _____ African Mango products _____ . Be careful when you select one of these products, however, because not all of them are effective or trustworthy.

75

Did You Know Which Fruit Can Burn About 9 Pounds In A Month?

1 You can **shed** 9 pounds in a month by eating African Mango.

v. (피, 눈물) 흘리다, (껍질, 옷) 벗다, 없애다, (빛, 냄새) 발하다 shed-shed-shed
n. 오두막, 가축우리, 창고 (이 문장에서는 '벗어버리다, 없애다')

2 Thankfully, this special mango [1] **reduces** bad cholesterol and [2] **burns** average

고맙게도 (문장 전체를 수식하는 부사) 주어 this special mango (3인칭 단수현재) 동사 [1] reduces, [2] burns
burn fat 지방을 연소시키다 burn calories 칼로리를 소비하다

2 inches of **belly** fat within a month.

한 달 내에 (no more than a month)

3 More thankfully, it is **cheap compared to** other diet foods, **supplements** or diet **pills**.

더욱 고맙게도   …와(to) 비교할 때   보충물, 보조제, 부록   알약, 정제
a. supplementary 추가의, 보충의

4 Of course it's a whole lot cheaper than **gym** membership **fees**.

휠씬, 더   더 싼 (비교급)   헬스클럽 회원 이용료 (gym = gymnasium 체육관)
fee (회원의) 회비, 수수료 charge (상품, 서비스) 요금 rate 요금, 임금 fare (버스 등 교통) 요금

5 It costs less than a dollar per serving, so it's cheaper than a can of soda.

…이하의   serving (제공되는) 1인분 양   소다 음료수 한 캔
helping 1인분 음식량   (soda 같은 불가산 명사는 포장/계량 단위로 센다.
two cups of water, three bags of sugar, a carton of milk)

6 Dr. Oz was the person who (made it famous) in America.

( )인 사람이 바로 주어이다 ↑ 수식   = African Mango
(I was the one who won the first prize back in high school. 고등학교 때 1등 상 탄 게 바로 나였다.)

7 He called it a "**breakthrough** supplement" and a "miracle

n. breakthrough 획기적인 발견, 돌파구
v. break through 돌파구를 찾다

in your medicine cabinet" on his The Dr. Oz Show on September 13, 2010.

약을 보관하는 찬장   방송 프로그램에서

8 Ever since then, many people have experienced its **awesome** effect.

그 때 이후   since + 현재완료 (have experienced)

9 For instance, Dr. Tanya Edwards, M.D. called African Mango **extract** a "miracle pill"

= for example 예를 들어   = 동격   의학박사 (Doctor of Medicine)   n. 발췌, 추출물 v. 발췌/추출하다
주어 called A B : 주어가 A(African Mango extract)를 B(miracle pill)라 불렀다

because she lost 7 pounds in a month with the help of it.

체중을 감량하다 (lose-lost-lost)   이것(it)의 도움으로
lose weight / lose 7 pounds (체중이 늘다 gain - gain weight, gian 7 pounds)

⑩ She said she didn't make any changes to her eating habits or exercise **routine**.

make changes to …에(to) 변화를 주다
평소 규칙적으로 하던 운동
daily routine 매일 하는 일 eating routine 평소 먹는 음식

⑪ With the recent popularity of African Mango,

…의 인기에 따라

there are dozens of African Mango products (being sold online).

there are (복수동사) dozens of (복수 명사)
dozens of 수십 개의 (dozen =12)

수식

products (which are) being sold 현재 팔리고 있는 제품들
(are being 현재 진행 + being sold 수동태)

⑫ Be careful when you select one of these products, however,

one of + 복수명사
콤마와 함께 however는 문장 중간에 쓰이지만
해석할 때 맨 앞에 '그러나'를 넣는 게 좋다.

because not all of them are effective or **trustworthy**.

부분 부정
모든 제품들(them=products)이 다 …인 건 아니다

trust 신뢰 + worthy (…받을 만한) – 신뢰할 만한, 믿을 수 있는

한 달 안에 9파운드를 빼주는 과일이 무엇인지 아세요?

❶ 아프리칸 망고를 먹으며 한 달에 9파운드를 뺄 수 있습니다.

❷ 고맙게도 이 특별한 망고는 나쁜 콜레스테롤을 줄여주고 한 달 안에 평균 2인치의 복부 지방을 연소시킵니다.

❸ 더욱 고마운 것은 다른 다이어트 음식, 보조제, 다이어트 약품과 비교했을 때 가격이 싸다는 겁니다.

❹ 물론 헬스클럽 회원 이용료보다 훨씬 더 쌉니다.

❺ 1회분 가격이 1달러도 못 되니까 음료수 한 캔보다 쌉니다.

❻ 이를 미국에서 유명하게 만든 사람은 오즈박사입니다.

❼ 그는 2010년 9월 13일 자신의 <닥터 오즈 쇼>에서 이를 "획기적 보조제" 그리고 "의약품 보관 찬장 안의 기적"이라 불렀습니다.

❽ 이후 많은 사람들이 아프리칸 망고의 놀라운 효과를 경험하고 있습니다.

❾ 예를 들어 의학 박사 타냐 에드워즈는 아프리칸 망고 추출물을 "기적의 알약"이라 불렀는데, 이것의 도움으로 한 달에 7파운드를 감량했기 때문입니다.

❿ 그녀는 식습관과 평소 하던 운동에 어떤 변화도 주지 않았었다고 합니다.

⓫ 최근 아프리칸 망고의 인기에 영합해 수십 종의 아프리칸 망고 제품이 온라인 상에서 팔리고 있습니다.

⓬ 이런 제품 중 하나를 고를 때 주의해야 하는데, 모든 제품이 다 효과적이고 믿을 만 한 건 아니기 때문입니다.

16 Did You Know Fat-Free Foods Are Not Always Good For Health?

If you put yourself on a diet, or you have a health problem requiring weight loss such as diabetes, watch out fat-free or fat-reduced foods, diet sodas and yogurt drinks. They sound healthy, but you had better not put these foods on your everyday menu because they may not be helpful for your diet or your health after all.

Fat-free or reduced-fat foods tend to be less flavorful than full-fat foods, which means they do not taste as good or as satisfying. So, if you set the table with these foods, you may have to eat more to feel full. In other words, these low-fat or zero-fat foods are likely to make you eat more than you need. Furthermore, foods labeled with the words like "light", "fat-free", "low-fat", "zero-calory" or the like are prone to contain various sweeteners like extra sugar or corn syrup to make up for their unsatisfying flavor.

Recently, Harvard research center published an article claiming that full-fat dairy products may lower the risk of diabetes. When it comes to books, you 'do not judge a book by its cover', but as for food, we would do well to 'judge food by its label.'

Words & Expressions

put oneself on a diet ...에게 다이어트를 시키다 **require** 요구하다 **weight loss** 체중 감량 **watch out** 조심하라 **fat-free** 무지방 **fat-redued** 지방을 줄인 (low-fat 저지방의) **flavorful** 풍미 있는, 맛이 좋은 **satisfying** 만족스러운 **set the table** 상을 차리다 **feel full** 배부르다고 느끼다 **in other words** 달리 표현하면 **furthermore** 게다가, 더욱이 **label** 상표를 붙이다, (상표 등에) 필요한 정보를 적어 넣다 **be prone to** ...하는 경향이 있다 **sweetener** 감미료 **corn syrup** 옥수수 시럽 **make up for** 벌충하다, 메우다 **don't judge a book by its cover** 책 표지만 보고 책을 판단하지 말라 (속담-외모만으로 판단하지 말라)

1. What can be the best title of this story?

    a. Must Choose Fat-Free Foods For Your Own Sake

    b. Be Aware : The Word 'Fat-Free' May Not Means 'Healthy'

    c. Fat-Free : Totally Different From Low-Fat

    d. Don't Judge Drinks By Their Labels

2. According to the passage, which sentence is <u>wrong</u>?

    a. Fat-free or fat-reduced foods may not be beneficial to your health.

    b. If you have diabetes, you may want to eat full-fat dairy product.

    c. Ordinarily, people who try to cut down on fat have a tendency to choose low-fat or fat-free foods.

    d. Zero-fat drinks are good but they contain more salt and fat than you think.

3. Choose the correct words for each sentence.

    a. We have to <u>make out of</u> / <u>make our own</u> / <u>make up for</u> the deficit with bonuses.

    b. If you want to <u>low</u> / <u>lower</u> / <u>lowing</u> the danger of premature birth, Omega-3 fatty acids may help.

    c. Kay was diagnosed with type 2 diabetes which <u>are</u> / <u>were</u> / <u>is</u> different from type 1 diabetes.

Answer **1.** b **2.** d **3.** make up for ┃ lower ┃ is

Listening Drill – Dictation

If you   , or you have a health problem   such as diabetes, watch out fat-free or fat-reduced foods, diet sodas and yogurt drinks. They sound healthy, but you   put these foods on your everyday menu because they may not be helpful for your diet or your health after all.

Fat-free or reduced-fat foods   be less flavorful than full-fat foods, which means they do not taste as good or as satisfying. So, if you   with these foods, you may have to eat more to feel full. In other words, these low-fat or zero-fat foods are likely to make you eat   . Furthermore, foods labeled with the words like "light", "fat-free", "low-fat", "zero-calory"   are prone to contain various sweeteners like extra sugar or corn syrup to   their   .

Recently, Harvard research center published an article claiming that full-fat dairy products may   . When it comes to books, you 'do not judge a book by its cover', but as for food, we would do well to 'judge food by its label.'

Did You Know Fat-Free Foods Are Not Always Good For Health?

① If you put yourself on a diet, or you have a health problem requiring weight loss

put ( ) on a diet ( )를 다이어트 시키다
put myself on a diet 내가 다이어트하다
put him on a diet 그를 다이어트하게 시키다

수식

problem which requires weight loss

체중 감량

(such as **diabetes**), watch out (**fat-free** or **fat-reduced** foods,

체중감량이 요구되는 건강문제의 예   watch out = look out, be careful 조심하다
diabetes 당뇨병 (복수가 아님)

diet sodas and yogurt drinks).

② They sound healthy, but you had better not put these foods on your everyday menu

had better 동사원형 : …하는 게 좋다   put ( ) on menu 식단에 ( )를 올리다
had better not 동사원형 : …하지 않는 게 좋다
they = (앞문장의 fat-free or fat-reduced food, diet sodas, yogurt drinks)

because they may not be helpful for (your diet or your health) **after all**.

도움이 되지 않을 수 있다   결국에는

③ (Fat-free or reduced-fat foods) **tend to** be less **flavorful** than full-fat foods

fat-free 지방이 없는   = be prone to …경향이 있다   less than 더 적은 (비교)
reduced-fat (원래 있던) 지방 양을 줄인 (light-fat 지방이 적은)

, which means they do not **taste** as good or as **satisfying**.

콤마 which means   taste as good 맛이 좋다   taste as satisfying 맛이 만족스럽다
계속 용법-순서대로 해석

④ So, if you set the table with these foods, you may have to eat more to feel full.

상(음식)을 차리다   …해야만 할 수도 있다   배부르다고 느끼다
집합명사 food에는 -s가 붙지 않고, 음식, 요리 종류를 뜻할 때는 foods로 쓸 수 있다.

⑤ In other words, (these low-fat or zero-fat foods) **are likely to** make

즉, 다시 (달리) 말하면   …할 가능성이 있다

you eat more than you need.

필요한 것 보다 더 먹다

⑥ Furthermore, foods labeled with (the words like "light", "fat-free", "low-fat",

게다가, 더욱이   수식   a. 가벼운, n. 빛   a. 자유로운, 없는   a. 뚱뚱한 n. 지방
= moreover   foods (which are) labeled with ( )
                ( )라는 라벨이 붙은 음식들

"zero-calory" or the like) **are prone to** contain various **sweeteners**

또는 그 밖의 것들   …하는 경향이 있다   주어 foods + 동사 are   감미료
(etc.)   = tend to   contain sweetners like ( ) to make up for 〈 〉
                                      〈 〉를 별충하기 위해 ( )같은 감미료를 함유하다

(like extra sugar or corn syrup) to **make up for** their unsatisfying **flavor**.

(모자라거나 빠진 부분) 벌충하다, 만회하다
= compensate for

satisfy 만족시키다 satisfying 만족스러운
dissatisfy 불만을 느끼다 unsatisfying 만족감을 주지 못하는
(동사로 unsatisfy는 잘 쓰이지 않는다.)

7 Recently, Harvard research center published an article claiming that

수식
that 이하라고 주장하는 글 article

(full-fat dairy products) may lower the risk of diabetes.

지방을 제거하지 않은 유제품   low a. 낮은 lower v. 낮추다

8 **When it comes to** books, you 'do not judge a book by its cover',

…에 관해서라면 (to + 명사) = As far as books are concerned

but as for food, we would do well to 'judge food by its label.'

do well to 동사 : …하는 게 현명하다   judge 판단하다 food 음식 by its label 라벨에 의해
(do good 이롭다, 도움이 되다)

무지방 음식이 항상 건강에 좋은 건 아니라는 사실 아세요?

1 만약 다이어트 중이거나 당뇨처럼 체중 감량이 요구되는 건강 문제를 안고 있다면, 무지방 또는 저지방 음식, 다이어트 음료와 요구르트 음료를 조심하세요.

2 이런 음식들은 건강에 좋은 것 같지만 매일 먹는 식단에 올리지 않는 게 좋은데, 이유는 다이어트와 건강에 도움이 안 될 수도 있기 때문입니다.

3 저지방 음식은 지방이 다 들어간 음식들에 비해 맛이 떨어지는 경향이 있는데, 이 말은 맛과 만족감이 좋지 않다는 뜻입니다.

4 그래서 이런 음식들로 상을 차릴 경우 배부른 느낌이 들려면 더 많이 먹어야 합니다.

5 달리 말하면, 저지방, 무지방 음식들은 필요 이상의 음식을 먹게 만듭니다.

6 게다가 "라이트", "무지방", "저지방", "제로 칼로리" 등과 같은 단어가 라벨에 적힌 음식들은 만족스럽지 못한 맛을 보충하기 위해 다양한 감미료와 과도한 설탕 또는 옥수수 시럽이 들어 있을 가능성이 높습니다.

7 최근 하버드 연구 센터는 한 기사를 통해 지방이 그대로 다 들어 있는 치즈나 요구르트 같은 유제품이 당뇨의 위험을 낮출 수도 있다고 주장합니다.

8 책에 관해서는 '책 표지만 보고 책을 판단하지 말아야' 하지만, 음식에 관해서는 '라벨을 보고 음식을 판단하는' 게 현명한 것 같습니다.

Did You Know **Koreans Are Not The Only People Who Enjoy Soondae?**

In Korea, Soondae has been a popular food for a long time. Amazingly, we can find foods very similar to Soondae in other countries.

Soondae is steamed pig's (or cow's) intestines stuffed with various ingredients. The common Korean Soondae generally contains cellophane noodles and pig's blood. Interestingly, people in Europe, North America, Latin America, and other Asian countries also enjoy this kind of food. It is called black pudding, blood pudding or blood sausage, depending on the country. Their ingredients and recipes are similar to Korean Soondae.

Cows and pigs are preferred by countries such as Korea, China and Germany. But Tibetan people have used yaks, and several European countries have made black pudding out of sheep's intestines and blood. Typical European-style black pudding is filled with meat, blood, fat, bread, onion, and barley.

However, nowadays, unlike Korea, sausages made of blood are not easy to find at local supermarkets or delis in western countries. It seems that westerners are no longer keen on food containing blood.

Words & Expressions

similar 비슷한 steam 증기, 증기로 익히다, 찌다 stuffed with ...로 속을 채운 cellophane 셀로판 (cellophane noodles 당면) barley 보리 nowadays 요즘 deli (= delicatessen) 식료품 가게, 식당 be keen on 좋아하다

Understanding Checkpoint

1. What is the main idea of the story?

    a. Unexpectedly, many people around the world enjoy foods similar to Korean Soondae.

    b. Soondae out of cows' intestines is more delicious than black pudding.

    c. European-style black pudding is filled with cellophane noodles and pig's blood.

    d. Generally, Europeans don't like food containing blood

2. You can make Soondae by _____ .

    a. cooking animals' intestines with lots of oil and spices

    b. steaming animals' intestines stuffed with cellophane noodles and pig's blood

    c. boiling sheep's intestines and blood in a large pan

    d. frying yaks' intestines filled with grains

3. Choose the correct words for each sentence.

    a. Some Europeans who love K-pop stars and Korean dramas are <u>keen on</u> / <u>likes to</u> / <u>desperate to</u> learning Korean.

    b. <u>Before long</u> / <u>Nowadays</u> / <u>For the time being</u> more and more children are addicted to computer games

    c. These products are widely <u>preferred</u> / <u>prefer</u> / <u>to prefer</u> by customers around the world.

Answer **1.** a **2.** b **3.** keen on ǀ Nowadays ǀ preferred

Listening Drill - Dictation

In Korea, Soondae _____ for a long time. Amazingly, we can find foods very similar to Soondae in other countries.

Soondae is steamed pig's (or cow's) intestines _____ various ingredients. The common Korean Soondae generally contains cellophane noodles and pig's blood. Interestingly, people in Europe, North America, Latin America, and other Asian countries also enjoy this kind of food. It is called black pudding, blood pudding or blood sausage, _____ . Their ingredients and _____ Korean Soondae.

Cows and pigs _____ countries such as Korea, China and Germany. But Tibetan people have used yaks, and several European countries have made black pudding _____ sheep's intestines and blood. Typical European-style black pudding is filled with meat, blood, fat, bread, onion, and _____ .

However, nowadays, _____ Korea, sausages made of blood are not easy to find at local supermarkets or _____ in western countries. It seems that westerners _____ food containing blood.

Did You Know Koreans Are Not The Only People Who Enjoy Soondae?

❶ In Korea, Soondae has been a popular food for a long time.

현재완료 + for 기간   오랫동안 …해왔다

❷ **Amazingly**, we can find foods (very **similar to** Soondae) in other countries.

놀랍게도 (surprisingly)   순대와 비슷한 음식

❸ Soondae is **steamed** pig's (or cow's) **intestines stuffed with** various **ingredients**.

steam (증기로) 찌다 simmer 끓이다 (boil)   수식   재료, 성분
saute 기름에 빨리 튀기다 fry 튀기다, 볶다   intestines (which are) stuffed with …로 채워진 창자
roast (오븐, 불) 굽다 bake (빵을) 굽다   intestine 창자, 장 (small intestine 소장 large intestine 대장)

❹ The common Korean Soondae **generally contains**

주어 Soondae (3인칭 단수 현재) 동사 contains   대개   향유하다

(cellophane noodles and pig's blood).

셀로파네 누들 (셀로판지처럼 투명한 전분 국수, 당면)

❺ Interestingly, people (in Europe, North America, Latin America,

주어 people 동사 enjoy   수식   people – ( )의 사람들

and other Asian countries) also enjoy this kind of food.

❻ It is called [1] black pudding, [2] blood pudding or [3] blood sausage,

It = (앞문장의) this kind of food
= food made of animals' intestines and blood

depending on the country.

나라에 따라 (다르다, 다양하다)

❼ Their ingredients and **recipes** are similar to Korean Soondae.

n. 요리법   유사하다, 비슷하다

❽ Cows and pigs are **preferred** by countries (such as Korea, China and Germany).

…에서 선호되다 (수동태)   German 독일의, 독일인 Germany 독일 (국가)

❾ But Tibetan people have used yaks, and several European countries

현재완료 (과거에서 지금까지) 사용해오고 있다

have made black pudding out of sheep's intestines and blood.

make ( ) out of 〈 〉 ( )를 〈 〉로 만들다

❿ (Typical European-style black pudding) **is filled with**

(주어) is filled with (재료)   수식   …로 (속이) 채워지다 (be stuffed with)

84

(meat, blood, fat, bread, **onion**, and **barley**).
　　　　　　　　　　　　　　　　 양파　　　　　　　 보리, wheat 밀

⑪ (However, nowadays, unlike Korea), sausages made of blood are **not easy to find**
　그러나　　　　요즘은　　　　 한국과 달리　　　　　　 ↑　　 수식　　　　　　 찾기 쉽지 않은
　이 문장을 가주어(it) / 진주어(to find) 구문으로 바꾸면　　 sausages (which are) made of blood
　It is not easy to find sausages made of blood.

at (**local** supermarkets or delis) in western countries.
　　동네 상점이나 음식점　　　　　　　　 deli = delicatessen (식료품점, 음식점)

⑫ It seems that westerners are no longer **keen on** (food containing blood).
　　　　　　　　　　　 food which contains blood 피가 함유된 음식 ↑　　 수식
　　　　　　　　　 be keen on 좋아하다 / be not keen on 좋아하지 않다 / be no longer keen on 더 이상 좋아하지 않다

한국인들만 순대를 즐기는 게 아니라는 거 아세요?

❶ 한국에서 순대는 오랫동안 인기 있는 음식이었습니다.

❷ 놀랍게도 다른 나라에서도 순대와 매우 비슷한 음식을 찾을 수 있습니다.

❸ 순대는 다양한 재료를 채워 넣어 익힌 돼지나 소의 창자입니다.

❹ 한국의 일반적인 순대는 대개 당면과 돼지 피로 만듭니다.

❺ 재미있게도, 유럽, 북아메리카, 라틴 아메리카는 물론 다른 아시아 국가들 역시 이런 종류의 음식을 즐겨왔습니다.

❻ 나라에 따라 블랙푸딩, 피푸딩, 또는 피 소시지라고 불립니다.

❼ 재료와 조리법은 한국의 순대와 비슷합니다.

❽ 한국, 중국, 독일과 같은 많은 나라들이 소와 돼지를 선호합니다.

❾ 하지만 티베트 사람들은 야크를 사용하고, 일부 유럽 국가들은 양의 창자와 피로 블랙푸딩을 만들어왔습니다.

❿ 전형적인 유럽 스타일의 블랙푸딩은 고기, 피, 지방, 빵, 양파, 보리 등을 채워 넣어 만듭니다.

⑪ 하지만 한국과는 달리, 오늘날 서구 국가들의 슈퍼마켓이나 음식점에서 피로 만든 소시지를 찾기가 쉽지 않습니다.

⑫ 서구인들은 피가 들어간 음식은 더 이상 좋아하지 않는 것 같습니다.

18 Did You Know Chinese People Eat Pigeon Soup?

Chinese people eat pigeon soup. Many gourmets find it delicious, and it is relatively easy to make : prepare pigeon meat, chives, salt and pepper and then boil them together.

Pigeon soup is not that surprising compared to other exotic Chinese foods. Chinese cuisine is famous for being diverse and having amazing ingredients. Chefs are said to use almost everything edible in their cooking including chicken hearts, monkey brains, bird's nests, bear paws, antlers, cockroaches, scorpions, cicadas, etc.

People around the world enjoy and appreciate Chinese exotic and creative foods. But, some of them are not easy for foreigners to enjoy, because they are too strange and unusual. For example, Stinky Tofu, made of fermented tofu, is popular in China but some cannot stand its strong odor. Also, it is not odd or strange to use animals' blood in Chinese dishes, while quite a few westerners think that's disgusting. Yet, many Chinese people allegedly believe that the blood of live snakes or turtles, and blood-dripping antlers are healthy foods.

Words & Expressions

gourmet 미식가 relatively 비교적 chive 차이브, 골파 boil 끓이다 exotic 이국적인 cuisine 요리, 요리법 diverse 다양한 chicken heart 닭의 심장, 겁쟁이 paw (동물) 발 antler 사슴 뿔 cockroach 바퀴벌레 scorpion 전갈 cicada 매미 appreciate 진가를 인정하다 creative 창의적인 ferment 발효하다, 발효 tofu 두부 can't stand 견딜 수 없다 odor 냄새 odd 이상한 dish 접시, 설거지 거리, 요리 disgusting 구역질나는 blood-dripping 피가 뚝뚝 떨어지는

86

1. What is the main idea of the story?

    a. The most horrible Chinese food is pigeon soup.

    b. Chinese food is diverse, creative and exotic.

    c. People who try to eat Stinky Tofu are likely to die of its terrible smell.

    d. Foreigners pretend to enjoy Chinese food but in fact, they don't.

2. According to the passage, which sentence is right?

    a. Many gourmets claim that pigeon soup is the most delicious food in China.

    b. The recipe of pigeon soup is quite simple but the ingredients cost very much.

    c. Chinese cuisines are nothing but normal so everyone can enjoy them without reserve.

    d. It seems that Chinese cooks are not afraid of using poisonous animals in their cooking.

3. Choose the correct words for each sentence.

    a. I'm so surprised that there are so many <u>surprise</u> / <u>surprising</u> / <u>surprised</u> six figure jobs out there.

    b. Many of my friends can <u>sip</u> / <u>take a dip</u> / <u>appreciate</u> fine wine and they are willing to pay hundreds of dollars to get a taste of it.

    c. Lady Gaga is famous for not only <u>eccentric</u> / <u>being eccentric</u> / <u>eccentricity</u> but also falling flat on her back during a show at Texas.

Listening Drill - Dictation

Chinese people eat pigeon soup. Many gourmets   , and it is relatively easy to make : prepare pigeon meat, chives, salt and pepper and then boil them together. Pigeon soup is not that surprising compared to other exotic Chinese foods. Chinese cuisine is famous for being diverse and having amazing ingredients. Chefs are said to   in their cooking including chicken hearts, monkey brains, bird's nests, bear paws, antlers, cockroaches, scorpions,   , etc.

People around the world enjoy and   Chinese exotic and creative foods. But, some of them are not easy for foreigners to enjoy, because they are too strange and unusual. For example, Stinky Tofu, made of   tofu, is popular in China but some   its strong odor. Also,   use animals' blood in Chinese   , while quite a few westerners think that's disgusting. Yet, many Chinese people   that the blood of live snakes or turtles, and   are healthy foods.

Did You Know Chinese People Eat Pigeon Soup?

1 Chinese people eat **pigeon** soup.

dove, pigeon 둘 다 비둘기인데 dove가 더 작은 종류

2 Many **gourmets** find it **delicious**, and it is **relatively** easy to make :

미식가 (t 묵음)　이것(it=pigeon soup)을 맛있다고 생각하다　비교적　　easy to make 만들기 쉬운
Gourmets think pigeon soup is delicious.　　　　　　　　　hard / difficult to make 만들기 어려운

$^{1)}$ prepare (pigeon meat, chives, salt and pepper) and then $^{2)}$ boil them together.

(閣) 만드는 방법 $^{1)}$ and then $^{2)}$　　　　　　　　　　　　them = 앞문장의 ( )

3 Pigeon soup is not that **surprising** compared to (other **exotic** Chinese foods).

그렇게 (surprising을 강조) 놀라운 ↑　수식　　　　　이국적인
　　　　　　　　　　　(다른 이국적인 중국 음식들과) 비교할 때

4 Chinese **cuisine** is famous for $^{1)}$ being **diverse** and $^{2)}$ having amazing ingredients.

요리법　　　　　　　　　　　　다양한
유명하다 (for + 명사 / -ing) famous for being… and (famous for) having

5 **Chefs** are said to use almost everything **edible** in their cooking including

요리사들은 사용한다고 한다 (be said to 동사)　　↑　수식
　　　　　　　　　　　…thing/one + 형용사 (someone important 중요한 사람 / something blue 파란 것 /
　　　　　　　　　　　everything visible 보이는 모든 것 / everyone present 현재 참석한 모든 사람)

(chicken hearts, monkey brains, bird's nests, bear **paws**, **antlers**,

chicken heart 겁쟁이, 닭의 심장　　　　　　paw 발톱이 있는동물의 발　hoof 발굽　사슴 뿔

cockroaches, scorpions, cicadas, etc.)

-ch로 끝나는 단어의 복수 -es (churches, peaches, ranches)

6 People around the world $^{1)}$ enjoy and $^{2)}$ **appreciate** Chinese

주어 + people 동사 1) enjoy, 2) appreciate　　　감상하다, 맛있게 먹다, 진가를 인정하다, 감사하다
　　　　　　　　　　　　　　　　　　　　(이 문장에서는 '맛있게 먹다, 또는 진가를 인정하다'의 의미)

(exotic and **creative**) foods.

창의적인

7 But, some of them are not easy for foreigners to enjoy,

be (not) easy for 사람 to 동사
누가 …하기에 쉽다 (쉽지 않다) = It's not easy for foreigners to enjoy some of them.

because they are too strange and **unusual**.

= some of Chinese foods

⑧ For example, **Stinky** Tofu, (made of **fermented** tofu), is popular in China

수식   ferment 발효, 발효하다
Stinky Tofu which is made of fermented tofu 발효 도부로 만든 취두부
stink v. 악취를 풍기다 n. 악취 stinky a. 악취나는

but some cannot **stand** its strong **odor**.

= some people   stink, reek, stench, odor 악취
stand v. 서다, (부정어와 함께) 참다, 견디다   smell 냄새 fragrance 향기

⑨ Also, it is not **odd** or strange to use animals' blood in Chinese **dishes**,

It (가주어) is not odd or (it is not) strange to동사 (진주어)   요리
사용하는 게(to동사) 이상하거나 특이한 게 아니다

while quite a few westerners think that's **disgusting**.

반면   = many   that = to use animals' blood in dishes   구역질 나는

⑩ Yet, many Chinese people **allegedly** believe that ¹⁾ the blood (of live snakes

that 이하를 믿는다고 한다   수식
(allegedly ad. …라는 주장에 의하면, 이른바)   살아있는 뱀이나 거북의 피

or turtles), and ²⁾ blood-dripping antlers are healthy foods.

⑧ Chinese people believe that 주어 ¹⁾, ²⁾ + 동사 are healthy foods.

중국인들이 비둘기 스프를 먹는다는 거 아세요?

① 중국인들은 비둘기 스프를 먹습니다.

② 많은 미식가들이 이를 맛있다고 생각하고 비교적 만들기도 쉬운데, 비둘기 고기, 차이브(골파), 소금과 후추를 준비한 뒤 이를 끓이면 됩니다.

③ 비둘기 스프는 중국의 다른 이색적인 음식과 비교할 때 그리 놀라운 음식이 아닙니다.

④ 중국 요리는 다양성과 놀라운 재료로 유명합니다.

⑤ 요리사들은 먹을 수 있는 건 거의 모든 걸 요리에 사용한다고 하는데, 닭 심장, 원숭이 뇌, 새 둥지, 곰 발바닥, 사슴 뿔, 바퀴 벌레, 전갈, 매미 등을 들 수 있습니다.

⑥ 전 세계 사람들은 중국의 이색적이고 창의적인 음식을 즐기고 칭찬합니다.

⑦ 하지만 그 중 어떤 음식들은 너무 이색적이고 특이해서 외국인들이 먹기 힘든 것도 있습니다.

⑧ 예를 들어 발효된 두부로 만든 취두부는 중국에서는 인기가 좋지만, 취두부의 강한 냄새를 견디지 못하는 사람도 있습니다.

⑨ 또 중국 요리에서 동물의 피를 사용하는 건 이상하거나 특이한 일이 아니지만, 상당한 서구인들은 이를 끔찍하다고 여깁니다.

⑩ 그러나 많은 중국인들은 살아 있는 뱀이나 거북의 피, 그리고 피가 뚝뚝 떨어지는 사슴뿔을 건강식이라고 믿습니다.

You can find a sandwich worth $200 in the UK. Naturally, you have to pay 100 pounds (almost 200 USD) for ordering this special sandwich. This triple-layered sandwich is made of bread, chicken, quail eggs, ham, white truffles and so on. Of course, only the finest ingredients are used. Despite being fat and greasy, food fanatics all over the world speak very highly of its awesome taste.

Do you think a $200 sandwich is expensive? There are many more expensive foods out there. Saffron, a kind of spice, costs at least over one thousand dollars per kilogram because it's very hard to get.

Spending over a thousand dollars on a spice sounds ridiculous, but there is something more ridiculous: whisky. This is not just any whisky, it is the most expensive whisky in the world. If you want to appreciate the rare taste of this 30-year-old whisky from the Macallan Fine Rare Vintage Collection, you may have to empty your bank account because the price per bottle is $38,000.

Words & Expressions

worth of ...가치의　naturally 당연히　pound 파운드 (계량 단위 1파운드-0.454kg, 영국의 화폐 단위)　triple-layed 3중 겹의, 3층의　quail 메추라기　truffle 송로버섯, 트뤼플　greasy 기름기 많은　food fanatic 음식 광신자　speak highly of ...를 칭찬하다　spice 향신료　hard to get 얻기(구하기) 어려운　sound ridiculous 어이없게 들린다　the rare taste of ...의 흔치 않은 맛　empty one's bank account 통장을 털다　the price per bottle 한 병 당 가격

Understanding Checkpoint

1. What is the main idea of the story?

    a. Spending thousands of dollars on one sandwich is a crazy thing to do.

    b. If you buy one bottle of the most expensive wine, you will go broke.

    c. There are unexpectedly expensive foods in the world.

    d. Greasy food is expensive but it's tasty.

2. If you want to order a $200 sandwich, you will have to _____ .

    a. go to the UK

    b. keep your stomach empty

    c. withdraw $38,000 from your bank account

    d. go bankrupt

3. Choose the correct words for each sentence.

    a. I got the speeding ticket because I didn't know the speed limit was 35 miles <u>per</u> / <u>every</u> / <u>in a</u> hour.

    b. No wonder those <u>bare</u> / <u>rare</u> / <u>scare</u> handicrafts were sold at a high price. There were only three of them in the entire planet.

    c. I wanted to speak <u>great</u> / <u>highly</u> / <u>good</u> of his work, but I spoke ill of it in spite of myself.

Answer **1.** c **2.** a **3.** per ׀ rare ׀ highly

Listening Drill – Dictation

You can find a sandwich _____ in the UK. Naturally, you have to pay 100 pounds (almost 200 USD) _____ this special sandwich. This triple-layered sandwich is made of bread, chicken, ____ eggs, ham, white truffles and so on. Of course, only _____ _____ are used. Despite being fat and greasy, food fanatics all over the world ____ _____ its awesome taste.

Do you think a $200 sandwich is expensive? There are many more expensive foods out there. Saffron, a kind of spice, costs at least over one thousand dollars per kilogram because _____ .

Spending over a thousand dollars on a spice _____ , but there is something more ridiculous: whisky. This is not just any whisky, it is the most expensive whisky in the world. If you want to _____ this 30-year-old whisky from the Macallan Fine Rare Vintage Collection, you may have to _____ because _____ is $38,000.

Did You Know There Is A Nearly $200 Sandwich?

1 You can find a sandwich (**worth** $200) in the UK.

수식 　　worth a. (얼마의) 가치가 있는
a sandwich which is worth $200 200달러 가치의 샌드위치

2 **Naturally**, you have to pay 100 pounds (almost 200 USD) for ordering

당연히 (No wonder)　　　　pay 돈 for (명사, 동명사) - 주문하는데 100파운드를 내다

this special sandwich.

3 This triple-layered sandwich **is made of** (bread, chicken, quail eggs, ham,

3층/단계의　　수식　　　　made of (물리적 변화) made from (화학적 변화)
(bi -2, tri- 3, quad- 4
bicycle 두발 자전거, triangle 삼각형, quadruple 네 배의)

white truffles **and so on**).

기타 등등 (= etc.)

4 Of course, only the finest ingredients are used.

가장 좋은 재료들만

5 Despite being (fat and **greasy**), food **fanatics** all over the world

기름기 많은　　　　fanatic 광신자 fan 팬
despite / in spite of + 동명사(-ing), 명사
despite 다음에 절(주어+동사), 동사가 올 수 없고, 형용사가 올 경우 being이 와야 한다.
= Despite the fact that this is fat and greasy

speak very highly of its **awesome** taste.

찬사를 보내다 (↔ speak ill of 비난하다, 나쁘게 말하다)

6 Do you think a $200 sandwich is **expensive**?

비싼 (↔ inexpensive)

7 There are many more expensive foods out there.

There 유도부사 주어 + are 복수 동사 + 복수 명사(주어) foods

8 Saffron, (a kind of spice), **costs at least over one thousand dollars per** kilogram

= 동격　　　값이 얼마가 들다　최소한　　1천 달러 이상　　per ..당 (per hour 1시간 당, per person 1인당,
　　　　　　　　　　　　　　　　　　　　　　　　　　　　　per gallon 1갤론당, per customer 고객 1명당)

because it's very hard to get.

9 (Spending over a thousand dollars on a spice) sounds **ridiculous**,

주어 ( ) 동사 sounds　동명사 주어 - 향신료 하나에 1천 달러 이상 돈을 쓰는 것 (3인칭 단수 현재)　sound ridiculous 어처구니없게 들리다
　　　　　　　　　　　　　　　　　　　　　　sound natural 자연스럽게 들리다 sound funny 웃기게 들리다
　　　　　　　　　　　　ridiculous a. 웃기는, 말도 안 되는 ridicule n. 조롱, 조소 (ludicrous a. 터무니없는 = ridiculous)

but there is something more ridiculous: whisky.

something + 형용사 　　　　= 동격
말도 안 되는 것 (something important 중요한 것)

⑩ This is not just any whisky, it is the most expensive whisky in the world.

그냥 아무 위스키가 아닌 　　　　음절이 긴 단어의 최상급 the most ____ / 음절이 짧은 단어의 최상급 -est
the most handsome guy / the cheapest jeans

⑪ If you want to **appreciate** the rare taste of this 30-year-old whisky

맛보다, 감상하다 　　　　　　　　　　　수식

하이픈(-) 연결표현은 형용사 (복수 의미라고 명사에 -s를 붙이지 않는다.)
This whisky is 30 years old. 이 위스키는 30년 되었다.
It is a 30-year-old whisky. 이것은 30년 된 위스키이다.

가정법 현재 If 주어 you 현재동사 want, 주어 you may have to 동사원형 empty

(from the Macallan Fine Rare Vintage Collection), you may have to

empty your bank account because the price per bottle is $38,000.

통장을 비우다 – 돈을 다 인출하다 　　　　한 병 당 (The price per pound is $5. 무게 1파운드 당 값은 5달러이다.)

약 200달러짜리 샌드위치가 있다는 거 아세요?

❶ 영국에서 200달러 가치의 샌드위치를 찾을 수 있습니다.

❷ 당연히 이 특별한 샌드위치를 주문하려면 100파운드 (미국 달러로 거의 200달러)를 지불해야 합니다.

❸ 세 겹으로 된 이 샌드위치는 빵, 닭고기, 메추라기 알, 햄, 화이트 트뤼플 등으로 만듭니다.

❹ 물론 최고의 재료만 사용됩니다.

❺ 기름지지만 전 세계 음식 마니아들은 최상의 맛이라며 극찬합니다.

❻ 샌드위치에 200달러라는 게 비싸다고 생각하나요?

❼ 세상에는 그보다 더 비싼 음식이 아주 많습니다.

❽ 일종의 향신료인 샤프란은 워낙 얻기 어려운 탓에 1kg에 최소 1천 달러 이상을 지불해야 합니다.

❾ 향신료 하나에 천 달러 이상을 쓴다는 게 어이없는 짓 같지만, 더 어이없는 게 있으니 바로 위스키입니다.

❿ 그냥 위스키가 아니라 전 세계에서 가장 비싼 위스키입니다.

⓫ 맥켈란 파인 레어 빈티지 컬렉션의 30년 된 이 위스키의 흔치 않은 맛을 감상하려면 통장을 털어야 할지도 모르는데,
한 병 당 가격이 38,000달러이기 때문입니다.

Coffee made of cat poo is the most expensive coffee? You might say, 'No way!' but many people would say, 'Yes way.' Poo, or we can say 'feces', is supposed to be smelly and gross, but this cat poo coffee is nothing like that. Cat Poo Coffee (called 'civet coffee' or 'Kopi Luwak') is more expensive and tastier than Starbucks'. But, who would pay around $20 for a single cup of coffee brewed from an animal's poo? Unexpectedly, quite a few coffee lovers are willing to wait in line to get a taste of it.

It is not brewed from regular coffee beans. Its special beans are collected from the feces of the civet, which is not exactly a cat, but a cat-like mammal. The civet eats the coffee cherries that fall off the trees, and defecates. Brewers search through the droppings and pick out the cherries that have passed through its digestive system. It is expensive because only about 230kg of the beans are produced each year in the whole of Indonesia.

Generally, customers praise its strong aftertaste. Considering its origin, no wonder it has a strong aftertaste. In spite of that, some people have no reservations about paying 20 bucks for a cup of poo coffee, since its flavor is just that good.

1. What can be the best title of this story?

    a. Eat Poo, Drink Poo, And Smell Poo

    b. Cat, The Mysterious Animal

    c. The Most Expensive Poo Ever

    d. Coffee From Poo : Not Smelly But Fragrant

2. According to the passage, which sentence is <u>wrong</u>?

    a. 'Feces' and 'poo' have the same meaning.

    b. Poo is supposed to be smelly and dirty, but cat poo is not dirty, just smelly.

    c. Coffee fanatics don't mind waiting in line to get a taste of Cat Poo Coffee.

    d. Special beans of Kopi Luwak can be found in the droppings of the civet.

3. Choose the correct words for each sentence.

    a. I have heard his lies quite a few <u>time</u> / <u>times</u> / <u>timing</u>. Can't believe whatever he says.

    b. The nearest supermarket is Kristine's Fresh Market <u>which</u> / <u>who</u> / <u>what</u> is owned by my sister.

    c. Considering that <u>his advanced age</u> / <u>his age advanced</u> / <u>as his advanced age</u>, he looks surprisingly young.

    d. Bobby Brown, ex-husband of Whitney Houston who was found dead in her hotel room, <u>mourn</u> / <u>mourns</u> / <u>mourning</u> Houston's death.

Answer **1.** d   **2.** b   **3.** times ǀ which ǀ his advanced age ǀ mourns

Listening Drill - Dictation

Coffee   cat poo is the most expensive coffee? You might say, 'No way!' but many people would say, 'Yes way.' Poo, or we can say '   ', is supposed to be smelly and gross, but this cat poo coffee   . Cat Poo Coffee (called 'civet coffee' or 'Kopi Luwak') is more expensive and tastier than Starbucks'. But, who would pay around $20   coffee brewed from an animal's poo? Unexpectedly, quite a few coffee lovers are willing to wait in line   .

It is not   regular coffee beans. Its special beans are collected from the feces of the civet, which is not exactly a cat, but a cat-like mammal. The civet eats the coffee cherries that fall off the trees, and   . Brewers search through the droppings and pick out the cherries that have   . It is expensive because only about 230kg of the beans are produced each year in the whole of Indonesia. Generally, customers praise its strong aftertaste. Considering its origin, no wonder it   . In spite of that, some people   paying 20 bucks for a cup of poo coffee, since its flavor is just that good.

Did You Know The Most Expensive Coffee Is Made Of Cat Poo?

1 (Coffee made of cat poo) is the most expensive coffee?

Coffee which is made of cat poo 고양이 똥으로 만든 커피
주어 coffee 동사 is

2 You might say, 'No way!' but many people would say, 'Yes way.'

원래 yes way라는 표현은 없지만 no way의 반대 표현으로 구어에서 종종 쓰인다.

3 Poo, (or we can say 'feces'), is supposed to be smelly and gross,

⌐ = 동격 ⌐ 또는 …라고도 말할 수 있는   be supposed to 동사 : …하기로 되어 있다, …해야 한다
poo, dropping, feces, excrement 대변   (It is supposed to be tasty, but it's not. 이거 맛있어야 하는데 그렇지 않다.)
smell 냄새(나다) smelly (안 좋은) 냄새가 나는   gross 총 (모두 합해서), 중대한, 역겨운, 무례한

but this cat poo coffee is nothing like that.

전혀 그렇지 않다

4 Cat Poo Coffee (called 'civet coffee' or 'Kopi Luwak') is more expensive

⌐ = 동격 ⌐   more beautiful, more difficult, more comfortable
                         / prettier, easier, uglier / smarter, fatter

and tastier than Starbucks'.

긴 음절의 비교급 more, 짧은 음절은 -er (y로 끝나면 y 지우고 -ier)

5 But, who would pay around $20 for (a single cup of coffee brewed from

pay 가격 for ( ) : ( )에 얼마를 내다   coffee (which was) brewed from… …에서 우려낸 커피

an animal's poo)?

6 Unexpectedly, quite a few coffee lovers are willing to wait in line to get a taste of it.

예상외로, 뜻밖에   = many (+ 복수명사)   기꺼이 ..하다   줄 서서 기다리다   맛보다
                                                              taste v. 맛보다 n. 맛 (get a taste에서는 명사)

7 It is not brewed from regular coffee beans.

보통의, 정기적인, 규칙적인 – 이 문장에서는 '보통의, 일반적인')

8 (Its special beans) are collected from the feces of the civet,

(소유격) 이것의 특별한 콩들   be collected from …에서 모아지다 (수동태)
= Civet coffee's special beans

which is not exactly a cat, but a cat-like mammal.

콤마 which 계속 용법   정확히 …는 아니고 not A but B : A가 아니고 B   n. 포유동물
단어 순서대로 해석

9 The civet ¹⁾ eats the coffee cherries (that fall off the trees), and ²⁾ defecates.

                          수식 │ 나무에서 떨어진 열매   배설하다

10 Brewers ¹⁾ search through the droppings and ²⁾ pick out the cherries (that

뒤져서 찾다   수식
                                    시벳의 소화계를 통과한 열매들 (시벳이 먹고 소화시켜 배설한 열매들)

have passed through its **digestive** system).
통과하다 　　 its (소유격) 　 소화계, 소화기관

⑪ It is expensive because (only about 230kg of the beans) are produced each year
because 이하 절의 주어 ( ) 겨우 약 230kg의 콩들, 동사 are 　　 be produced 수동 – 생산되다

in the whole of Indonesia.
인도네시아 전역에서

⑫ Generally, customers **praise** its strong aftertaste.
praise v. 찬양/칭송하다 n. 칭송, 칭찬 　　 after (후, 나중) + taste (맛) – 뒷맛
= speak highly of, compliment

⑬ **Considering** its origin, no wonder it has a strong aftertaste.
이것(시벳 커피)의 근원을 감안할 때 　　 (It is) no wonder (that) : ⋯는 당연하다, 놀랍지 않다

⑭ In spite of that, some people have no **reservations** about paying
that (앞서 나온 시벳 커피에 대한 내용)에도 불구하고 　　 reservation 1. 예약 2. 의구심, 거리낌
in spite of + that (명사) ⋯하는데 주저하지 않다 　 have no reservations about -ing 물건에 얼마를 내다
(have no reservations (반드시 복수형) 거리낌 없다 / make a reservation 예약하다)

20 bucks for a cup of poo coffee, since its **flavor** is just that good.
pay 가격 for 물건 　　 = because 　 맛, 향미 　　 good을 강조하는 that (그만큼, 그 정도로)

---

❶ 고양이 똥으로 만든 커피가 가장 비싼 커피?

❷ 여러분은 '말도 안 돼!' 라고 말할지 모르지만, '말이 된다'고 할 사람이 많습니다.

❸ '배설물'이라고도 하는 똥은 냄새 나고 더러워야 하지만 고양이 똥 커피는 전혀 그렇지 않습니다.

❹ 고양이 똥 커피 (시벳 커피 또는 코피 루왁)는 스타벅스 커피 보다 더 비싸고 더 맛있습니다.

❺ 하지만 20달러나 내고 동물 똥에서 추출한 커피 한 컵을 먹겠다는 사람이 누가 있을까요?

❻ 의외로, 상당한 커피 애호가들이 그 맛을 보기 위해 기꺼이 줄을 서서 기다립니다.

❼ 이 커피는 평범한 커피콩에서 추출하지 않습니다.

❽ 특별한 콩은 시벳(사향고양이)의 똥에서 모을 수 있는데, 시벳은 정확히 고양이는 아니고 고양이와 비슷한 포유동물입니다.

❾ 시벳은 나무에서 떨어진 커피 열매를 먹고 똥을 쌉니다.

❿ 커피 만드는 사람들은 똥을 뒤져 시벳의 소화 기관을 통과한 열매를 골라냅니다.

⑪ 이 커피가 비싼 이유는 매년 인도네시아 전체에서 겨우 230kg 정도만 생산되기 때문입니다.

⑫ 보통 고객들은 이 커피의 강한 뒷맛에 찬사를 보냅니다.

⑬ 어디에서 나온 것인지 감안할 때 뒷맛이 강할 만도 하지요.

⑭ 그럼에도 불구하고 조금도 주저하지 않고 똥 커피 한 컵에 20달러를 내는 사람들이 있는데, 풍미가 그만큼 좋기 때문입니다.

Chapter 03

Beauty

MP3

21 Did You Know Botox Is A Kind Of Poison?

Botox is the most popular non-surgical cosmetic procedure. Allegedly, millions of people have been getting Botox injections every year. Botox is the brand name of botulinum toxin A, and botulism is a serious form of food poisoning. The typical symptom of botulism is paralysis. In some cases, paralysis of botulism can be very dangerous, even fatal. Interestingly, Botox injections are a diluted form of botulism which is injected into facial muscles because they can paralyze or weaken the muscles that form wrinkles. For instance, when a person gets the injection into the muscles around the brows, those muscles can not contract for a period of time. They are paralyzed. After being given Botox injections, people can see the effects of the injections within a few hours to a couple of days.

Unfortunately, the amazing effects of Botox do not last long. If you want to maintain a wrinkle-free look throughout the year, you have to get the injections 3 to 4 times a year since the effects last about three to five months.

Words & Expressions

non-surgical 비수술적인, 수술을 하지 않는 cosmetic procedure 미용 시술 injection 주입, 주사 undergo (수술, 시술) 받다 botulism 보툴리누스 식중독 food poisoning 식중독 typical symptom 전형적인 증상 paralysis 마비 (v. paralyze) fatal 치명적인 dilute 희석하다, 흐리게 하다 facial muscles 얼굴 근육 weaken 약하게 하다 (a. weak 약한) contract 수축하다 (n. contraction 수축, 계약) for a period of time 한 동안 last 지속하다 throughout the year 일년 내내

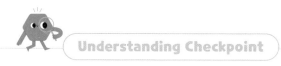

1. What is the main idea of the story?

    a. It is very dangerous and foolish to get Botox injections.

    b. Botox is the most expensive but popular non-surgical cosmetic procedure.

    c. Botox is fatal because it can paralyze the muscles.

    d. Botox is a diluted form of botulism which is a kind of dangerous toxin.

2. If you get a Botox injection into the muscles around your eye brows, _____ .

    a. those muscles will be paralyzed

    b. you will go blind due to infection caused by the toxin

    c. your wrinkle-free skin will last for 5 years

    d. your facial muscles will contract very quickly.

3. Choose the correct words for each sentence.

    a. I think the right side of my body is <u>paralysis</u> / <u>paralyzed</u> / <u>paralyze</u>. I can't move my right hand.

    b. Some patients with type 1 diabetes have to get insulin <u>infections</u> / <u>injections</u> / <u>induction</u> on a daily basis.

    c. Just be patient for a while. He will be here <u>for</u> / <u>in</u> / <u>with</u> a minute.

Answer 1. d 2. a 3. paralyzed | injections | in

Botox is the most popular   . Allegedly, millions of people have been getting Botox injections every year. Botox is the brand name of botulinum toxin A, and botulism is   food poisoning. The   of botulism is paralysis. In some cases, paralysis of botulism can be very dangerous, even fatal. Interestingly, Botox injections are   botulism which is injected into facial muscles because they can   the muscles that form wrinkles. For instance, when a person   into the muscles around the brows, those muscles can not contract   . They are paralyzed. After being given Botox injections, people can see the effects of the injections

    .

Unfortunately, the amazing effects of Botox do not last long. If you want to maintain a wrinkle-free look   , you have to get the injections 3 to 4 times a year since   three to five months.

Did You Know Botox Is A Kind Of Poison?

1 Botox is [1] the most **popular** [2] non-**surgical cosmetic** procedure.

가장 인기 있고   비수술적인 (non 아닌 + surgical 외과 수술의)

cosmetic a. 성형의 n. 화장품 + procedure

n. 절차, 수술 = 성형수술 (plastic surgery)

2 **Allegedly**, (millions of people) have been getting Botox **injections** every year.

알려진 바에 의하면   수백만 명   현재완료 have been + 진행 been getting   n. 주사, 투입

dozens of people 수 십 명 hundreds of people 수백 명 thousands of people 수천 명

tens of thousand 수만 명 hundreds of thousands 수십만 명

3 Botox is the brand name of (botulinum toxin A), and botulism is a serious form

보톡스는 (보툴리눔 독소 A의) 상표이다.

of **food poisoning**.

식중독

4 (The typical **symptom** of botulism) is **paralysis**.

증상   paralysis n. 마비 paralyze v. 마비시키다

주어 symptom 동사 is   analysis n. 분석 analyze v. 분석하다

5 In some cases, (paralysis of botulism) can be very dangerous, even **fatal**.

주어 paralysis 동사 can   심지어 치명적인

fatal a. 치명적인, 죽음을 초래하는

fatality n. 사망자, 치사율

6 Interestingly, Botox injections are a **diluted** form of botulism (which is

                                              수식

희석된 형태 (명사 form)   form which is injected into facial muscles

얼굴 근육에 주입되는 (보툴리눔의) 희석된 형태

injected into facial muscles) because they can [1] **paralyze** or [2] **weaken**

Botox injections (복수)

the muscles (that form **wrinkles**).

        수식 | 주름을 형성하는 근육 (여기서 form은 동사)

7 For instance, when a person gets the injection into (the muscles around

= for example 예를 들어   주사를 맞다   눈썹 주위 근육에

the brows), those muscles can not **contract** (for a period of time).

수축하다   일정 기간 동안

8 They are paralyzed.

앞문장의 those muscles (= the muscles around the brows)

⑨ After being given Botox injections, people can see the **effects** of the injections

주절의 주어 people 일치, 생략   효과를 보다
= After people are given Botox injections

within a few hours to a couple of days.

몇 시간에서 이틀 내에 (<u>from</u> a few hours <u>to</u> a couple of days - from 생략) a couple of = 2

⑩ Unfortunately, ⟨the amazing effects of Botox⟩ do not **last** long.

주어 effects (복수) + 동사 do not   오래 지속하다 (↔ 오래 지속하지 않다 do not last long)
                                              짧은 기간 지속하다 last briefly

⑪ If you want to maintain a wrinkle-free look throughout the year, you have to get

가정법 현재   주름 없는 (free 자유로운, 없는)   일년 내내
                           oil-free, fat-free 무지방의, trouble-free 문제없는, sugar-free 무가당의, dury-free 면세의

the injections 3 to 4 times a year since the effects last about three to five months.

일 년에 (일년마다 a year = per year) 3-4번   3달에서 5달

보톡스가 일종의 독이라는 거 아세요?

❶ 보톡스는 가장 인기 있는 비수술적인 미용 시술입니다.

❷ 알려진 바에 의하면 매년 수백만의 사람들이 보톡스 시술(주사)을 받는다고 합니다.

❸ 보톡스는 보툴리눔 독소 A의 상표로, 보툴리눔 식중독은 심각한 식중독의 한 형태입니다.

❹ 보툴리눔 식중독의 전형적인 증상은 마비입니다.

❺ 어떤 경우 보툴리눔 식중독으로 인한 마비는 대단히 위험해서, 심지어 치명적일 수도 있습니다.

❻ 흥미롭게도, 보툴리눔 식중독을 희석시킨 것을 얼굴에 주입하는 게 보톡스 시술인데, 이것이 주름을 형성하는 근육을 마비시키거나 약화시키기 때문입니다.

❼ 예를 들어 눈썹 주위 근육에 이 시술을 받는다면, 주변 근육은 일정 기간 동안 수축할 수 없게 됩니다.

❽ 근육이 마비된 것입니다.

❾ 보톡스 주입을 받고 난 후, 사람들은 몇 시간에서 이틀 이내에 시술의 효과를 볼 수 있습니다.

❿ 불행히도 보톡스의 놀라운 효과는 오래 지속되지 않습니다.

⓫ 일 년 내내 주름 없는 모습을 유지하고 싶다면 일 년에 3-4회 시술을 받아야 하는데, 효과가 3달에서 5달 정도만 유지되기 때문입니다.

First, you need to find the right cleanser for your skin. You can find a good cleanser for your skin type at drugstores or local cosmetic shops. The number one mistake people make when it comes to a facial wash is thinking expensive ones are always better. But that is not always true. There is no need to spend over 50,000 won on a costly name-brand wash. However, you had better not choose bar soap because it generally dries out the skin.

And don't forget not to wash or cleanse too often. Nothing more than washing once or twice a day with a proper cleanser is needed. In the morning, just a splash of lukewarm water is enough.

One more thing : use a small amount of cleanser (just a dime-sized bit is sufficient to cleanse your face) and rinse with lukewarm water. Be careful not to wash your face with hot or cold water. Both can have a bad effect on your skin.

1. What can be the best title of this story?

    a. The More You Wash, The Clearer Skin You Can Get

    b. Cleanser : The Biggest Enemy For Your Skin

    c. How To Wash Your Face & How To Choose Your Cleanser

    d. All You Need To Know About Bar Soap

2. According to the passage, which sentence is <u>wrong</u>?

    a. You had better not use bar soap and not wash your face more than twice a day.

    b. No need to spend lots of money on expensive cleansers.

    c. You can find an appropriate cleanser for your skin type only at drugstores.

    d. You don't have to use any soap or cleanser when washing your face in the morning.

3. Choose the correct words for each sentence.

    a. I <u>do</u> / <u>make</u> / <u>have</u> mistakes all the time but I try not to repeat the mistakes of the past.

    b. When it comes <u>about shopping</u> / <u>to shopping</u> / <u>to shop</u>, my boyfriend is an expert.

    c. Since my eye are blurry, I have to be careful <u>to not</u> / <u>not to</u> / <u>to not to</u> bump into something or someone.

Answer **1.** c **2.** c **3.** make ǀ to shopping ǀ not to

First, you need to find the right cleanser for your skin. You can find a good cleanser for your skin type   or local cosmetic shops.

      when it comes to a facial wash is thinking expensive ones are always better. But that is   . There is no need to spend over 50,000 won on a costly name-brand wash. However, you   bar soap because it generally dries out the skin.

And don't forget not to wash or cleanse too often.   washing   with a proper cleanser is needed. In the morning, just a splash of   is enough.

One more thing : use   cleanser (just   is sufficient to cleanse your face) and rinse with lukewarm water. Be careful not to wash your face with hot or cold water. Both can   your skin.

Did You Know The Basic Tips For Cleansing?

1 First, you need to find the right **cleanser** for your skin.

clean a. 깨끗한 cleanse v. 깨끗하게 하다 cleanser n. 세안제
detergent n. (세탁, 주방용) 세제

2 You can find a good cleanser for your skin type at **drugstores** or

= pharmacy 약국 (drugstore는 화장품 같은 것도 판매)

local cosmetic shops.

3 The number one mistake (people make) when it comes to a facial wash is

수식 | 사람들이 저지르는 실수   …에 관해서라면 (to + 명사, 동명사)
주어 mistake 동사 is ⇒ 실수는 …라고 생각하는 것이다 thinking

thinking (**expensive** ones are always better).

비싼 게 항상 더 좋다 (ones = facial washes 얼굴용 세안제들)

4 But that is not always true.

부분 부정 - 항상 …인 건 아니다

5 There is no need to spend over 50,000 won on a **costly** name-brand wash.

…할 (to 동사) 필요는 없다   spend 값 (over 50,000 won) on 물건 : 물건에 얼마를 지출하다
costly a. 비싼 (-ly로 끝나지만 형용사)
(-ly로 끝나는 형용사 : friendly, lovely, ugly, lonely, deadly, timely)

6 However, you had better not choose bar soap because it generally **dries out** the skin.

had better의 부정 : had better not 동사원형   말라버리게 하다
: …하지 않는 게 더 낫다   soap 불가산 명사로 -s 복수 형태로 쓰지 않는다.
two soaps (X) two bars of soap (O)

7 And don't forget not to 1) wash or 2) cleanse too often.

don't forget 잊지 마라
to 부정사의 부정은 to 앞에 부정어 not to wash (O), to not wash (X)
don't forget not to wash 안 씻는 거 잊지 마라 (안 씻어라)

8 Nothing (more than washing once or twice a day with a proper cleanser) is needed.

주어 nothing 아닌 것, 동사 is needed 필요하다 = 필요하지 않다 (적당한 세안제로 하루 한 두 번 이상 씻는 것)
⇒ 두 번 이상 씻는 건 필요하지 않다

9 In the morning, just a **splash** of **lukewarm** water is enough.

첨벙 끼얹다, 물을 끼얹은 방울
boiling 끓는 〉 hot 뜨거운 〉 lukewarm 미지근한 〉 room temperature 상온의
〉 cold 차가운 〉 freezing 얼음장 같은

⑩ One more thing : ¹⁾ use a small amount of cleanser (just a dime-sized bit

( )의 적은 양 a small amount of ( )　　　　　다임 동전 크기
( )의 많은 양 a large amount of ( )

is sufficient to cleanse your face) and ²⁾ **rinse** with lukewarm water.

be sufficient to 동사 : …하기에 충분하다　　　　　헹구다　(wash v. 씻다　rinse v. 헹구다　rub v. 문지르다)

⑪ Be careful not to wash your face with (hot or cold) water.

Be careful not to wash 씻지 않도록 조심하라 (to 부정사의 부정은 to 앞에 not)

⑫ Both can have a bad effect on your skin.

= hot water or cold water

have an effect on …에 영향을 미치다 (= affect)
have a bad effect on …에 나쁜 영향을 미치다 = affect negatively
have a good effect on …에 좋은 영향을 미치다 = affect positively

〔 세안을 위한 기본 팁을 아세요? 〕

❶ 먼저 자기 피부에 맞는 클렌저(세안제품)를 찾을 필요가 있습니다.

❷ 약국이나 동네 화장품 가게에서 자기 피부 타입에 맞는 좋은 클렌저를 찾을 수 있습니다.

❸ 피부 세안에 관해 사람들이 가장 많이 저지르는 실수는 비싼 제품이 항상 좋다고 생각하는 것입니다.

❹ 하지만 언제나 그런 건 아닙니다.

❺ 고가의 유명 브랜드 세안 제품 하나에 5만원 이상의 돈을 쓸 필요는 없습니다.

❻ 하지만 고체 비누는 고르지 않는 게 좋은데, 일반적으로 고체 비누가 피부를 건조시키기 때문입니다.

❼ 그리고 너무 자주 씻거나 세안하지 말아야 한다는 걸 잊지 마세요.

❽ 적당한 클렌저로 하루에 한 두 번 세안하면 되지 그 이상은 필요 없습니다.

❾ 아침에는 미지근한 물만 한 번 뿌리듯 세안하는 걸로 충분합니다.

⑩ 한 가지 더. 클렌저 양을 적게 사용하고 (얼굴을 닦는데 다임 동전 하나 크기면 충분) 미지근한 물로 헹궈 냅니다.

⑪ 뜨겁거나 찬 물로 닦지 않도록 주의하세요.

⑫ 두 가지 모두 피부에 안 좋은 영향을 미칠 수 있습니다.

Many diet and weight loss industries have been pocketing huge amounts of money because many people are willing to open their wallets for weight-loss products. People just want to lose weight easily and these products work.

Among the many diet products, fat burners are gaining huge popularity, since these help users lose weight in a short time period without sweaty exercises or the horrible pain of dieting. The problem is that not everybody who spends money on fat burners tastes the joy of losing weight. So before choosing fat burners, consider the following points:

- Is it effective? - The fat burners are supposed to help you lose fat, not just water.

- Is it safe? - Check whether the ingredients are clinically safe and if there are any side effects. Choose only FDA-approved products.

- Are consumers satisfied with the product? - Review other users' opinions before buying. Hundreds of companies making and selling fat burners have been busted by the FDA for false advertising and using unhealthy ingredients.

Words & Expressions

fat burner 지방 연소 보조 제품 weight loss industry 체중 감량 산업 pocket 주머니에 넣다, 챙기다 be willing to 기꺼이 …하다 open one's wallet (돈을 내려고) 지갑을 열다 weight-loss product 체중 감량 제품 work 효과가 있다 gain popularity 인기를 얻다 in a short time period 짧은 시간 내에 sweaty 땀이 나는 (sweat 땀) pain 고통 (pang, agony) taste the joy of …의 기쁨을 맛보다 effective 효과적인 clinically 의학적으로 (clinic 병원, 진료) side effect 부작용 customer 고객 approved 승인을 받은 bust 단속하다 (be busted 단속에 걸리다) false advertisement 허위광고

1. What is the main idea of the story?

    a. People who want to lose weight easily need to buy fat burners.

    b. When choosing a fat burner, select the effective, safe and customer-approved one.

    c. All diet products including fat burners must have been approved by the FDA.

    d. Companies who advertise their products falsely must be busted by the FDA.

2. Fat burners are gaining popularity since _____ .

    a. they are cheaper than diet pills

    b. they promise a miracle for a reasonable price

    c. all of them are approved by the FDA and clinically safe

    d. these can help users burn their fat in a not-so-difficult way.

3. Choose the correct words for each sentence.

    a. Surprisingly, his company <u>pocket</u> / <u>pocketed</u> / <u>pockets</u> nearly $3 million last year.

    b. Why are you never <u>satisfied with</u> / <u>satisfy about</u> / <u>satisfied by</u> anything in your life?

    c. If you cheat on a test, you will <u>bust</u> / <u>be buste</u> / <u>to bust</u> faster than you can say 'I'm busted!'

Answer **1.** b   **2.** d   **3.** pocketed ∣ satisfied with ∣ be busted

Listening Drill – Dictation

Many diet and weight loss industries have been pocketing huge amounts of money because many people _____ open their wallets for weight-loss products. People just want to _____ easily and these products _____.

Among the many diet products, fat burners _____ , since these help users lose weight in a short time period without sweaty exercises or the horrible pain of dieting. The problem is that not everybody who _____ fat burners _____ losing weight. So before choosing fat burners, consider the following points:

- Is it effective? - The fat burners are supposed to help you lose fat, not just water.

- Is it safe? - Check whether the ingredients are _____ and if there are any side effects. Choose only FDA-approved products.

- Are consumers _____ the product? - Review other users' opinions before buying. Hundreds of companies making and selling fat burners _____ the FDA for false advertising and using unhealthy ingredients.

Did You Know How To Choose The Right Fat Burner?

1 (Many **diet** and **weight loss** industries) have been pocketing **huge** amounts of money

주어 ( ) 동사 have 현재완료 have been + 진행 been pocketing

엄청난 금액의 돈 = lots of money
pocket n. 주머니 v. 주머니에 챙기다, 넣다

because many people are willing to open their wallets for weight-loss products.

기꺼이 …하다   지갑을 열다 = spend money

2 People just want to **lose weight** easily and these products **work**.

체중 감량 – lose / 체중 증가 – gain
gain weight 체중이 늘다 lose weight 체중이 줄다

work v. 일하다, 효과가 있다
It works wonders. 기적적인 효과가 있다.

3 Among the many diet products, fat burners are gaining huge **popularity**,

둘 사이 between, 둘 이상 among
between you and me 너와 나 사이 / among these people 이 사람들 사이

gain popularity 인기를 얻다 (popular a. 인기 있는)

since these help users lose weight in a short time period

fat burners   짧은 기간 안에
help 목적어(users) 동사원형(lose)
사용자들 users이 살을 뺄 수 있도록 lose 돕다 help

without [1] sweaty exercises or [2] the horrible pain of dieting.

짧은 기간 안에 땀 흘리는 운동   짧은 기간 안에 끔찍한 다이어트의 고통

4 The problem is that not everybody (who spends money on fat burners)

수식

문제는 that… 이다   that 절의 주어 (not) everybody 동사 tastes – 모두가 ( )의 맛을 보는 건 아니다

tastes (the joy of losing weight).

taste the joy of …의 즐거움을 맛보다   체중감량의 즐거움

5 So before choosing fat burners, consider the following points:

before you choose …(명령문 주어 you 생략)

6 - Is it **effective**? -

a. 효과적인 (↔ ineffective)

7 The fat burners **are supposed to** help you lose (fat, not just water).

be supposed to 동사원형 help 목적어 you 동사원형 lose   (물이 아니라 지방)

8 - Is it safe? -

9 Check [1] whether the **ingredients** are **clinically** safe

확인할 점(check) [1] 과 [2]   성분, 재료, 요소   의학적으로 (clinic 병원, 진료)
재료가 의학적으로 안전한지 여부 whether (or not 아닌지–생략)

and ²⁾ if there are any **side effects**.
부작용

⑩ Choose only FDA-approved products.
FDA 승인을 받은 (approved 승인된, 공인된)
FDA : Food and Drug Administration 미식품의약국

⑪ - Are **consumers satisfied with** the product?
인칭주어 be satisfied with 주어가 …에 만족하다 (I am satisfied with this bread. 나는 이 빵에 만족한다.)
비인칭주어 be satisfying 주어는 만족스럽다. (This bread is satisfying. 이 빵은 만족스럽다.)

⑫ - Review other users' opinions before buying.
명령문 주어 you 생략   주절의 주어와 일치, 생략 ⇒ You review… before you buy

⑬ Hundreds of companies (making and selling fat burners) have been busted by the FDA
┗━━━ 수식 ━━━┛
현재 완료 have been 수동태 been busted by
현재 완료 have been 수동태 been busted by(지방 연소제를 제조하고 판매하는) 수백의 회사들 (주어) + have 동사

for ¹⁾ false advertising and ²⁾ using **unhealthy** ingredients.
busted for (적발되는 이유) ^{1), 2)}
be busted by ( ) for 〈 〉: 〈 〉 때문에 ( )에 의해 적발되다. 전치사 for 다음에 명사나 동명사만 올 수 있다.)

┌ 올바른 지방 연소제를 어떻게 선택해야 하는지 아세요? ┐

❶ 다이어트와 체중 감량 산업이 엄청난 돈을 챙기는 건 많은 사람들이 체중 감량 제품에 기꺼이 지갑을 열기 때문입니다.

❷ 사람들은 그저 쉽게 체중을 감량하고 싶은데 이런 제품들은 효과가 있습니다.

❸ 많은 다이어트 제품들 중에 지방 연소제가 엄청난 인기를 얻고 있는데, 이유는 이 제품들은 땀 흘리는 운동이나 끔찍한 다이어트의 고통 없이 짧은 시간에 체중을 감량할 수 있게 도와주기 때문입니다.

❹ 문제는 지방 연소제에 돈을 쓰는 사람들 모두가 체중 감량의 기쁨을 맛보는 건 아니라는 점입니다.

❺ 그래서 지방 연소제를 선택하기 전에 다음 사항을 고려해야 합니다.

❻ - 효과적인가? -   ❼ 지방 연소제는 지방을 빼줘야지 물만 빼주면 안 됩니다.

❽ - 안전한가? -   ❾ 성분이 의학적으로 안전한지, 부작용은 없는지 확인해야 합니다.

❿ FDA 승인을 받은 제품을 선택합니다.

⑪ - 소비자들이 그 제품에 만족하는가? -   ⑫ 구매 전에 다른 사용자들의 의견을 살펴보세요.

⑬ 지방 연소제를 만들어 판매하는 수백 군데의 업체들이 허위 광고와 건강에 해로운 재료를 사용해서 FDA에 적발되고 있습니다.

24 Did You Know Three 'Don'ts' For Your Healthy And Smooth Skin?

Don't smoke. If you are a smoker and don't have any intention of quitting smoking in the near future, you had better prepare to get wrinkly and dry skin. Experts say sun exposure and smoking are the two main causes of skin damage. Kate Moss is the perfect example. Although she looks fabulous in pictures and many skin experts have taken care of her skin with costly cosmetics, her bare skin is horrible because she is a longtime smoker.

Don't forget to moisturize. Skin needs moisture to stay healthy and smooth. Moisture-rich products and moisturizers help your skin lock in moisture. And the best way to use moisturizers is to apply them while your skin is still damp.

Don't tan. Tanned skin looks great, but unfortunately tanned skin is damaged skin. Repeated or constant tanning or sunburn can not only accelerate the aging of the skin but also increase the risk of skin cancer.

Words & Expressions

smoker 흡연자 don't have any intention of –ing ...할 의사가 없다 (= have no intention of –ing) in the near future 가까운 미래에 wrinkly 주름투성이의 (wrinkle 주름) exposure 노출 fabulous 멋진, 근사한 costly 비싼 naked 벌거벗은 naked skin 맨 피부 longtime 오랫동안의, 여러 해의 moisturize 수분을 주다 (moisture 수분 moisturizer 보습제) smooth 부드러운, 매끈한 moisture-rich 수분이 풍부한 apply 적용하다, (화장품) 바르다 damp 축축한 tan 피부를 태우다, 선탠하다 repeated 반복적인 constant 끊임없는, 계속되는 sunburn 햇볕에 의한 화상 accelerate 가속화하다 longtime 오랜, 장기간의

1. What is the main idea of the story?

    a. In order to get smooth skin, do not smoke or tan and do moisturize.

    b. The most important thing to do for smooth skin is to moisturize.

    c. Tanning and smoking are the main causes of skin cancer.

    d. Kate Moss looks fabulous because she has used high-priced cosmetics.

2. According to the passage, which sentence is right?

    a. A non-smoker is highly likely to have wrinkly and dry skin.

    b. Kate Moss' bare skin is bad because she has smoked for a long time.

    c. Skin experts recommend that you should apply moisturizers while taking a bath.

    d. Repeated tanning is a good solution to skin cancer.

3. Choose the correct words for each sentence.

    a. How can I <u>steady cool</u> / <u>stay cool</u> / <u>keep cool</u> in scorching hot temperatures?

    b. Boy, I feel sorry for you because your workload looks <u>brutally</u> / <u>brutality</u> / <u>brutal</u>.

    c. My wife has no intention of quitting <u>smoke</u> / <u>smoking</u> / <u>smoked</u> and that makes me crazy.

Answer **1.** a **2.** b **3.** stay cool ǀ brutal ǀ smoking

Listening Drill – Dictation

Don't smoke. If you are a smoker and   quitting smoking in the near future, you had better prepare to   . Experts say sun exposure and smoking are the two main causes of skin damage. Kate Moss is the perfect example. Although she   in pictures and many skin experts   her skin with costly cosmetics, her   is horrible because she is a longtime smoker. Don't forget to moisturize. Skin needs moisture to   . Moisture-rich products and moisturizers help your skin lock in moisture. And the best way to use moisturizers is to   them while your skin is still damp. Don't tan. Tanned skin looks great, but unfortunately tanned skin is damaged skin.   or constant tanning or sunburn can not only   of the skin but also   .

113

Did You Know Three 'Don'ts' For Your Healthy And Smooth Skin?

① Don't **smoke**.

n. 연기 v. 담배를 피우다 (이 문장에서는 동사 '담배를 피우다') smoker 흡연자 smoking 흡연

② If you [1] are a smoker and [2] don't have any **intention** of **quitting** smoking

have an intention of –ing …할 의사가 있다   그만두다, 중지하다
don't have any intention of –ing / have no intention of –ing …할 의사가 없다

in the near future, you had better prepare to get (wrinkly and dry) skin.

가까운 미래에, 조만간   had better + 동사원형 : …하는 게 좋다 prepare to 동사 ..할 준비를 하다

③ Experts say [1] sun **exposure** and [2] smoking are the two main causes of skin **damage**.

노출   손상, 피해

Experts say (that) 주어 [1] and [2] (태양 노출과 흡연) 동사 are

④ Kate Moss is the perfect example.

⑤ Although [1] she looks fabulous in pictures and [2] many skin experts

Although [1], [2] – [1]과 [2]에도 불구하고

have **taken care of** her skin (with **costly** cosmetics),

현재완료 have taken(pp) take care of 관리하다, 돌보다   비싼 화장품들로
cost v. 값이 얼마 하다 costly a. 비싼 (expensive)

her bare skin is horrible because she is a longtime smoker.

화장 안 한 맨 피부
bare 화장하지 않은 (bare feet 맨발 bare hands 맨손 – 하지만 '맨눈'은 bare eyes로 쓰지 않고 naked eyes)

⑥ Don't forget to **moisturize**.

v. 수분을 주다
Don't forget to 동사원형 : 미래에 할 일을 잊지 마라 (Don't forget to lock the door. 문을 잠그는 걸 잊지 말고 잠가라.)
Don't forget –ing : 이미 일어난 일을 잊지 마라 (Don't forget locking the door. 문을 잠갔다는 사실을 잊지 마라.)

⑦ Skin needs **moisture** to stay (healthy and smooth).

n. 수분, 습기   stay healthy 건강이 유지되다 and stay smooth 부드러움이 유지되다

⑧ (Moisture-rich products and **moisturizers**) help your skin lock in moisture.

수식   보습제   가두다
수분이 풍부한 (Vitamin C-rich 비타민C가 풍부한)   주어 ( ) 동사 help 목적어 your skin 동사원형 lock

⑨ And the best way to use moisturizers is (to **apply** them

주어 way + 동사 is = 방법은 ( )이다   적용하다, (화장품) 바르다
way to 동사 …하는 방법 – the best way to use 사용하는 최상의 방법, the better way to eat. 먹는 더 좋은 방법

while your skin is still **damp**).

a. 축축한

⑩ Don't **tan**.

햇볕에 태우다

⑪ Tanned skin looks great, but unfortunately tanned skin is damaged skin.

look 형용사 …로 보이다　　　　　　　　　　선탠이 된 (수동-tanned)
look fabulous 멋지게 보이다 look old 늙어 보이다　　　　　　손상된 (수동 damaged)

⑫ (Repeated or constant tanning or sunburn) can not only **accelerate** the aging

　　　　　　　　　　　수식　　↑　　　　　　　　　　가속화하다 + 피부 노화
Repeated tanning or constant tanning or sunburn
주어 ( ) 동사 can not only ( ) but also ( )

of the skin but also **increase** the risk of skin cancer.

increase 증가시키다 + 피부암의 위험

〔 건강하고 매끄러운 피부를 위해 하지 말아야 할 '세 가지'가 무엇인지 아세요? 〕

❶ 담배를 피우지 마세요.

❷ 만약 당신이 흡연자이고 조만간 담배를 끊을 생각이 없다면, 주름지고 메마른 피부를 갖게 될 각오를 하는 게 좋습니다.

❸ 전문가들은 태양 노출과 흡연이 피부 손상의 주요 두 가지 원인이라고 말합니다.

❹ 케이트 모스가 완벽한 예입니다.

❺ 모스는 사진에서는 근사해 보이고 많은 피부 전문가들이 비싼 화장품으로 피부 관리를 해주고 있음에도 불구하고, 모스의 맨 피부가 끔찍한 건 그녀가 오랜 흡연자이기 때문입니다.

❻ 보습을 잊지 마세요.

❼ 건강하고 매끈한 피부를 유지하려면 수분이 필요합니다.

❽ 수분이 많이 함유된 제품과 보습제는 피부의 수분이 빠져나가지 않게 막는데 도움이 됩니다.

❾ 최선의 보습제 사용 방법은 피부가 촉촉할 때 바르는 것입니다.

⑩ 선탠을 하지 마세요.

⑪ 선탠한 피부가 보기에는 좋지만, 불행히도 선탠한 피부는 손상된 피부입니다.

⑫ 반복적으로 또는 지속적으로 선탠하거나 태양에 피부를 그을리면 피부 노화가 가속될 뿐만 아니라 피부암의 위험도 높아집니다.

Women who have long and damaged hair are most likely to have problems with split ends. Split ends happen when the tips of hairs lose their outer protective layer. The best and only way to remove current split ends is to cut them off. But if you don't want to trim your hair frequently, refer to the following information.

First, do not use heated hair devices such as blow dryers, curling irons, hair straighteners, etc. These hot air tools dry out your hair and heat is the main cause of split ends. So try not to use them or at least reduce the amount of time that you use them for. Second, lessen how often you dye your hair or get a perm. Both can damage hair, so avoid bleaching, dyeing or getting a perm too often. Third, be careful when brushing. Brushing when it is wet, or brushing too often, or brushing with a fine-toothed comb can harm your hair. Inappropriate brushing can break pieces of your hair and eventually cause split ends. So do not brush wet hair, and use a wide-toothed comb.

Understanding Checkpoint

1. What is the main idea of the story?

    a. Long hair means damaged hair with split ends.

    b. Heated hair devices have nothing to do with hair damage.

    c. If you take precautions, split ends can be prevented.

    d. A wide-toothed comb is always better than a fine-toothed comb.

2. People who hate to trim their hair frequently but have problems with split ends _____ .

    a. tend to brush their hair with a wide-toothed comb

    b. must dye their hair as often as possible

    c. have to use a fine-toothed comb

    d. had better not use curling irons and hair straighteners

3. Choose the correct words for each sentence.

    a. A proper exercise is a fine way <u>losing</u> / <u>to lose</u> / <u>for lost</u> weight and stay healthy.

    b. <u>In order not to</u> / <u>In order to not</u> / <u>In not order to</u> break a large loaf of bread into pieces, she carried it with both hands.

    c. How <u>often</u> / <u>much</u> / <u>long</u> do you work out? Let me guess. Twice a week?

    d. The Smiths are <u>dying</u> / <u>dyeing</u> / <u>dyed</u> their hair black at the hair salon.

Answer **1.** c **2.** d **3.** to lose ǀ In order not to ǀ often ǀ dyeing

Women who have long and damaged hair   have problems with split ends. Split ends   when the tips of hairs lose their outer protective layer.   remove current split ends is to   . But if you don't want to trim your hair frequently, refer to the following information.

First, do not use heated hair devices such as blow dryers, curling irons, hair straighteners, etc. These   dry out your hair and heat is the main cause of split ends. So try not to use them or at least   that you use them for. Second,   how often you dye your hair or get a perm. Both can damage hair, so avoid bleaching, dyeing or getting a perm too often. Third, be careful   . Brushing when it is wet, or brushing too often, or brushing with a fine-toothed comb can harm your hair.   brushing can   of your hair and eventually cause split ends. So do not brush wet hair, and use a wide-toothed comb.

117

Did You Know How To Prevent Split Ends?

1 (Women who have long and damaged hair) are most likely to have problems

주어 women(복수) + 동사 are   be likely to 동사 …할 가능성이 높다
                                                       be most likely to 동사 …할 가능성이 가장 높다

with split ends.

갈라진 머리끝

2 Split ends happen when (the tips of hairs) lose their **outer** protective **layer**.

복수 명사 주어 (tips) + lose + their – 모두 복수 형태   외부의, 외관의   층
                                              집합명사 hair는 복수 –s로 쓰지 않지만 머리카락 한 올일 때 복수 –s를 쓸 수 있다.

3 (The best and only way to remove **current** split ends) is to cut them off.

                    ↑ 수식   a. 현재의   cut them (= split ends) off ( )를 잘라내다
        The best way to remove… and the only way to remove…   주어는 ends가 아니라 way (단수) + is

4 But if you don't want to **trim** your hair **frequently**, refer to the following information.

              (머리카락, 나뭇가지) 다듬다   자주, 빈번하게   (명령– you 생략) 참조하라

5 First, do not use heated hair devices (such as blow dryers, curling irons,

                    열이 나는 모발 장비의 예 ( )

hair **straighteners**, etc.)

        straight a. 곧은 straighten v. 곧게 하다 straightener n. 곧게 펴는 것

6 These hot air tools dry out your hair and heat is the main cause of split ends.

                    가운데 and를 중심으로 독립적 두 문장으로 구성   …의 주요 원인

7 So [1] try not to use them or at least [2] **reduce** the amount of time (that you use

        to 부정사의 부정 try not to 동사   v. 줄이다 (= lessen) 시간의 양, 사용하는 총 시간 ↑   수식
        명령문 [1] try not to… [2] reduce …

them for).

이 문장의 them은 앞서 소개된 heated hair devices

8 Second, **lessen** how often you [1] dye your hair or [2] get a perm.

              얼마나 자주 …하는 지를 (횟수를) 줄이다   염색하다 dye hair, 파마하다 get a perm
              lessen 줄이다 lesson 수업, 교훈   permanent a. 영구적인 n. 파마 v. 파마하다

9 Both can damage hair, so **avoid** (**bleaching**, **dyeing** or getting a perm) too often.

                    avoid + ing …를 피하다   염색
                    bleach 탈색/표백하다 (breach 위반, 붕괴, 파괴)

10 Third, be careful when brushing.

        명령문 You (must) be careful when you brush. (when brushing – 주절의 주어와 일치, 생략)

⑪ ¹⁾ Brushing when it is wet, or ²⁾ brushing too often, or ³⁾ brushing
　　동명사 주어 ¹⁾ or ²⁾ or ³⁾ 동사 can

with a fine-toothed comb can harm your hair.
　　　　　빗살(tooth)이 가는/촘촘한(fine)

⑫ 〔Inappropriate brushing〕 can ¹⁾ break pieces of your hair
　　주어 ( ) 동사 can break … and (can) cause　　산산조각내다, 박살내다

and eventually ²⁾ cause split ends.
　　eveuntually 결국 eventual 궁극적인, 최종의

⑬ So ¹⁾ do not brush wet hair, and ²⁾ use a wide-toothed comb.
　　명령문 ¹⁾ do not brush… and ²⁾ use (주어 you 생략)　　빗살이 (toothed) 넓은 (wide)　(b묵음) 빗

갈라지는 머리끝을 방지하는 방법을 아세요?

① 길고 손상된 모발을 가진 여성은 머리끝이 갈라지는 문제를 겪을 가능성이 아주 높습니다.

② 머리 끝 부분이 외부 보호층을 잃으면 머리끝이 갈라지게 됩니다.

③ 현재 갈라진 끝 부분을 제거하는 최상의, 그리고 유일한 방법은 잘라내는 것입니다.

④ 하지만 자주 머리카락을 다듬고 싶지 않다면, 아래 정보를 참조하세요.

⑤ 먼저, 바람으로 말리는 드라이어, 컬링 아이론, 헤어 스트레이트너 등 열을 이용한 모발 기구를 사용하지 않습니다.

⑥ 이렇게 뜨거운 모발 용품들은 머리카락을 마르게 만들고, 열은 머리끝이 갈라지는 주요 원인입니다.

⑦ 그래서 이러한 용품을 사용하지 않도록, 최소한 이를 사용하는 시간을 줄이도록 노력합니다.

⑧ 두 번째로 염색 또는 파마 횟수를 줄입니다.

⑨ 두 가지 모두 모발을 손상시킬 수 있으니 탈색, 염색 또는 퍼머를 너무 자주 하지 않도록 합니다.

⑩ 세 번째, 빗질할 때 주의합니다.

⑪ 머리카락이 젖었을 때 빗질하거나 너무 자주 빗질하거나 촘촘한 빗으로 빗질하는 것 모두 모발을 손상시킬 수 있습니다.

⑫ 부적절한 빗질은 모발을 부수고 결과적으로 머리끝이 갈라지는 원인이 됩니다.

⑬ 그러니 젖은 머리를 빗지 말고 빗살이 넓은 빗을 사용합니다.

Honey is an effective bacteria killer. So honey has been used as a wound dressing because it can kill bacteria and help heal wounds. Bacteria in wounds are not the only kind honey can kill. Honey can kill bacteria on your skin.

In fact, honey is one of the best ways to get clear and smooth skin. Thanks to honey's amazing healing properties - such as containing enzymes, antioxidants and anti-bacterial agents, - a honey facial mask is effective at removing acne scars, reducing redness, and moisturizing. In addition, it is very easy and simple. All you need is natural unfiltered honey.

First, wash your face. Make sure remove all makeup and that your hands are clean. Apply the honey to your face. When applying the honey, slowly rub the honey all over your face. Leave the honey on your face for about 15 minutes. Wash your face with warm water until all the honey is removed, and lastly with cool water to close your pores. Apply a honey mask 2-3 times a week or as desired.

1. What is the main idea of the story?

    a. Honey had been used to treat wounds but not any more.

    b. Honey can kill bacteria in wounds so we have to use honey as medicine.

    c. Filtered honey is not so effective compared to unfiltered honey.

    d. It is a good idea to use honey to treat acne or acne scars.

2. According to the passage, which sentence is right?

    a. In the past, people used honey only as a sweetener in replacement of sugar.

    b. Honey can kill all kinds of bacteria in the world thanks to antioxidants.

    c. If you have acne scars on your face, honey facial mask may be helpful.

    d. Honey facial mask needs lots of ingredients and costs much.

3. Choose the correct words for each sentence.

    a. You should read the directions carefully before <u>making</u> / <u>getting</u> / <u>applying</u> this ointment.

    b. 'Have a meeting <u>three times a month</u> / <u>seven times a week</u> / <u>24 hours a day</u>?' You mean, we will have a meeting everyday?

    c. Meg is <u>not the only one</u> / <u>the only person</u> / <u>not someone</u> who can speak Spanish among us. Actually several people can speak Spanish as much as she does.

Answer **1.** d   **2.** c   **3.** applying ∣ seven times a week ∣ not the only one

Listening Drill – Dictation

Honey is an effective bacteria killer. So honey   a wound dressing because it can kill bacteria and help   . Bacteria in wounds   honey can kill. Honey can kill bacteria on your skin.

In fact, honey is one of the best ways to get clear and smooth skin. Thanks to honey's amazing healing properties - such as containing   , antioxidants and anti-bacterial agents, - a honey facial mask   removing acne scars, reducing redness, and moisturizing. In addition, it is very easy and simple.   natural unfiltered honey.

First, wash your face.   remove all makeup and that your hands are clean. Apply the honey to your face.   , slowly rub the honey all over your face.   the honey on your face for about 15 minutes. Wash your face with warm water until all the honey is removed, and lastly with cool water to close your pores. Apply a honey mask 2-3 times a week or   .

Did You Know The Sweetest Way To Control Acne?

1 Honey is an **effective** bacteria killer.

effect n. 영향, 효과   박테리아, 세균 (bacterium의 복수형)
effective a. 효과적인

2 So honey has been used as a **wound** dressing

현재완료 has been + 수동태 been used   n. 상처, 부상 (injury) scar n. 흉터 cut n. 베인 상처

because it can ¹⁾ kill bacteria and ²⁾ help **heal** wounds.

help + heal 동사원형 – 치유를 돕다

3 (Bacteria in wounds) are not the only kind (honey can kill).

상처 속 박테리아 (복수 주어) + are   수식
– 상처의 박테리아는 꿀이 죽일 수 있는 유일한 종류가 아니다   유일한 종류가 아닌 (kind a. 친절한 n. 종류)

4 Honey can kill bacteria on your skin.

피부 위 / 표면 – on

5 In fact, honey is one of the best ways to get (clear and smooth) skin.

one of the 복수 명사 + 단수 동사   way to 동사 …하는 방법

6 Thanks to honey's amazing healing **properties** - such as containing (**enzymes**,

덕분에 + 명사(구)   properties의 예 - such as   효소
due to, because of + 명사(구) – 때문에   property 속성, 특징, 재산, 부동산

antioxidants and anti-bacterial **agents**), - a honey facial mask is effective at

anti항(抗)+ oxidant산화제   agent 대리인, 중개인, 물질   🉐 be effective at _ing ¹⁾ ²⁾ ³⁾ …에 효과적이다

¹⁾ removing **acne scars**, ²⁾ reducing redness, and ³⁾ moisturizing.

여드름

7 In addition, it is very easy and simple.

게다가 = moreover

8 (All you need) is natural unfiltered honey.

주어 ( ) – 네가 필요한 모든 것 (all – 단수 취급) + is

9 First, wash your face.

10 Make sure ¹⁾ remove all **makeup** and ²⁾ that your hands are clean.

확실하게 하다
🉐 명령문 (주어 you 생략) make sure ¹⁾ (that) … and ²⁾ that …
두 가지 that 이하를 확실하게 하라

⑪ **Apply** the honey to your face.
1. (로션, 연고) 바르다 (to) 2. (이력서, 직책 등) 지원하다 (for)

⑫ When [1] applying the honey, slowly [2] rub the honey all over your face.
📘 명령문 when you [1] apply honey, [2] rub   얼굴 전체에
주절의 주어와 일치, 생략-능동적인 행동이므로 applying

⑬ Leave the honey on your face for about 15 minutes.
v. …인 상태로 두다, 떠나다 (leave-left-left)   for (기간 …동안) + about (약) + 15 minutes – 약 15분 동안
left leave의 과거형, 왼쪽
leaves 동사 leave의 3인칭 단수 현재형, leaf (잎)의 복수

⑭ Wash your face [1] with **warm** water (until all the honey is removed),
따뜻한 / lukewarm 미지근한   꿀이 전부 제거될 때까지

and lastly [2] with cool water to close your **pores**.
마지막으로 (wash your face) with cool water   구멍, 모공

⑮ Apply a honey mask 2-3 times a week or as desired.
바르다   2 times a week = twice a week 일주일에 두 번   = as it is desired, as you desire 원하는 대로
3 times a week 일주일에 세 번 (once a week 일주일에 한 번)

(여드름은 관리하는 가장 달콤한 방법이 무엇인지 아세요?)

❶ 꿀은 효과적인 박테리아 킬러입니다.

❷ 그래서 꿀은 상처 도포제로 사용되고 있는데, 꿀이 박테리아를 죽이고 상처가 낫는데 도움이 되기 때문입니다.

❸ 꿀은 상처의 박테리아만 죽일 수 있는 게 아닙니다.

❹ 꿀은 여러분 피부의 박테리아도 죽일 수 있습니다.

❺ 사실 꿀은 깨끗하고 매끄러운 피부를 얻는 가장 좋은 방법 중 하나입니다.

❻ 이를테면 효소와 산화방지제, 항세균제를 함유한 꿀의 놀라운 치유적 속성들 덕분에 꿀 페이셜 마스크는 여드름 흉터를 없애고 붉어지는 현상을 완화시키며 보습에도 효과적입니다.

❼ 게다가 아주 쉽고 간단합니다.   ❽ 필요한 건 걸러지지 않은 천연 꿀 뿐입니다.

❾ 먼저 얼굴을 씻습니다.   ❿ 반드시 화장을 완전히 지우고 손을 깨끗이 해야 합니다.

⑪ 얼굴에 꿀을 바릅니다.   ⑫ 바를 때 얼굴 전체에 꿀을 천천히 문지르며 바릅니다.

⑬ 그리고 약 15분 정도 그대로 꿀을 얼굴에 둡니다.

⑭ 꿀을 완전히 씻어낼 때 까지 따뜻한 물로 얼굴을 씻고 마지막으로 모공을 닫기 위해 시원한 물로 씻습니다.

⑮ 꿀 마스크는 일주일에 2-3번, 혹은 원하는 대로 시행합니다.

You can get your teeth whitened by your dentist. Professional whitening is the most effective and quickest way to get whiter teeth, but it costs you a lot. However, there are several inexpensive ways to get whiter teeth. Here are three tips for whiter teeth.

Brush And Rinse Often : Brushing your teeth is essential to keeping your teeth clean and white. So be sure to brush and rinse more than twice a day.

Avoid Drinking Colored Beverages : Colored beverages, such as coffee, tea, cola, wine and juice, make you get yellow-stained teeth. So be sure to brush your teeth after drinking these beverages, not to mention trying to use a straw.

Stop Smoking. : No matter how often you get professional whitening treatments, and no matter how hard you try not to get yellow teeth, your teeth will get yellow again if you keep smoking. Cigarette smoke contains tar and many other chemicals which discolor your teeth. That is why some heavy and long-term smokers' teeth often appear not yellow but brown.

Words & Expressions

dentist 치과의사 professional 전문적인 whitening 화이트닝, 미백 effective 효과적인 inexpensive 비싸지 않은 brush 솔질하다 rinse 헹구다 essential 필수적인 plaque 명판, 플라 그 beverage 음료 stain 얼룩, 더러움 tint 엷은 색, 색조 (tinted 엷은 색이 낀) straw 지푸라기, 빨대 minimize 최소화하다 chemical 화학물질 discolor 변색시키다

1. What can be the best title of this story?

    a. No Way To Get Whiter Teeth

    b. What You Can Do For Getting Whiter Teeth

    c. Smokers' Teeth : Teeth Of Hell

    d. A Smoker Found Unconscious After Brushing

2. Smokers cannot help getting yellow tinted teeth because _____ .

    a. they hate all dentists and don't get a checkup

    b. cigarette smoke can discolor their teeth

    c. they never brush or rinse their teeth after eating

    d. they can't afford to get professional whitening

3. Choose the correct words for each sentence.

    a. My knees were swollen and bruised because I <u>got hurt</u> / <u>get to hurt</u> / <u>got hurted</u> by a soccer ball.

    b. If you keep <u>to shop</u> / <u>shop</u> / <u>shopping</u>, I'm sure you will be broke soon.

    d. I love his good character and his appearance, <u>as long as</u> / <u>not to mention</u> / <u>no matter how</u> his thick wallet.

Answer **1.** b   **2.** b   **3.** got hurt ⏐ shopping ⏐ not to mention

Listening Drill – Dictation

You can _____ by your dentist. Professional whitening is the most effective and quickest way to get whiter teeth, but _____ . However, there are several inexpensive ways to get whiter teeth. Here are three tips for whiter teeth.

Brush And Rinse Often : Brushing your teeth _____ keeping your teeth clean and white. So be sure to brush and rinse _____ .

Avoid Drinking Colored Beverages : _____ , such as coffee, tea, cola, wine and juice, make you get yellow-stained teeth. So be sure to brush your teeth after drinking these beverages, _____ trying to use a straw.

Stop Smoking. : _____ you get professional whitening treatments, and no matter how hard you try not to get yellow teeth, your teeth will get yellow again if you keep smoking. Cigarette smoke contains tar and _____ which discolor your teeth. That is why some _____ smokers' teeth _____ not yellow but brown.

Did You Know Three Tips For White Teeth?

1 You can get your teeth whitened by your **dentist**.

white a. 흰색의 n. 흰색 whiten v. 희게 만들다 whitening n. 미백   치과의사
get을 이용한 수동태 get + pp + by (get injured 부상당하다 get hired 고용되다 get paid 월급 받다)

2 **Professional** whitening is the most effective and quickest way to get whiter teeth,

전문적인   긴 음절 the most + 형용사 (the most effective 가장 효과적인)   더 흰 치아를 갖다
                  짧은 음절 형용사 -est (quickest 가장 빠른)

but it **costs** you a lot.

cost v. 돈이 얼마 들다 (cost-cost-cost) It cost him $100. 그는 이것에 100달러를 냈다. (과거)
It = professional whitening

3 However, there are several **inexpensive** ways (to get whiter teeth).

유도부사 there + 복수 동사 are + 복수 명사(진주어) ways   비싸지 않은   ↑   수식   ↓ 더 흰 치아를 갖는 방법들 (way to 동사)

4 Here are three **tips** for whiter teeth.

tip 조언, 충고, 뾰족한 끝부분, 팁 (봉사료), 기울어지다
(fingertip 손가락 끝부분, leave a tip on the table 탁자에 팁을 남기다, tip the cup to the left 왼쪽으로 컵을 기울이다)
there처럼 here 역시 단수/복수 동사 모두 올 수   Here are some apples. 여기 사과들이 있다. (are-apples)
있는데, 이어지는 진주어에 따라 달라진다.   Here is the book you wanted to buy. 여기 네가 사고 싶어했던 책이 있다. (is-the book)

5 Brush And Rinse Often :

6 (Brushing your teeth) is **essential** to keeping your teeth (clean and white).

이를 닦는 것 - 동명사 주어   be essential to + 명사/동명사   keep + 목적어 (teeth) + 형용사 (clean and white)
                  필수적이다   : 목적어를 ( )하게 유지하다

7 So be sure to ¹⁾ brush and ²⁾ rinse more than twice a day.

= make sure + 동사원형   하루에 (a day) 두 번 (twice) 이상 more than

8 **Avoid** Drinking Colored **Beverages** :

avoid + ing …하는 것을 피하다   n. 음료
(avoid to drink (X))

9 Colored beverages, (such as coffee, tea, cola, wine and juice),

Colored beverages의 예 ( ) - 주어, make 동사

make you get yellow-**stained** teeth.

stain 얼룩지게 하다, 얼룩, 더러움
make 사역동사 + 동사원형 get (..하도록 시키다, 하게 만들다) He made me go on a diet. 그는 내가 다이어트하게 만들었다.

10 So be sure to brush your teeth after drinking these beverages,

명령문 You be sure to brush, after you drink… (주절의 주어와 일치, 생략)

not to mention trying to use a **straw**.

…는 말할 필요도 없고 (+ 명사, 동명사)   1. 빨대 2. 지푸라기

not to mention과 비슷한 의미이지만 let alone은 부정문, 부정적인 의미에서 쓰인다.

He is a good singer, not to mention a talented actor. 그는 훌륭한 가수이고, 재능있는 배우인 건 말할 필요도 없다.

I can't swim in the pool, let alone in the river. 나는 수영장에서 수용할 수 없고 강에서는 말할 필요도 없다.

⑪ Stop Smoking. :

⑫ No matter how often you get professional whitening **treatments**,

아무리 자주 often …한다 할지라도 (no matter how 형용사 + 주어 + 동사)   치료, 시술

and no matter how hard you try not to get yellow teeth,

아무리 열심히/대단히 hard …한다 할지라도

your teeth will get yellow again if you keep smoking.

keep + ing 계속 …하다

⑬ Cigarette smoke **contains** (tar and many other **chemicals**) which **discolor** your teeth.

v. ~이 들어 있다, 함유되어 있다   수식   dis(부정) + color(n. 색깔, v. 색칠하다)

chemicals의 추가 설명 which 이하 – 치아를 변색시키는 화학품들

⑭ That is why (some heavy and long-term smokers' teeth) often appear

why이하 주어는 teeth (복수)

not yellow but brown.

not A but B : A가 아니라 B

흰 치아를 갖기 위한 세 가지 팁을 아세요?

① 치과 의사를 통해 치아를 희게 만들 수 있습니다.

② 전문 미백은 치아를 하얗게 만드는 가장 효과적이고 빠른 방법이지만 돈이 많이 듭니다.

③ 하지만 저렴하게 흰 치아를 가질 수 있는 몇 가지 방법이 있습니다.

④ 여기 흰 치아를 위한 세 가지 팁을 소개합니다.

⑤ 자주 양치하고 입을 헹군다. :   ⑥ 양치는 치아를 깨끗하고 희게 유지하는데 필수적입니다.

⑦ 그래서 반드시 하루에 두 번 이상 양치하고 입을 헹구도록 합니다.   ⑧ 색깔이 있는 음료 마시는 걸 피한다. :

⑨ 색깔이 있는 음료, 예를 들어 커피, 차, 콜라, 포도주, 그리고 주스 같은 음료는 노랗게 얼룩진 치아를 갖게 합니다.

⑩ 그러니 빨대를 이용하려고 노력하는 건 말할 필요도 없고, 이런 음료를 마신 후에는 반드시 양치를 하세요.

⑪ 금연한다. :   ⑫ 전문 미백 치료를 아무리 자주 받는다 해도, 치아가 노랗게 되지 않게 아무리 열심히 노력한다 해도, 계속 담배를 피우면 다시 치아가 노랗게 될 것입니다.

⑬ 담배 연기에는 치아를 변색시키는 타르와 많은 화학 물질이 들어 있습니다.

⑭ 오랫동안 많은 담배를 피운 애연가들의 치아가 노란 정도가 아니라 갈색으로 보이기도 하는 건 이 때문입니다.

28 Did You Know Why Removing Love Handles Is Difficult?

"Love handles" is a slang term for deposits of extra fat at the sides of the waistline. We don't know how this sweet term was given to the saggy and flabby area on the sides. Whether its term is sweet or not, love handles bulging over your waistline doesn't look good.

Many people want to trim only the love handle fat at your sides. But most of them say it's almost impossible to get rid of them. You can't have flat abs without getting your entire body into shape. Those chunks of fat are super stubborn. That's why you have to raise your metabolism by doing aerobic exercise to burn that extra fat. If you don't have the time or money to join a gym, there's no need to worry. Doing jumping jacks or running in place for about half an hour at home can be a good cardio workout for you. Of course, doing some other exercises that focus on the sides while doing basic exercise can help you remove love handles more effectively.

Words & Expressions

love handle 처진 뱃살, 늘어진 옆구리 살 slang 은어 deposit 축적물 side 옆, 옆구리 waistline 허리선 saggy 축 처진 flabby 힘없이 늘어진 bulge 튀어나오다, 불거져 나오다 trim 다듬다, 오려내다 get rid of 제거하다 flat 납작한 get into shape 건강한(맵시 있는) 몸매를 유지하다 chunk 덩어리 stubborn 완강한, 고집 센 metabolism 신진대사 aerobic 유산소의 (aerobic exercise = cardio exercise/workout 유산소운동) jumping jack 팔 벌려 뛰기 run in place 제자리에서 뛰다 cardio (달리기 등 유산소 운동처럼) 심장을 강화시키는 운동 effectively 효과적으로

128

Understanding Checkpoint

1. What can be the best title of this story?

    a. Solutions to Love Handles

    b. To Be Flabby Or To Be Saggy

    c. Effective Cardio Workouts For Everyone

    d. Remove Love Handles : A Mission Impossible

2. According to the passage, which sentence is right?

    a. Love handles are deposits of extra fat around the neck.

    b. The term 'love handles' is lovely because love handles look lovely.

    c. You have to get your body into shape before trying to get a flat ab.

    d. Doing exercises that focus only on the sides is effective to remove love handles.

3. Choose the correct words for each sentence.

    a. After giving birth, I have this ugly <u>flabby</u> / <u>chubby</u> / <u>stubby</u> belly.

    b. Please tell me how and when to <u>do</u> / <u>make</u> / <u>have</u> exercises.

    c. You must decide <u>while</u> / <u>whether</u> / <u>weather</u> you go to the theater or stay home with your kids.

Answer   1. a   2. c   3. flabby | do | whether

Listening Drill - Dictation

"Love handles" is _____ deposits of extra fat _____ the waistline. We don't know how this sweet _____ the saggy and flabby area on the sides. Whether its term is sweet or not, love handles _____ your waistline doesn't look good.

Many people want to _____ at your sides. But most of them say it's almost impossible to get rid of them. You can't _____ without getting your entire body into shape. Those chunks of fat are _____. That's why you have to _____ by doing aerobic exercise to burn that extra fat. If you don't have the time or money to join a gym, there's no need to worry. Doing jumping jacks or running in place _____ at home can be a good cardio workout for you. Of course, doing some other exercises that focus on the sides while _____ can help you remove love handles more effectively.

129

Did You Know Why Removing Love Handles Is Difficult?

1 "Love handles" is a **slang term** for **deposits** of **extra fat** at the sides of the waistline.

···에 해당하는 (의미하는) 은어　　　　　여분의 지방　　허리선 양 옆쪽에 (양 옆이라서 복수 sides)
deposit 보증금, 예금, 침전물, 쌓여있는 것

2 We don't know how this sweet term was given to the (**saggy** and **flabby**) area

어떻게/어쩌다 ···인지 모르다　　　　　(용어가 ···에) 주어지다 (수동태)　　축 처진　　힘없이 늘어진
how 이하 문장은 의문문이 아니기 때문에 주어와 동사가 도치되지 않는다.
I knew how he did it. 그가 어떻게 했는지 나는 알았다. (how 명사절)
How did he do it? 그는 어떻게 한 거야? (how 의문문)

on the sides.

3 Whether its term is sweet or not, (love handles **bulging** over your waistline)

whether ··· or not ···이든 아니든　　　　　　　수식
이 문장의 주어 love handles (복수) 동사 doesn't look　　love handles which bulge over··· 불룩 나온 러브 핸들

doesn't look good.

4 Many people want to **trim** only the love handle fat at your sides.

다듬다, 잘라내다　오직 ···만

5 But most of them say it's almost impossible to **get rid of** them.

앞문장의 people (옆구리 러브핸들만 빼고 싶다는 사람들)　　　　　= remove 제거하다, 없애다
가주어 it, 진주어 to get rid of

6 You can't have flat **abs** without getting your entire body into shape.

can't + without 이중 부정 – ···없이 ···할 수 없다　get into shape (몸매) 균형 있게 가꾸다 (get out of shape 몸매/체형 균형이 깨지다)
abs = abdominal muscles 복근　　　　　　　　　　(stay fit 균형 있게 가꾼 몸매를 유지하다)
have flat abs 납작한 배를 갖다 (복근이 실제 하나일 리 없으므로 일반적으로 복수형 abs로 쓴다.)

7 Those **chunks** of fat are super **stubborn**.

주어는 fat이 아니라 chunks (복수) + are　　　고집이 센, 질긴

8 That's why you have to raise your **metabolism** by doing aerobic **exercise**

rise 스스로 올라가다 (The Sun rises. 태양이 뜬다.)　신진대사　　(유산소) 운동하다 do (aeroic) exercise
raise 올리다 (raise a hand 손을 들다, raise a question 문제를 제기하다)

to burn that extra fat.

9 If you don't have the (time or money) to join a gym, there's no need to worry.

수식　　　　체육관에 가다, 헬스클럽에 등록하다

10 1) Doing jumping jacks or 2) running in place for about half an hour at home can be

동명사 주어 1) doing, 2) running + 동사 can　　　　　　약 about 반 시간 half an hour 동안 for

a good cardio **workout** for you.

유산소 운동 (cardio 심장강화 운동, '심장의-' 접두사)

⑪ Of course, (doing some other exercises that focus on the sides

동명사 주어 doing ( ), 동사 can　　　수식　　　옆구리에 집중한 다른 운동들

while doing basic exercise) can help you remove love handles more effectively.

while you do … (주어 일치, 생략)　　　　help + 동사원형 remove 제거하는데 도움이 되다

러브 핸들을 제거하는 게 왜 어려운지 아세요?

❶ 러브 핸들은 허리선의 옆구리에 붙은 여분의 지방 축적물을 뜻하는 은어입니다.

❷ 어쩌다 옆구리의 힘없이 늘어진 부위가 이렇게 사랑스러운 이름을 갖게 되었는지는 모를 일입니다.

❸ 이름이 사랑스럽든 아니든 허리 밖으로 불거져 나온 러브 핸들은 전혀 좋아 보이지 않습니다.

❹ 많은 이들이 옆구리의 러브 핸들 지방만 빼길 원합니다.

❺ 하지만 대부분이 이를 제거하기가 거의 불가능하다고 말합니다.

❻ 몸 전체의 체형을 관리하지 않고 평평한 배를 가질 수는 없습니다.

❼ 그 지방 덩어리들은 보통 질긴 게 아니니까요.

❽ 이것이 과도한 지방을 연소시키려면 유산소 운동으로 신진대사를 올려야 하는 이유입니다.

❾ 체육관에 갈 시간이나 돈이 없어도 걱정할 필요 없습니다.

❿ 집에서 팔 벌려 뛰기나 제자리에서 30분 정도 뛰는 것도 좋은 유산소 운동이 됩니다.

⑪ 물론 기본 운동을 하면서 옆구리에 초점을 맞춘 다른 운동을 해주는 건 러브 핸들을 더 효과적으로 제거하는데 도움이 됩니다.

Did you know that dyeing your hair blonde can make you look older than you are? It can, since lighter hair color doesn't always go well with all shades of skin color. As we get older, our skin generally becomes yellowish and paler, and that is why it's not a very good idea to go blonde for people who are getting old but don't want to look old.

If you want to dye your hair in order to look younger than you are, had better consider dyeing your hair dark brown, reddish brown or black, since matching your hair to your skin tone is highly likely to make you look older than you are. As getting older usually leads to getting paler skin, it might be a good choice to dye your hair a color that's a little bit darker.

Believe it or not, many Asians dye their hair black as they get older, and that surely makes them look younger than they are.

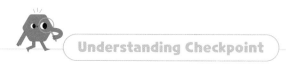

1. What can be the best title of this story?

    a. Dye Your Hair, And Your Hair Will Die

    b. Hair Colors Make You Look Younger Or Older

    c. Always Avoid Dyeing Your Hair Blonde

    d. Getting Old Means Getting Pale

2. For old people, it's not a nice idea to dye their hair blonde because _____ .

    a. none of them want to dye their hair dark brown

    b. people with pale skin have to go blonde for their own good

    c. matching their hair to their yellowish skin tone makes them look older

    d. old people always want to look old, not young

3. Choose the correct words for each sentence.

    a. Have you heard a guy who died while <u>dyeing</u> / <u>dying</u> / <u>dyed</u> his hair purple?

    b. I am afraid things aren't <u>making</u> / <u>going</u> / <u>becoming</u> well with the project.

    c. She arrived at the scene wearing her pinkish gown <u>around nineish</u> / <u>at nine sharp</u> / <u>at one to nine</u>. I don't remember the exact time.

    d. People who eat continuously tend to be <u>having</u> / <u>getting</u> / <u>doing</u> fatter and bigger.

Answer **1.** b **2.** c **3.** dyeing ǀ going ǀ around nineish ǀ getting

Listening Drill – Dictation

Did you know that   can make you   you are? It can, since lighter hair color doesn't always   all shades of skin color.   , our skin generally becomes yellowish and paler, and that is why it's not a very good idea to   for people who are getting old but don't want to look old.

If you want to dye your hair in order to look younger than you are, had better consider dyeing your hair dark brown, reddish brown or black, since matching your hair to your skin tone   make you look older than you are. As getting older usually   getting paler skin,   dye your hair a color that's a little bit darker.

Believe it or not, many Asians dye their hair black as they get older,   them look   .

133

Did You Know What Hair Colors Can Make You Look Younger?

1 Did you know that (dyeing your hair blonde) can make you look older than

that절 이하 주어 ( ) 동명사 주어 (염색하는 것)   사역동사 make + 동사원형 look
…보이도록 하다 / 보이게 하다

you are?

2 It can, since (lighter hair color) doesn't always **go** well **with** all **shades**

It can make you look older than you are.   not always 부분부정   …와(with) 잘 어울리다   shade 그늘, 빛 가리개, 색조
항상 …인 건 아니다

of skin color.

3 we **get older**, our skin generally becomes (yellowish and **paler**), and

get old 나이 들다   become yellowish 노르스름해지다 / become paler 더 창백해지다
get older 나이가 더 들다 (look old 늙어 보이다 / look older 더 늙어 보이다)

that is why it's not a very good idea to go blonde

금발로 하다 (go bald 대머리가 되다 go blind 눈이 멀다
go crazy 미치다 go bankrupt 파산하다 go bad 상하다)

for people who ¹⁾ are getting old but ²⁾ don't want to look old.

⬆ 수식   (톱) ¹⁾ 늙어가는 사람들 ²⁾ 늙어 보이고 싶지 않은 사람들

4 If you want to dye your hair in order to look younger than you are,

현재(실제)보다 더 어려 보이기 위해서

had better **consider** dyeing your hair (dark brown, **reddish** brown or black),

had better + 동사원형 consider 고려하는 게 좋다   불그스름한 (yellowish, pinkish, greenish, blackish)
consider + -ing (동명사) …할 것을 고려하다

since (**matching** your hair to your skin **tone**) is highly likely to make you look

동명사 주어 ( )   색조   사역동사 make + 동사원형 look
머리카락과 피부톤을 맞추는 것 + is   현재보다 너를 더 늙어 보이게 하다

older than you are.

5 As (getting older) usually leads to (getting paler skin), it might be a good choice

(나이 드는 것) …로 이어지다   (더 창백한 피부가 되는 것)   it 가주어 (이것은 좋은 선택일 수 있다)

to dye your hair a color (that's a little bit darker).

⬆ 수식

to dye your hair 진주어 (염색하는 것)
dye 목적어 (hair) + 색깔 (a color that…) 머리카락을 that이하 색깔로 염색하다

❻ Believe it or not, many Asians dye their hair black as they get older,

믿거나 말거나   dye + 목적어 (hair) + 색깔 (black)

and that surely makes them look younger than they are.

　　　 = 늙을수록 머리카락을 검게 염색하는 것
　　　 사역동사 make + 목적어 them + 동사원형 look : ···보이게 하다

어떤 머리카락 색깔이 젊어 보이게 만드는 아세요?

❶ 머리카락을 금발로 염색하면 실제보다 더 늙어 보일 수 있다는 사실을 아세요?

❷ 그럴 수 있는데, 이는 밝은 색 머리카락이 모든 색조와 언제나 잘 어울리는 건 아니기 때문입니다.

❸ 나이가 들면 보통 우리 피부는 노르스름해지고 더 창백해지는데, 이런 이유로 나이가 들지만 늙어 보이고 싶지 않은 사람이 금발을 하는 건 그다지 좋은 생각이 아닙니다.

❹ 실제보다 더 젊어 보이려고 머리카락을 염색하고 싶다면, 머리카락 색깔과 피부 톤을 맞추면 실제보다 더 늙어 보일 가능성이 높아지므로 진한 갈색, 붉은 갈색, 또는 검정색 염색을 고려해보세요.

❺ 나이가 들면 일반적으로 피부가 더 창백해지므로, 좀 진한 색깔로 머리카락을 염색하는 게 좋은 선택이라 할 수 있습니다.

❻ 믿거나 말거나지만, 많은 아시아인들은 나이가 들면 검정색으로 머리카락을 염색하는데 이들은 실제보다 확실히 더 젊어 보입니다.

As you get older, your skin becomes loose. Your eye lids are not an exception. If the area below the eyes becomes saggy, bags will appear under the eyes. That's why they are called 'eye bags' because they are a kind of bag formed under the eyes. Of course, a plastic surgeon can lift saggy under-eye skin by surgery. But, there is a way to prevent saggy skin under the eyes without paying any money. Several facial exercises can help you improve your "bags under the eyes" problem.

1. Place your index fingers on the area under the eye. Try to lift the muscle of the eye with your fingers without wrinkling the skin around your brows. Maintain this pose for one second and repeat 15-20 times.

2. With the three middle fingers of each hand, tap lightly around your under-eye area. Tap from the outer corners of the eye to the inner corners, three to four times a day.

Words & Expressions

loose 헐거운 eye lid 눈꺼풀 exception 예외 saggy 늘어진 bag 주머니, 주머니처럼 늘어진 살 appear 나타나다 form 형성하다, 만들다 plastic surgeon 성형외과 의사 lift 들어 올리다 by surgery 수술로 facial exercise 안면 운동 improve 개선하다, 좋아지게 하다 place 놓다, 두다 index finger 검지 wrinkle 주름지게 하다 brow = eye brows 눈썹 stay in a pose 자세를 유지하다 repeat 반복하다 tap 가볍게 두드리다 under-eye are 눈 밑 부위

Understanding Checkpoint

1. What is the main idea of the story?

    a. Getting old means getting loose skin.
    b. Some facial exercises can improve "bags under the eyes" problem.
    c. When exercising, index fingers are the most important.
    d. There is no way to remove eye bags other than plastic surgery.

2. According to the passage, which sentence is <u>wrong</u>?

    a. Eye bags are formed under the eyes.
    b. Plastic surgery can remove eye bags but it costs you.
    c. Tapping gently the under-eye area may be helpful for "bags under the eyes" problem.
    d. When doing facial exercises, you must use only index fingers.

3. Choose the correct words for each sentence.

    a. Can they take my personal information without <u>to let</u> / <u>let</u> / <u>letting</u> me know?
    b. My boss wants to <u>give</u> / <u>place</u> / <u>submit</u> an ad in the newspapers and magazines.
    c. Can I walk from here <u>until</u> / <u>with</u> / <u>to</u> the moon? Or should I ride a bicyle?

Answer   **1.** b   **2.** d   **3.** letting | place | to

Listening Drill & Dictation

As you get older, your skin   . Your eye lids are not an exception. If the area below the eyes becomes saggy, bags will   under the eyes. That's why they are called 'eye bags' because they are a kind of bag   under the eyes. Of course, a plastic surgeon can lift saggy under-eye skin   . But,   prevent saggy skin under the eyes   . Several facial exercises can help you improve your "bags under the eyes" problem.

1.   your index fingers on the area under the eye. Try to lift the muscle of the eye with your fingers without wrinkling the skin around your brows.   for one second and repeat 15-20 times.

2. With the three middle fingers of each hand,   around your under-eye area. Tap from the outer corners of the eye to the inner corners,   .

137

Did You Know There Are Exercises For Eye Bags?

1 As you get older, your skin becomes loose.
    나이가 더 들다   헐거워/느슨해지다 loose a. 헐거운, 느슨한 lose v. 잃다

2 Your **eyelids** are not an exception.
    eye눈 + lid뚜껑   …도 예외가 아니다 (마찬가지이다)
    = 눈꺼풀

3 If (the area below the eyes) becomes **saggy**, bags will appear under the eyes.
              수식   축 처진, 늘어진
    주어는 eyes가 아니라 area (단수) + becomes (단수동사)

4 That's why they are called 'eye bags' because they are a kind

    of bag (**formed** under the eyes).
           수식
    bag (which is) formed 형성된

5 Of course, **a plastic surgeon** can **lift** (saggy under-eye) skin by **surgery**.
    성형외과 의사   v. 올리다, 해제하다   수식
    lift skin by surgery 수술로 피부를 올리다
    plastic surgery (cosmetic surgery) 성형수술 surgeon 외과 의사

6 But, there is a way to **prevent** saggy skin (under the eyes)
    …할 방법이 있다   막다, 예방하다   수식

    without paying any money.
    돈 내지 않고

7 (Several facial exercises) can help you **improve**
                        help 목적어 you + 동사원형 improve – 개선하는데 너에게 도움이 된다

    your "bags (under the eyes)" problem.
           수식

8 1. **Place** your **index fingers** on the area (under the eye).
    place n. 장소 v. 놓다 (이 문장에서는 동사)   수식
    엄지 thumb, 집게손가락/검지 index finger (forefinger),
    중지 middle finger 약지 ring finger 새끼손가락 pinkie

9 Try to lift the muscle of the eye with your fingers without **wrinkling**
                                    주름지지 않게 하고서
                                    (without은 전치사이기 때문에 명사/동명사가 이어진다.)

138

(the skin around your brows).

　　　↑　　수식　　│　눈썹 주위의 피부

⑩ 1) **Maintain** this **pose** for one second and 2) repeat 15-20 times.

　　명령형, 유지하다　　　　　　　for 기간 – 1초간

　　　　　　　　pose v. 자세를 취하다, (문제, 위협) 제기하다, 뻐기다 n. 자세

⑪ 2. With the three middle fingers of each hand, **tap** lightly around

　　　　　　가운데 세 손가락들 (검지, 중지, 약지)　　　　　　가볍게 lightly + 두드리다 tap

your under-eye area.

⑫ Tap from (the outer corners of the eye) to (the **inner** corners),

　　　from A to B (눈 바깥 구석)에서 (안쪽 구석)으로 : A에서 B로　　　　안쪽의

three to four times a day.

(from) three (times) to four times + a day 세 번에서 네 번 (3-4회) + 하루에

〔 처진 눈 밑 살을 위한 운동이 있다는 거 아세요? 〕

❶ 나이가 들면 피부가 느슨해집니다.

❷ 눈꺼풀도 예외는 아닙니다.

❸ 눈 아랫부분이 처지면 주머니 같은 게 눈 밑에 생깁니다.

❹ 그래서 이를 처진 눈 밑 살 (눈 밑 주머니)이라고 부르는데, 눈 아래에 형성된 일종의 주머니이기 때문입니다.

❺ 물론 성형외과 의사가 수술로 쳐진 눈꺼풀을 올려줄 수 있습니다.

❻ 하지만 돈을 내지 않고도 쳐지지 않은 눈꺼풀을 가질 수 있는 방법이 있습니다.

❼ 몇 가지 안면 운동이 '눈 밑 살 문제'를 개선하는데 도움이 될 수 있습니다.

❽ 1. 검지를 아래 눈꺼풀에 올립니다.

❾ 눈썹 주변 피부에 주름을 만들지 않고 손가락으로 아래 눈꺼풀 근육을 올려보세요.

⑩ 그 자세를 1초 유지하고 15-20회 반복합니다.

⑪ 2. 각 손의 가운데 세 손가락을 이용하여 눈 아래 부위를 가볍게 두드립니다.

⑫ 눈 모서리의 바깥쪽에서부터 안쪽으로 두드리는 게 좋고 하루에 3-4회 실시합니다.

Chapter 04

People

MP3

31 Did You Know That Calment's Secret Of Longevity Was Chocolate?

Jeanne Louise Calment was born in 1875 and died in 1997 in Arles, France. She died at the age of 122 years old. To be more exact, she lived 122 years and 164 days. Calment was listed in the Guinness Book of Records in 1988 and 1995. Surprisingly, she lived longer than her only child and her only grandchild. She lived long enough to meet Vincent van Gogh when she was young. Later, she recalled him as "a dirty, badly dressed and disagreeable man."

When people asked her about her secrets to her longevity, she said that the secrets might have been olive oil and chocolate. She was a longtime smoker, and allegedly not crazy about health. But, she was healthy enough to ride a bicycle at the age of 100, and she could take care of herself, by herself, until she was 110 years old. However, after causing a small fire while cooking in her flat, she was moved to a nursing home. She said she used lots of olive oil in her cooking and rubbed olive oil into her skin. And she ate about one kilogram of chocolate every week.

Words & Expressions

be born in (년도) ...에 태어나다 die in (년도) ...에 사망하다 longevity 장수, 오래 삶 lifetime 일생, 평생
recall 기억하다, 회고하다 badly dressed 옷을 잘 못 입은 disagreeable 불쾌한 a longtime smoker 오랜 흡
연자 flat (영국) 아파트 a nursing home 양로원, 요양소 rub 비비다, 바르다

Understanding Checkpoint

1. What is the main idea of the story?

    a. Calment's secret of longevity is chocolate and olive oil.

    b. Calment could live longer than her grandchild thanks to riding a bicycle.

    c. After meeting Gogh, Calment decided to live long.

    d. Rubbing olive oil into the skin is the secret of longevity.

2. When Calment met Gogh, _____ .

    a. she envied Gogh because he was older than her

    b. Gogh was not a clean or neat guy

    c. she was 122 years old

    d. she didn't want to share her chocolate with him

3. Choose the correct words for each sentence.

    a. My little twin brothers have been crazy <u>about</u> / <u>at</u> / <u>of</u> baseball since they were 5.

    b. It's safe to say that he is a <u>dirty</u> / <u>disagreeable</u> / <u>messy</u> man because he is always being rude, offensive and unamiable.

    c. His colleagues recalled him <u>of</u> / <u>as</u> / <u>with</u> a nice and friendly guy and an excellent programmer.

    d. What I want to <u>board</u> / <u>ride</u> / <u>make</u> is a big huge dinosaur, but all I have is an old bicycle.

Answer **1.** a **2.** b **3.** about ⏐ disagreeable ⏐ as ⏐ ride

Listening Drill – Dictation

Jeanne Louise Calment _____ 1875 and died in 1997 in Arles, France. She died _____ 122 years old. To be more exact, she lived 122 years and 164 days. Calment was listed in the Guinness Book of Records in 1988 and 1995. Surprisingly, she _____ her only child and her only grandchild. She lived long enough to meet Vincent van Gogh when she was young. Later, she _____ "a dirty, badly dressed and _____ man."

When people asked her about _____ , she said that the secrets _____ olive oil and chocolate. She was a longtime smoker, and allegedly not crazy about health. But, she was healthy enough to _____ at the age of 100, and she could take care of herself, _____ , until she was 110 years old. However, after causing a small fire while cooking in her flat, she was moved to a nursing home. She said she used lots of olive oil in her cooking and _____ . And she ate about one kilogram of chocolate every week.

Did You Know That Calment's Secret Of Longevity Was Chocolate?

1 Jeanne Louise Calment **was born in** 1875 and **died in** 1997 in Arles, France.
태어나다 (수동) be born in 년도 　　사망하다 (능동) die in 년도

2 She died **at the age of** 122 years old.
몇 살의 나이에

3 To be more exact, she lived 122 years and 164 days.
= more exactly speaking 더 정확히 말하면

4 Calment **was listed** in the Guinness Book of Records in 1988 and 1995.
… 목록에 오르다 (수동)

5 Surprisingly, she **lived longer than** (her only child and her only grandchild).
…보다 오래 살다 (비교)　　only 단 한 명의
= She outlived her only child and her only grandchild. (outlive 더 오래 살다)

6 She lived **long enough to** meet Vincent van Gogh when she was young.
…할 정도로 충분히 오래
tall enough to become a model 모델 될 정도로 충분히 키가 큰
smart enough to solve the problem 문제를 풀 정도로 충분히 똑똑한

7 Later, she **recalled** him as "a dirty, badly dressed and **disagreeable** man."
recall A as B : A를 B로 회상/기억하다　　옷을 잘 못 입은　　무뚝뚝한, 불쾌한 (↔ agreeable 기분좋은, 쾌활한)
well dressed 옷을 잘 입는

8 When people asked her about her secrets to her **longevity**,
…의 비밀 (to)　　long a. 긴, 오랜 ad. 오랫동안 v. 간절히 바라다
longevity n. 장수

she said that the secrets might have been (olive oil and chocolate).
과거의 일 추측 …였을지도 모른다 (might have pp)

9 She was [1] a longtime smoker, and **allegedly** [2] not **crazy about** health.
She was a long… and (she was) not crazy…　　be crazy about 열광하다, 광적으로 좋아하다
allegedly 알려진 바에 의하면 (reportedly 보도된 바에 의하면)

10 But, she was healthy enough to ride a bicycle at the age of 100,
healthy enough to ride… 탈 정도로 꽤 건강한　　탈 것을 탈 때 - ride (ride-rode-ridden)
(ride a horse, ride a train, ride a scooter)

and she could **take care of** herself, by herself, until she was 110 years old.
스스로를 돌보다　　by oneself 스스로, 혼자서

⑪ However, after causing a small fire while cooking in her **flat**,

주절의 주어 she와 일치, 생략 (능동 -ing) (영국) 아파트 a. 평평한
= after she caused a small fire while she was cooking

she was moved to a **nursing home**.

be moved to 누군가 주어를 …로 이사시키다 (수동)
nursing home 양로원 refugee camp 난민수용소 shelter 보호소
sanitarium (질병 회복)요양원 asylum 장기요양 정신병원

⑫ She said she ¹⁾ used lots of olive oil in her cooking and ²⁾ rubbed olive oil into her skin.

she used … and (she) rubbed … cooking 요리 rub oil into skin
cook v. 요리하다 n. 요리사 피부에 대고 오일을 문지르다

⑬ And she ate about ⟨one kilogram of chocolate⟩ every week.

= She ate ( ) per week. 매주 ( )를 먹었다. chocolate 불가산명사 (초콜릿 과자의 의미일 때는 가산명사)
two kilograms of chocolate (o) two chocolates (x)
five bars of chocolate = five chocolate bars (o) 초콜릿바 5개

〔 칼멘의 장수 비결이 초콜릿이라는 거 아세요? 〕

❶ 잔 루이스 칼멘은 프랑스 아를에서 1875년에 태어나 1997년에 사망했습니다.

❷ 122살의 나이로 세상을 떠난 겁니다.

❸ 더 정확히 말하면 122년 164일을 살았습니다.

❹ 칼멘은 1988년과 1995년에 기네스 세계 기록에 올랐습니다.

❺ 놀랍게도 그녀는 하나 밖에 없는 자식과 하나 밖에 없는 손주보다 더 오래 살았습니다.

❻ 그녀는 어린 시절 빈센트 반 고흐를 만났을 정도로 오래 살았습니다.

❼ 나중에 그녀는 고흐를 '더럽고 옷을 잘 못 입었으며 무뚝뚝한 남자'로 기억했습니다.

❽ 사람들이 그녀에게 장수 비결을 물었을 때 그녀는 비법이 올리브기름과 초콜릿일지도 모른다고 말했습니다.

❾ 그녀는 오랜 흡연자였고 알려진 바에 의하면 건강에 지나치게 신경 쓰지도 않았다고 합니다.

❿ 하지만 100살 때 자전거를 탈 정도로 꽤 건강했고, 110살 때까지 혼자서 생활할 수 있었습니다.

⑪ 하지만 아파트에서 요리하다 작은 화재를 낸 이후, 그녀는 양로원으로 이주했습니다.

⑫ 그녀는 음식에 올리브기름을 많이 사용했으며 피부에 올리브기름을 발랐다고 합니다.

⑬ 또 매주 1kg 정도의 초콜릿을 먹었다고 합니다.

Karen Butler, the 56-year-old American woman and lifelong resident of Oregon, developed an Irish accent after oral surgery. She had never been abroad, and never learned or tried to learn an Irish accent. But, when she awoke from sedation in 2009, she started speaking in an Irish accent. Actually, her accent is a mix of Irish, British, Scottish and Australian. Anyway, the way she spoke was definitely not an American style.

Doctors suspect that she may be suffering from a rare case of foreign accent syndrome (FAS). This may sound like a 'hurriedly and newly coined terms', but this kind of speech disorder really exists, though it is very much rare. FAS is usually caused by some type of brain damage such as a stroke or brain hemorrhage.

You can find other cases of FAS. A Norwegian woman also developed FAS after being hit by a bomb fragment during World War II. When she woke up, she was said to speak in a German accent. An American man also started speaking in a Scandinavian accent after a stroke. But, his accent faded after several months.

Words & Expressions

oral 구강의, 입의 lifelong 일평생 resident 주민 abroad 해외의 awaken 깨어나다 sedation 진정제가 투여된 상태 coin 동전, (용어, 표현)만들다 rare 흔치 않은 speech disorder 언어장애 stroke 뇌졸중 hemorrhage 출혈 Norwegian 노르웨이의, 노르웨이인의 fragment 파편, 조각 fade 색이 바래다, 점점 사라지다

1. What is the main idea of the story?

   a. FAS is a totally new term coined by a Norwegian woman.

   b. There are thousands of people who suffer from FAS in the world.

   c. Karen Butler developed a foreign accent after oral surgery.

   d. If you were hit by something, you would speak in a German accent.

2. According to the passage, which sentence is right?

   a. Karen Butler has been living in Oregon since she was born in Oregon.

   b. FAS is always caused by bomb fragments.

   c. Allegedly, a large number of North Americans suffer from FAS.

   d. Ms. Butler got an Irish accent as a result of years of training.

3. Choose the correct words for each sentence.

   a. I plan to be famous both at home and <u>outside</u> / <u>abroad</u> / <u>foreign</u>.

   b. We must act with great haste because a <u>strike</u> / <u>stork</u> / <u>stroke</u> is a medical emergency.

   c. The soldier has started bleeding after <u>shot</u> / <u>being shot</u> / <u>shoot</u> by his enemy.

          Answer 1. c 2. a 3. abroad ㅣ stroke ㅣ being shot

Karen Butler, the 56-year-old American woman and lifelong resident of Oregon,   an Irish accent after oral surgery. She   , and never learned or tried to learn an Irish accent. But, when she   sedation in 2009, she started speaking in an Irish accent. Actually, her accent is a mix of Irish, British, Scottish and Australian. Anyway,   was definitely not an American style.

Doctors   that she may be suffering from a rare case of foreign accent syndrome (FAS). This may sound like a 'hurriedly and   ', but this kind of speech disorder really exists, though it is very much rare. FAS is usually caused by some type of brain damage such as a stroke or   .

You can find other cases of FAS. A Norwegian woman also developed FAS   a bomb fragment during World War II. When she woke up, she was said to speak in a German accent. An American man also   a Scandinavian accent after a stroke. But, his accent   after several months.

Did You Know What Happened To Karen Butler After Oral Surgery?

1 Karen Butler, (the 56-year-old American woman and lifelong **resident** of Oregon),

= 동격

주어 Karen Butler 동사 developed

평생 lifelong 거주자 resident

developed an Irish **accent** after **oral** surgery.

아일랜드 억양이 생기다 British accent 영국식 억양　　a. 구강의, 구두의

develop v. 성장/발달하다, 개발하다, (병, 문제)생기다 (이 문장에서는 세 번째 의미)

2 She had [1) never been **abroad**, and [2) never (learned or tried to learn) an Irish accent.

[1) 외국에 나가본 적이 없다

[2) 배웠거나 배우려 시도한 적이 없다 (과거 완료 부정 had never pp)

3 But, when she awoke from **sedation** in 2009, she started speaking in an Irish accent.

진정제에서 깨어나다

start - -ing / to 동사 모두 가능 : ⋯하기 시작하다

sedate a. 차분한, 조용한 sedative n. 진정제 sedation n. 진정제가 투여된 상태

4 Actually, her accent is a mix of (Irish, British, Scottish and Australian).

( )의 혼합

5 Anyway, the way (she spoke) was **definitely** not an American style.

수식

그녀가 말하는 방식 (주어) + 동사 was

절대 아닌

6 Doctors suspect that she may be **suffering from** a **rare** case of

질병을 앓다

( )라는 흔하지 않은 경우(질병)

rare a. 흔하지 않은, 진귀한, 고기를 거의 익히지 않은

(foreign accent **syndrome** (FAS)).

7 This may sound like a '(hurriedly and newly) **coined terms**',

= foreign accent syndrome

수식　　수식

(성급하게 그리고 새롭게) 만들어진 용어 – 급조한 신조어

coin n. 동전 v. (용어를) 만들다 term n. 용어

but (this kind of speech **disorder**) really exists, though it is very much rare.

주어 ( ) disorder (3인칭 단수현재) + 동사 exists

(신체기능의) 장애

8 FAS is usually caused by some type of brain damage (such as a **stroke** or

⋯에 의해 야기되다 (be caused by 수동태)

brain damage (뇌손상)의 예 : ( )

brain hemorrhage).

출혈 (= bleeding)

9 You can find other cases of FAS.

other + 복수명사

⑩ A Norwegian woman also **developed FAS** after being hit by a bomb **fragment**

develop FAS : FAS라는 질병이 생기다

파편, 조각

주절의 주어 a Norwegian woman 일치, 생략

– 파편에 맞은 수동이므로 be pp (hit)

= after she was hit by a bomb fragment

during World War II.

⑪ When she woke up, she was said to speak in a German accent.

깨어나다 ···라고 한다 독일어 억양으로 말하다 (speak German 독일어를 하다)

(wake-woke-woken)

⑫ An American man also started speaking in a Scandinavian accent after a stroke.

스칸디나비아 억양으로 말하다 뇌졸중 이후

⑬ But, his accent **faded** after several months.

서서히 사라지다, 희미해지다

구강 수술 후 카렌 버틀러에게 어떤 일이 생겼는지 아세요?

❶ 일평생 오리곤 주민으로 살아온 56세의 미국인 여성 카렌 버틀러는 구강 수술 후 아일랜드 억양이 생겼습니다.

❷ 그녀는 외국에 나간 적도 없고, 아일랜드 억양을 배운 적도, 배우려고 시도한 적도 없습니다.

❸ 하지만 2009년 진정제에서 깨어났을 때 그녀는 아일랜드 억양으로 말하기 시작했습니다.

❹ 사실 그녀의 억양은 아일랜드에 영국식, 스코트랜드식 그리고 호주식이 섞여있었습니다.

❺ 어쨌든 그녀가 말하는 방식이 미국식이 아닌 건 확실합니다.

❻ 의사들은 그녀가 희귀한 경우인 외국인 억양 증후군(FAS)을 앓을 지도 모른다고 추측하고 있습니다.

❼ '급하게 새로 만들어낸 용어'처럼 들릴지도 모르겠는데, 매우 희귀하긴 하지만 이런 종류의 언어 장애가 정말 존재합니다.

❽ FAS는 일반적으로 뇌졸중 또는 뇌출혈 등 일종의 뇌 손상으로 야기됩니다.

❾ FAS의 다른 예들도 찾을 수 있습니다.

❿ 한 노르웨이인 여성 역시 2차 세계대전 중 폭탄 파편에 맞은 후 외국인 억양 증후군이 생겼습니다.

⓫ 그녀가 정신을 차렸을 때 그녀는 독일식 억양으로 말했다고 합니다.

⓬ 미국인 남성 역시 뇌졸중을 앓은 후 스칸디나비아 식 억양으로 말하기 시작했습니다.

⓭ 하지만 그의 억양은 몇 달 후 없어졌습니다.

In 2011, a pair of Russian teenage girls, Irina and Anya, and their family members were shocked because they found out that these two girls had been accidentally switched at birth, which means each girl's parents were not the real parents. Their mothers gave birth just 15 minutes apart in the same hospital in 1999. After being born, two baby girls were given the wrong name tags by employees of the hospital.

The whole thing started when Irina's father thought his daughter might not be his daughter because she looked nothing like him. A DNA test showed that neither of Irina's parents was her natural parent. With the help of the local police, Irina's mother started to search her real daughter, who was living just a few miles away.

Although two girls were happy to meet their real parents, they didn't want to leave the family they had grown up with. So, nothing changed for these two families.

But, the hospital had to deal with a big change because both families decided to sue the hospital, demanding about $160,000 in damages. Nothing hurts like the truth, especially for that hospital.

Words & Expressions

teenage 십대의 accidentally 우연히, 사고로 switch 바꾸다 at birth 태어날 때 name tag 이름표
employee 직원 natural parents 친부모 sue 고소하다 demand 요구하다 damage 손해배상금 nothing
hurts like the truth 진실만큼 아픈 (고통스러운) 건 없다-속담

Understanding Checkpoint

1. What is the main idea of the story?

a. Never give birth in Russia since all Russian hospitals are horrible.

b. Finding natural parents is utmost important.

c. The DNA test was supposed to be accurate but it wasn't.

d. Two Russian girls who were switched at birth found their real parents.

2. The accident that happened to Irina and Anya _____ .

a. was a simple mistake of employees of the hospital

b. became the main cause of the civil war

c. was so tragic that Irina's parents had to divorce

d. made the hospital go bankruptcy

3. Choose the correct words for each sentence.

a. My boss who is famous for being short-tempered <u>yells</u> / <u>demands</u> /<u>says</u> an immediate and clear explanation.

b. If there were <u>damages</u> / <u>damage</u> / <u>much damages</u> to pay, I should sell my car.

c. Neither of them <u>studies</u> / <u>study</u> / <u>studying</u> hard to pass the exam even though they have much time to study.

Answer **1.** d **2.** a **3.** demands ǀ damages ǀ studies

Listening Drill – Dictation

In 2011, _____ Russian teenage girls, Irina and Anya, and their family members _____ because they found out that these two girls had been _____ switched _____ , which means each girl's parents were not the real parents. Their mothers gave birth just 15 minutes apart in the same hospital in 1999. _____ , two baby girls were given the wrong name tags by employees of the hospital.

The whole thing started when Irina's father thought his daughter _____ because she looked nothing like him. A DNA test showed that neither of Irina's parents was her natural parent. With the help of the local police, Irina's mother started to search her real daughter, who was living just a few miles away.

Although two girls were happy to meet their real parents, they didn't want to leave the _____ . So, nothing changed for these two families.

But, the hospital had to _____ because both families decided to sue the hospital, _____ about $160,000 _____ . Nothing hurts like the truth, especially for that hospital.

151

Did You Know How These Russian Girls Got The Wrong Parents?

1 In 2011, (a pair of Russian teenage girls, Irina and Anya, and their family members)
주어 ( ) 동사 were shocked   = 동격

were shocked because they found out that these two girls had been **accidentally**
인칭 주어 be shocked : 주어가 놀랐다   that 이하를 알게 되었다   accidentally = by accident 우연히, 사고로
He was shocked by the news. 그는 뉴스에 충격을 받았다   과거완료 had been + 수동태 been switched
비인칭 주어 be shocking : 주어는 놀랍다 The news was shocking. 뉴스는 충격적이다.

switched at birth, which means each girl's parents were not the real parents.
출생 시   콤마 + 관계대명사 which (계속 용법) 출생 때 사고로 바뀌었는데, 이 말은…라는 뜻이다

2 Their mothers gave birth just 15 minutes apart in the same hospital in 1999.
출산하다   15분 차이로 (apart (시간, 공간) 떨어져)
give birth to a girl 딸을 낳다

3 After being born, two baby girls were given the wrong name tags
주절의 주어 two baby girls와 일치, 생략   be given ( ) by …에 의해 ( )이 주어지다 (수동태- 주어가 ( )를 받다)
= After two baby girls were born

by **employees** of the hospital.
고용된 사람, 직원 (employer 고용한 사람, 고용주)

4 The whole thing started when Irina's father thought his daughter might not be
이 모든 일은 … 일 때 시작되었다   아닐 수도 있다 (추측)

his daughter because she looked nothing like him.
그를 전혀 닮지 않다, 비슷하지 않다

5 A DNA test showed that (neither of Irina's parents) was her natural parent.
검사는 that 이하로 나왔다   = not one of the two   = biological parent 낳은 부모
neither of …어느 쪽도 아니다 (둘 중 아무도 아니므로 단수로 취급) + was (단수동사)

6 With the help of the local police, Irina's mother started to **search** her real daughter
…의 도움으로   start to 부정사 / -ing 모두 가능 – 찾기 시작했다

, who was living just a few miles away.
콤마 + 관계대명사 who (계속 용법) – 진짜 딸을 찾기 시작했는데, 그 딸은 불과 몇 마일 거리에 살고 있었다

7 Although two girls were happy to meet their real parents,
be 감정형용사 + to 부정사 (감정의 원인) …해서 행복하다
be happy to meet 만나서 행복하다 be sad to fail the exam 시험에 떨어져서 슬프다

they didn't want to leave the family (they had grown up with).
                          ↑ 수식
그들이 함께 성장한 가족 the family that they had grown up with
leave (leave-left-left) 떠나다, 뒤에 남겨두다 (이 문장에서는 '떠나다')

⑧ So, nothing changed for these two families.
변한 건 없다 (something changed 무언가 변했다)

⑨ But, the hospital had to **deal with** a big change because both families decided
다루다, 처리하다

to **sue** the hospital, demanding about $160,000 in **damages**.
sue 고소하다, 재판을 청구하다   demand 금액 in damages 손해배상으로 얼마를 요구하다
litigate 소송하다 prosecute 기소하다   damages 손해배상금 (항상 복수형) / damage 손상, 피해

⑩ Nothing hurts like the truth, especially for that hospital.
진실만큼 상처를 주는 건 없다 (속담)

(어떻게 이 러시아 소녀들이 엉뚱한 부모와 살게 되었는지 아세요?)

❶ 2011년, 러시아인 십대 소녀 두 명인 아이리나와 아냐, 그리고 가족들은 두 소녀들이 우연히 태어날 때 바뀌었다는 걸 알고 깜짝 놀랐는데, 이 말은 각 소녀의 부모가 진짜 부모가 아니라는 뜻입니다.

❷ 이들의 어머니들은 1999년 같은 병원에서 15분 간격으로 출산했습니다.

❸ 태어난 후 두 아기 딸들은 병원 직원에 의해 엉뚱한 이름표를 받았던 것입니다.

❹ 이 모든 일은 아이리나의 아버지가 딸이 자기 딸이 아닐 수도 있다고 생각하면서 시작되었는데 딸이 아버지와 전혀 닮지 않았기 때문이었습니다.

❺ DNA 테스트 결과 아이리나의 부모 중 누구도 아이리나의 친부모가 아니라고 나왔습니다.

❻ 지방 경찰의 도움으로 아이리나의 어머니는 친딸을 찾기 시작했는데, 그 딸은 불과 몇 마일 거리에 살고 있었습니다.

❼ 두 소녀는 친부모를 만나 기뻤지만, 그들이 함께 성장했던 가족을 떠나길 원치 않았습니다.

❽ 그래서 이 두 가족에게 변한 건 없었습니다.

❾ 하지만 병원은 엄청난 변화를 준비해야 했는데, 두 가족이 병원을 상대로 16만 달러의 손해배상을 청구하기로 결정했기 때문입니다.

❿ 특히 그 병원에게 있어서 진실만큼 고통스러운 것은 없는 것 같습니다.

She was kind of famous because she was a queen. She's not just any normal queen, such as Queen Elizabeth. She was the queen of plastic surgery. And again, she's not just any normal queen of plastic surgery - she was the queen of the worst plastic surgery nightmare.

Unusually, she was changed from a beauty into a beast by plastic surgery. You know, generally it is the other way around. More unusually, it was not an accident to get a monster-looking face. It was her choice.

Allegedly, she spent a handsome amount of money on surgery over the years to look like a cat. Why? Because her rich husband liked his pet cats very much, and she didn't want to lose his love. So, she decided to change her face to look like a cat. And she did. However, her husband divorced her anyway.

Even after divorce, she couldn't stop getting plastic surgery. She underwent small cosmetic procedures, such as an eyebrow lift and Botox, until she passed away at 84 on December 31, 2024. Not surprisingly, she didn't classify these as plastic surgeries.

Anyway, thank God her husband loved cats, not rabbits or elephants.

Words & Expressions

queen 여왕 normal 일반적인 plastic surgery 성형수술 nightmare 악몽 unusually 특이하게도 beast 야수 the other way around 반대로, 거꾸로 a handsome amount of money 엄청난 금액의 돈 over the years 수 년 간 divorce 이혼하다

Understanding Checkpoint

1. What can be the best title of this story?

    a. Wildenstein : Changed Into The Beast To Look Like A Cat

    b. The Queen Of Plastic Surgery : Who Wouldn't Like Her?

    c. Complete Flipflop : From The Monster To The Beauty Queen

    d. The Ultimate Cat Lover Turned Into A Cat

2. According to the passage, which sentence is <u>wrong</u>?

    a. Wildenstein was famous for the worst plastic surgery nightmare.

    b. Wildenstein allegedly spent a fortune on plastic surgery.

    c. Wildenstein seemed to be seriously addicted to plastic surgery.

    d. Wildenstein was loved by her husband and his pet cats.

3. Choose the correct words for each sentence.

    a. I can't stop <u>to eat</u> / <u>eat</u> / <u>eating</u> sweets whenever I am stressed out, although I am diabetic.

    b. Butter is healthier than margarine? I though it was <u>another</u> / <u>the other</u> / <u>others</u> way around.

    c. Maybe I should allow him to train my dog because I have nothing to <u>loose</u> / <u>lose</u> / <u>lost</u>.

Answer **1.** a **2.** d **3.** eating ׀ the other ׀ lose

Listening Drill - Dictation

She was   because she was a queen. She's not just any normal queen, such as Queen Elizabeth. She was the queen of   . And again, she's not just any normal queen of plastic surgery - she was the queen of the worst plastic surgery nightmare.

Unusually, she   a beauty   a beast by plastic surgery. You know, generally it is   . More unusually, it was not an accident to get a monster-looking face. It was her choice.

Allegedly, she spent   money on surgery over the years to look like a cat. Why? Because her rich husband liked his pet cats very much, and she didn't want to lose his love. So, she decided to change her face to look like a cat. And she did. However, her husband   .

Even after divorce, she   plastic surgery. She underwent small cosmetic procedures, such as an eyebrow lift and Botox, until she passed away at 84 on December 31, 2024. Not surprisingly, she didn't classify these as plastic surgeries.

Anyway,   her husband loved cats, not rabbits or elephants.

Did You Know Why Jocelyn Wildenstein Is Famous?

1 She was **kind of** famous because she was a queen.
좀, 약간 (sort of) / a kind of ..의 종류

2 She's **not just any normal** queen, such as Queen Elizabeth.
보통의 (일반적인) …아닌   한국어와 어순이 반대 – 엘리자베스 여왕
                              조지왕 – king George 헨리 왕자 prince Henry

3 She was the queen of **plastic surgery**.
= cosmetic surgery 성형수술

4 And **again**, she's not just any normal queen of plastic surgery –
다시 한 번, 또 다시

she was the queen of the worst plastic surgery **nightmare**.
bad - worse - worst 최악의 (최상급 the)   악몽, 악몽처럼 끔찍한 일(것)

5 Unusually, she was **changed** from a beauty **into** a beast by plastic surgery.
be changed by …로 인해 바뀌다 (수동태)   from A into B : A에서 B로
The beauty and the beast 미녀와 야수 (이야기) a beauty 미녀, a beast 야수

6 You know, generally it is **the other way around**.
정반대

7 More unusually, it was not an accident to get a monster-looking face.
가주어 it, 진주어 to get   괴물처럼 보이는

8 It was her **choice**.
choose v. 선택하다 (choose-chose-chosen) choice n. 선택 a. 질이 좋은, 고급의 chosen a. 선택 받은

9 Allegedly, she spent (a **handsome** amount of money) on surgery over the years
알려진 바에 의하면   spend 돈 on : …에 돈을 쓰다   handsome a. 잘생긴, (돈) 상당한 양의
                       a handsome amount of money = a hefty sum of money 많은 금액의 돈
                       I paid handsomely for this little ring. 이 작은 반지에 나는 거액을 냈다.

to look like a cat.   **10** Why?
고양이처럼 보이기 위해서

11 Because [1] her rich husband liked his pet cats very much,
              a. 부유한, 풍부한 (enrich (영양소) 강화하다, 풍요롭게 하다)

and [2] she didn't want to lose his love.
lose-lost-lost (잃다)

⑫ So, she decided to change her face to look like a cat.

⑬ And she did.
= change her face

⑭ However, her husband **divorced** her anyway.
divorce v. 이혼하다 n. 이혼   어쨌든 간에

⑮ Even after **divorce**, she couldn't stop getting plastic surgery.
(수술) 받는 것을 멈출 수 없었다 (계속 수술을 받았다)

⑯ She underwent small cosmetic procedures, such as an eyebrow lift and Botox,
lift v. 들어올리다 n. 승강기, (차) 태워주기, 들어올리기 (성형수술에서 lift는 처진 피부를 위로 끌어당기는 것)

until she passed away at 84 on December 31, 2024.
84세의 나이로 사망할 때까지

⑰ Not surprisingly, she didn't **classify** these **as** plastic surgeries.
놀랍지 않게도   classify A as B : A를 B라고 분류하다   these - eyebrow lift or Botox
surprisingly 놀랍게도   classified a. 기밀의, 주제별로 분류된

⑱ Anyway, thank God her husband loved cats, not rabbits or elephants.
다행이다, 신에게 감사할 일이다

(조슬린 와일든스타인이 왜 유명한지 아세요?)

❶ 그녀는 여왕이라서 좀 유명했습니다.   ❷ 엘리자베스 여왕 같은 일반적인 여왕이 아니었습니다.

❸ 그녀는 성형수술의 여왕이었습니다.

❹ 또 그냥 일반적인 성형수술의 여왕이 아니라, 그녀는 최악의 성형수술 악몽의 여왕이었습니다.

❺ 이상하게도 그녀는 성형수술로 미녀에서 야수로 바뀌었습니다.

❻ 그 반대가 일반적인데도 말입니다.   ❼ 더 이상한 건 그녀가 괴물 같은 얼굴이 된 게 사고가 아니라는 겁니다.

❽ 그건 그녀의 선택이었습니다.

❾ 알려진 바에 의하면 그녀는 수년 간 고양이처럼 보이기 위한 수술에 엄청난 금액의 돈을 썼다고 합니다.   ❿ 왜냐고요?

⓫ 그녀의 돈 많은 남편이 애완 고양이들을 아주 좋아했고 그녀는 그의 사랑을 잃고 싶지 않았기 때문이었습니다.

⓬ 그래서 그녀는 고양이처럼 보이도록 얼굴을 바꾸기로 결심했습니다.   ⓭ 그리고 그렇게 했습니다.

⓮ 그런데도 남편은 그녀와 이혼했습니다.   ⓯ 심지어 이혼 이후에도 그녀는 성형수술 받는 걸 멈출 수 없었습니다.

⓰ 그녀는 2024년 12월 31일 84세로 사망할 때까지 눈썹 리프팅이나 보톡스 같은 소소한 성형 시술을 받았습니다.

⓱ 놀랍지 않게도 그녀는 이런 것들은 성형수술로 치지 않았습니다.

⓲ 아무튼 그녀의 남편이 토끼나 코끼리가 아닌 고양이를 좋아해서 다행입니다.

Hollywood stars are too rich to give birth like everybody else does. Here are two rich star couples who gave birth in an unusual way.

The first too-rich Hollywood star couple is Beyonce Knowles and her hubby Jay-Z. They shelled out a whopping $1.3 million to rent an entire floor at the Lenox Hill Hospital in Manhattan. Hospital staff couldn't use their cell phones when working, since they might take disallowed pictures of the precious baby girl. Additionally, that floor's security cameras were covered to protect the couple's privacy, not to mention that a bunch of personal bodyguards stood at every corner of the building.

Renting a whole floor of a hospital is nothing compared to this couple. In 2006, the couple known as Brangelina flew to Namibia to give birth to their baby girl. This super star couple and their unable-to-be-ugly baby were guarded by the 'government' of Namibia. The government gave their security personnel the right to punch or arrest anyone who tried to violate the couple's privacy. Furthermore, any journalists without proper permits were forbidden to enter the country. Of course, Jolie and Pitt spent a fortune during their stay in Namibia, including a hefty donation.

1. What is the main idea of the story?

a. Brangelina couple is the richest and weirdest couple ever.

b. Beyonce married Jay-Z since he owns a hospital in Manhattan.

c. Some Hollywood stars don't spare their money when it comes to protecting their privacy.

d. Jolie and Pitt asked the government of Namibia to forbid using cell phones.

2. To protect their privacy, Brangelina couple _____ .

a. flew to Namibia and gave birth to a girl there

b. tried to arrest anyone who tried to punch their baby girl

c. threatened the government of Namibia

d. rent an entire floor of the hospital in Namibia

3. Choose the correct words for each sentence.

a. Brian struggles with arithmetic, <u>not to mention</u> / <u>not to mention that</u> / <u>not needy to mention</u> of his other subjects.

b. Korry was caught in another <u>spacious</u> / <u>whopping</u> / <u>extensive</u> lie. She is a born liar.

c. The photographer <u>made</u> / <u>took</u> / <u>had</u> pictures of victims and put those pictures in the newspaper.

Answer **1.** c   **2.** a   **3.** not to mention ǀ whopping ǀ took

Listening Drill – Dictation

Hollywood stars are _____ like everybody else does. Here are two rich star couples who gave birth _____ .

The first too-rich Hollywood star couple is Beyonce Knowles and her hubby Jay-Z. They _____ a whopping $1.3 million to _____ at the Lenox Hill Hospital in Manhattan. Hospital staff couldn't use their cell phones when working, since they might _____ of the precious baby girl. Additionally, that floor's security cameras were covered to protect the couple's privacy, not to mention that personal bodyguards stood _____ the building.

Renting a whole floor of a hospital is nothing compared to this couple. In 2006, the couple known as Brangelina flew to Namibia to give birth to their baby girl. This super star couple and their unable-to-be-ugly baby _____ the 'government' of Namibia. The government gave their security personnel the right to punch or arrest anyone who tried to _____ . Furthermore, any journalists without proper permits were forbidden to enter the country. Of course, Jolie and Pitt _____ during their stay in Namibia, including a hefty donation.

Did You Know How Hollywood Rich Stars Gave Birth?

❶ Hollywood stars are too rich to **give birth** (like everybody else does).

too 형용사 to 동사 너무 …해서 …할 수 없다 – 너무 부자라서 (일반인이 하듯) 출산할 수 없다
부정어 not이 없지만 부정문이다.   give birth (to) …를 낳다, 출산하다

❷ Here are two rich star couples (who gave birth in an unusual way).

a couple 2명 / two coupels 4명　　↑　　수식　　　　　평범하지 않은 방식으로
커플(부부)가 두 쌍 two couples이므로 총 4명　　( )한 부자 스타커플 두 쌍

❸ The first too-rich Hollywood star couple is (Beyonce Knowles and her hubby Jay-Z).

하이픈(-)으로 연결된 형용사 too-rich 너무 부자인　　　　　　　　　　　= husband
so rich 매우 부자인 too rich (과도하게) 너무 부자인
이 문장의 주어는 couple (한 쌍-단수), 동사 is (두 쌍 two couples 부터 복수 취급)

❹ They **shelled out** a whopping $1.3 million to **rent** an entire **floor**

많은 돈을 쓰다　　　무려, 자그마치 (= staggering)　　　v. 돈을 내고 빌리다, 세를 내다 n. 집세 (그냥 빌리는 경우는 lend)
shell out + 돈 + to 동사 : …하려고 돈을 쓰다　　　　　　　　　floor 층, 바닥
돈/금액 앞에 a를 쓰지 않지만 whopping 형용사의 수식을 받았기 때문에 a whopping $1.3 million으로 썼다.

at the Lenox Hill Hospital in Manhattan.

❺ Hospital staff couldn't use their cell phones when working,

Hospital staff는 집합명사 (병원 직원 집단) – 단수 동사가 오지만 they의 의미로 쓸 수 있다.
　　　　　　주절의 주어 hospital staff와 일치, 생략 / 능동적인 행위 working = when they worked / when they were working

since they might take **disallowed** pictures of the **precious** baby girl.

사진 찍다 – take 동사를 쓴다 (take pictures/photos, take a picture/photo)　　precious 소중한, 귀중한
disallowed 허가받지 않은 – take disallowed pictures 허가 받지 않은 사진을 찍다

❻ Additionally, that floor's security cameras were covered to protect

　　　　　　　　　　　　　　　　　(수동태) …하기 위해 가려지다 be covered to 동사

the couple's privacy, **not to mention** that (**a bunch of** personal bodyguards)

(평서문) that이하는 말할 것도 없고　a bunch of 일단의, 무리의 + 복수 명사
that + 주어 + 동사 (절)

stood at every corner of the building.

every + 단수 명사 + 단수 동사
every, each는 항상 단수 취급

❼ (Renting a whole floor of a hospital) **is nothing compared to** this couple.

동명사 주어 ( ) 병원의 한 층을 다 빌리는 것 + 동사 is　　…에 비하면 아무것도 아니다

❽ In 2006, (the couple known as Brangelina) flew to Namibia to **give birth to**

　　　　　　↑　　수식　　　　　　fly to …로 날아가다, 비행하다
　　　　　Brangelina로 알려진 커플 (Brad+Angelina)

their baby girl.

⑨ (This super star couple and their unable-to-be-ugly baby) were guarded by

주어 ( ) (복수) + were　　　　　　하이픈(-)으로 연결된 형용사 :　　　수동태 be guarded by …에 의해 경호를 받다
　　　　　　　　　　　　　　　　(부모의 외모를 감안할 때) 못생길 수 없는

the 'government' of Namibia.

⑩ The government gave their security personnel the right to (punch or **arrest**)

주어 give 사람 + the right to 동사　　　　　right to punch or right to arrest
: …할 수 있는 권리를 누구에게 주다　　　　때릴 권리 또는 체포할 권리

anyone who tried to **violate** the couple's privacy.

…하려는 누구라도　　　　v. 위반하다 (n. vloation 위반, 침입)
　　　　　　　　　　　사생활을 보호하다 protect privacy / 사생활을 침해하다 violate privacy

⑪ Furthermore, (any journalists without proper permits) were forbidden

　　　　　　　　　　　수식
　　　　　　　　　　　　　　　　　　　　be forbidden 금지되다 (수동) = be banned
주어 ( ) journalists 적당한 허가증이 없는 언론인들 + were
journalists who didn't have proper permits　　permit v. 허가하다 n. 허가증 permission n. 허가

to enter the country.

⑫ Of course, Jolie and Pitt spent a fortune during their stay in Namibia,

spend (돈, 시간) 쓰다 = spend lots of money

including a **hefty donation**.

'거액'을 의미할 때 hefty, handsome이 자주 쓰인다.
거액을 기부하다 donate a hefty amount of money, donate handsomely

> 할리우드 스타들은 어떻게 출산했는지 아세요?

❶ 할리우드 스타들은 너무 부자라서 일반인들처럼 출산할 수 없습니다.

❷ 평범하지 않은 방식으로 출산한 돈 많은 할리우드의 부부 두 쌍을 소개합니다.

❸ 너무 돈이 많은 첫 번째 할리우드 스타 커플은 비욘세 놀즈와 남편 제이지입니다.

❹ 이들은 무려 천삼백만 달러를 들여 맨하탄의 레녹스 힐 병원의 한 층 전체를 빌렸습니다.

❺ 병원 직원들은 병원에서 일하는 동안 휴대 전화를 사용할 수 없었는데, 이는 허락 없이 그들의 소중한 딸 아기의 사진을 찍을 수 있기 때문입니다.

❻ 물론 그 층의 보안 카메라 모두 이 커플의 사생활 보호를 위해 가려졌고, 건물 구석구석마다 수많은 개인 경호원들이 보초를 선 건 말할 것도 없습니다.

❼ 병원 한 층을 다 빌린 것도 이 커플에 비하면 아무것도 아닙니다.

❽ 2006년 브란젤리나로 알려진 커플은 아기 딸을 낳기 위해 나미비아로 날아갔습니다.

❾ 이 수퍼스타 커플과 예쁘지 않을 수 없는 이들의 아기는 나미비아 '정부'의 경호를 받았습니다.

❿ 정부는 이들의 개인 경호원들에게 이들의 사생활을 침해하려는 사람에게 주먹을 날리거나 체포할 수 있는 권한을 주었습니다.

⑪ 그리고 적당한 허가증이 없는 언론인은 아예 입국을 금지했습니다.

⑫ 물론 졸리와 피트는 나미비아에 머무는 동안 거액의 기부를 포함해 상당한 돈을 썼습니다.

36

Did You Know What Nelson Mandela, Edgar Allan Poe, Leo Tolstoy Have In Common?

Johann Sebastian Bach

Other than these, Louis Armstrong (a jazz musician and a trumpeter), Johann Sebastian Bach (a German composer), Marilyn Monroe (an actress), Babe Ruth (a baseball player) also have this in common with them, too. These great people with great achievements were all orphans. They must have had a hard time when they were young, but as far as leaving their names in history was concerned, being orphans didn't matter to them.

Some people have a strong bias against orphans. They believe that orphans are highly likely to go wrong emotionally and financially, and tend to be bad or troubled people, like criminals. Orphans do have difficulties surviving in our society, since many of them don't receive parents' proper care, protection, or guidance. But, that doesn't mean every orphan has no choice but to become a bad or troubled person, just as some non-orphans might be. Some of them become greater people than those raised by both parents under very good conditions.

Words & Expressions

have in common 공통점이 있다 trumpeter 트럼펫 연주자 composer 작곡자 orphan 고아 leave one's name in the history 역사에 이름을 남기다 have a strong bias against ...에 대해 (부정적인) 편견을 가지다 emotionally 정서적으로, 감정적으로 financially 경제적으로 criminal 범죄자 under very good conditions 좋은 조건에서

162

1. What is the main idea of the story?

a. It is impossible for orphans to leave their names in history as great figures.

b. All orphans are supposed to become great people and they do.

c. There are many orphans who turned out to be great figures in history.

d. The financial support for orphanages is utmost important.

2. According to the passage, which sentence is <u>wrong</u>?

a. There are many great people who were orphans but achieved great things.

b. Orphans are children who don't have rich parents or relatives.

c. Not all orphans become bad criminals.

d. It's possible for orphans to leave their names in history.

3. Choose the correct words for each sentence.

a. Some people claim that Greece is highly <u>to like</u> / <u>like</u> / <u>likely</u> to leave Euro due to the financial crisis.

b. Viki is a racist so she has a bias <u>for</u> / <u>against</u> / <u>to</u> African-Americans and Asians as well.

c. As far as me and my cousin <u>is</u> / <u>are</u> / <u>was</u> concerned, it doesn't matter whenever you go.

Answer **1.** c   **2.** b   **3.** likely ¦ against ¦ are

these, Louis Armstrong (a jazz musician and a trumpeter), Johann Sebastian Bach (a German composer), Marilyn Monroe (an actress), Babe Ruth (a baseball player) also _____ with them, too. These great people _____ were all orphans. They _____ when they were young, but as far as leaving their names in history was concerned, being orphans _____ .
Some people have a strong bias _____ orphans. They believe that orphans _____ emotionally and financially, and tend to be bad or troubled people, like criminals. Orphans do _____ in our society, since many of them don't receive parents' proper care, protection, or guidance. But, _____ every orphan has no choice but to become a bad or troubled person, just as some non-orphans might be. Some of them become greater people than those raised by both parents _____ very good conditions.

Did You Know What Nelson Mandela, Edgar Allan Poe, Leo Tolstoy Have In Common?

❶ Other than these, Louis Armstrong (a jazz musician and a trumpeter),

제목에 나온 사람들(these) 외에 　　　　　= 동격

Johann Sebastian Bach (a German **composer**), Marilyn Monroe (an **actress**),

= 동격 　　　　　　　　　　　　　= 동격

compose v. 작곡하다, 구성하다 composition 구성요소, 작곡 composer 작곡가

Babe Ruth (a baseball player) also **have** this **in common with** them, too.

= 동격 　　　　(이것이라는) 공통점이 있다 (have something in common)
↔ have nothing in common 공통점이 없다

❷ (These great people with great **achievements**) were all **orphans**.

수식 　　　　achieve v. 달성하다, 성취하다 achievement 달설, 성취
주어 ( ) - achievements가 아니라 people이 주어 + were 　　orphan 고아

❸ They must have **had a hard time** when they were young,

must have pp 　　have a hard time 어려움을 겪다
: …임에 틀림없다 (강한 추측)

but as far as (leaving their names in history) was concerned,

as far as ( ) be concerned …에 관해서라면
be동사는 ( )에 맞춘다. 동명사 leaving (남기는 것-단수)이 주어-단수동사 was

being orphans didn't **matter** to them.

고아라는 것 (동명사주어) 　　　문제가 되다, 중요하다
Nothing matters. 문제될 거 없다.

❹ Some people have a strong **bias** against orphans.

…에 반하여 (강한) 편견을 갖다　　bias n. 편견 biased a. 치우친

❺ They believe that orphans [1] are highly likely to go wrong (**emotionally** and

(앞문장) 고아에 강한 편견을 가진 사람들 　　　　　　　잘못되다 (감정적으로, 경제적으로)
orphans [1] are and [2] tend

financially), and [2] tend to be (bad or troubled) people, (like **criminals**).

나쁜 bad 사람이나 문제가 있는 troubled 사람이 되기 쉽다 (tend to)　　criminal 범죄자, 범인

❻ Orphans do **have difficulties** surviving in our society, since many of them

본동사 have를 강조하는 do 　　　　　　　　그들(orphans) 중 다수
have difficulty -ing …하는데 어려움이 있다
have difficulty sleeping 자는데 어려움이 있다

don't receive parents' [1] proper **care**, [2] **protection**, or [3] **guidance**.

돌봄　　　보호　　　　　지도

⑦ But, that doesn't mean every orphan has no choice but to become
　　앞문장(that)이 …를 의미하는 건 아니다　　　　　to 이하 할 수밖에 없다 (every + has 단수)

a (bad or troubled) person, just as some non-orphans might be.
　　　　　　　　고아가 아닌 사람들 non-orphans 일부 역시 그럴 수 있듯이

⑧ Some of them become greater people than those (raised by both parents
= some orphans　　　　　비교급 greater than ..보다 위대한　　↑　　수식
　　　　　　　　　　　　　　　　　　　　　　　　those (who were) raised by …에 의해 양육 받은 사람들

under very good conditions).
굉장히 좋은 환경에서 (condition 조건, 상태)

넬슨 만델라, 에드가 알렌 포, 레오 톨스토이의 공통점이 무엇인지 아세요?

❶ 이들 외에도, 루이 암스트롱 (재즈 음악가, 트럼펫 연주가), 요한 세바스찬 바흐 (독일 작곡가), 마릴린 먼로 (배우) 베이브 루스 (야구 선수) 역시 이들과 공통점을 갖고 있습니다.

❷ 엄청난 업적을 이룬 엄청난 이 사람들 모두 고아였습니다.

❸ 이들은 어렸을 때 어려운 시절을 보냈을 게 분명하지만, 역사에 이름을 남기는데 있어서 고아라는 건 이들에게 아무 문제가 되지 않았습니다.

❹ 어떤 사람들은 고아에 관해 강한 편견을 가지고 있습니다.

❺ 이들은 고아들이 정서적, 경제적으로 잘못될 가능성이 매우 높기 때문에 범죄자처럼 나쁜 사람 또는 문제를 가진 사람이 되기 쉽다고 믿습니다.

❻ 고아들 중 많은 경우 부모의 적절한 보살핌과 보호, 지도를 받지 못하기 때문에 사회에서 살아가기가 어려운 게 사실입니다.

❼ 하지만 그렇다고 모든 고아가 나쁜 사람이나 범죄자가 될 수밖에 없다는 뜻은 아니고, 고아가 아닌 몇몇 사람들도 마찬가지 입니다.

❽ 어떤 고아들은 아주 좋은 환경에서 양쪽 부모의 양육을 받고 자란 사람보다 더 훌륭하게 자라기도 합니다.

37

Did You Know **How Much This Eating Champion Weighs?**

Sonya Thomas (a Korean-born American, with the Korean name Lee Sun-kyung), a.k.a. The Black Widow, is the world champion eater.

She has won a whopping 37 times in eating competitions since 2003. In almost every eating competition she participated in, she set unbelievable world records. Her eye-popping and mouth-watering records are as follows:

11 pounds of cheesecake in 9 minutes in 2004, 183 chicken wings in 12 minutes in 2011, 65 hard boiled eggs in 6 minutes and 40 seconds in 2003, 44 lobsters totaling 11.4 pounds of lobster meat in 12 minutes in 2005, 38 Moonpies in 8 minutes in 2010, 552 oysters in 10 minutes in 2005, 6 and a half extra large slices of cheese pizza in 15 minutes in 2004, 41 Hot Dogs and Buns in 10 minutes in 2009, 183 Buffalo Wings in 12 minutes in 2011.

As everybody already must have noticed, she has never been a picky eater. She eats moon pies, tacos, clams, baked beans, anything; you name it, she can eat it.

What's surprising here is her size. She is 152 cm tall and weighs 47kg.

1. What can be the best title of this story?

    a. Surprising Secrets To Become The Eating Champion

    b. The Eating Champion's Unbelievable Body Size

    c. Sonya Thomas, The Worst Eating Champion Ever

    d. Why She Called The Black Widow

2. In 2004, Sonya Thomas ate _____ .

    a. hard boiled eggs and lobsters

    b. Buffalo wings and BBQ chicken wings

    c. cheese pizza and cheesecake

    d. Tacos, clams, baked beans

3. Choose the correct words for each sentence.

    a. I planned to <u>take part in</u> / <u>participate</u> / <u>join to</u> a race but I gave up because of injury.

    b. I have to buy the book titled 'How to stop being a <u>heavy eater</u> / <u>picky eater</u> / <u>light eater</u>' since my daughter says everything is yucky except chocolate.

    c. Almost every well in the village is drying out because it hasn't rained for <u>three and half</u> / <u>three and a half</u> / <u>three a half</u> years.

Answer **1.** b **2.** c **3.** take part in | picky eater | three and a half

Listening Drill – Dictation

Sonya Thomas (a Korean-born American, with the Korean name Lee Sun-kyung), a.k.a. The Black Widow, is the world champion eater.

She has won _____ 37 times in eating competitions since 2003. In almost every eating competition s_____ , she set unbelievable world records. Her eye-popping and _____ records are as follows:

11 pounds of cheesecake in 9 minutes in 2004, 183 chicken wings in 12 minutes in 2011, 65 _____ in 6 minutes and 40 seconds in 2003, 44 lobsters _____ 11.4 pounds of lobster meat in 12 minutes in 2005, 38 Moonpies in 8 minutes in 2010, 552 _____ in 10 minutes in 2005, 6 and a half _____ cheese pizza in 15 minutes in 2004, 41 Hot Dogs and Buns in 10 minutes in 2009, 183 Buffalo Wings in 12 minutes in 2011.

As everybody already must have noticed, she _____ . She eats moon pies, tacos, clams, baked beans, anything; you _____ it, she can eat it. _____ is her size. She is 152 cm tall and weighs 47kg.

Learning Spotlight

Did You Know How Much This Eating Champion Weighs?

① Sonya Thomas (a Korean-born American, with the Korean name Lee Sun-kyung),

= 동격 　 한국 태생의 　 수식 　 한국 이름으로

a.k.a. The Black Widow, is the world champion eater.

= also known as …라고도 알려진

② She has won a whopping 37 times in eating **competitions** since 2003.

현재완료 has pp(won) 상을 타다, (경쟁) 이기다 win-won-won 　 competition 경쟁, 대회

a + 수를 수식하는 형용사 + 수 (a whopping 500 tickets 무려 5천장의 표 a staggering 200% 자그마치 200%)

③ (In almost every eating competition she **participated in**),

수식 　 participate in = take part in 참가하다

그녀가 참가한 대회 competition that she participated in

she set unbelievable world records.

set records 기록을 세우다 break records 기록을 깨다

④ Her (eye-popping and mouth-watering) records are as follows:

눈이 튀어나오고 입에 군침이 도는 　 다음과 같은

pop-eyed (놀라) 눈이 휘둥그레진 Popeye 뽀빠이 (시금치를 먹으면 힘이 생긴다는 만화 캐릭터)

⑤ 11 pounds of cheesecake in 9 minutes in 2004,

⑥ 183 chicken wings in 12 minutes in 2011,

⑦ 65 hard boiled eggs in 6 minutes and 40 seconds in 2003,

삶은 달걀 soft boiled eggs 반숙 달걀 sunny side-up eggs 노른자가 위로 오게 익힌 계란 후라이

⑧ 44 lobsters (totaling 11.4 pounds of lobster meat) in 12 minutes in 2005,

수식 　 랍스터 살(고기)만 …파운드

랍스터 44마리 총

⑨ 38 Moonpies in 8 minutes in 2010,

마시멜로가 들어간 (초코파이와 비슷한) 파이 (mooncake 중국 추석 음식 월병)

⑩ 552 **oysters** in 10 minutes in 2005,

굴 (clam 조개, mussel 홍합, barnacle 따개비)

⑪ 6 and a half extra large slices of cheese pizza in 15 minutes in 2004,

반 (1/2) 　 피자 조각을 셀 때는 pizza에 -s를 붙이지 않고 조각 slice에 -s를 붙인다.

6 and a half slices 6조각 + 반 조각

⑫ 41 Hot Dogs and Buns in 10 minutes in 2009,

⑬ 183 Buffalo Wings in 12 minutes in 2011.

⑭ As everybody already must have **noticed**, she has never been a **picky** eater.

must have pp 강한 추측- 알아차렸을 게 분명하다   입맛이 까다로운 / 음식을 가리는 사람
현재완료의 부정 - have와 pp 사이에 부정어

⑮ She eats moon pies, tacos, clams, baked beans, anything; you name it, she can eat it.

네가 이름을 말하는 거 무엇이든 (name v. 이름을 대다)

⑯ (What's surprising here) is her size.

주어 ( ) 여기서 놀라운 점 + 동사 is
The thing that is surprising here에서 선행사 the thing을 포함한 관계대명사로 what이 쓰임

⑰ She ¹⁾ is 152 cm tall and ²⁾ **weighs** 47kg.

키가 몇이다 : 주어 be ( ) tall.   체중이 얼마이다 : 주어 weigh ( ) - 주어 she가 3인칭 단수 현재 weighs

---

(먹기 대회 우승자의 몸무게가 얼마인지 아세요?)

❶ 블랙 위도우로 알려진 소냐 토마스 (한국 태생의 미국인으로 한국 이름은 이선경)는 먹기 대회 세계 챔피언입니다.

❷ 그녀는 2003년부터 먹기 대회에서 무려 37번이나 우승했습니다.

❸ 그녀는 참여한 거의 모든 먹기 대회에서 믿기 힘든 세계 기록을 달성했습니다.

❹ 눈이 튀어 나올 만하고 입에 군침이 도는 그녀의 기록은 다음과 같습니다.

❺ 2004년 9분 동안 11파운드의 치즈 케이크,   ❻ 2011년 12분 동안 닭 날개 183개,

❼ 2003년 6분 40초 동안 삶은 달걀 65개,   ❽ 2005년 12분 동안 랍스터 44개 고기 무게로 총 11.4파운드,

❾ 2010년 8분 동안 문파이 38개,   ❿ 2005년 10분 동안 굴 552개,

⓫ 2004년 15분 동안 초대형 치즈 피자 6 1/2조각,   ⑫ 2009년 10분 동안 핫도그와 번즈 41개,

⑬ 2011년 12분 동안 버팔로 윙 183조각.

⑭ 다들 눈치 챘겠지만, 그녀는 한 번도 식성이 까다로운 적이 없습니다.

⑮ 문 파이, 타코, 조개, 베이크드 빈즈, 무엇이든 그녀는 먹을 수 있습니다.

⑯ 여기서 놀라운 건 그녀의 사이즈입니다.   ⑰ 그녀는 152cm 키에 체중은 47kg입니다.

Ferdinand Cheval (1836-1924) was a French mailman who built 'Le palais Ideal' (The Ideal Palace) in Hauterives, which has been officially protected as a cultural landmark of the France for its extraordinary architecture.

Cheval was a poor, uneducated mailman. He just delivered letters to people. But after he tripped on a stone in the street, his life began to change. He said the shape of the stone inspired him. The next day, he returned to the same spot where he picked up the special stone to pick some more. After that, Cheval collected stones and carried them home for the next 33 years. These stones became the building materials for his amazing Ideal Palace.

At first, he carried them in his pocket, but later he used a basket and then a wheelbarrow. It took him 33 years to complete his own dream palace. He just did it by himself with his bare hands. Cheval died a year after finishing building it. He was buried in his palace, as he wished.

Now, it's open to the public, and visitors around the world become speechless due to the fact that this marvelous piece of architecture was built by one old man with stones.

Understanding Checkpoint

1. What is the main idea of the story?

    a. Amazingly, Cheval built the Ideal Palace by himself with bare hands.

    b. Cheval was the most prominent architect in France.

    c. Cheval tried to prove that stones can be excellent building materials.

    d. Cheval made visitors speechless by carrying so many stones with bare hands.

2. According to the passage, which sentence is right?

    a. Cheval delivered letters all day long so he couldn't do anything.

    b. Cheval could build the Ideal Palace since he was a professional architect.

    c. Cheval had collected tons of stones for his collection.

    d. When Cheval was alive, he wanted to be buried in his own dream palace.

3. Choose the correct words for each sentence.

    a. Your paintings left me <u>talkative</u> / <u>speechless</u> / <u>unspeakable</u>. It was just fantastic.

    b. These books are for underprivileged children <u>which</u> / <u>what</u> / <u>who</u> can't afford to buy books.

    c. <u>It made me spend a while</u> / <u>It took me a while</u> / <u>I spent the time</u> to learn how to play the guitar.

Answer   **1.** a   **2.** d   **3.** speechless ǀ who ǀ it took me a while

Listening Drill – Dictation

Ferdinand Cheval (1836-1924) was a French mailman who built 'Le palais Ideal' (The Ideal Palace) in Hauterives, which   as a cultural landmark of the France for its   architecture.

Cheval was a poor, uneducated mailman. He just   to people. But after he   in the street, his life began to change. He said the shape of the stone   him. The next day, he returned to the same spot where he picked up the special stone to pick some more. After that, Cheval collected stones and carried them home   33 years. These stones became the building materials for his amazing Ideal Palace.

At first, he carried them in his pocket, but later he used a basket and   a wheelbarrow.   33 years to complete his own dream palace. He just did it by himself   . Cheval died a year after finishing building it. He was buried in his palace, as he wished.

Now, it's open to the public, and visitors around the world become speechless due to the fact that this marvelous   was built by one old man with stones.

Did You Know How Cheval The Mailman Built 'Le Palais Ideal'?

1 Ferdinand Cheval (1836-1924) was a French mailman (who built 'Le palais

mailman에 대한 추가설명 who 이하 ↑ 수식

Ideal' (The Ideal Palace) in Hauterives), which has been officially protected as

= 동격

콤마 + which (계속 용법) 현재완료 has been + 수동태 been protected
수동태에서 부사 위치 : be 부사 pp (been officially protected)

a cultural landmark of the France for its extraordinary architecture.

주요 건물 extra (추가의) + ordinary (일상적인, 평범한) – 비범한, 놀라운

2 Cheval was a (poor, uneducated) mailman.

가난하고 교육 받지 못한 | 수식 ↑
educated 교육을 받은 highly educated 고등 교육을 받은
poorly educated 교육을 잘 받지 못한

3 He just delivered letters to people.

배달하다, 출산하다, 넘겨주다, (판결)내리다 (여기서는 '배달하다')

4 But after he tripped on a stone in the street, his life began to change.

trip v. 여행하다, 발을 헛디디다, 넘어지다 n. 여행, 헛디딤 trip on a stone 돌에 걸려 넘어지다
after tripping on a stone, his life began to change로 쓰면 안 되는데,
주절의 주어 his life와 after절의 주어 he가 일치하지 않기 때문에 주어를 생략할 수 없다.

5 He said (the shape of the stone) inspired him.

동사 inspire의 주어는 (stone이 아니라) shape – 그에게 영감을 준 건 돌의 '모양'
inspire 영감을 주다

6 The next day, he returned to the same spot where (he picked up

(그가 특별한 돌을 주워 올린) 같은 장소   ↑ 수식 | spot n. 점, 얼룩, 장소 v. 찾아내다
He returned to 장소 to pick some more. 더 줍기 위해서 (어느 장소로) 돌아갔다
pick up ...을 얻다, 집어 올리다

the special stone) to pick some more.

7 After that, Cheval [1] collected stones and [2] carried them home for the next 33 years.

슈발은 [1] 돌을 모으고 [2] 이를 집에 가져갔다   for + 기간 – 이후next 33년 동안

8 These stones became the building materials for his amazing Ideal Palace.

건축 자재/재료   궁전

9 At first, he carried them in his pocket, but later he used a basket and then a wheelbarrow.

처음에는   돌을 옮긴 수단 pockets – basket – wheelbarrow

⑩ It took him 33 years to complete his own dream palace.
사람이 …하는데 시간이 얼마 걸리다 : 가주어 it + take + 사람 + 기간 + to동사
(It took me three hours to get there. 내가 거기 가는데 3시간 걸렸다.)
take - 시간이 얼마 걸리다, 사진을 찍다, 약을 복용하다

⑪ He just did it by himself (with his **bare** hands).
by oneself 혼자서   맨손으로 (bare feet 맨발 / bare skin 맨 피부 / naked eyes 맨눈)

⑫ Cheval died a year after finishing building it.
주절의 주어와 일치, 생략 after he finished building the Ideal Palace
동명사를 취하는 동사 : finish, avoid, spend (finish building O / finish to build X)

⑬ He was buried in his palace, as he wished.
be buried 묻히다 (수동태)   그가 소망한 대로
bury v. 묻다 (bury-buried-buried) burial n. 매장, 장례식

⑭ Now, it's open to the public, and (visitors around the world) become **speechless**
대중에 공개된   visitors become speechless 방문객들은 말문이 막힌다   speak v. 말하다 speech n. 연설
speechless a. (놀람, 기쁨, 공포) 말문이 막힌

due to the fact that (this **marvelous** piece of architecture) was built by

due to + 명사, 동명사   be built by …의해 건설되다 (수동태)
due to the fact that + 주어 + 동사(절)   build - built - built

one old man with stones.

우체부 슈발이 어떻게 '발레 이데알'을 건축했는지 아세요?

❶ 페르디낭 슈발 (1836-1924)은 오뜨리브에 '발레 이데알' (이상의 궁전)을 건축한 프랑스인 우체부인데, 이는 파리의 문화적 지형물이며 특별한 건축물로 공식적인 보호를 받고 있습니다.

❷ 슈발은 가난하고 교육을 받지 못한 우체부였습니다.   ❸ 그는 그저 편지를 배달할 뿐이었습니다.

❹ 그러나 거리에서 돌에 발이 걸린 이후, 그의 인생은 바뀌기 시작했습니다.

❺ 그는 그 돌의 모양이 그에게 영감을 주었다고 말했습니다.

❻ 다음 날, 그는 특별한 돌을 주웠던 장소에 더 많이 줍기 위해 돌아가 보았습니다.

❼ 이후 슈발은 33년 동안 돌을 모아 집으로 가져갔습니다.

❽ 바로 그 돌들이 그의 놀라운 '이상의 궁전' 건축 재료가 되었습니다.

❾ 처음에는 주머니에 돌을 넣어 나르다가 나중에는 바구니와 손수레를 이용했습니다.

❿ 그가 자신만의 꿈의 궁전을 완공하는데 33년이 걸렸습니다.   ⓫ 그가 혼자서 맨손으로 이루어낸 것입니다.

⓬ 건축을 끝낸 후 일 년 뒤에 슈발이 사망했습니다.   ⓭ 그는 원하던 대로 자신의 궁전에 묻혔습니다.

⓮ 현재 이곳은 대중에 공개되고 있는데, 전 세계의 방문객들은 이 놀라운 건축물이 한 노인에 의해 돌로 지어졌다는 사실에 말을 잇지 못합니다.

Did You Know Why Lali Was Worshipped As A Reincarnated God?

Lali was born on March 11, 2008 in Northern India. When she was born, people believed she was a reincarnation of the god Ganesh, the Hindu god who is half person and half elephant. Not only local neighbors but also people around the world came to her little village to meet her. Many of them offered her parents money to ask for her blessing. This is very helpful for them because her young parents earned less than $2 a day, like many other neighbors in their village.

What was so special about this baby? Lali was born with two faces. She had one body and one head like other babies, but unlike other babies, she had two faces on one head. So she had four eyes, two noses, and two mouths. Her young parents didn't agreed to let the hospital perform a free CT scan or an MRI on her head. Lali's father said, "I accepted whatever God gives."

A baby with two faces is very much rare but Lali was not the only baby with two faces. In 2011, another baby with two faces was born in Pakistan.

Words & Expressions

reincarnation 환생 local neighbor 동네 이웃 offer 제공하다 blessing 축복 earn 돈을 벌다 like other babies 다른 아기들처럼 perform a CT scan CT 촬영을 하다 for free 공짜로 very much rare 매우 희귀한, 굉장히 드문

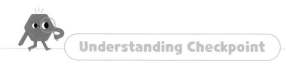

1. What is the main idea of the story?

    a. Lali's parents must be arrested for not paying Lali's hospital bill.

    b. God Ganesh, the God of Elephants, has two faces like Lali.

    c. A baby with two faces was worshipped since people believed she was a god.

    d. There was no other babies with two faces except Lali.

2. Lali was treated as the most special baby in her village because _____ .

    a. she could earn money unlike other babies

    b. her appearance was very unique

    c. she could have a free CT scan

    d. she really was a reincarnation of the God Ganesh

3. Choose the correct words for each sentence.

    a. How can I clean my house in <u>further than</u> / <u>fewer than</u> / <u>less than</u> one hour?

    b. His visit surprised me since his visits were <u>mere</u> / <u>rare</u> / <u>scare</u> occasions.

    c. Megan broke up with Bill <u>because</u> / <u>although</u> / <u>when</u> she though Bill wasn't the only pebble on the beach.

Answer **1.** c   **2.** b   **3.** less than | rare | because

Lali was born _____ March 11, 2008 in Northern India. When she was born, people believed she was _____ the god Ganesh, the Hindu god who is half person and half elephant. Not only local neighbors but also people around the world came to her little village to meet her. Many of them offered her parents money to _____ . This is very _____ them because her young parents _____ less than $2 a day, like many other neighbors in their village.

_____ this baby? Lali was born with two faces. She had one body and one head like other babies, but _____ other babies, she had two faces on one head. So she had four eyes, two noses, and two mouths. Her young parents didn't agreed to let the hospital perform a free CT scan or an MRI on her head. Lali's father said, "I accepted _____ God gives."

A baby with two faces is _____ but Lali was _____ with two faces. In 2011, another baby with two faces was born in Pakistan.

Did You Know Why Lali Was Worshipped As A Reincarnated God?

1 Lali was born on March 11, 2008 in Northern India.

be born on 월 일, 년도 (언제) 태어나다

2 When she was born, people believed she was a **reincarnation** of

···의 환생 reincarnate v. 환생하다, 다시 태어나다
(rebirth, be reborn, be born again)

(the god Ganesh), (the Hindu god who is half person and half elephant).

= 동격   ↑ 수식   인도의 여러 신들 중 하나이기 때문에 God가 아닌 소문자 god로 썼다
반은 사람, 반은 코끼리인 힌두의 신

3 (Not only local **neighbors** but also people around the world) came

not only A but also B : A 뿐 아니라 B도 (A와 B 모두)

주어 ( ) 동사 came
주어 came to her village to meet her.

to her little village to meet her.

4 Many of them **offered** (her parents) money to ask for her blessing.

offer ( ) money ( )에게 돈을 제공하다   ···를 구하다, 달라고 하다

5 This is very helpful for them because her young parents earned less than $2 a day,

help v. 돕다 helpful a. 도움이 되는   ..보다 적게 (적은 돈을) 벌다 (비교)
helpless a. 무력한, 속수무책의

like many other neighbors in their village.

···와 마찬가지로   마을의 다른 주민들처럼 other + 복수명사 neighbors

6 What was so special about this baby?

7 Lali was born with two faces.

be born with ···를 갖고 태어나다 He was born with a silver spoon in his mouth.
그는 입에 은수저를 물고 태어났다. (부잣집에서 태어났다.)

8 She had one body and one head (**like** other babies),

... 처럼 (다른 아기들처럼)

but (**unlike** other babies), she had two faces on one head.

...와는 달리 (다른 아기들과 달리)

9 So she had four eyes, two noses, and two mouths.

10 Her young parents didn't agreed to let the hospital **perform** a **free** (CT scan

let (사역동사) + 동사원형 : 시키다, ···하도록 하다   공짜 검사 두 가지 : CT scan, MRI
Let me do it. 내가 그것을 하게 해주십시오.   perform a CT scan / perform an MRI

or an MRI) on her head.

⑪ Lali's father said, "I accepted whatever God gives."

신이 주는 건 무엇이든 = anything that God gives

⑫ (A baby with two faces) is very much rare but Lali was not the only baby

수식

주어 ( ) faces가 아니라 baby (단수) + is　　　　　　드문, 희귀한　　　　유일한 …는 아니다 (다른 누군가/무언가 더 있다)

with two faces.

⑬ In 2011, (another baby with two faces) was born in Pakistan.

수식

주어 ( ) faces가 아니라 baby (단수) + was

⟨ 랄리가 왜 환생한 신으로 숭배 받았는지 아세요? ⟩

❶ 랄리는 2008년 3월 북부 인도에서 태어났습니다.

❷ 소녀가 태어났을 때 사람들이 랄리를 반은 인간, 반은 코끼리인 힌두신 가네쉬가 환생했다고 믿었습니다.

❸ 동네 사람들 뿐 아니라 전세계의 사람들이 랄리를 만나러 작은 마을로 왔습니다.

❹ 대부분의 사람들은 랄리의 축복을 받고자 부모에게 돈을 주었습니다.

❺ 그건 랄리의 부모에게 큰 도움이 되었는데, 이유인즉 랄리의 젊은 부모는 그 마을의 다른 이웃들처럼 하루에 2달러도 못 벌기 때문입니다.

❻ 이 아기의 무엇이 그렇게 특별했을까요?

❼ 랄리는 얼굴이 두 개로 태어났습니다.

❽ 랄리는 다른 아기들처럼 하나의 몸과 하나의 머리를 갖고 있지만, 다른 아기들과는 달리 하나의 머리에 얼굴이 두 개입니다.

❾ 그래서 눈이 네 개, 코가 두 개, 입도 두 개입니다.

❿ 랄리의 젊은 부모는 병원이 무료로 랄리의 뇌를 CT 스캔하거나 MRI를 찍어주겠다는 걸 거부했습니다.

⑪ 랄리의 아빠는 이렇게 말했습니다. "나는 신이 주신 건 무엇이든 그대로 받아들이겠습니다."

⑫ 두 얼굴을 가진 아기는 매우 희귀하지만 랄리만이 두 얼굴을 가진 아기는 아닙니다.

⑬ 2011년 파키스탄에서도 두 얼굴을 가진 아기가 태어났습니다.

Unfortunately, Billie Bob Harrell Jr., who held the only winning ticket to a Texas Lotto jackpot of $31 million in 1997, took his own life in 1999.

In 1997, Harrell and his family were having a hard time since Harrell was not good at earning money. So, he bought a lottery ticket, dreaming of hitting the jackpot. He did hit the jackpot, and it made him a millionaire. His hard times were officially over.

He was so rich that he bought many things, such as big houses, a ranch, and fancy cars. Also, he contributed a large sum of money. When somebody needed financial help, Harrell was there with cash. He just spent his time spending and lending money. However, his spending habits were getting more and more out of control. Family, friends, even strangers took advantage of him, while Harrell kind of enjoyed being used by them. Before long, his marriage began to crack and his bank account began to dry up.

Twenty months after hitting pay dirt, Harrell shot himself in his bedroom. After his death, his family members fought over the remaining money. But, there was not even enough money left to pay the taxes on his bank accounts.

Words & Expressions

winning ticket 당첨 복권 jackpot (도박, 복권) 거액의 상금 take one's own life 스스로 목숨을 끊다 have a hard time 어렵게 지내다 a lottery ticket 복권 hit the jackpot 대박을 터트리다 millionaire 백만장자 officially 공식적으로 ranch 농장 contribute 기부하다 cash 현금 lend 빌려주다 spending habit 소비습관 out of control 통제불능의 take advantage of ...를 이용/악용하다 crack 금이 가다 bank account 예금 계좌 hit pay dirt 노다지를 발견하다, 갑자기 큰 부자가 되다 shot oneself 스스로에게 총을 쏘다, 권총 자사를 하다 fight over ...를 두고 (가지려고) 싸우다 pay taxes 세금을 내다

Understanding Checkpoint

1. What can be the best title of this story?

    a. How To Win The Lottery & Change Your Life

    b. Billie Bob Harrell, The Good Samaritan

    c. The Tragic End Of The Lottery Winner

    d. 20 Tips For Becoming A Lottery Winner

2. According to the passage, which sentence is <u>wrong</u>?

    a. Billie Bob Harrell Jr. committed suicide two years after winning the lottery.

    b. Even strangers tried to take advantage of Billie even though he was poor.

    c. When Billie died, his money was almost gone.

    d. Thanks to the lottery ticket, Billie went from rags to riches.

3. Choose the correct words for each sentence.

    a. I am pretty good at solving others' problems but I am not so good <u>to solve</u> / <u>at solving</u> / <u>with solving</u> my own. Wonder why.

    b. I had to spend two whole hours <u>doing</u> / <u>to do</u> / <u>do</u> my homework.

    c. Two waiters were fired because they <u>fought over</u> / <u>struggled with</u> / <u>battled each other</u> some tips from customers.

Answer 1. c 2. b 3. at solving | doing | fought over

Listening Drill – Dictation

Unfortunately, Billie Bob Harrell Jr., who held the only winning ticket to a Texas Lotto jackpot of $31 million in 1997, _____ in 1999.

In 1997, Harrell and his family were having a hard time since Harrell _____ money. So, he bought a lottery ticket, dreaming of hitting the jackpot. He did _____, and it made him a millionaire. His hard times _____ .

He was so rich that he bought many things, such as big houses, a ranch, and fancy cars. Also, he _____ a large sum of money. When somebody needed financial help, Harrell was there with cash. He just spent his time spending and lending money. However, his spending habits were getting more and more out of control. Family, friends, even strangers _____ him, while Harrell kind of _____ them. Before long, his marriage began to crack and his bank account began to dry up.

Twenty months _____, Harrell shot himself in his bedroom. After his death, his family members _____ the remaining money. But, there was _____ to pay the taxes on his bank accounts.

179

Did You Know How Billie Bob Harrell, The Lottery Winner, Died?

① **Unfortunately**, Billie Bob Harrell Jr., (who held the only **winning** ticket to

= 동격   hold the (only) winning ticket to …의 (유일한) 당첨권을 쥐다

a Texas Lotto **jackpot** of $31 million in 1997), **took his own life** in 1999.

take one's own life = commit suicide 자살하다

② In 1997, (Harrell and his family) were **having a hard time**

과거 진행형 were having   have a hard time 어려움을 겪다

since Harrell was not good at earning money.

= because   be good at -ing …하는 걸 잘 하다 (be not good at -ing …하는 걸 못 하다)

③ So, he bought a lottery ticket, dreaming of hitting the jackpot.

…를 꿈꾸며   대박을 터트리다, 큰 상금을 타다
분사구문 while he was dreaming of (of + 명사, 동명사)

④ He did hit the jackpot, and it made him a **millionaire**.

동사 hit을 강조한 강조의 조동사   it(그가 대박을 터트린 것)은 그를 백만장자로 만들었다.
조동사에 인칭, 시제 등을 표현하므로 과거 did로 쓰였다. (강조의 do 동사 다음에는 항상 동사원형이 온다.)

⑤ His hard times were officially over.

힘든 시기, 가난한 시절   be officially over 공식적으로 끝나다 (over 끝난 The party was over. 파티는 끝났다.)

⑥ He was so rich that he bought many things, (such as big houses, a ranch,

so 형용사 that 너무 …해서 that 하다 : 너무 부자라서 많은 것들을 샀다

and **fancy** cars).

a. 멋진, 고급의 v. 원하다, (이성에게) 끌리다 n. 공상, 상상 fancy cars 고급 자동차들

⑦ Also, he **contributed** a large sum of money.

공헌/기여하다, 기부하다   거액의 = a hefty sum of

⑧ When somebody needed financial help, Harrell was there with cash.

경제적 도움   현금을 들고

⑨ He just spent his time [1] spending and [2] lending money.

spend (시간, 돈) 쓰다 (+ -ing) he spent his time [1] spending money and [2] lending money.
돈을 쓰고 돈을 빌려주는데 그의 시간을 보내다
lend 빌려주다 borrow 빌리다 - Please lend me some money. I want to borrow money from you.
나에게 돈을 빌려주세요. 나는 당신에게 돈을 빌리고 싶습니다.

⑩ However, his spending habits were getting (more and more) **out of control**.

과거진행 (be -ing) were getting (점점 더) get out of control 통제불능이 되다

⑪ (Family, friends, even strangers) took advantage of him,
take advantage of ( ) : ( )를 이용해먹다

while Harrell kind of enjoyed being used by them.
약간, 어느 정도   enjoy + ing (enjoy being) / 수동태 be pp (being used by)
그들에 의해 이용당하는 것을 좀 즐겼다

⑫ Before long, his marriage began to crack and his bank account began to dry up.
오래 지나지 않아서   금이 가다, 갈라지다   은행계좌, 예금계좌   말라버리다
(long before 오래 전에)

⑬ Twenty months after hitting pay dirt, Harrell shot himself in his bedroom.
after Harrell hit pay dirt (주절의 주어와 일치, 생략)   shoot oneself 자신에게 총을 쏘다
hit pay dirt 횡재하다, 대박나다   (shoot-shot-shot)

⑭ After his death, his family members fought over the remaining money.
fight over ( ) : ( )를 두고/서로 가지겠다고 싸우다
Fred and John fought over Jane, although Jane is not interested in either of them.
제인은 둘 중 아무에게도 관심이 없는데, 프레드와 존은 제인을 두고 싸웠다.

⑮ But, there was not even enough money left to pay the taxes on his bank accounts.
심지어 even 세금 낼 to pay the taxes 돈도 충분히 남지 않았다 not even enough money left

복권 당첨자 빌리 밥 하렐이 어떻게 사망했는지 아세요?

❶ 불행히도 1997년 3천1백만 달러가 걸린 텍사스 로또의 유일한 당첨 복권을 소유했던 빌리 밥 하렐 주니어는 1999년 자살했습니다.

❷ 1997년, 하렐이 돈을 잘 벌지 못해 하렐과 그의 가족은 힘들게 생활했습니다.

❸ 그래서 그는 대박의 꿈을 안고 복권을 구매했습니다.   ❹ 그는 정말 대박을 터트렸고 덕분에 백만장자가 되었습니다.

❺ 그의 힘든 시절은 공식적으로 끝난 것입니다.

❻ 그는 너무 부자라 큰 집들, 농장, 멋진 자동차 등 많은 것을 사들였습니다.

❼ 그리고 상당한 돈을 기부했습니다.   ❽ 경제적인 도움이 필요한 사람에게는 현금을 든 하렐이 있었습니다.

❾ 그는 돈을 쓰고 빌려주는데 시간을 보냈습니다.   ❿ 그러다 그의 소비 습관은 점점 통제불능이 되어갔습니다.

⑪ 가족, 친구, 심지어 모르는 사람들도 그를 이용했고, 하릴은 이들에게 이용당하는 걸 좀 즐기기도 했습니다.

⑫ 얼마 지나지 않아 그의 결혼 생활에 금이 가기 시작했고 그의 통장도 마르기 시작했습니다.

⑬ 대박을 터트린 지 20개월 후, 하렐은 자기 침실에서 권총으로 자살했습니다.

⑭ 그가 사망한 후 그의 가족들은 남은 그의 돈을 두고 싸웠습니다.

⑮ 하지만 그의 통장에 남은 돈은 세금 내기에도 부족했습니다.

Chapter 05

Animals & Nature

MP3

41 Did You Know **Not All Spiders Make Webs?**

Spiders are not insects. Unlike insects, spiders have two body parts, no antennae, no wings, and four pairs of legs. Insects have three body parts, 2 antennae, wings and three pairs of legs. Other arachnids, such as scorpions and ticks, have eight legs like spiders.

Not all spiders make webs. Only about half of all spiders use webs to catch prey. Certain spiders, like wolf spiders and crab spiders, just wait and pounce on prey from a close distance. Some spiders make webs, but their webs are not for hunting. Jumping spiders use webs to make resting places, and wolf spiders make egg sacs with their silk.

Maybe some of you watched the movie 'Charlotte's Web', and learned that spiders suck the juices, or we can say 'liquefied meat', from their prey rather than eating or crunching them. Some spider species do fill their stomach by sucking, but some species actually eat their prey by chewing with the jaws.

Words & Expressions

insect 곤충 antennae 더듬이(antenna의 복수형) arachnid 거미류 scorpion 전갈 tick 진드기 web 거미
줄 prey 먹이 pounce (공격하며) 덮치다 (on) at a close distance 가까운 거리에서 sac (동식물 체내의) 주머
니 egg sac 알주머니 suck 빨다 liquefied 액화된 crunch 와그작 씹다 species 종 fill one's stomach 위장
을 채우다 chew 씹다 jaw 턱

Understanding Checkpoint

1. What can be the best title of this story?

    a. Facts About Spiders You May Misunderstand

    b. Differences Between Spiders And Arachnids

    c. Charlotte's Web : The Must Watch Movie

    d. How To Make Liquefied Meat

2. Jumping spiders and wolf spiders _____ .

    a. use their webs to catch prey

    b. don't use webs at all

    c. don't use their webs when catching prey

    d. have three pairs of wings and no antennae

3. Choose the correct words for each sentence.

    a. At the crime scene, the police found human bones along with <u>two pair of glasses</u> / <u>two pairs of glasses</u> / <u>two glasses</u> and a watch.

    b. You can <u>behold</u> / <u>watch</u> / <u>look</u> some free movies online.

    c. This information about tax exemption is not <u>to</u> / <u>for</u> / <u>with</u> tax collectors but for tax payers.

Answer **1.** a **2.** c **3.** two pairs of glasses ∣ watch ∣ for

Listening Drill – Dictation

Spiders are not insects. Unlike insects, spiders have two body parts, no _____ , no wings, and _____ legs. Insects have three body parts, 2 antennae, wings and three pairs of legs. Other _____ , such as scorpions and ticks, have eight legs like spiders.

Not all spiders make webs. Only _____ all spiders use webs to catch prey. Certain spiders, like wolf spiders and crab spiders, just wait and pounce on prey from a close distance. Some spiders make webs, but their webs are not for hunting. Jumping spiders use webs to _____ , and wolf spiders _____ with their silk.

Maybe some of you watched the movie 'Charlotte's Web', and learned that spiders suck the juices, or we can say '_____ meat', from their prey _____ eating or crunching them. Some spider species do _____ by sucking, but some species actually eat their prey by _____ .

185

Did You Know Not All Spiders Make Webs?

1 Spiders are not **insects**.

insect 곤충 bug 벌레 worm (땅속) 벌레, 유충(larva)

2 Unlike insects, spiders have ¹⁾ two body parts, ²⁾ no antennae, ³⁾ no wings,

곤충들과 달리   spiders have no antennae or wings   더듬이 antenna (단수) antennae(복수)
= spiders don't have any antennae or wings   유충 larva (단수) larvae (복수)

and ⁴⁾ four pairs of legs.

pair = 2   a pair of = 2, four pairs of = 8
(a pair는 2의 의미지만 단수(pair)로 취급하고 two pairs of.. 이상은 복수(pairs)로 취급해서 복수 동사가 온다.)

3 Insects have three body parts, 2 antennae, wings and three pairs of legs.

three 3 X pair 2 = 6

4 Other arachnids, (such as **scorpions** and **ticks**), have eight legs like spiders.

거미류 other + 복수형 arachnids   전갈   진드기   four pairs of legs

5 Not all spiders make **webs**.

부분 부정 - 모든 거미들이 ..한 건 아니다   web 거미줄

6 (Only about half of all spiders) use webs to catch **prey**.

모든 거미들 all spiders 중 단지 only 약 about 반 half 정도 about   prey n. 먹이 (predator 포식자)

7 Certain spiders, (like wolf spiders and crab spiders), just ¹⁾ wait and

= 동격   어떤 거미들의 예 ( )

²⁾ pounce on prey from a close distance.

…에 (on) 달려들다   가까운 거리에서   close v. 닫다 a. 가까운

8 Some spiders make webs, but their webs are not for hunting.

사냥을 위함이 아닌 (not for playing 놀이를 위함이 아닌)

9 Jumping spiders use webs to make **resting** places,

쉴 곳을 만들다

and wolf spiders make egg sacs with their silk.

알주머니를 만들다   sac (동식물의 체내) 주머니, sack 부대, 자루, 봉지), sag 가운데가 처지다, 약해지다

10 Maybe some of you ¹⁾ watched the movie 'Charlotte's Web', and

영화, TV 등을 시청/감상하다 - watch, see (look, behold 등은 쓰지 않는다)
look at the screen 화면을 보다, watch a movie 영화를 감상하다
view a documentary 다큐를 시청하다 (오락, 감상의 의미가 약함)

²⁾ learned that spiders **suck** the juices, (or we can say '**liquefied** meat'),

suck v. 빨다, 엉망이다

= 동격

or we can say 또는 …하고도 할 수 있다
liquefy v. 액화되다 liquid n. 액체 liquidity n. 유동성, 환금성 liquor 독한 술
LPG liquefied petroleum gas 액화 석유 가스

from their prey rather than eating or crunching them.

instead of(대신에) 의미의 전치사라서 동명사(-ing)가 왔다.

⑪ Some spider **species** do fill their **stomach** by sucking, but

종   동사 fill을 강조하는 강조 조동사 do   빨아서
            fill stomach 위장을 채우다

some species actually eat their prey by chewing with the jaws.

species, series, means, corps – 단수/복수 형태 동일   씹어서

(모든 거미가 거미줄을 만드는 건 아니라는 사실 아세요?)

❶ 거미는 곤충이 아닙니다.

❷ 다른 곤충들과는 달리 거미는 몸이 두 부분이고, 더듬이와 날개가 없고 다리는 네 쌍입니다.

❸ 곤충은 몸이 세 부분이고 2개의 더듬이, 날개, 다리는 세 쌍입니다.

❹ 전갈, 틱과 같은 다른 거미류 역시 거미처럼 8개의 다리를 갖고 있습니다.

❺ 그리고 모든 거미가 거미줄을 만드는 건 아닙니다.

❻ 모든 거미 중 반 정도는 거미줄로 먹이를 잡습니다.

❼ 늑대 거미나 게 거미 같은 거미들은 그냥 기다렸다 가까운 거리에서 먹이에게 달려듭니다.

❽ 어떤 거미는 거미줄을 만들긴 하지만 사냥을 위한 건 아닙니다.

❾ 깡충거미는 쉴 곳을 만들기 위해 거미줄을 사용하고, 늑대 거미는 거미줄로 알주머니를 만듭니다.

❿ 여러분 중 어떤 분들은 '샬롯의 거미줄' 영화를 보고 거미가 먹이를 먹거나 씹는 게 아니라 주스, 또는 '물처럼 만든 고기'를 빨아 먹는다는 사실을 배웠을 겁니다.

⑪ 어떤 거미 종류는 빨아서 배를 채우지만, 어떤 종류는 실제 턱으로 씹어서 먹이를 먹기도 합니다.

No one can survive without breathing, and we need oxygen to breathe. It is said the human population hit 8 billion in 2024. That means the amount of oxygen we need is beyond your imagination.

Then, where does our oxygen come from? Oxygen is produced through photosynthesis in green plants, such as trees and flowers. South America's Amazon rain forest, a.k.a "the lungs of the world", is allegedly the single largest oxygen generator in the world. Some say it is providing more than 20% of the Earth's total oxygen.

But some disbelieve this, saying less than 10% of the world's oxygen is from the Amazon rain forest, and that the rest of it comes from the ocean. In fact, the ocean plants, such as algae and plankton, generate an enormous amount of oxygen through photosynthesis. The exact amount is under debate, but some scientists claim that at least 50% of the world's atmospheric oxygen comes from the ocean.

For now, nobody knows whether the ocean produces more oxygen than the Amazon or not. But, one thing is for sure about oxygen. If we do not protect green plants on land and in the ocean, 8 billion human beings cannot survive.

Words & Expressions

breathe 호흡하다, 숨 쉬다   oxygen 산소   human population 인구   beyond one's imagination ...의 상상을 초월하는   photosynthesis 광합성   be against ...에 반하다, 반대하다   algae 조류   plankton 플랑크톤   generate 생산하다   be under debate 논란의 여지가 있다   atmospheric 대기의

Understanding Checkpoint

1. What is the main idea of the story?

    a. We have to protect the Amazon rain forest because it is the main source of the earth's oxygen.

    b. Some claim the ocean is the largest oxygen generator, but it's unclear that the ocean generates more oxygen than the Amazon.

    c. All scientists agree that the single largest oxygen generator is the ocean.

    d. We have to calculate the exact amount of oxygen produced by algae.

2. According to the passage, which sentence is right?

    a. We cannot survive without Amazon rain forest since it's the lungs of the world.

    b. Oxygen comes only from the ocean, that's why we have to protect the ocean.

    c. Scientists found out the exact amount of oxygen produced by the ocean.

    d. Green plants on land are not the only oxygen generator.

3. Choose the correct words for each sentence.

    a. I hope this meeting can <u>provide us</u> / <u>provide</u> / <u>provide with</u> an opportunity to talk about our problem.

    b. Take a deep <u>breathe</u> / <u>breath</u> / <u>breathing</u> when you get nervous. That will help you relax.

    c. Becoming rich <u>over</u> / <u>beyond</u> / <u>with</u> your wildest dream does not make you happy.

Answer **1.** b **2.** d **3.** provide ǀ breath ǀ beyond

Listening Drill – Dictation

No one can survive _____, and we need oxygen to breathe. It is said the human population _____ in 2024. That means the amount of oxygen we need is _____.

Then, where does our oxygen come from? Oxygen is produced through _____ in green plants, such as trees and flowers. South America's Amazon rain forest, a.k.a "the lungs of the world", is allegedly _____ oxygen generator in the world. Some say it is providing more than 20% of the Earth's total oxygen.

But some disbelieve this, saying less than 10% of the world's oxygen is from the Amazon rain forest, and that _____ comes from the ocean. In fact, the ocean plants, such as algae and plankton, generate an enormous amount of oxygen through photosynthesis. The exact amount _____, but some scientists claim that at least 50% of the world's _____ comes from the ocean.

For now, nobody knows _____ the ocean produces more oxygen than the Amazon or not. But, one thing _____ oxygen. If we do not protect green plants on land and in the ocean, 8 billion human beings cannot survive.

Did You Know Where Oxygen Comes From?

① No one can **survive** without breathing, and we need **oxygen** to breathe.

이중부정 – 숨을 안 쉬고 살아남을 수 있는 사람은 없다   산소   breath n. 숨, 호흡 breathe v. 숨을 쉬다
= 숨을 쉬어야 산다   cloth n. 옷(감) clothe v. 옷을 입히다
bath n. 목욕 bathe v. 목욕하다

② It is said the human **population** hit 8 billion in 2024.

…라고 한다   n. 인구, 주민수   도달하다 (hit 8 billion 80억이 되다 hit 40 40살이 되다)

③ That means (the amount of oxygen we need) is beyond your imagination.

앞 문장(인구가 80억)의 의미는 ( ) the amount + is   상상을 초월하는 (unimaginable)
beyond the wildest dream 꿈꾸거나 원하던 것보다 더 좋은

④ Then, where does (our oxygen) **come from**?

주어 our oxygen이 3인칭 단수현재 + does (의문문이라 주어와 동사 도치)
의문사 where 동사does + 주어   come from …에서 나오다

⑤ Oxygen is produced through **photosynthesis** in green plants, (such as trees

…를 통해 생산되다 (수동)   광합성   녹색 식물의 예 ( )

and flowers).

⑥ (South America's Amazon **rain forest**), (a.k.a "the lungs of the world"), is **allegedly**

열대우림   = 동격   알려진 /전해지는 바에 의하면
a.k.a. also known as …라고도 알려진

the single largest oxygen **generator** in the world.

유일한 + 가장 큰 (최상급)   generate v. 만들다, 발생시키다 generation n. 발생, 세대 generator n. 발전기
the second tallest 두 번째로 가장 큰

⑦ Some say it is providing (more than 20% of the Earth's total oxygen).

= the Amazon rain forest   지구 전체 산소 total oxygen의 20% 이상 more than

⑧ But some disbelieve this, saying (less than 10% of the world's oxygen) is from

= some disbelieve this and they say that   지구 산소의 10% 미만less than   be from …에서 나오다

the Amazon rain forest, and that the rest of it comes from the ocean.

아마존에서 나오는 10% 미만의 산소를 제외한 나머지 산소

⑨ In fact, the ocean plants, (such as **algae** and plankton),

ocean plants의 예 ( )   조류, 해조 (algebra 대수학-혼동 주의)

generate an **enormous** amount of oxygen through photosynthesis.

v. 생산하다   엄청난 양의 산소 (= a large amount of)   광합성을 통해
enormous 엄청난 (= huge, gigantic, humongous)

⑩ The exact amount is under debate, but some scientists claim that
　　　　　　　　　　　논쟁의 여지가 있다 (확실히 모른다)

(at least 50% of the world's **atmospheric** oxygen) comes from the ocean.
최소한at least 전세계 대기 속 산소의 50% (3인칭 단수 현재) + comes
　　　　　　　　　　　　　atmosphere n. (지구) 대기 atmospheric a. 대기의

⑪ For now, nobody knows whether (the ocean produces more oxygen than
현재(지금)로는, 당장은　　　　( )인지 아닌지 whether or not 아무도 모른다 nobody knows
　　　　　　　　　　　　whether (the ocean <u>produces</u> more oxygen than the Amazon <u>does</u>) or not

the Amazon) or not.

⑫ But, one thing is for sure about oxygen.
　　　　　　　　한 가지는 확실하다

⑬ If we do not protect green plants on land and in the ocean,
가정법 현재 if 주어 동사현재형, 주어 may, can… 동사원형　　　　green plants on land and (green plants) in the ocean

8 billion human beings cannot survive.
　　　　　　　　　　　　survive v. 살아남다, 생존하다 survival n. 생존

산소가 어디에서 나오는지 아세요?

❶ 숨을 쉬지 않고 살 수 있는 사람은 없기 때문에 우리는 숨을 쉴 산소가 필요합니다.

❷ 2024년에 인구가 80억 명에 도달했다고 합니다.　　　❸ 이 말은 우리가 필요로 하는 산소의 양이 상상을 초월한다는 뜻입니다.

❹ 그럼 산소는 어디에서 오는 것일까요?　　　❺ 산소는 나무나 꽃 같은 녹색 식물의 광합성을 통해 생산됩니다.

❻ "지구의 폐"라고도 알려진 남아메리카 아마존 열대 우림은 전 세계의 단일 최대 산소 발전소라고 합니다.

❼ 어떤 이들은 이곳에서 지구의 전체 산소 중 20% 이상을 제공한다고 말합니다.

❽ 하지만 어떤 이들은 이를 믿지 않고, 세계 산소량의 10% 미만이 아마존 열대 우림에서 나오고 나머지는 바다에서 나온다고 말합니다.

❾ 실제로 조류와 플랑크톤 같은 해양 식물이 광합성을 통해 엄청난 양의 산소를 생산합니다.

❿ 정확한 양은 논란의 여지가 있지만, 일부 과학자들은 전 세계 대기권 산소의 최소 50%가 바다에서 나온다고 주장합니다.

⑪ 현재 바다에서 아마존보다 더 많은 산소를 생산하는지 여부는 아무도 모릅니다.

⑫ 하지만 산소에 관해 확실한 것이 하나 있습니다.

⑬ 만약 우리가 육지와 바다의 녹색 식물을 보호하지 않으면 80억 인구는 생존할 수 없다는 것입니다.

43 Did You Know Cockroaches Kept As Pets?

Usually, cockroaches avoid people. They wander around the house at night to find something to eat. If they are caught by people, they will surely get sprayed with deadly poison. Quite a few people are willing to open their wallets to get rid of them in their houses.

But, a certain type of cockroach is kept and raised in the house as a pet. Unlike other kinds of cockroaches, this kind is able to make a hissing sound and doesn't have any wings. This big herbivore doesn't bite the hand that feeds it, since it is far from being aggressive, although its size is pretty big for an insect, reaching about 3 inches. That's why some people want to keep it as a pet.

It is the Madagascar hissing cockroach, also simply called 'Hisser'. Mostly they eat fruits and vegetables, and can live up to 5 years if well cared for. If you want to keep them as pets and you live in Florida, you will need to get a permit from the state. In the US, several states require permits to keep them as pets.

Words & Expressions

cockroach 바퀴벌레 avoid 피하다 wander 배회하다, 돌아다니다 deadly 치명적인 open one's wallet 지갑을 열다 get rid of 제거하다 make a hissing sound 쉭쉭 소리를 내다 herbivore 초식동물 don't bite the hand that feeds you 너에게 먹이를 주는 손을 물지 마라 (속담) aggressive 공격적인 if well cared for 잘 관리 받으면 get permits 허가를 받다

192

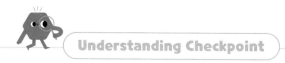

1. What is the main idea of the story?

    a. We have to eliminate cockroaches at all costs.

    b. Don't forget to get permits if you want to keep cockroaches as pets.

    c. The Madagascar hissing cockroach is the best pet.

    d. A certain kind of cockroach is being loved by people as a pet.

2. Hisser can be a good pet because _____ .

    a. people can catch it easily

    b. it is mild and gentle

    c. it carries all kinds of germs

    d. it looks like a hissing snake

3. Choose the correct words for each sentence.

    a. I'm glad every student <u>want to</u> / <u>is willing to</u> / <u>giving</u> chip in for charity.

    b. My boy is too small <u>as</u> / <u>for</u> / <u>to</u> his age but he acts like an adult.

    c. I am not able <u>for attending</u> / <u>to attend</u> / <u>of attendant</u> the meeting since something more important came up this morning.

Answer **1.** d **2.** b **3.** is willing to | for | to attend

Usually, cockroaches avoid people. They wander around the house   to find something to eat. If they are caught by people, they will surely   with deadly poison.   are willing to open their wallets to get rid of them in their houses.

But, a certain type of cockroach   in the house as a pet. Unlike other kinds of cockroaches, this kind is able to make a hissing sound and doesn't have any wings. This big   doesn't bite the hand that feeds it, since it is far from being aggressive, although its size is   , reaching about 3 inches. That's why some people want to keep it as a pet.

It is the Madagascar hissing cockroach,   'Hisser'. Mostly they eat fruits and vegetables, and can   5 years   . If you want to keep them as pets and you live in Florida, you will need to   from the state. In the US, several states require permits to keep them as pets.

193

Did You Know Cockroaches Kept As Pets?

1 Usually, **cockroaches avoid** people.

ch로 끝나는 단어의 복수 +es – cockroaches, churches, peaches
avoid v. 피하다

2 They wander around the house at night to find something to eat.

(정처없이) 돌아다니다

밤에 at night, 새벽에 at dawn, 정오에 at noon, 자정에 at midnight
아침에 in the morning, 오후에 in the afternoon, 저녁에 in the evening

3 If they are caught by people, they will surely get sprayed with **deadly** poison.

be + pp 수동 : 잡히다   get + pp 수동 : 스프레이로 뿌려지다
가정법 현재 if 주어 동사 현재형 are, 주어 will 동사 원형   deadly a. 치명적인

4 Quite a few people **are willing to** open their wallets to **get rid of** them

= many + 복수명사(people)   기꺼이 ...하다   = remove
                    제거하기 위해 to get rid of 지갑 열기를 to open wallets 마다하지 않다 be willing to

in their houses.

5 But, (a certain type of cockroach) is ¹⁾ kept and ²⁾ raised in the house as a **pet**.

주어( ) type 단수 + is   is kept (붙잡아 보관되어 지고) and (is) raised (길러지다) – 수동   반려동물
바퀴벌레의 특정 종류

6 Unlike other kinds of cockroaches, this kind ¹⁾ is able to make a hissing sound

이 종류 (이 종류의 바퀴벌레) this kind is able to make… and doesn't have

and ²⁾ doesn't have any wings.

= have no wings 날개가 없다

7 This big **herbivore** doesn't bite the hand that feeds it,

초식동물   Don't bite the hand that feeds you. 너에게 먹을 것을 주는 손을 물지 마라 (속담)
              속담을 인용해서 주인을 공격하지 않는다는 뜻으로 사용

since it is far from being **aggressive**, although its size is pretty big for an insect,

be far from –ing (동명사)   a. 공격적인   …치고 for 꽤 pretty 큰 big
…와는 거리가 멀다, 전혀 …아니다

reaching about 3 inches.

its size reaches about 3 inches (주어 its size가 일치해서 생략)
reach (크기, 거리) …에 달하다, 미치다

8 That's why some people want to keep it as a pet.

That's why 주어+동사 : 이것이 …인 이유인 것이다.

9 It is the Madagascar hissing cockroach, also simply called 'Hisser'.

also (it is) simply called 이것은 또한 …로 불리다 (수동)

⑩ Mostly they ¹⁾ eat (fruits and vegetables), and ²⁾ can live up to 5 years
　　　　　　　　　　　　　　　　　　　　　　　　　　(최대 5년) 까지 살다

　　if well **cared for**.
　　잘 보살핌을 받으면 = if they are well cared for (주어 일치 생략)
　　　　　　care for 돌보다 care about 관심을 갖다, 좋아하다

⑪ If ¹⁾ you want to keep them as pets and ²⁾ you live in Florida,
　　🔁 가정법 현재 if ¹⁾ you want to … and ²⁾ you live …, you will need

　　you will need to get a permit from the state.
　　　　　　　　　　　　허가증을 받다

⑫ In the US, several states require permits to keep them as pets.
　　　　　　　　　　　허가증을 요구하다, 허가증을 받으라고 요구하다

애완동물로 길러지는 바퀴벌레를 아세요?

❶ 일반적으로 바퀴벌레들은 사람들을 피합니다.

❷ 먹을 것을 찾아 밤에 집 안을 돌아다니지요.

❸ 만약 사람들에게 걸리면 치명적인 독 스프레이 세례를 받을 게 확실합니다.

❹ 상당히 많은 사람들이 집 안의 바퀴벌레를 없애기 위해 기꺼이 지갑을 엽니다.

❺ 하지만 어떤 종류의 바퀴벌레는 애완동물로 집 안에서 길러집니다.

❻ 다른 종류의 바퀴벌레들과는 달리, 이 종류는 쉭쉭 소리를 낼 수 있고 날개가 없습니다.

❼ 큰 초식동물인 이 바퀴는 약 3인치 정도로 벌레 치고 크기가 큰 편이지만 공격적이지 않아서 먹이 주는 사람의 손을 물지 않습니다.

❽ 그래서 어떤 사람들은 이 바퀴벌레를 애완동물로 키우길 원합니다.

❾ 이는 마다가스카르 히싱 바퀴벌레로, 간단히 '히서'라고도 불립니다.

⑩ 대부분 과일과 야채를 먹고, 잘 돌보아 주면 5년까지 살 수 있습니다.

⑪ 당신이 이 바퀴벌레를 애완동물로 키우고 싶은데 플로리다에 살고 있다면, 주(state)의 허가를 받아야 할 것입니다.

⑫ 미국에서 몇몇 주가 이들을 애완동물로 키우려면 허가를 받도록 요구하고 있습니다.

The thorough preparation and training are not enough to climb the Himalayas. You also have to grab your wallet if you don't want to just return home without having done anything. It is called 'peak royalty.' It differs depending on peaks. If you plan to climb peaks up to 6,500m, you must pay US $500. If you intend to go for peaks between 6501m-7000m, you will be charged US $2,000. Peaks above 7,001m cost you US $3,000. If you want to try to climb peaks in restricted areas, you have to go through the severest and harshest training, as well as withdraw US $4,000 from your bank account. Thankfully, these peak royalties are charged per group of 12 people. Don't say "phew" too soon, because there are other expenses. US $400 will be charged as the environmental levy for each expedition, and US $500 will be charged for the Liaison Officers' equipment.

Even after going through the training and putting some money in your pocket, you have to do something else to climb the Himalayas, especially the Mt. Everest. You must get a permit from the Nepalese government and submit an application along with a recommendation from the concerned government or mountaineering association.

Understanding Checkpoint

1. What is the main idea of the story?

    a. All you need to climb the Himalayas is to get a permit from the government.

    b. $4,000 is enough to pay all expenses to climb the Himalayas.

    c. It costs a lot to climb the Himalayas.

    d. Paying peak royalties is absurd and unfair.

2. According to the passage, which sentence is <u>wrong</u>?

    a. Climbing the Himalayas is not as simple as it sounds.

    b. Peak royalties differ depending only on the size of expedition teams.

    c. Before trying to climb the Himalayas, you have to prepare some documents.

    d. People who want to climb peaks above 7,001m have to pay roughly US $4,000.

3. Choose the correct words for each sentence.

    a. I have never received a <u>through</u> / <u>thorough</u> / <u>thoroughly</u> evaluation on this matter.

    b. . You will <u>charge</u> / <u>be charged</u> / <u>charging</u> $500 or more per pair.

    c. That's <u>good</u> / <u>enough</u> / <u>all</u>. We don't have enough time to do this. Please stop whining.

Answer **1.** c **2.** b **3.** thorough ｜ be charged ｜ enough

Listening Drill – Dictation

    and training are not enough to climb the Himalayas. You also have to grab your wallet if you don't want to just return home . It is called 'peak royalty.' depending on peaks. If you plan to climb peaks up to 6,500m, you must pay US $500. If you peaks between 6501m-7000m, you will be charged US $2,000. Peaks above 7,001m cost you US $3,000. If you want to try to climb peaks in restricted areas, you have to go through the severest and harshest training, withdraw US $4,000 from your bank account. Thankfully, these peak royalties are 12 people. Don't say "phew" too soon, because . US $400 will be charged as the for each expedition, and US $500 will be charged for the Liaison Officers' equipment.

Even after going through the training and putting some money in your pocket, you have to do something else to climb the Himalayas, especially the Mt. Everest. You must get a permit from the Nepalese government and along with a recommendation from the or mountaineering association.

Did You Know You Have To Pay Fee Before Climbing The Himalayas?

1 (The thorough preparation and training) are not enough to climb the Himalayas.
철저한 (through와 혼동 주의)   to…하기에 충분하지 않다

2 You also have to grab your **wallet** if you don't want to just return home
지갑 챙기다, 돈을 준비하다   don't … without 이중 부정 = 긍정 (아무것도 이루지 않은 채 돌아오고 싶다면 – 무언가 이루고 돌아오고 싶다면)
wallet 지갑 (신용카드, 약간의 현금) purse 지갑 (wallet 보다 큰) pouch (지갑 보다는) 작은 가방

without having done anything.
아무것도 한 게 없는 상태로

3 It is called 'peak royalty.'
peak 정상 + royalty 사용료

4 It differs **depending on** peaks.
…에 따라 depdending on 다르다 differ
differ v. 다르다 different a. 다른 difference n. 다름

5 If you plan to climb peaks up to 6,500m, you must pay US $500.
(최대) …까지

6 If you **intend to** go for peaks between 6501m-7000m, you will be **charged** US $2,000.
시도하다   요금이 부과되다 (수동)   charge 1. (요금, 값) 청구하다
2. 기소,고소하다 3. 비난하다 4. 공격하다 5. (임무, 책임) 맡기다 5. (배터리) 충전하다 6. (총알) 장전하다

7 (Peaks above 7,001m) cost you US $3,000.
주어 peaks (복수) + cost : (돈이) 얼마 든다 It costs you 돈 : 이것 it 때문에 네가 얼마의 돈을 지불하다

8 If you want to try to climb peaks in **restricted** areas,
제한구역 (아무나 못 들어가는 통제 구역)

you have to go through (the **severest** and **harshest**) training,
go through training 훈련을 통과하다(마치다)   harsh 혹독한 the harshest 가장 혹독한
severe 심한 the severest 가장 심한

as well as withdraw US $4,000 from your bank **account.**
뿐만 아니라   withdraw 돈 from bank account 통장에서 돈을 인출하다   은행계좌
withdraw 물러나다, 철수하다, (돈) 인출하다 withdrawal 철수, 인출

9 Thankfully, these peak royalties are charged per group of 12 people.
고맙게도, 다행히   그룹 하나 당 요금이 부과되다   per group of 12 people 12명 한 그룹 당
per capita 1인당 per unit 한 개당

10 Don't say "phew" too soon, because there are other **expenses.**
휴 (안도의 숨을 내쉴 때 소리)   어떤 일에 드는 비용 (other + 복수형)

⑪ US $400 will be **charged** as the environmental **levy** for each **expedition**,

charge 돈(값)을 청구하다 environmental 환경의 + levy (세금) 추가 부담금 = 환경부담금

for each expedition 각 원정마다, 원정 갈 때마다 (each)

and US $500 will be charged for the Liaison Officers' equipment.

liaison officer 연락 담당관 (liaison office 연락 사무소)

⑫ Even after [1] **going through** the training and [2] putting (some money) in your pocket,

주절의 주어 you 일치, 생략   go through 통과하다   put ( ) in one's pocket ( )를 주머니에 챙기다

Even after you go … and put

you have to do something else to climb the Himalayas, especially the Mt. Everest.

다른 무언가를 하다

⑬ You must [1] get a permit from the Nepalese government and [2] submit an **application**

…로부터 허가를 얻다   신청서를 제출하다

발급 받아야 할 것 a permit from the Nepalese government 허가증

along with a **recommendation** from the **concerned** (government or

…와 함께, 더불어   추천서   관련된, 담당의

(여러 국가가 히말라야 산맥과 관련되어 있으므로 가려는 산맥을 담당하는 국가의 정부 또는 산악 협회의 추천서 필요)

제출해야 할 것 an application, a recommendation 신청서, 추천서

mountaineering **association**).

협회

히말라야에 등반하기 전에 돈을 내야 한다는 거 아세요?

❶ 히말라야에 등반하는데 철저한 준비와 훈련만으로는 부족합니다.

❷ 아무것도 하지 않고 그냥 집으로 돌아오고 싶지 않다면 지갑을 챙겨야 합니다.

❸ 이를 '정상 로열티'라고 부릅니다.   ❹ 이는 정상이 어디냐에 따라 다릅니다.

❺ 만약 6,500미터 이하의 정상을 오를 계획이라면, 미국 달러로 500달러를 내야 합니다.

❻ 6,501미터에서 7,000미터 사이의 정상에 도전할 생각이라면, 2,000달러를 내야 합니다.

❼ 7,001미터 이상의 정상일 경우 3,000달러를 내야 합니다.

❽ 만약 제한 구역 내의 정상에 오르고자 시도하고 싶다면, 가장 혹독하고 어려운 훈련을 거쳐야 하고 통장에서 4,000달러도 인출해야 합니다.

❾ 다행스러운 건, 이 로열티는 12명으로 이루어진 한 그룹 당 내는 돈입니다.

❿ 다른 추가 비용도 있으니까 너무 빨리 '휴-'하지 마십시오(안도의 한숨을 쉬지 마십시오).

⑪ 매번 원정 때마다 환경 부담금 400달러, 연락 담당관 장비 비용 500달러도 내야 합니다.

⑫ 훈련도 하고 주머니에 돈도 챙겨 넣은 이후에도 히말라야, 특히 에베레스트 산을 오르려면 해야 할 일이 더 있습니다.

⑬ 네팔 정부로 부터 허가를 받아야 하고, 지원서와 함께 당국 정부의 추천서 혹은 등반협회의 추천서를 제출해야 합니다.

Did You Know Bats' Droppings Are Valuable To Humans?

Bats' droppings are so valuable that we do not call them just 'excrement' or 'dung', but give them the name of 'guano.' What's so special about their droppings? They are nutrient-rich droppings, which means humans use them as good fertilizers. Guano commonly refers to the excrement of bats. But, more exactly speaking, guano is the feces of bats, seals, and sea birds such as pelicans. Guano fertilizer has been popular due to its high levels of phosphorus and nitrogen. In addition, compared to other kinds of droppings, the odor of guano isn't so bad. So, many farmers prefer guano fertilizer to chemical fertilizers.

In spite of that, some critics say it's not a good thing to take bat guano from caves. When people collect bat guano, they disturb bats' habitat and make them anxious and uneasy. It is said that some bats often drop their babies because of anxiety.

Words & Expressions

valuable 가치 있는 excrement 배설물 dung 똥 guano 구아노 (박쥐, 바다새의 배설물) dropping 배설물
nutrient-rich 양분이 풍부한 fertilizer 비료 be commonly referred to as 일반적으로 ...로 불리다 cave
동굴 feces 배설물 phosphorus 인 nitrogen 질소 odor 냄새 chemical fertilizer 화학비료 critic 비판하
는 사람

Understanding Checkpoint

1. What can be the best title of this story?

    a. Don't Waste Wastes From Bats

    b. Which Is Worse : Bats' Droppings? Or Seals' Droppings?

    c. Bats Drop Not Droppings But Babies

    d. The Way To Find Good Fertilizers

2. The odor of guano is _____ compared to other kinds of droppings.

    a. too good to go by

    b. not so bad

    c. obnoxious

    d. like a fragrant flower

3. Choose the correct words for each sentence.

    a. When he asked me to sit down, I said I <u>preferred to be</u> / <u>prefer to</u> / <u>preferring</u> stand.

    b. Sorry but I don't know what exactly you are <u>referring</u> / <u>referring to</u> / <u>reffered</u>.

    c. Don't forget to collect fertilized eggs from the hen house and to buy some <u>fertilize</u> / <u>fertilizers</u> / <u>fertilizing</u>. I need to fertilize the garden.

<u>**Answer**</u> **1.** a **2.** b **3.** prefer to ⏐ referring to ⏐ fertilizers

Listening Drill – Dictation

Bats' droppings are _____ we do not call them just 'excrement' or 'dung', but give them the name of 'guano.' What's so special about their droppings? They are _____ droppings, which means humans use them as _____ . Guano _____ the excrement of bats. But, more exactly speaking, guano is the feces of bats, seals, and sea birds such as pelicans. Guano fertilizer _____ due to its high levels of _____ and _____ . In addition, _____ other kinds of droppings, the odor of guano isn't so bad. So, many farmers prefer guano fertilizer to chemical fertilizers.

In spite of that, some critics say _____ take bat guano from caves. When people collect bat guano, they disturb bats' habitat and make them anxious and uneasy. It is said that some bats often drop their babies _____ .

201

Did You Know Bats' Droppings Are Valuable To Humans?

1 Bats' **droppings** are so **valuable** that we do not call them just 'excrement'

(특히) 새, 짐승의 똥   so 형용사 that : 너무 …해서 that 이하이다.
= excrement, dung, feces 배설물   not call … but give (not A but B) ..라 부르지 않고 …를 주다

or 'dung', but give them the name of 'guano.'

bats' droppings   give the name of ( ) : ( )라는 이름을 주다

2 What's so special about their droppings?

3 They are **nutrient**-rich droppings, which means humans use them

영양분이 풍부한 = highly nutritious   which가 앞 문장 전체(단수)를 받으므로 동사는 means
rich 풍부한 (vitamin-rich 비타민이 풍부한)

as good **fertilizers**.

fertilize 1. 수정시키다 2. 비료를 주다
(fertilizer 비료 fertilized egg 수정란)

4 Guano commonly refers to the excrement of bats.

일반적으로 commonly 가리킨다 refer to

5 But, more exactly speaking, guano is the feces of (bats, seals, and sea birds

더 정확하게 말하면 (exactly speaking 정확하게 말하면)   feces 복수형인데 보통 복수형으로 사용
(specifically speaking 구체적으로 말하면 frankly speaking 솔직하게 말하면)

such as pelicans).

6 Guano fertilizer has been **popular due to** its high levels of (phosphorus and nitrogen).

현재완료 have pp (has been)   인과 질소
= because of …때문에 + 명사/명사구

7 In addition, **compared to** other kinds of droppings, (the **odor** of guano) isn't so bad.

다른 종류들 other kinds의 배설물과 비교할 때 compared to   냄새 (특히 '악취' ↔ fragrance 향기)

8 So, many farmers prefer guano fertilizer to chemical fertilizers.

prefer A to B : B보다 A를 더 선호하다 (to 다음에 동사가 아닌 명사/동명사) (prefer to 동사원형 …를 선호하다)
I prefer to read books to to watch movies. (X)   prefer A to B에서 A와 B 형태를 일치시키려 to가 반복되었다.
I prefer reading books to watching movies. (O)
I prefer to read books rather than watch movies. (O)

9 In spite of that, some **critics** say it's not a good thing to take bat guano from **caves**.

= Despite that   critic 비판하는 사람   가주어 it, 진주어 to take   cave 동굴
that 앞 부분 내용 (화학 비료보다 구아노 비료가 선호되다)

⑩ When people collect bat guano, they [1] **disturb** bats' **habitat** and

disturb v. 방해하다　　habitat n. 서식지　inhabit v. 살다, 거주하다
disturbance n. 방해　　habitant/inhabitant 거주민　habit n. 습관

[2] make them (**anxious** and uneasy).

make + 목적어 + 형용사 : 목적어를 …하게 만들다
그들(them = bats)을 불안하고 불편하게 만들다
anxious a. 불안한

⑪ It is said that some bats often drop their babies because of **anxiety**.

…라고 한다　　　　　　　　　　　　　　　　　　　　불안 때문에 = due to anxiety (because of 명사 / because 절)
anxiety n. 불안

〔 박쥐 똥이 인간에게 가치가 있다는 거 아세요? 〕

❶ 박쥐 똥은 너무 가치가 있어서 그냥 '배설물' 또는 '똥'이라 부르지 않고 '구아노'라는 이름을 붙여주었습니다.

❷ 그들의 똥이 뭐가 그리 특별할까요?

❸ 영양가가 풍부한 똥이라 인간이 사용할 수 있는 훌륭한 비료가 됩니다.

❹ 구아노는 일반적으로 동굴 바닥에서 수집된 박쥐 배설물을 의미합니다.

❺ 하지만 더 정확히 말하면 구아노는 펠리칸 같은 바닷새, 박쥐, 물개의 배설물입니다.

❻ 구아노 비료는 인과 질소 함량이 높아서 인기가 좋습니다.

❼ 게다가 다른 종류의 똥과 비교할 때 구아노 냄새는 그리 지독하지 않습니다.

❽ 그래서 많은 농부들이 화학비료보다 구아노 비료를 더 좋아합니다.

❾ 그럼에도 불구하고 일부 비판가들은 동굴에서 박쥐 구아노를 가져오는 게 좋은 일이 아니라고 말합니다.

❿ 사람들이 박쥐 구아노를 모을 때, 박쥐의 서식지를 혼란시키고 박쥐들을 불안하고 어수선하게 만듭니다.

⓫ 어떤 박쥐는 불안감 때문에 아기를 떨어뜨린다고 합니다.

46 Did You Know **How Hot The Hottest Hot Spring In The World Is?**

Brace yourself before putting your foot into this hot spring. It is literally a 'hot' spring - hot enough to boil some eggs. You can find the hottest hot spring in the world in Serbia. Its temperature is a whopping 111°C.

That is surely hot, but the largest hot spring can be found in another continent. The Frying Pan Lake in New Zealand is the world's largest hot spring. The second largest is in Dominica, and the name is the Boiling Lake. We don't know who named them, but their names express themselves very well since both of them are not only large but also very hot - hot enough to be described as 'frying' and 'boiling.'

Here's another amazing hot spring. It yields approximately 250 liters of hot water per second. This monstrous hot spring is actually a geyser in Yellowstone National Park in the US and its name is the Excelsior Geyser Crater.

The Tamagawa Hot Spring holds the record of the highest flow rate in Japan. It has a flow rate of 150 liters per second. Its width is 3m and the temperature of its water is 98°C.

Words & Expressions

brace oneself 마음의 각오를 하다 boil 끓이다 hot spring 온천 temperature 온도 continent 대륙
frying pan 후라이팬 the second largest 두 번째로 큰 것 yield 생산하다 approximately 대략 per second
초 당 monstrous 괴물 같은 geyser 간헐천 flow rate 유량 width 폭

Understanding Checkpoint

1. What is the main idea of the story?

    a. There are hot springs holding amazing records in the world.

    b. If you want to boil some eggs, go to the Boiling Lake.

    c. Japan's hot springs are not so hot, just big.

    d. The Excelsior Geyser Crater is called the monster hot spring.

2. According to the passage, which sentence is right?

    a. Hot springs in Japan are much hotter than hot springs in Yellowstone National Park.

    b. The second largest hot spring in the world is in New Zealand.

    c. The Boiling Lake was misnamed because its water is not hot but cold.

    d. The Excelsior Geyser Crater is famous for yielding so much hot water.

3. Choose the correct words for each sentence.

    a. It took me hours to measure the <u>height</u> / <u>width</u> / <u>depth</u> of a football field all by myself.

    b. I bought the book about Mother Teresa to know about the <u>surprised</u> / <u>surprising</u> / <u>surprise</u> life of hers.

    c. There is a <u>yielding</u> / <u>yield</u> / <u>yielded</u> sign next to the wheat field yielding 3 tones a hectare.

Answer **1.** a **2.** d **3.** width ∣ surprising ∣ yield

Listening Drill - Dictation

    _____ before putting your foot into this hot spring. It is _____ a 'hot' spring - _____ some eggs. You can find the hottest hot spring in the world in Serbia. Its temperature is a whopping 111°C.

That is surely hot, but the largest hot spring can be found _____. The Frying Pan Lake in New Zealand is the world's largest hot spring. The second largest is in Dominica, and the name is the Boiling Lake. We don't know who named them, but their names _____ very well since both of them are not only large but also very hot - hot enough to _____ 'frying' and 'boiling.'

Here's another amazing hot spring. It _____ approximately 250 liters of hot water _____. This monstrous hot spring is actually a _____ in Yellowstone National Park in the US and its name is the Excelsior Geyser Crater.

The Tamagawa Hot Spring holds the record of the highest flow rate in Japan. It has a flow rate of 150 liters per second. Its width is 3m and the _____ is 98°C.

205

Did You Know How Hot The Hottest Hot Spring In The World Is?

1 Brace yourself before putting your foot into this hot spring.

brace oneself · · · · · · 명령문의 주어 you 일치, 생략 - before you put··· · · · · · hot 뜨거운 spring 샘 - 온천
마음을 단단히 먹다, 마음의 준비를 하다

2 It is **literally** a 'hot' spring - hot enough to **boil** some **eggs**.

문자 그대로, 말 그대로 · · · · · · ···할 만큼 충분히 뜨거운 · · · boil eggs 계란을 익히다 boiled egg 삶은 계란
(literally speaking 문자 그대로 말하자면)

3 You can find the hottest hot spring in the world in Serbia.

짧은 음절 최상급 the + -est
(마지막 자음이 2번 오는 경우 the hottest, the biggest, the fattest, the thinnest)

4 Its **temperature** is a whopping 111°C.

its 소유격 the hottest hot spring's temperature　a + 숫자를 수식하는 형용사 whopping / staggering / mere + 숫자
temperature n. 온도　　a whopping one million dollars 무려 1백만 달러 / a mere two dollars 겨우 2달러
숫자를 수식하는 형용사가 없다면 a가 오지 않는다. ··· temperature is 111°C

5 That is surely hot, but the largest hot spring can be found in another **continent**.

large - larger - the largest　　be found 찾아지다 (수동)　　n. 대륙

6 (The Frying Pan Lake in New Zealand) is the world's largest hot spring.

후라이팬 (튀기거나 볶는 팬), 여기서는 온천 이름
fry 튀기다, 볶다 + pan 팬 (넓은 조리기구)
steam 삶다 boil 끓이다 roast 굽다 heat 따뜻하게 하다, 데우다

7 The second largest is in Dominica, and the name is the Boiling Lake.

두 번째로 큰 것 = the second largest hot spring　　　　boil v. 끓다 n. 종기　lake 호수

8 We don't know who named them, but their names express themselves very well

동사 이름을 짓다　　　　　　명사 이름

since (both of them) are not only large but also very hot –

= because　상기 언급된 두 온천들 (복수)　클 뿐 아니라 뜨겁기도

hot enough to be described as 'frying' and 'boiling.'

···라 묘사되기에 (수동) 충분할 정도로 뜨거운

9 Here's another **amazing** hot spring.

another + 단수명사 / other + 복수명사
amazing a. 놀라운

10 It **yields approximately** (250 liters of hot water) per second.

대략　　　　　　　　　　　　　　per second 1초당 per hour 1시간에 per day 하루에
yield 1. (농작물, 결과)내다, 산출하다 2. 항복하다 3. 양도하다 4. 양보하다 (이 문장에서는 '내다, 산출하다')

⑪ This **monstrous** hot spring is actually a **geyser** in Yellowstone National Park

monster n. 괴물 monstrous a. 괴물 같은   간헐천

in the US and its name is the Excelsior Geyser Crater.

the name of a geyser (간헐천의 이름-소유격)

⑫ The Tamagawa Hot Spring holds the record of the highest flow rate in Japan.

기록을 보유하다   가장 높은 유량 (물의 흐름)
set the record 기록을 세우다 break the record 기록을 깨다

⑬ It has a flow rate of 150 liters per second.

1초 당 150리터의 물 흐름

⑭ Its **width** is 3m and the temperature of its water is 98°C.

소유격 – 타마가와 온전의 넓이width   소유격 – 타마가와 온천의 물
wide a. 넓은 widen v. 넓게 하다 width n. 넓이

(세계에서 가장 뜨거운 온천이 얼마나 뜨거운지 아세요?)

❶ 그 온천에 발을 넣기 전에 마음의 준비를 단단히 해야 합니다.

❷ 말 그대로 '뜨거운' 샘인데, 얼마나 뜨거운지 계란을 삶을 수 있을 정도입니다.

❸ 세상에서 가장 뜨거운 온천은 세르비아에 있습니다.   ❹ 온도는 무려 섭씨 111도라고 합니다.

❺ 그 정도면 상당히 뜨겁지만 가장 큰 온천은 다른 대륙에서 찾을 수 있을 수 있습니다.

❻ '프라잉 팬 레이크'가 세상에서 가장 큰 온천입니다.

❼ 두 번째로 큰 것은 도미니카에 있고, 이름은 '보일링 레이크'입니다.

❽ 누가 이름을 지었는지는 모르지만, 프라잉 팬 레이크와 보일링 레이크라는 이름은 온천을 아주 잘 표현하는 이름인데,
이유인 즉 둘 다 클 뿐만 아니라 '프라잉(튀기는)'과 '보일링(끓는)'이라 묘사될 정도로 꽤 뜨겁기 때문입니다.

❾ 여기 또 다른 놀라운 온천이 있습니다.   ❿ 이 온천은 1초당 뜨거운 물이 약 250리터나 나온다고 합니다.

⑪ 괴물 같은 이 온천은 사실 미국의 옐로우스톤 국립공원에 있는 간헐천으로 이름은 엑셀시오 가이저 크레이터입니다.

⑫ 타마가와 온천은 일본에서 가장 많은 유량 기록을 가지고 있습니다.

⑬ 이 온천은 1초에 150리터의 물이 흘러옵니다.   ⑭ 온천 폭은 3미터, 물의 온도는 섭씨 98도입니다.

47 Did You Know Why The Quagga, A Half Zebra And Half Horse, Was Extinct?

The quagga, which was once found in great numbers in the plains of Africa, went extinct because people hunted them for meat and hides. So, it was we humans who drove them to extinction.

The quagga was different from other zebras. It had distinct stripes only on the front part of its body. In the middle part of its body, the stripes faded into a plain brown. So, the quagga looked like a zebra and a horse at the same time.

Scholars were confused about how to categorize this species. Sadly, before they had made any decision about its species, the quagga became extinct. The last wild quagga was thought to have been shot and disappeared in the late 1870s, and the very last quagga kept in captivity in Amsterdam died in 1883. But, scientists have continued to study about it with its DNA. As a matter of fact, the quagga was the first extinct animal which left behind its DNA. Recently, genetic engineers revealed that the quagga was not a separate species. It had diverged from the plains zebra.

Words & Expressions

in great numbers 대량으로, 많은 수의 extinct 멸종한 plain n. 평원(prairie 초원) a.밋밋한, 무늬가 없는 hide n. 가죽 v. 숨다 extinction 멸종 stripe 줄무늬 fade 흐려지다 plain brown 평범한 갈색 categorize 분류하다 species 종 become extinct 멸종하다 in the wild 야생에서 capture 잡다 diverge 갈라지다, 나뉘다

Understanding Checkpoint

1. What is the main idea of the story?

    a. The quagga was totally different from the plains zebra.

    b. Ever since the quagga became extinct, scientists have studied about the cause of its extinction.

    c. The quagga looks the same as the zebra but its species was different.

    d. The quagga driven to extinction by human beings was the first extinct animals left behind its DNA.

2. In order to get _____, people had hunted the quagga at will.

    a. grass in the plains

    b. other zebras and horses

    c. meat and hides

    d. its DNA samples

3. Choose the correct words for each sentence.

    a. The hunters tried to catch seals for their <u>hides</u> / <u>hid</u> / <u>hide</u> but seals hid under the ice.

    b. Those who <u>did</u> / <u>came</u> / <u>made</u> a decision to stay inside the house wouldn't leave the house.

    c. National treasures taken by Japan during the Japanese colonial era had <u>come</u> / <u>came</u> / <u>coming</u> back to Korea in 2001.

    d. Sue wore a <u>plains</u> / <u>plain</u> / <u>plainly</u> T-shirt, on the other hand, Demi wore a fancy colorful gown.

Answer **1.** d **2.** c **3.** hides ׀ made ׀ come ׀ plain

Listening Drill - Dictation

The quagga, which was once found _____ in the plains of Africa, went extinct because people hunted them for meat and _____. So, it was we humans who _____.

The quagga was different from other zebras. It had distinct stripes only on the front part of its body. In the middle part of its body, the stripes _____ a plain brown. So, the quagga looked like a zebra and a horse _____.

Scholars were confused about how to categorize this species. Sadly, before they had _____ about its species, the quagga became extinct. The last wild quagga was thought to have been shot and disappeared in the late 1870s, and the very last quagga _____ in Amsterdam died in 1883. But, scientists have continued to study about it with its DNA. As a matter of fact, the quagga was the first extinct animal which _____ its DNA. Recently, genetic engineers revealed that the quagga was not _____. It had _____ the plains zebra.

Did You Know Why The Quagga, A Half Zebra And Half Horse, Was Extinct?

1 The quagga, (which was once found in great numbers in the plains of Africa),

= 동격   once 한 때, 이전에 be found 발견되다 in great numbers 많이 the plains 평원 (-s)

went **extinct** because people hunted them for (meat and hides).

go extinct 멸종하다 (extinct a. 멸종한 extinction n. 멸종)   hide n. 가죽 v. 숨다 (hide-hid-hidden)
(go bald 대머리가 되다 go green 환경친화적이 되다 go blind 장님이 되다 go wild 통제불능이 되다)

2 So, it was we humans who drove them to **extinction**.

강조 It is/was ( ) who …한 건 바로 ( )이다.   drive몰다 그들을(them= the quagga) 멸종으로 to extinction
It was you who broke my phone. 내 전화기 고장 낸 게 바로 너였구나.

3 The quagga was different from other zebras.

…와 다르다 (differ v. 다르다 different a. 다른)

4 It had **distinct** stripes only on the front part of its body.

a. 또렷한, 분명한 명확한 줄무늬   오직 앞부분에만 (on 표면 위)

5 In the middle part of its body, the stripes faded into a **plain** brown.

…로(into) 흐려지다   n. 평원
a. 분명한, 꾸미지 않은, 못생긴, 무늬가 없는

6 So, the quagga looked like (a zebra and a horse) **at the same time**.

…처럼 보이다   동시에 (at once 한 번에)

7 Scholars were **confused** about how to **categorize** this **species**.

사람 주어 + be confused 주어가 헷갈려하다   분류하다   종
how to 동사 …하는 방법

8 Sadly, (before they had made any decision about its species), the quagga

결정하다 make a decision = decide
주절의 주어 the quagga와 일치하지 않아서 생략하지 않음

became extinct.

= go extinct 멸종하다

9 The last wild quagga was thought to have [1] been shot and [2] disappeared

마지막 야생 콰가   = be said to   현재완료 [1] 총에 맞아 have been shot [2] 사라졌다 have diappeared

in the late 1870s, and (the very last quagga kept in captivity in Amsterdam) died

very – 강조   수식   야생, 동물원 다 포함해 진짜 마지막 콰가
주어 ( ) …quagga that was kept in captivity 포획된 콰가 + died

in 1883.

⑩ But, scientists have continued to study about it with its DNA.

continue는 to부정사, 동명사 다 가능   = the quagga

⑪ As a matter of fact, the quagga was the first extinct animal (which left behind its

사실상 (in fact, actually)   뒤에 남기다

DNA).

⑫ Recently, **genetic** engineers **revealed** that the quagga was not a **separate** species.

유전공학자들   밝히다 (uncover)   a. 별개의, 서로 다른, 독립된

genetic a. 유전의 genetic engineering 유전공학   v. 분리되다, 헤어지다

⑬ It had **diverged from** the plains zebra.

…에서(from) 갈라지다, 나누어지다

반은 얼룩말, 반은 말인 콰가가 왜 멸종했는지 아세요?

❶ 한 때 아프리카 초원에서 많은 수가 발견되었던 콰가는 사람들이 고기와 가죽을 얻기 위해 사냥하는 바람에 멸종했습니다.

❷ 그러니까 콰가를 멸종으로 몬 건 바로 우리 인간입니다.

❸ 콰가는 다른 얼룩말과는 다릅니다.   ❹ 몸 앞부분에만 선명한 줄무늬가 있었습니다.

❺ 몸의 중간 부분에서 줄무늬가 흐려지면서 그냥 갈색이 됩니다.

❻ 그래서 콰가는 얼룩말과 말을 동시에 닮았습니다.   ❼ 학자들은 이 종을 어떻게 분류할지 몰랐습니다.

❽ 안됐지만, 학자들이 이 종에 대한 어떤 결정도 내리기 전에, 콰가가 멸종되었습니다.

❾ 마지막 야생 콰가는 1870년대 후반에 총에 맞아 사라진 것으로 알려져 있고, 암스테르담의 동물원에 있던 진짜 마지막 콰가는 1883년에 사망했습니다.

❿ 하지만 과학자들은 콰가의 DNA로 콰가에 대한 연구를 계속하고 있습니다.

⑪ 사실 콰가는 DNA를 남긴 최초의 멸종 동물입니다.

⑫ 최근 유전공학자들은 콰가가 분리된 종이 아니라는 것을 밝혀냈습니다.

⑬ 콰가는 초원 얼룩말에서 나온 종이었습니다.

Whales have been very useful to the bone for human beings, both figuratively as well as literally speaking.

Whales provide us with tons of meat. Considering their enormous size, it's no wonder they can give us an enormous amount of meat. They also provide us with their whalebones. Whalebone, also called baleen, is a kind of brush-looking filter inside the mouth of teethless whales. Whales eat tons of krill by filtering sea water through their whalebones. Whalebones have been variously used for a long time, such products as umbrellas, brushes, women's corset, fishing rods, and more.

The most important thing whales provide us is oil. In the past, whale oil was widely used as fuel in oil lamps and as candle wax. It was once a major food source for some people of the Pacific Northwest. Even today, it is still used in soap making and leather dressing. Most whale oil comes from blubber (sea animals' fat), but humans can take oil from their baleen, meat, organs, bones, and even blood. From now on, maybe we should call them 'the giving whales.'

Words & Expressions

useful 유용한 to the bone 뼈까지, 철저하게 figuratively 비유적으로 literally speaking 문자 그대로 말해서 provide 제공하다 (with) whalebones 고래수염 (baleen) teethless 이가 없는 filter 필터, 걸러내다 variously 다양하게 corset 코르셋 fishing rod 낚싯대 a major food source 주요 식량원 soap making 비누 제작 leather dressing 가죽 무두질 blubber 바다 동물의 지방

Understanding Checkpoint

1. What is the main idea of the story?

    a. Whale meat is delicious and highly nutritious.

    b. Whales are endangered animals so we must protect them.

    c. Whales have been useful for humans in various ways.

    d. We must call whales 'the giving whales.'

2. According to the passage, which sentence is right?

    a. Whales have been useful for human beings for a long time.

    b. In many countries, in all ages, people have enjoyed eating whale meat.

    c. Whalebones are still widely used as a major food source.

    d. Whalebones are absolutely different from baleen.

3. Choose the correct words for each sentence.

    a. The problem is that many government officials are deeply corrupt <u>through</u> / <u>to</u> / <u>into</u> the bone.

    b. Since you insulted me in front of my family, <u>from time to time</u> / <u>from now on</u> / <u>till the end</u> you and I are no longer friends.

    c. <u>Literally</u> / <u>Figuratively</u> / <u>Comparatively</u> speaking, you look like a hungry lion which has been starved for weeks.

    d. The giving tree provided the boy <u>for</u> / <u>with</u> / <u>to</u> fruits and branches.

Answer **1.** c **2.** a **3.** to ∣ from now on ∣ Figuratively ∣ with

Listening Drill – Dictation

Whales have been very useful to the bone for human beings, both literally speaking.

Whales   tons of meat.   their enormous size, it's no wonder they can give us an enormous amount of meat. They also provide us with their whalebones. Whalebone, also called baleen, is a kind of brush-looking filter   teethless whales. Whales eat tons of krill by filtering sea water through their whalebones. Whalebones   for a long time, such products as umbrellas, brushes, women's corset, fishing rods,   .

The most important thing whales provide us is oil. In the past, whale oil   as fuel in oil lamps   candle wax. It was once a major food source for some people of the Pacific Northwest. Even today, it is still used in soap making and leather dressing. Most whale oil comes from blubber (sea animals' fat), but humans can take oil from their baleen, meat,   , bones, and even blood.   , maybe we should call them 'the giving whales.'

Did You Know Whales Are Useful To The Bone?

1 Whales have been very useful **to the bone** for human beings,

뼈까지, 철저하게 (be soaked to the bone. 뼛속까지/완전히 젖다)

both **figuratively** as well as **literally** speaking.

both A as well as B : B뿐 아니라 A   literally 문자 그대로 literally speaking (비유 없이) 있는 그대로 말해서
(both A and B (A, B 모두)와 같은 의미)
          figuratively 비유적으로 figuratively speaking 비유적으로 말해서

2 Whales **provide** us **with** tons of meat.

provide ( ) with… : ( )에게 …를 제공하다

3 **Considering** their **enormous** size, it's no wonder they can give us

그들(고래)의 엄청난 크기를 감안할 때   놀랄 일도 아니다
          enormous a. 거대한(=huge)

an enormous amount of meat.

엄청난 양의 = a huge amount of

4 They also provide us with their whalebones.

5 Whalebone, (also called baleen), is a kind of brush-looking filter inside

| = 동격 |

a kind of 일종의 / kind of 약간, 좀

the mouth of **teethless** whales.

이가 없는

6 Whales eat (tons of krill) by filtering sea water through their whalebones.

걸러서 ( )를 먹는다   …를 통해 through 걸러서 by filtering

7 Whalebones have been **variously** used for a long time, in

현재완료 수동태 have been 부사 pp   오랫동안   be used in …에서 사용되다
          variously ad. 다양하게

such products as (umbrellas, brushes, women's corset, fishing rods, and more).

( )와 같은 상품들   fishing 낚시+rod 막대기 = 낚싯대 그 외 더 있다

8 (The most important thing whales provide us) is oil.

수식

thing that whales provide us 고래가 우리에게 제공하는 것
긴 음절 단어의 최상급 the most ( )   주어( ) thing + is (단수)
긴 음절 the most handsome man, 짧은 음절 the biggest cake

9 In the past, whale oil was widely used as (**fuel** in oil lamps) and as (candle wax).

수동태 be 부사 pp   be used as …로 사용되다
          fuel n. 연료

⑩ It was once a major food source for some people of the Pacific Northwest.
(더 이상 현재는 그렇지 않지만) 과거 한 때

⑪ Even today, it is still used in $^{1)}$ soap making and $^{2)}$ **leather** dressing.
수동태 be 부사 pp   📘 be used in $^{1)\ 2)}$ $^{1)}$과 $^{2)}$에서 사용되다   hide 동물의 가죽 leather 무두질한 가죽

⑫ Most whale oil **comes from** blubber (sea animals' fat), but humans can
···에서 오다, 나오다   바다 동물의 지방, 블러버

extract oil from (their baleen, meat, organs, bones, and even blood).
···를 ( )에서 추출하다, 뽑아내다
extract n. 발췌, 초록, 추출 v. 뽑아내다, 억지로 떨어내다

⑬ From now on, maybe we should call them 'the giving whales.'
Shel Silverstein의 〈The Giving Tree 아낌없이 주는 나무〉 제목 인용

> 고래가 뼈까지 유용하다는 거 아세요?

❶ 고래가 인간에게 뼈까지 철저하게 유용하다는 건 비유적으로 한 말이든 축어적인 한 말이든 다 맞는 말입니다.

❷ 고래는 우리에게 수 톤의 고기를 제공합니다.

❸ 고래의 엄청난 크기를 감안할 때 고래가 엄청난 양의 고기를 제공한다는 건 놀랄 일도 아닙니다.

❹ 그리고 고래는 우리에게 고래수염(baleen)도 제공해왔습니다.

❺ 이는 치아가 없는 고래 입 안에 있는 솔처럼 생긴 일종의 필터입니다.

❻ 고래는 고래수염을 통해 바닷물을 걸러 수 톤의 크릴새우를 먹습니다.

❼ 고래수염은 우산, 솔, 여성 코르셋, 낚싯대 등과 같은 제품에서 오랫동안 다양하게 이용되어 왔습니다.

❽ 고래가 우리에게 제공하는 가장 중요한 건 기름입니다.

❾ 과거에 고래 기름은 램프의 발광제와 양초 왁스로 널리 애용되었습니다.

❿ 한 때 태평양 북서지역의 일부 사람들의 주요 식량자원이기도 했습니다.

⑪ 지금도 비누 제작과 가죽 무두질에 고래 기름이 쓰이고 있습니다.

⑫ 대부분의 고래 기름은 블러버 (해양 동물의 지방)에서 나오지만, 인간은 고래의 수염, 고기, 내장, 뼈, 심지어 혈액에서도 기름을 뽑아냅니다.

⑬ 지금부터 우리는 고래를 '아낌없이 주는 고래'라고 불러야 할 것 같습니다.

Not all animals feel sad, but some animals have shown signs of grief.

When one of elephants dies, other elephants stand around the dead body and stare at it for a while. And if a mother elephant loses her baby, she won't leave her dead baby, and will touch it with her trunk from time to time.

In the case of chimpanzees and gorillas, they also feel sad when they lose their babies and vice versa. There was a baby chimpanzee who lost his mom. This baby chimp's sorrow was so deep that he refused to eat any food. Finally, he starved to death.

Parrots, which are faithful to their mates, also show sadness. When the mate dies, the other parrot seems disheartened and distressed by grief. Sometimes, they do not eat for a long time. Dogs are also said to grieve when sad things happen, like the death of their mate or owner.

216

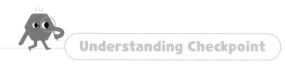

1. What is the main idea of the story?

    a. Some animals show signs of grief because they have feelings of grief.

    b. Parrots feel sad when they lose their mates.

    c. All elephants grieve when their babies die.

    d. Chimpanzees and gorillas have so much in common.

2. _____ feel sad and show their grief.

    a. All animals

    b. Certain animals

    c. Only Elephants

    d. Most birds

3. Choose the correct words for each sentence.

    a. Tim and I promise to live together until <u>dead</u> / <u>death</u> / <u>die</u> separates us.

    b. I share my room with Jeff <u>from time to time</u> / <u>now more than ever</u> / <u>for the first time</u> and that makes me crazy.

    c. When I put down my pink trunk by a tree trunk to change clothes into swimming trunks, an elephant came close to me and touched my pink trunk with its <u>trunk</u> / <u>trunks</u> / <u>a trunk</u>.

    d. His dog is famous for being faithful <u>with</u> / <u>to</u> / <u>for</u> his owner. My dog? Definitely not.

Answer **1.** a **2.** b **3.** death death ┃ from time to time ┃ trunk ┃ to

Not all animals feel sad, but some animals   .

When one of elephants dies, other elephants stand around the dead body and   it for a while. And if a mother elephant   , she won't leave her dead baby, and will touch it with her trunk from time to time.

In the case of chimpanzees and gorillas, they also feel sad when they lose their babies   . There was a baby chimpanzee who lost his mom. This baby chimp's   he refused to eat any food. Finally, he   .

Parrots, which   their mates, also   . When the mate dies, the other parrot   and distressed by grief. Sometimes, they do not eat for a long time. Dogs are also said to grieve when sad things happen, like   or owner.

217

Did You Know Animals Do Feel Sad?

① Not all animals feel sad, but some animals have shown signs of **grief**.

부분부정 – 모든 동물이 …인 건 아니다 (not all… but some)　　　　　　　　　n. 슬픔, 비탄 (grieve v. 슬퍼하다)

② When one of elephants dies, other elephants [1] stand around the dead body and

one of 복수명사 : …중 하나 (단수) + dies

[2] **stare at** it for a while.

(빤히) 쳐다보다, 응시하다

③ And if a mother elephant loses her baby, she [1] won't leave her dead baby,

if 주어 + 동사(현재), 주어 will + 동사원형 (will not leave, will touch)
주어 a mother elephant가 3인칭 단수 현재시제 – loses

and [2] will touch it with her **trunk** (from time to time).

코끼리의 코, 나무 기둥, 남성용 사각 팬티 (사각 수영복)
여행가방 트렁크, 자동차 트렁크

④ In the case of chimpanzees and gorillas, they also feel sad

…의 경우에
in case of …의 경우 (가상의 미래) : in case of fire 불이 날 경우
in case (혹시) …경우를 대비하여 : in case it rains 비가 올 경우를 대비해서, just in case 만약을 대비해서, 혹시 몰라서

when they lose their babies and **vice versa**.

반대의 경우도 그렇다 (부모가 새끼를 잃는 경우의 반대 ⇒ 새끼가 부모를 잃을 때)

⑤ There was a baby chimpanzee (who lost his mom).

↑ 수식 │ 엄마를 잃은 아기 침팬지

⑥ (This baby chimp's sorrow) was so deep that he **refused** to eat any food.

주어 ( ) sorrow + was　　　　so 형용사 that 절 : 너무 …해서 that
　　　　　　　　　　　　　　　　　refuse v. 거부하다, 거절하다

⑦ Finally, he **starved to death**.

* be starved to death 외부적 요인/강요에 의해 굶어 죽는 경우
He was almost starved to death before he was rescued. 구조되기 전 그는 거의 아사 직전이었다.
* starve to death 단순히 먹지 않아서/못 먹어서 굶어 죽는 경우
Many animals starve to death during harsh winters. 많은 동물들이 혹독한 겨울에 굶어 죽는다.
문제에서는 침팬지가 스스로 먹기를 거부한 것이므로 be starved to death가 아닌 starved to death

⑧ Parrots, (which are faithful to their **mates**), also show sadness.

↑ 수식 │ 짝에게 충실한 앵무새　　　mate 짝, 배우자

⑨ When the mate dies, the other parrot seems (**disheartened** and distressed)

dis (부정) + hearten (용기를 북돋우다) – 낙심시키다

(둘 중 하나, 그리고) 나머지 하나 the other (단수) + seems

I have two pens. One is red, and the other is blue.

나에게 펜이 둘이다. 하나는 빨강, 나머지 하나는 파랑이다.

by grief.

⑩ Sometimes, they do not eat for a long time.

⑪ Dogs are also said to **grieve** when sad things happen, (like the death of their mate

슬퍼한다고 한다 　　　v. 슬퍼하다 grief n. 슬픔　　슬픈 일 sad things의 예 ( )

or owner).

(동물도 슬픔을 느낀다는 거 아세요?)

❶ 모든 동물이 슬픔을 느끼는 건 아니지만 일부 동물은 슬픔을 표현합니다.

❷ 코끼리 중 한 마리가 죽으면 다른 코끼리들은 시체 주위에 둘러서서 한동안 동료를 바라봅니다.

❸ 그리고 엄마 코끼리는 아기를 잃으면 죽은 아기 곁을 떠나지 않고 가끔씩 코로 아기를 만집니다.

❹ 침팬지와 고릴라의 경우, 이들 역시 아기를 잃거나 그 반대의 경우 슬픔을 느낍니다.

❺ 엄마를 잃은 아기 침팬지가 있었습니다.

❻ 그 아기 침팬지의 슬픔이 얼마나 심했는지 먹기를 거부했습니다.

❼ 마침내 아기는 굶어 죽었습니다.

❽ 배우자에게 헌신적인 앵무새 역시 슬픔을 표현합니다.

❾ 짝이 죽으면 남은 앵무새는 슬픔으로 상심하고 고통스러운 듯 보입니다.

❿ 가끔은 오랫동안 먹지 않기도 합니다.

⑪ 개들 역시 짝이나 주인의 죽음처럼 슬픈 일이 생기면 슬퍼한다고 합니다.

Sharks can make themselves look dead. It's understandable for opossums to "play opossum." This comes as no surprise. But sharks "play opossum?"

To be exact, sharks don't "play opossum" of their own accord. But, they can enter the state of paralysis, and it is called 'tonic immobility' (a kind of apparent death).

Not all sharks display tonic immobility, but some sharks enter and remain in this state for about 10 to 15 minutes when inverted. During tonic immobility, sharks show no response when touched. Yet, after 15 minutes of lifeless-looking state, they recover consciousness, turn themselves over quickly, and swim away. So, you can make some sharks helpless for several minutes by turning them upside down; I mean, if you can. No one knows what causes this weird state.

Some scientists take advantage of this phenomenon to study sharks. Interestingly, scientists are not the only ones who use this tactic to take control over sharks. While hunting, killer whales often manage to invert sharks to eat them more easily.

Understanding Checkpoint

1. What is the main idea of the story?

    a. You can make sharks helpless by turning them into opossums.

    b. In the state of tonic immobility, sharks can't swim fast.

    c. Some sharks can play opossum.

    d. If you invert sharks, they will eat you up.

2. According to the passage, which sentence is <u>wrong</u>?

    a. In the state of tonic immobility, sharks can't do anything.

    b. Some sharks play opossum, but some don't.

    c. Killer whales often try to invert sharks while hunting them.

    d. Tonic immobility lasts for 15 hours.

3. Choose the correct words for each sentence.

    a. This shiny shirt will make me <u>look</u> / <u>looking</u> / <u>to look</u> good and young.

    b. <u>Paralysis</u> / <u>Paralyze</u> / <u>Paralyzed</u> happens when something goes wrong with your body, especially your brain and muscles.

    c. Tim was crying out loud while <u>waited</u> / <u>waiting</u> / <u>to wait</u> for his mom.

Answer 1. c 2. d 3. look ∣ Paralysis ∣ waiting

Listening Drill – Dictation

Sharks can make themselves _____. It's understandable for opossums to "play opossum." _____. But sharks "_____?"

To be exact, sharks don't "play opossum" _____. But, they can enter _____, and it is called 'tonic immobility' (a kind of apparent death).

Not all sharks display tonic immobility, but some sharks enter and remain in this state for about 10 to 15 minutes _____. During tonic immobility, sharks _____ when touched. Yet, after 15 minutes of lifeless-looking state, they recover consciousness, turn themselves over quickly, and swim away. So, you can make some sharks helpless for several minutes by turning them upside down; I mean, if you can. No one knows what causes this weird state.

Some scientists _____ this phenomenon to study sharks. Interestingly, scientists _____ use this tactic to _____ sharks. While hunting, killer whales often manage to invert sharks to eat them more easily.

Did You Know Sharks Can Play Opossum?

❶ Sharks can make themselves look dead.

사역동사 make + 동사원형 look dead 죽은 듯 보이게 만들다

❷ It's understandable for opossums to "play opossum."

주머니쥐 흉내를 내다 (= play dead 죽은 척하다)
주머니쥐는 opossum인데 '주머니쥐 흉내를 내다, 죽은 척 하다' 표현에서는 'possum'을 쓴다.
play opossum으로 쓰는 경우가 있는데 '죽은 척 하다'는 'play possum'이 맞다. (지문에서는 opossum을 흉내낸다는 의미로 사용)
play dumb 모르는 척 하다, 시치미 떼다 play dirty 비열하게 행동하다 play house 소꿉놀이/엄마아빠 놀이하다

❸ This comes as no surprise.

놀랍지 않다

❹ But sharks "play opossum?"

❺ To be exact, sharks don't "play opossum" of their own accord.

정확하게는   스스로, 자발적으로

❻ But, they can enter the state of paralysis,

마비상태   n. 마비 paralyze v. 마비시키다

and it is called 'tonic immobility' (a kind of apparent death).

= 동격   apparent …인 듯 보이는 + death 죽음 = 가사(假死)
tonic 기운을 돋우는 것 + immobility 부동상태, 정지
- 긴장성 부동 (일시적으로 움직이지 못함)살아 있지만 겉으로 죽은 듯 보이는 상태

❼ Not all sharks display tonic immobility, but some sharks [1] enter and [2] remain

부분 부정   나타내다, 보이다   그런 상태(가사)에 [1] 들어가 [2] 유지하다

in this state (for about 10 to 15 minutes) when inverted.

기간 for dir 10-15분간   주절의 주어 some sharks와 일치, 생략
when they(= some sharks) are inverted 그들이 뒤집히면

❽ During tonic immobility, sharks show no response when touched.

= sharks don't show any response   when they are touched (주절의 주어와 일치, 생략)
아무 반응을 보이지 않다 (be nonresponsive)

❾ Yet, after 15 minutes of lifeless-looking state, they recover consciousness,

죽은 것처럼 보이는 상태   의식을 회복하다   n. 의식

[1] turn themselves over quickly, and [2] swim away.

몸을 뒤집다   수영해서 멀리 가버리다

❿ So, you can make some sharks helpless for several minutes by

make ( ) helpless by … : …하여 ( )를 무력하게 만들다

turning them upside down; I mean, if you can.
위아래가 뒤집히게 turn upside down = invert 뒤집다

⑪ No one knows what causes this **weird** state.
　　　　　　　　　　　　　　　　　　a. 기이한
　　　　　선행사를 포함한 관계대명사 what – 무엇이 이런 이상한 상태를 야기하는지를

⑫ Some scientists **take advantage of** this **phenomenon** to study sharks.
　　　　　　　자기에게 유리하도록 이용하다　　　　　현상 (복수 phenomena phenomenal a. 경이적인, 감탄할 만한)

⑬ Interestingly, scientists are not the only ones (who use this **tactic**
　　　　　　　　　…하는(이 전략을 사용하는) 유일한 사람들이 아니다 ↑　　　수식

to take control over sharks).
　　　　통제하다

⑭ While hunting, killer whales often **manage to** invert sharks to eat them
주절의 주어 killer whales과 일치, 생략　　　　　　어찌어찌, 힘겹게 …하다
while they hunt 사냥할 때

more easily.

상어가 주머니쥐 흉내를 낼 수 있다는 거 아세요?

❶ 상어는 자신을 죽은 것처럼 보이게 할 수 있습니다.　　❷ 주머니쥐가 죽은 척 한다는 건 이해할만합니다.

❸ 놀랄 일도 아니지요.　　　　　　　　　　　　　❹ 하지만 상어가 주머니쥐 흉내를?

❺ 정확히 말하면 상어는 스스로 주머니쥐 흉내(죽은 척하기)를 내지 않습니다.

❻ 하지만 마비 상태에 들어가긴 하는데, 이를 '긴장성 부동'이라고 합니다. (일종의 가사상태)

❼ 모든 상어가 긴장성 부동을 보이는 건 아니지만 일부 상어는 몸이 뒤집히면 이런 상태가 되어 10분에서 15분정도 유지합니다.

❽ 긴장성 부동 상태일 때 상어는 누가 건드려도 반응을 보이지 않습니다.

❾ 물론 죽은 것처럼 보이는 이 15분이 지난 후 상어는 정신을 차리고 얼른 몸을 뒤집어 수영해 가버립니다.

❿ 그래서, 할 수만 있다면, 상어를 뒤집어 놓으면 몇 분 동안 상어를 무력하게 만들 수 있습니다.

⑪ 무엇이 이런 이상한 상태를 유발하는지는 아무도 모릅니다.

⑫ 일부 과학자들은 상어를 연구하는데 이 현상을 이용합니다.

⑬ 재미있게도 과학자들만 상어를 통제하려고 이를 이용하는 게 아닙니다.

⑭ 범고래들은 사냥할 때 쉽게 상어를 잡아먹기 위해 종종 상어를 뒤집습니다.

Chapter 06

Myth Or Fact

MP3

The most common myth about the cold is that vitamin C can prevent a cold. Many people are convinced that a large amount of vitamin C will prevent a cold or at least relieve cold symptoms. So parents used to make their kids eat fruits containing lots of vitamin C when they catch a cold.

Doctors and scientists have conducted many studies and experiments to test this common cold myth. The results said, that's just a myth. Currently, there is no conclusive data to prove that a large amount of vitamin C prevents a cold. But, the vitamin may still alleviate cold symptoms even though there is no clear evidence of this.

If you want to get over a cold sooner, a bowl of hot chicken soup can help. Chicken soup for colds is not a myth; it is a fact backed up with solid medical evidence, as it has an anti-inflammatory effect.

For your information, taking too much vitamin C for too long may not be good for your health. Far from being good for health, it could be harmful, because the excessive doses of vitamin C can cause diarrhea, which is very much dangerous especially for elderly people and young children.

Understanding Checkpoint

1. What is the main idea of the story?

a. 'Taking a large amount of vitamin C prevents a cold' is a myth.

b. Vitamin C is cheap but not effective, chicken soup is effective but pricey.

c. As far as vitamin C is concerned, more, is better.

d. Taking vitamin C too much causes diarrhea.

2. A bowl of hot chicken soup can help you get over a cold sooner since _____ .

a. there is no an anti-inflammatory effect in it

b. its anti-inflammatory properties are effective for a cold

c. it can cause diarrhea and be harmful

d. it has lots of good stuffs such as vitamin C

3. Choose the correct words for each sentence.

a. It is said humans yawn in order to <u>alleviate</u> / <u>waste</u> / <u>removal</u> oxygen deficiency.

b. I thought he never <u>got over</u> / <u>made over</u> / <u>came over</u> the death of his sister.

c. In one of the experiments <u>performed</u> / <u>conducted</u> / <u>taken</u> by HC Research Center, the shocking result was released.

Answer **1.** a **2.** b **3.** alleviate ǀ got over ǀ conducted

Listening Drill - Dictation

The most common myth about the cold is that vitamin C can prevent a cold. Many people _____ a large amount of vitamin C will prevent a cold or at least _____ . So parents used to make their kids eat fruits containing lots of vitamin C when they _____ .

Doctors and scientists have conducted many studies and experiments to test this common cold myth. The results said, that's just a myth. _____ , there is no conclusive data to prove that a large amount of vitamin C prevents a cold. But, the vitamin may still _____ cold symptoms even though _____ this.

If you want to get over a cold sooner, a bowl of hot chicken soup can help. Chicken soup for colds is not a myth; it is _____ solid medical evidence, as it has an _____ .

For your information, taking too much vitamin CC for too long may not be good for your health. _____ good for health, it could be harmful, because the excessive doses of vitamin C can cause _____ , which is very much dangerous especially for elderly people and young children.

227

Did You Know A Myth About The Common Cold?

1 (The most common **myth** about the cold) is that vitamin C can **prevent** a **cold**.

n. 신화, 근거 없는 이야기　　주어 ( ) cold가 아니라 myth + 동사 is　　v. 예방하다, 막다　a. 추운 n. 감기

2 Many people are **convinced** that (a large amount of vitamin C) will

be convinced 설득당하다 (수동태)　많은 양의 비타민 C (an enormous amount of 아 너 크고 많은 어감)
convince 확신시키다, 설득하다 (I convinced her. 나는 그녀를 설득했다. She was convinced. 그녀는 확신했다.)

¹⁾ prevent a cold or at least ²⁾ **relieve** cold **symptoms**.

많은 양의 비타민 C가 ¹⁾ 예방하고 최소한 ²⁾ 경감시키다　　　n. 증상
relieve v. 경감/완화시키다, 안도하다 (n. relief)
relieve pain 통증을 줄이다 What a relief. 다행이다.

3 So parents used to make their kids eat fruits (containing lots of vitamin C)

used to …하곤 하다 + 동사원형　　　　　수식
사역동사 make + 목적어 + 동사원형 eat : 목적어에게 …하도록 시키다
fruits that contain lots of vitamin C 비타민C를 많이 함유한 과일들

when they **catch a cold**.

감기에 걸리다 (= get a cold, have a cold)

4 Doctors and scientists have **conducted** many (studies and **experiments**) to **test**

conduct experiments to test … ..검사하기 위해 실험을 실시하다
conduct – 연구/조사하다, 지휘하다, 행동하다, 처리하다　experiment n. 실험

this common cold myth.

일반 감기 (독감 influenza, influ – 줄여서 flu라고 한다.)
우리말에는 코감기, 목감기 이런 표현이 있는데, 영어로 표현할 때는 보통 증상을 말한다.
I have a cold, and my nose is runny. 감기 걸려서 콧물이 난다. (코감기에 걸렸다.)
I caught a cold, and now my throat hurts. 감기 걸려서 목이 아프다. (목감기에 걸렸다.)

5 The results said, that's just a myth.

결과가 …라고 나왔다. 결과는 이렇다

6 Currently, there is no **conclusive** data to prove that a large amount of

that 이하를 증명할 결정적인 자료는 없다
conclude v. 결론을 내리다 conclusion n. 결론, 결말 conclusive a. 결정적인

vitamin C prevents a cold.

7 But, the vitamin may still **alleviate** cold symptoms even though

alleviate 줄이다, 경감하다 + cold 감기 + symptoms 증상들 = lessen, relieve

there is no clear evidence of this.

명확한 증거는 없다　there is no evidence (불가산 명사 / 단수)

8 If you want to **get over** a cold sooner, (a bowl of hot chicken soup) can help.

어려움을 극복하다(overcome), 병이 낫다　　　soup 불가산명사 – 계량 단위로 복수 표현
get over 병이 낫다 / get better 병세가 좋아지다　　two bowls of soup 수프 2그릇 (O) two soups (X)

⑨ (Chicken soup for colds) is not a myth; it is a fact (**backed up** with
주어 ( ) colds가 아니라 soup + is

수식
it is a fact that is backed up with ⋯로 뒷받침된 사실

solid medical evidence), as it has an anti-**inflammatory** effect.
단단한, 고체의, 확고한, 속이 꽉 찬, 빈틈없는   because   anti (반대) inflammatory 염증의 effect 효과
(solid evidence 확고한 증거)   – 소염효과 (inflammation n. 염증 inflammatory a. 염증의)
This is heavily backed up with solid evidence. 이는 확실한 많은 증거가 뒷받침되어 있다.

⑩ For your information, (taking too much vitamin C for too long)
참고로 = FYI   ( ) 주어 taking 복용하는 것   너무 많은 비타민C를, 너무 오래

may not be good for your health.
⋯일 수도 있다 조동사 may의 부정 – may not + 동사원형

⑪ Far from being good for health, it could be **harmful**, because
건강에 좋기는 커녕 far from + ing ⋯이기는 커녕. ⋯가 아니라   a. 해로운

(the **excessive doses** of vitamin C) can cause **diarrhea**, which is
dose (약) 1회 복용양   diarrhea 설사 (loose bowels) / 변비 constipation   콤마 + which 계속 용법 (설사를 유발하는데, 이는⋯)
(portion, helping, serving 음식 1인분 양)

very much dangerous especially for (elderly people and young children).
= the elderly 어르신들

(일반 감기에 관한 낭설을 아세요?)

❶ 감기에 관한 가장 흔한 낭설은 비타민 C가 감기를 예방한다는 것입니다.

❷ 많은 사람들은 많은 양의 비타민 C는 감기를 예방하거나 최소한 감기 증상을 완화시킨다고 확신합니다.

❸ 그래서 부모들은 아이가 감기에 걸리면 비타민 C가 많이 함유된 과일을 먹입니다.

❹ 의사들과 과학자들은 감기에 관해 널리 알려진 낭설을 확인하기 위해 많은 연구와 실험을 해왔습니다.

❺ 그 결과 그건 낭설일 뿐입니다.

❻ 현재까지 많은 양의 비타민 C가 감기를 예방한다고 증명된 결정적인 자료는 없습니다.

❼ 명확한 증거는 없지만 비타민이 감기 증상을 경감시킬 수도 있습니다.

❽ 감기를 빨리 낫고 싶다면 따뜻한 닭고기 스프 한 그릇이 도움이 될 수 있습니다.

❾ 감기에 닭고기 스프를 먹는 건 낭설이 아니라 확실한 의학적 증거가 뒷받침된 사실인데, 닭고기 스프에 소염 효과가 있기 때문입니다.

❿ 참고로 비타민 C를 너무 많이, 너무 오랫동안 섭취하면 건강에 좋지 않을 수 있습니다.

⓫ 건강에 좋은 건 고사하고 오히려 해로울 수 있는데 과도한 양의 비타민 C는 설사를 유발하기 때문으로, 설사는 특히 연로한 어르신들과 어린이들에게 매우 위험합니다.

It is better to eat a small amount of food prior to starting a workout, because fuel is required to provide the needed energy for your body. You can get that fuel from food and drinks. A proper portion of food will prepare your muscles for the activities that are to come. Fill up your tank with some fruits or drinks, such as bananas, nuts, or a cup of water.

There are other myths about exercise. People believe that you must stretch before a workout. But, several studies have showed that stretching sometimes leads to injury, since lengthened muscle fibers are more susceptible to a strain.

Also, some women fear that if they work out, their fat will turn into muscle. They believe that lifting weights will surely make their bodies bulky and muscular. But, fat and muscle tissues are totally different, so that's an absolute myth and a lame excuse for not working out.

Words & Expressions

prior to ...전에 workout 운동 (exercise) fuel 연료 provide 제공하다 proper portion of ...의 적당한 양 activity 활동 that is(are) to come 이제 다가올, 가까운 미래의 stretch 늘이다, 스트레 칭하다 lead to injury 부상으로 이어지다 lengthen 늘이다 muscle fiber 근섬유 susceptible 민감한, 예민한 strain 부담, 압박, 염좌 lifting weights 역기 들기 bulky 우람한, 덩치 큰 muscly 근육이 발달한 tissue 조직 lame excuse 말도 안 되는 변명

1. What is the main idea of the story?

    a. Eating something is very important to everyone, especially athletes.

    b. Before a workout, eat the proper amount of food and be careful about stretching.

    c. See what you eat before doing something hard.

    d. Eat less and exercise more.

2. According to the passage, which sentence is right?

    a. It would be better to eat some food before an exercise. Nuts can be a good choice.

    b. You have to stretch your legs and arms out several times right after a workout.

    c. The most recommended food for you before an exercise is a bunch of bananas.

    d. Fat tissues can turn into muscle tissues, that's why female athletes are muscly.

3. Choose the correct words for each sentence.

    a. Maria is nice and smart but her new boyfriend is so <u>tall</u> / <u>handsome</u> / <u>lame</u>.

    b. These sugary snacks make me fat, and this pair of jeans <u>make</u> / <u>makes</u> / <u>made</u> me look fat.

    c. I want to check out the latest movies that <u>is</u> / <u>are</u> / <u>was</u> to come.

Answer 1. b   2. a   3. lame ǀ makes ǀ are

Listening Drill – Dictation

It is better to eat a small amount of food   starting a workout, because fuel is required to   for your body. You   food and drinks.   food will prepare your muscles for the activities that are to come. Fill up your tank with some fruits or drinks, such as bananas, nuts, or a cup of water.

There are other myths about exercise. People believe that you must stretch   . But, several studies have showed that stretching sometimes   , since lengthened muscle fibers   strain.

Also, some women fear that if they work out, their fat will   muscle. They believe that lifting weights will surely make their bodies bulky and muscular. But, fat and muscle tissues   , so that's an absolute myth and   not working out.

Did You Know 'Never Eat Before An Exercise' Is A Myth?

1 It is better to eat (a small amount of food) **prior to** starting a workout,

to…하는 게 더 좋다   적은 양의 음식   …전에, 이전에 (+ 명사, 동명사)
a large amount of food 많은 양의 음식   wash hands prior to eating 먹기 전 손 씻다

because **fuel** is required to **provide** (the needed energy) for your body.

…하는데 필요하다(수동) 필요한 에너지   provide ( ) for …위해 ( )를 제공하다

2 You can get that fuel from (food and drinks).

3 (A proper **portion** of food) will prepare your **muscles**

주어 ( ) food가 아니라 portion
portion n. 음식의 1인분, (큰 것의) 부분 v. 나누다, 분배하다

for the activities (that are to come).

활동들   수식   이제 다가 올 예정인
that의 선행사 activities가 복수 + are

4 **Fill up** your tank with some fruits or drinks, (such as bananas, nuts,

…로 연료탱크를 채우라   = 동격   fruits or drinks의 예
Fill'er up. (주유소) 가득 채워주세요. (Fill it up, please. 또는 Full tank, please.가 더 많이 쓰인다.)

or a cup of water).

5 There are other myths about **exercise**.

There are복수 + other + myths복수   n. 운동, 연습문제 v. 운동하다

6 People believe that you must **stretch** before a **workout**.

v. 스트레칭하다   n. 운동 (= exercise)

7 But, several studies have **showed** that stretching sometimes **leads to** injury,

연구studies가 showed 보여준다   that절의 주어 stretching + 동사 leads   lead to injury 부상으로 이어지다
몇몇 연구에 의하면 that절.. 이다. (study, result 등 표현과 함께 the result said that… 등으로 쓰이기도 하는데,
show 동사가 더 많이 쓰인다. According to the studies, The studies showed that…)

since (lengthened muscle fibers) are more **susceptible to** a strain.

길게 늘어난 근육 섬유들   be susceptible to 명사 …에 취약하다, 걸리기 쉽다
strain / sprain 모두 명사 의미 중 '염좌, 좌상'이 있는데
sprain 인대 ligament가 다친 경우
strain 근육 muscle, 인대 tendon가 다친 경우

8 Also, some women fear that if they **work out**, their fat will turn into muscle.

가정법 현재 if 주어 they + 동사 현재 work out, 주어 their fat + will + 동사원형 turn
work out v. 운동하다 (work out at the gym 체육관에서 운동하다)
workout n. 운동 (have an intense workout 강렬한 운동을 하다)

232

⑨ They believe that ⟨lifting weights⟩ will surely make their bodies

　　　　　　　　동명사 주어　역기를 드는 것　　　　　　　　make 목적어 형용사 : 목적어를 ..하게 만들다
　　　　　　　　lift weights 역기를 들다 weightlifting 역도

⟨**bulky** and **muscular**⟩.

　a. 우람한, 덩치 큰　muscle 근육 muscular 근육질의

⑩ But, ⟨fat and muscle **tissues**⟩ are totally different, so that's [1] an **absolute** myth

　　　　　　　　　　　　　　주어 ( ) 동사 are　　　　　　　　　　　　　　　　　　순전한, 완전한

and [2] a lame excuse for not working out.

　　궁색한 변병　운동을 하지 않는 데 대한(for)
　　lame 절름발이의, 변변치 않은, 설득력 없는, 후진

'운동 전에 먹으면 안 된다'는 게 낭설이라는 거 아세요?

❶ 운동을 시작하기 전에 적은 양의 음식을 먹는 게 좋은데, 이유는 몸에 필요한 에너지를 공급하려면 연료가 필요하기 때문입니다.

❷ 그 연료는 음식과 음료에서 얻을 수 있습니다.

❸ 적당한 양의 음식은 근육이 이제 시작할 활동을 준비할 수 있게 합니다.

❹ 바나나, 견과, 물 한 컵 등 약간의 과일과 음료로 연료 탱크를 채우세요.

❺ 운동에 관한 낭설이 더 있습니다.

❻ 사람들은 운동 전에 반드시 스트레칭을 해야 한다고 믿습니다.

❼ 하지만 몇몇 연구에 따르면 가끔은 스트레칭이 부상으로 이어지기도 하는데, 늘어난 근육 섬유가 염좌에 더 취약해지기 때문입니다.

❽ 몇몇 여성들은 운동하면 지방이 근육이 될까 두려워합니다.

❾ 그들은 역기를 들면 근육질의 우람한 몸이 된다고 생각합니다.

❿ 하지만 지방과 근육 조직은 완전히 다르기 때문에 그건 말도 안 되는 낭설이고, 운동을 하지 않으려는 궁색한 변명입니다.

Reading in dim light, and reading very small print for a long time, are not causes of eye damage. Of course, your eyes will surely feel tired, exhausted, uncomfortable, or become bloodshot by doing that. But, those bad reading habits will not cause permanent eye damage. Nevertheless, eye fatigue is not good for your eye heath. Doctors do not exclude the possibility that eye fatigue from overuse or misuse can ruin your eyesight. Also, the way you use your eyes early in life can affect your vision. In order to reduce eye fatigue, read books or newspapers in a well-lit room, and take a break from time to time to let your eyes rest for a while.

Likewise, sitting too close to the TV and wearing someone else's glasses also will not hurt your eyes. Sitting close to the TV may lead to nearsightedness, but there is no evidence that these two behaviors cause permanent damage to your eyes.

There is another myth about eyes : carrots. Carrots are rich in beta carotene, which is changed into vitamin A in the body. Vitamin A is crucial for maintaining normal vision, so vitamin A deficiency is a main cause of blindness. Despite this, eating supplementary carrots will not improve your eyesight.

Words & Expressions

dim 흐린, 어둑한 exhausted 지친 bloodshot 핏발이 선 permanent 영구적인 eye fatigue 눈의 피로
exclude 배제하다, 제외하다 overuse 남용하다 abuse v. 오용하다 n. 남용, 오용 early in life 인생 초기에, 어
렸을 때 reduce 줄이다 well-lit 조명이 잘 된 likewise 마찬가지로 nearsightedness 근시 crucial 필수적인
deficiency 결핍, 부족 supplementary 보충의, 추가의

1. What can be the best title of this story?

a. How To Protect Your Eyes From The TV

b. Keep An Eye On Your Eyes : Danger Everywhere

c. Unexpected Facts About Vitamin A

d. Facts & Myths About Eyes

2. If you want to reduce eye fatigue, you must _____ .

a. wear others' glasses

b. overuse or misuse your eyes whenever possible

c. rest your eyes from time to time

d. read books in a dim-lit room

3. Choose the correct words for each sentence.

a. I wanted this affair to be settled without <u>bloodshot</u> / <u>bloodshed</u> / <u>bloodstained</u>.

b. Mr. Baker let me join his team <u>despite</u> / <u>despite that</u> / <u>despite of the fact that</u> my many faults.

c. We don't <u>include</u> / <u>exclude</u> / <u>preclude</u> the possibility of life on Mars even though there is no definite proof.

Answer **1.** d **2.** c **3.** bloodshed ｜ despite ｜ exclude

Listening Drill – Dictation

Reading   , and reading very small print for a long time, are not causes of eye damage. Of course, your eyes will surely   , exhausted, uncomfortable, or become bloodshot by doing that. But, those bad reading habits will not cause permanent eye damage. Nevertheless, eye fatigue is not good for your eye heath. Doctors

                that eye fatigue from overuse or misuse can   . Also, the way you use your eyes early in life can affect your vision. In order to   ,
read books or newspapers in a   , and take a break from time to

             .

          , sitting too close to the TV and wearing someone else's glasses also will not hurt your eyes. Sitting close to the TV may lead to nearsightedness, but there is no evidence that these two behaviors cause permanent damage to your eyes.

There is another myth about eyes : carrots. Carrots are rich in beta carotene, which is changed into vitamin A in the body. Vitamin A   maintaining normal vision, so   is a main cause of blindness. Despite this, eating supplementary carrots will not improve your eyesight.

Did You Know Reading In Dim Light Is Not The Cause Of Eye Damage?

1 [1] Reading in **dim** light, and [2] reading very small print for a long time, are
동명사 주어 [1] 어둑한 빛에서 읽는 것 [2] 작은 글자를 오랫동안 읽는 것 (주어가 2개) + are (복수)

not **causes** of eye **damage**.
　　n. 원인　　　　손상, 손해 (damages 손해배상금(돈)일 때는 -s 항상 복수형)

2 Of course, your eyes will surely [1] feel (**tired**, **exhausted**, **uncomfortable**),
　　　　　　　　　　　　　　　　　feel ( )…를 느끼거나 or become bloodshot 충혈되다

or [2] become bloodshot by doing that.
　　　　　　　　그렇게 함으로써 (전치사 by + 동명사) doing = reading in dim light, reading small print

3 But, (those bad reading habits) will not cause **permanent** eye damage.
　　those + habits 그런 습관들 (복수)　　　　　　v. 원인이 되다 (①번 문장에서는 명사, 여기서는 동사)
　　　　　　　　　　　　　　　　　　　　　　permanent a. 영구적인

4 Nevertheless, eye **fatigue** is not good for your eye heath.
그럼에도 불구하고, 그렇긴 하지만　　　피로　　= is bad for

5 Doctors do not **exclude** the possibility that
　　　　　　　　　　　가능성을 배제하다 exclude 배제하다 include 포함하다 conclude 결론내다

eye fatigue from (overuse or misuse) can **ruin** your **eyesight**.
주어 eye fatigue 동사 can ruin　　　　　v. 망치다, 손상시키다　　n. 시력
　　over과도한 + use 사용　　mis 잘못된 + use 사용

6 Also, (the way you use your eyes early in life) can **affect** your **vision**.
　　　　　　　　↑　수식　　　　　　　　　　= have an effect 영향을 미치다
　　주어 (어린 시절 눈을 사용한 방식) eyes, life가 아니라 the way + 동사 can affect　　　vision n. 시력(= eyesight), 통찰력

7 In order to **reduce** eye fatigue, [1] read (books or newspapers) in a well-lit room,
　　v. 줄이다 (= decrease)　　well-lit 조명이 잘 된 / poorly-lit, dimly-lit 조명이 안 좋은, 어두운
　　　　　　　　　　　　light a. 가벼운, 밝은, 옅은 n. 빛, 전등, (성냥)불 v. 빛을 밝히다, 불을 붙이다 (light-lit/lighted)

and [2] **take a break** (from time to time) to let your eyes rest for a while.
쉬다, 멈추다　　　　　　　　　　　사역동사 let + 목적어 eyes + 동사원형 rest – 눈을 쉬게 하다
　　　　　　　　　　　　　　　　rest n. 휴식 v. 쉬다 (take a rest) 문장에서는 동사

8 Likewise, (sitting too close to the TV) and (wearing someone else's glasses) also
　　　　동명사 주어 ( ), and ( )　　wear 얼굴, 몸에 두르다, 걸치다 – wear a hat 모자 쓰다, wear socks 양말 신다
　　　　　　　　　　　　　　wear a necklace 목걸이하다, wear an eye patch 안대하다, wear a bandage 붕대감다

will not **hurt** your eyes.
= won't　　v. 손상을 주다(= damage, ruin)

⑨ (Sitting close to the TV) may lead to **nearsightedness**, but there is no evidence

TV 가까이 앉는 것 – 동명사 주어   근시로 이어지다   (farsightedness 원시)   there is 단수동사 + 불가산명사 evidence

that these two behaviors cause permanent damage to your eyes.

    ¹⁾ sitting too close to the TV   v. 원인이 되다, 야기하다
    ²⁾ wearing someone else's glasses

⑩ There is another myth about eyes : carrots.

there is 단수동사 + another + myth 단수명사

⑪ Carrots are rich in beta carotene, which is changed into vitamin A in the body.

    ··· 풍부하다   rich a. 부유한, 풍부한(in)   콤마 which (계속 용법) ···로 바뀌다

⑫ Vitamin A is **crucial** for maintaining normal vision,

    필수적이다 (be essential for)   maintain normal vision 정상 시력을 유지하다

so vitamin A **deficiency** is a main cause of blindness.

    비타민A 결핍증   n. 원인   blind a. 눈이 보이지 않는   blindness n. 실명 go blind 실명하다

⑬ Despite this, (eating **supplementary** carrots) will not **improve** your eyesight.

= in spite of this   추가로 당근을 먹는 것 – 동명사 주어   개선하다, 좋아지게 하다
이럼에도 불구하고   supplement n. (영양제) 보충제, (신문) 증보판, (여행 등) 추가요금 v. 보충/추가하다

> 어두운 불빛에서 글을 읽는다고 시력이 손상되는 건 아니라는 거 아세요?

❶ 어두운 불빛에서 글을 읽거나 아주 작은 글자를 오랫동안 읽는 게 시력이 손상되는 원인은 아닙니다.

❷ 물론 그렇게 하면 눈이 분명 피로하고 힘들고 불편해지며 충혈 됩니다.

❸ 하지만 그런 나쁜 독서 습관이 눈에 영구적인 손상을 가하는 건 아닙니다.

❹ 그럼에도 불구하고 눈의 피로는 눈 건강에 좋지 않습니다.

❺ 의사들은 남용이나 오용으로 인한 눈의 피로가 시력을 망칠 가능성을 배제하지 않습니다.

❻ 그리고 어린 시절 눈을 어떻게 사용하느냐가 시력에 영향을 미칠 수 있습니다.

❼ 눈의 피로를 줄이려면, 조명이 잘 된 방에서 책이나 신문을 읽고 눈이 잠깐 쉴 수 있도록 가끔씩 쉬는 시간을 가집니다.

❽ 마찬가지로 텔레비전에 너무 가까이 앉거나 남의 안경을 쓰는 것 역시 눈을 손상시키는 건 아닙니다.

❾ 텔레비전에 가까이 앉으면 근시가 생기겠지만, 이런 두 가지 행동이 눈에 영구 손상을 입힌다는 증거는 없습니다.

❿ 눈에 관한 낭설이 하나 더 있는데, 바로 당근입니다.

⓫ 당근은 베타카로틴이 풍부한데, 이는 몸 안에서 비타민 A로 바뀝니다.

⓬ 비타민 A는 정상 시력을 유지하는데 필수적이라서 비타민 A 부족은 실명의 주요 원인입니다.

⓭ 그렇지만 당근을 먹는다고 시력이 좋아지는 건 아닙니다.

You know not all commercials are true. Whitening toothpastes wash the surfaces of your teeth stained by coffee, tea and food. Abrasive ingredients in the toothpaste remove the stains. This makes your teeth look whiter, not makes them white. So, what the commercials say is not only a myth, but also a kind of exaggerative advertisement.

There is another myth that toothpastes are all the same. That is a myth. Some toothpastes contain more abrasive materials, dyes, alcohol and artificial sweeteners and flavors than others. Some contain fluoride, some don't. According to the experts, toothpastes with no alcohol, no dyes, and less abrasives are better.

Additionally, many people believe that fluoride toothpastes are better than non-fluoride toothpastes. That is not a myth, because it is true that the use of fluoride is closely related to fewer dental cavities. However, the common tooth paste myth of 'the more I use, the better' is not true. The more paste you use, the more money you waste. The important things are the way you brush your teeth, the quality of the toothpaste and the brush - not the amount of the paste and foam.

Words & Expressions

whitening 표백, 희게 함 commercial a. 상업의 n. 상업 광고 방송 surface 표면 stain 얼룩, 얼룩지게하다 abrasive 연마제의, 거친 exaggerative 과장하는 advertisement 광고 dye 염료, 염색하다 artificial 인공적인 flavor 향, 향미료 fluoride 불소 cavity 구멍 dental cavity 충치 quality 질, 품질 foam 거품

1. What is the main idea of the story?

    a. Must buy fluoride toothpastes for your teeth.

    b. An exaggerative advertisement is a serious crime.

    c. Tooth pastes are all different but their price is all the same.

    d. Whitening tooth pastes only make teeth look whiter, not make them white.

2. According to the passage, which sentence is <u>wrong</u>?

    a. Not all commercials are true and commercials of whitening toothpastes are not an exception.

    b. Whitening toothpastes do not make your teeth white to the core.

    c. All whitening toothpastes contain the same amount of fluoride.

    d. The important thing is the way you brush your teeth, not the price of the toothpaste.

3. Choose the correct words for each sentence.

    a. <u>What</u> / <u>When</u> / <u>Who</u> you just said is one of the most foolish remarks I have ever heard.

    b. The 4U center, a bona fide <u>no-profit</u> / <u>non-profit</u> / <u>not-profit</u> organization, is now recruiting volunteers.

    c. While some of her notes were spread all over the desk, some <u>didn't</u> / <u>wasn't</u> / <u>weren't</u>.

                         Answer **1.** d   **2.** c   **3.** What | non-profit | weren't

Listening Drill – Dictation

You know not all commercials are true. Whitening toothpastes wash the surfaces of your teeth   coffee, tea and food.   in the toothpaste remove the stains. This makes your teeth look whiter, not makes them white. So,   is not only a myth, but also a kind of   .

There is another myth that toothpastes are all the same. That is a myth. Some toothpastes contain more abrasive materials, dyes, alcohol and and flavors than others. Some contain fluoride, some don't. According to the experts, toothpastes with no alcohol, no dyes, and less abrasives are better.

              , many people believe that fluoride toothpastes are better than non-fluoride toothpastes. That is not a myth, because it is true that the use of fluoride is closely related to   . However, the common tooth paste myth of 'the more I use, the better' is not true. The more paste you use,   . The important things are   you brush your teeth, the quality of the toothpaste and the brush - not the amount of the paste and   .

Did You Know Whitening Toothpastes Do Not Whiten Your Teeth?

1 You know not all commercials are true.

부분 부정 - 모두가 다 사실이 아니다 (사실도 있고 아닌 것도 있다).
commercial n. 광고 a. 상업의

2 (Whitening toothpastes) wash the surfaces of your teeth stained by

주어 ( ) 동사 wash - 주어는 …를 닦는다   단순히 닦는 건 wash, 칫솔로 솔질을 하는 건 brush   ↑ 수식 ┃ ( )로 얼룩진 치아
surface n. 표면, 외관

(coffee, tea and food).

3 (Abrasive ingredients in the toothpaste) remove the stains.

주어 ( ) toothpaste가 아니라 ingredients + 동사 remove   stain v. 얼룩지게 하다 n. 얼룩 (remove the stains 얼룩을 제거하다)
(주어가 3인칭, 현재시제지만 복수라서 removes가 오면 안 된다.)   stain remover 얼룩 제거제 stainless 얼룩이 지지않는, 스테인리스

4 This makes your teeth look whiter, (not makes them white).

주어 this (3인칭 단수현재) + 사역동사 makes + 목적어 your teeth + 동사원형 look
너의 치아가 …보이게 만든다 (치아가 희어지게 만드는 게 아니라)   this : (앞 문장) 연마제 성분이 얼룩을 제거하는 것

5 So, (what the commercials say) is not only a myth, but also

선행사를 포함한 관계대명사 what (단수) + is
the thing that the commercials say 광고가 말하는 것

a kind of exaggerative advertisement.

일종의 a kind of 과대광고 exaggerative advertisement (허위 광고 false ad)

6 There is another myth that toothpastes are all the same.

there is 단수동사 + another + myth 단수명사   be all the same 다 똑같다 (the가 꼭 들어간다.)

7 That is a myth.

8 Some toothpastes contain more (abrasive materials, dyes, alcohol and artificial

Some toothpastes contain more ( ) than others. 일부 치약은 다른 치약보다 ( )이 더 들어있다   a. 인공적인, 억지로 꾸민
contain v. 함유하다, (감정을) 억누르다   dye n. 염료 v.염색하다

sweeteners and flavors) than others.

artificial sweetners and (artificial) flavors 인공의 감미료 & 향미료
flavor n. 향, 향미료, 맛

9 Some contain fluoride, some don't.

= some toothpastes (복수)   = don't contain fluoride

10 According to the experts, (toothpastes with no alcohol, no dyes, and less abrasives)

…에 의하면 (to + 명사)   주어 ( ) abrasives가 아니라 toothpastes + 동사 are   abrasive n. 연마제
no alcohol 무알콜, no dyes 무색소, less abrasive (다른 제품에 비해 양이) 적은 연마제

are better.

⑪ **Additionally**, many people believe that
게다가 (= in addition, besides)

fluoride toothpastes are better than **non-fluoride** toothpastes.
더 낫다, 더 좋다 (good-better-best) non 없는, 아닌 + fluoride 불소 : 불소가 없는
non-smoker 비흡연자, non-stop 멈추지 않는, 직행버스, non-negotiable 협상불가의
non profit 비영리의 nonfiction 실화 nonsense 말이 안 되는 말

⑫ That is not a myth, because it is true that (the use of fluoride) is closely related to
that 이하 문장의 주어 ( ) use 불소의 사용 + 동사 is   밀접하게 관련이 있다 (to)
수동태 be 부사 pp

··· the use of fluoride is closely related to fewer dental cavities than in individuals who do not use fluoride.
불소의 사용은 더 적은 충치와 밀접한 관련이 있다 – 불소를 사용하지 않는 사람들의 충치보다

fewer **dental cavities**.
dental 치아의 + cavity 구멍 = tooth decay 충치

⑬ However, (the common tooth paste myth of 'the more I use, the better') is not true.
주어 ( ) myth (···라는 낭설), 동사 is   수식

⑭ The more paste you use, the more money you **waste**.
the 비교급, the 비교급 ···일수록 더 ···이다   v. 낭비하다, 버리다 n. 낭비, 쓰레기 (이 문장에서는 동사)

⑮ The important things are [1] the way you brush your teeth, [2] the **quality** of
중요한 점 두 가지 [1] 양치 방법   v. 솔질하다   quality 질, 품질 quantity 양
[2] 치약과 칫솔의 품질

(the toothpaste and the brush) - not the amount of the (paste and foam).
n. 솔, 칫솔   중요하지 않은 점 한 가지 – 치약과 거품의 양

미백 치약이 치아를 희게 만들지 않는다는 거 아세요?

❶ 모든 광고가 다 사실은 아니라는 거 아실 겁니다.   ❷ 미백 치약은 커피, 차, 음식으로 얼룩진 치아의 표면을 닦아줍니다.
❸ 치약 속의 연마제 성분이 얼룩을 제거하는 것 뿐 입니다.   ❹ 그건 치아를 더 희게 보이도록 만들 뿐, 치아를 희게 만드는
건 아닙니다.   ❺ 그러니까 광고에서 하는 말은 낭설일 뿐 아니라 일종의 과대광고입니다.

❻ 치약은 다 그게 그거라는 낭설이 있습니다.   ❼ 낭설입니다.   ❽ 어떤 치약은 다른 치약에 비해 연마성분, 염색제, 알
코올, 감미료나 향이 더 많이 들어있습니다.   ❾ 또 어떤 것은 불소가 들었고, 어떤 건 들어있지 않습니다.   ❿ 전문가들
에 의하면 알코올과 염색제가 없고 연마제가 적게 들어 있는 게 좋은 치약입니다.

⑪ 덧붙이자면 많은 사람들이 불소가 없는 것보다 있는 게 좋은 치약이라고 믿습니다.   ⑫ 이건 낭설이 아닌데, 불소 사용
이 충치와 밀접한 관련이 있기 때문입니다.   ⑬ 그러나 '더 많이 사용할수록 좋다'는 일반적인 치약 낭설은 사실이 아닙니다.
⑭ 치약은 더 많이 사용할수록 돈만 더 낭비할 뿐입니다.   ⑮ 중요한 건 양치 방법, 치약과 칫솔의 품질이지, 치약과 거품의
양이 아닙니다.

241

Some people think coffee will help them sober up. They think if they drink a cup of coffee after drinking, the alcohol will wear off sooner than normal, or at least they can hide the effects of alcohol behind caffeine. But that's a myth. No matter how much coffee you drink, a slow reaction time and poor judgement caused by alcohol cannot be worn off or hidden by caffeine.

Furthermore, the rumor about coffee's effect of increasing energy is also a myth. The reason why they feel that coffee makes them feel energized is that they think they feel less sleepy after drinking coffee. It is true that coffee does make you wake up and be more alert, because caffeine is a stimulant. So, you can work better or study late at night with the help of coffee.

The relation between anemia and coffee, however, is not a myth. As a matter of fact, coffee can cause a loss of vitamins and minerals such as vitamin C, calcium, zinc and iron. So, If you suffer from anemia (iron deficiency), you should steer clear of coffee.

Words & Expressions

sober a. 술 취하지 않은 v. 정신이 들게 하다 wear off (서서히, 닳아) 없어지다, 사라지다 a slow reaction time 느린 반응 속도 energize 열기, 활력을 돋우다 stimulant 자극제 anemia 빈혈 calcium 칼슘 zinc 아연 iron 철 iron deficiency 철분 결핍 steer clear of 피하다

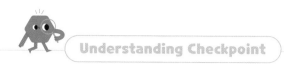

1. What is the main idea of the story?

   a. The caffeine in coffee is just a stimulant, not a cure-all.

   b. If you don't drink coffee while studying, you can't get a good grade.

   c. Coffee is absolutely dangerous because caffeine is a stimulant.

   d. You can hide the effects of alcohol behind caffeine.

2. Anemia and coffee _____ .

   a. have nothing to do with each other

   b. have something in common

   c. have something to do with each other

   d. are not related to each other

3. Choose the correct words for each sentence.

   a. How long does it take for anesthesia to <u>wear off</u> / <u>go out</u> / <u>sober up</u>?

   b. How many children are <u>suffered by</u> / <u>suffering into</u> / <u>suffering from</u> hunger today?

   c. No matter what song you sing and no matter <u>how</u> / <u>what</u> / <u>when</u> good you do, I will not chose you as the winner.

Answer **1.** a **2.** c **3.** wear off | suffering from | how

Some people think coffee will help them   . They think if they drink a cup of coffee after drinking, the alcohol will wear off sooner than normal, or at least they can hide the effects of alcohol behind caffeine. But that's a myth. No matter how much coffee you drink, a slow reaction time and   caused by alcohol cannot   or hidden by caffeine.

Furthermore, the rumor about coffee's   is also a myth.   they feel that coffee makes them feel energized is that they think they   after drinking coffee. It is true that coffee does make you wake up and be more alert, because caffeine is a stimulant. So, you can work better or study late at night with the help of coffee.

              anemia and coffee, however, is not a myth. As a matter of fact, coffee can   vitamins and minerals such as vitamin C, calcium, zinc and iron. So, If you   (iron deficiency), you should   coffee.

243

Did You Know Coffee Won't Help You Sober Up?

1 Some people think coffee will help them **sober up**.

help + 목적어 them + 동사원형 sober up (술 깨다)
Please help me finish this. 이걸 끝내게 나를 도와주십시오.

2 They think if they **drink** a cup of coffee (after **drinking**), the alcohol will **wear off**

coffee 불가산명사　　　　주절의 주어와 일치, 생략 – after they drink alcohol　　서서히 없어지다
two cups of coffee (O) two coffees (X)
첫번째 drink는 '커피/음료/물 마시다' 두번째 drinking은 '술을 마시다, 음주하다'

sooner than normal, or at least they can **hide** (the **effects** of alcohol) behind caffeine.

정상(일반적인 속도)보다 빠르게　　　　　　　　　　　v. 감추다　알코올의 효과　　　　　　　카페인 뒤로
effect n. 영향, 효과 affect v. 영향을 미치다(= have an effect on)

3 But that's a myth.

4 No matter how much coffee you drink, (a slow **reaction** time and

아무리 많이 …한다해도　　　　　　　　　주절의 주어 ( ) 알코올에 의해 야기된 [1] 늦어진 반응 시간 [2] 안 좋은 판단력

poor judgement caused by alcohol) cannot be [1] worn off or [2] hidden by caffeine.

　　　　　↑　수식　　　　　　　　　수동태 be worn off 없어지다 be hidden by caffeine 카페인에 의해 숨겨지다
poor a. 가난한, 형편없는, 빈약한 (poor eyesight 안 좋은 시력, poor quality 저질)

5 Furthermore, (the rumor about coffee's effect of **increasing** energy) is also a myth.

주어 ( ) energy가 아니라 the rumor (에너지를 높이는 커피의 효과에 대한 소문) + 동사 is
increase 증가시키다, 늘리다

6 The reason (why they feel that coffee makes them feel **energized**) is that

( )는 why 의문문이 아니라 명사절 – 커피가 힘이 난다고 느끼게 한다고 느끼는 이유
The reason (why…) is that : (왜 …인지) 이유는 that 이하 절이다　　사역동사 make + 목적어 them + 동사원형 feel

they think they feel less sleepy after drinking coffee.

덜 졸리게 느끼다 (커피를 먹지 않았을 때 보다–비교급) after they drink coffee (주절의 주어와 일치, 생략)
여기서 drink는 '(물/음료) 마시다'

7 It is true that coffee **does make you** [1] **wake up** and [2] be more **alert**,

강조의 조동사 do에 3인칭 단수 주어의 현재형이 반영되어 does + 동사원형 make
사역동사 make + 동사원형 [1] wake up, [2] be alert 잠이 깨게 만들고 정신을 맑게 만든다

because caffeine is a **stimulant**.

stimulate v. 자극하다 stimulation n. 자극 stimulant n. 자극제, 각성제

8 So, you can [1] **work better** or [2] **study late at night** (with the help of coffee).

(커피를 먹지 않은 때와 비교할 때) [1] 더 잘 일하고 [2] 밤늦게까지 공부하다　　　　　　커피의 도움으로

244

⑨ (The relation between anemia and coffee), however, is not a myth.

주어 ( ) coffee가 아니라 the relation (커피와 빈혈과의 관계) + 동사 is

⑩ As a matter of fact, coffee can cause a loss of (vitamins and minerals)

in fact 사실 야기하다 cause + ( )의 손실 a loss of ( )

such as vitamin C, calcium, zinc and iron.

커피로 인해 손실되는 비타민과 미네랄의 예 such as

⑪ So, If you **suffer from anemia** (iron **deficiency**), you should **steer clear of** coffee.

병을 앓다, …로 고생하다   = 동격   n. 결핍, 부족   피하다

I suffer from anemia. (O) 나는 빈혈이 있다.

I am suffered from anemia. (X) (undergo (수술을 받다)의 경우처럼 수동태로 쓰지 않는다.)

anemia 빈혈 = iron deficiency 철분부족

커피가 술 깨는데 도움이 안 된다는 거 아세요?

❶ 어떤 사람들은 커피가 술 깨는데 도움이 된다고 생각합니다.

❷ 그들은 술 마신 후 커피 한 잔을 마시면 술기운이 평소보다 빨리 없어지거나 최소한 카페인 뒤로 술기운을 숨길 수 있다고 생각합니다.

❸ 하지만 그건 낭설입니다.

❹ 아무리 많은 커피를 마셔도, 알코올로 인한 느린 반응 시간과 판단력은 카페인으로 없어지지도 않고 감출 수도 없습니다.

❺ 게다가 커피가 힘을 북돋는다는 소문 역시 낭설입니다.

❻ 커피가 힘을 나게 해준다고 느끼는 이유는 커피를 마시면 잠이 덜 온다고 느끼기 때문입니다.

❼ 커피가 잠을 깨고 정신을 차리게 하는 건 맞지만, 그건 카페인이 자극제이기 때문입니다.

❽ 그래서 커피의 힘으로 밤늦게까지 일을 하거나 공부할 수 있는 것입니다.

❾ 하지만 빈혈과 커피의 관계는 낭설이 아닙니다.

❿ 실제 커피는 비타민 C, 칼슘, 아연, 철분 같은 비타민과 미네랄 손실을 야기합니다.

⓫ 그래서 빈혈(철분 결핍)이 있다면 커피를 피해야 합니다.

Back in the 90s, a person who had lots of time sent phony e-mails to people claiming that Shell Oil issued a warning about the danger of using cell phones at gas stations. Since then, quite a lot people have blamed cell phones for sudden gasoline fires. However, Shell Oil didn't issue such a warning, and Shell said they have 'never heard of such incidents.'

The investigations proved that the cause of sudden fires at the pumps was actually static electricity. According to the experts, static electricity emitted from cell phones is not strong enough to ignite the gasoline, which means the idea that 'cell phones cause fires at the pumps' is just a myth. But, using or turning on your cell phone can possibly release some static electricity. Although it's not enough to ignite anything, gas station owners and cell phone manufacturers tend to take the safer road. So, they ask their customers not to use cell phones while pumping gas, saying 'better safe than sorry.'

FYI, the warning that 'smoking can cause a fire at a gas station' is definitely not a myth. Never smoke at the gas station.

Words & Expressions

phony 가짜의, 위조된 **issue a warning** 경고하다 **gas station** 주유소 (the pump) **blame** 비난하다, .. 탓으로 돌리다 **investigation** 조사 **static electricity** 정전기 **emit** (빛, 전기, 소리, 가스) 내다 **ignite** 점화하다, 불을 붙이다 **manufacturer** 제조업자 **cell phone** (= celluar phone) 휴대폰 **take the safer road** 안전한 길을 선택하다 **FYI** 참고로 (for your information)

1. What can be the best title of this story?

    a. Warning! Don't Even Think Of Using Cell Phones At The Pumps

    b. Smokers, The Real Suspect

    c. Another Myth Busted - You Can Smoke At The Pumps!

    d. Sudden Gasoline Fires : What Is To Blame?

2. According to the passage, which sentence is right?

    a. Shell Oil issued a warning about the danger of using cell phones at the pumps.

    b. The cause of sudden fires at the pumps was static electricity released from cell phones.

    c. You need strong static electricity to ignite the fire.

    d. 'Smoking while pumping gas is dangerous' is a total myth.

3. Choose the correct words for each sentence.

    a. No need to hurry up. You have <u>a large number of</u> / <u>lots of</u> / <u>as many as</u> time.

    b. Dont' blame me <u>on</u> / <u>for</u> / <u>to</u> this. You just want to find someone to blame for your mistake.

    c. How can you <u>possible</u> / <u>possibly</u> / <u>possibility</u> know what I said to my boss? I just talked to him a minute ago.

Answer 1. d   2. c   3. lots of | for | possibly

Listening Drill - Dictation

    in the 90s, a person who had lots of time   to people claiming that Shell Oil   about the danger of using cell phones at gas stations. Since then, quite a lot people have blamed cell phones for sudden gasoline fires. However, Shell Oil didn't issue such a warning, and Shell said they have 'never heard of such incidents.'

The investigations proved that the cause of sudden fires at the pumps was actually   . According to the experts, static electricity   cell phones is not strong enough to ignite the gasoline, which means the idea that 'cell phones cause fires at the pumps' is just a myth. But, using or   can possibly release some static electricity. Although it's   anything, gas station owners and cell phone manufacturers tend to   . So, they ask their customers not to use cell phones while pumping gas, saying '   .'

FYI, the warning that 'smoking can   at a gas station' is definitely not a myth. Never smoke at the gas station.

Did You Know Cell Phones Have Nothing To Do With Gas Station Fires?

❶ Back in the 90s, (a person who had lots of time) sent **phony** e-mails

주어 (어느 시간 많은 사람)　　수식　　　　　　　　　　　가짜의, 위조의 (fake)

send an e-mail to …에게 이메일을 보내다　send letters to …에게 편지들을 보내다

to people claiming that Shell Oil **issued** a warning about

(이메일에) …라 주장하며　　　　…에 대한 경고를 발표하다 (경고하다)

(the danger of using cell phones at **gas stations**).

주유소에서 휴대폰 사용의 위험성　　　　= the pump 주요소

❷ Since then, (quite a lot people) have blamed cell phones for sudden gasoline **fires**.

그 때 이후　　　　　　　　　　　　blame A for B : B에 대해 A를 비난하다 (책임을 돌리다)

fire n. 화재, 불, 난방기 v. 발포하다, 해고하다 (gasoline fire 가솔린에 의한 화재)

❸ However, Shell Oil didn't issue such a warning, and

그런 such 경고를 a warning를 발표/공표하다

issue v. 발표/공표하다, 발행하다 n. 주제, 안건, 문제 (이 문장에서는 '공표하다')

Shell said they have 'never heard of such incidents.'

have never heard of (현재완료) 그런 사고에 대해 들은 적이 없다

❹ The **investigations** proved that (the cause of sudden fires at the pumps) was

that 이하 절의 주어 ( ) pumps가 아니라 the cause (주유소에서의 갑작스런 화재 원인) + 동사 was

actually **static electricity**.

정전기

❺ According to the experts, (static electricity **emitted** from cell phones) is

수식

주어 ( ) phones가 아니라 electricity (휴대폰에서 방출된 정전기) + 동사 is

not strong enough to **ignite** the gasoline, which means (the idea that

…할 만큼 충분히 강하지 않은　　　　　　콤마 which (계속용법)　　　= 동격

(앞문장) 가솔린에 불을 붙일 만큼 강하지 않다는 건데, 이 말은 … 뜻이다

주어 ( ) pumps가 아니라 the idea + 동사 is

'cell phones cause fires at the pumps') is just a myth.

❻ But, (using or **turning on** your cell phone) can **possibly**

동명사 주어 – 사용하는 것using과 켜는 것turning on　　　아마, 가능한

turn on 켜다 turn off 끄다

release some static electricity.

정전기를 내보내다

❼ Although it's not enough to ignite anything,

불을 붙이기에 충분하지 않은　ignite v. 불을 붙이다　ingnition n. 점화

(gas station owners and cell phone **manufacturers**) tend to take the safer road.

주어 ( ) + 동사 tend to …경향이 있다 + 동사원형 take   제조 업자, 생산 회사   더 안전한 길(방식)을 가다, 더 안전하게 하다

❽ So, they ask their **customers** not to use cell phones while pumping gas,

customer 손님, 고객   to부정사의 부정은 to 부정사 앞   while they pump gas (주유 중에)
consumer 소비자   주절의 주어 they와 일치, 생략

saying 'better safe than sorry.'

…라고 말하며   후회하는 거 보다 안전한 게 낫다 (속담)

❾ **FYI**, (the warning that 'smoking can cause a fire at a gas station') is

참고로 | = 동격 | 주어 ( ) the warning (흡연이 주유소에 화재를 야기할 수 있다는 경고) + 동사 is
for your information = FYI

definitely not a myth.

분명히, 틀림없이

❿ Never smoke at the gas station.

v. 담배를 피우다 n. 연기

---

❶ 과거 90년대에, 어느 시간 많은 사람이 사람들에게 가짜 이메일을 보내면서 쉘 오일 회사가 주요소에서 휴대폰 사용의 위험에 대해 경고했다고 주장했습니다.

❷ 그 때 이후 꽤 많은 사람들이 갑작스런 가솔린 화재를 휴대폰 때문이라고 비난하고 있습니다.

❸ 하지만 쉘 오일 측은 그런 경고를 한 적이 없으며, '그런 사고에 대해서도 들은 바 없다'고 밝혔습니다.

❹ 화재 조사 결과 주유소에서의 갑작스런 화재 원인은 사실 정전기로 밝혀졌습니다.

❺ 전문가들에 의하면 휴대폰은 불을 붙일 정도의 강력한 정전기를 발산하지 않는데, 이는 '휴대폰이 주유소에서 화재를 일으 켰다'는 말이 낭설이라는 뜻입니다.

❻ 하지만 휴대폰을 사용하거나 켤 때 정전기가 나올 가능성이 있긴 있습니다.

❼ 그 양이 불을 붙일 정도로 강하지는 않지만, 주유소 주인과 휴대폰 제조업자들은 안전한 길로 가길 선호합니다.

❽ 그래서 이들은 고객들이 주유 중 휴대폰을 사용하지 않기를 당부하며 '불편해도 안전한 게 낫다'고 말합니다.

❾ 참고로 '주유소에서 흡연은 불을 낼 수 있다'는 말은 절대 낭설이 아닙니다.

❿ 주유소에서는 절대 금연입니다.

57 Did You Know **You Should Not Tilt Your Head Back When Your Nose Is Bleeding?**

There are several medical myths you may want to know. When you have a nosebleed, it's not a very good idea to tilt your head back. Many people believe this will help stop the bleeding, but it's just a myth since it may actually cause blood to run into the throat and lead you to feel nauseous and vomit. The right way to stop a nosebleed is to tip your head forward and pinch your nostrils firmly with your fingers.

People think that when you are sick, you should lie down. Generally, it is true. But, sometimes it can be a myth, especially in the case of a heart attack. It sounds right that a person who is having a heart attack should lie down immediately, but lying down can make it more difficult to breathe. When having a heart attack, sitting with your knees bent is better than lying down before going to the hospital.

One more thing : quite a few parents still warn their kids not to swallow chewing gums. They believe those gums will stick to the intestines, but that's a myth. It is true that the gum base remains indigestible, but it passes out of the digestive system harmlessly.

Words & Expressions

medical 의학의 nosebleed 코피 tilt 기울이다 nausea 메스꺼움 vomit 토하다 pinch 꼬집다 nostril 콧구멍 firmly 꽉, 힘주어 immediately 당장 swallow v. 삼키다 n. 참새 indigestible 소화되지 않은 digestive system 소화기관

1. What is the main idea of the story?

    a. Heart attack patients have to tilt their head back whenever possible.

    b. If you want your blood to run into the throat, buy a pack of chewing gum.

    c. Incorrect medical information can be dangerous or even fatal.

    d. When you suffer from a disease, you should lie down.

2. You will feel nauseous and vomit if you _____ .

    a. pinch your nose too firmly

    b. lie down in case of a heart attack

    c. tilt your head back when you have a nosebleed

    d. swallow chewing gums

3. Choose the correct words for each sentence.

    a. I almost threw <u>out</u> / <u>up</u> / <u>away</u> after listening to Paul's cheesy pick-up lines such as 'your legs must be tired because you've been running through my mind all day.'

    b. <u>Bleed</u> / <u>Bleeding</u> / <u>Blood</u>, a.k.a. hemorrhaging, means the loss of blood.

    c. First lay your book on the table and <u>lie</u> / <u>lying</u> / <u>laid</u> down on the couch.

Answer **1.** c **2.** c **3.** up ∣ Bleeding ∣ lie

Listening Drill – Dictation

There are several medical myths you may want to know. When you _____ , it's not a very good idea to _____ . Many people believe this will _____ , but it's just a myth since it may actually cause blood to run into the throat and lead you to _____ and vomit. The right way to stop a nosebleed is to tip your head forward and pinch your nostrils firmly with your fingers.

People think that when you are sick, you should lie down. Generally, it is true. But, sometimes it can be a myth, especially _____ a heart attack. _____ that a person who is having a heart attack should lie down immediately, but lying down can _____ breathe. When having a heart attack, sitting with your knees bent is better than _____ before going to the hospital.

One more thing : quite a few parents still warn their kids not to swallow chewing gums. They believe those gums will stick to the intestines, but that's a myth. It is true that the gum base _____ , but it passes out of the _____ harmlessly.

Did You Know You Should Not Tilt Your Head Back When Your Nose Is Bleeding?

❶ There are several medical myths (you may want to know).

There are 복수 동사 + myths 복수 명사 　　　　　↑ 수식 　　　…myths that you may want to know – 당신이 알고 싶어할 낭설

❷ When you have a nosebleed, it's not a very good idea to tilt your head back.

코피가 나다 (복수형 have nosebleeds라고도 쓴다.) 　　　　　　　　　머리를 뒤로 젖히다 tilt v. 기울이다, 젖히다
가주어 it, 진주어 to tilt your head back 　　　　　　　　　　(tilt a head forward 머리를 앞으로 숙이다)
it's not a good idea to… to…는 좋은 생각이 아니다 =Tilting your head back is not a good idea.

❸ Many people believe this will help stop the bleeding, but it's just a myth

= to tilt a head back 　　　help + 동사원형 stop – 멈추게 하는데 도움이 되다
bleeding n. 출혈 bleed 피를 흘리다

since it may actually [1] cause blood to run into the throat and

주어 it (머리를 뒤로 젖히는 것) 동사 [1] cause and [2] lead 　　흐르다
cause ( ) to… ( )가 …하게 하다 (초래/야기하다)

[2] lead you to (feel nauseous and vomit).

lead ( ) to… : ( )를 …로 인도하다　to feel nauseous 메스꺼움을 느끼고 and (to) vomit 구토하다

❹ (The right way to stop a nosebleed) is to [1] tip your head forward and [2] pinch

↑ 수식 　　　주어 ( ) the right way + 동사 is　올바른 방법 [1] 앞으로 머리를 기울이고 and [2] 콧구멍을 집는다

your nostrils firmly with your fingers.

firm n. 회사 a. 딱딱한, 확고한 firmly ad. 단호히, 확고히

❺ People think that when you are sick, you should lie down.

lie v. 눕다(lie-lay-lain lying) 거짓말하다 (lie-lied-lied lying)
lay v. (lay-laid-laid laying) 두다, 깔다, 알을 낳다 a. 문외한의
lie down (자리에) 눕다 lay down (무언가를 어디에) 내려놓다

❻ Generally, it is true.

일반적으로, 대개

❼ But, sometimes it can be a myth, especially in the case of a heart attack.

심장마비의 경우 (구체적인 상황을 특정해서 가정하므로 the가 들어가야 맞다.)
in case of a heart attack 만약 심장마비가 생길 경우 (아직 발생하지 않은 일 가정)
in case of 만약 …한다면 / in case …에 대비하여

❽ It sounds right that (a person who is having a heart attack) should lie down

that절은 맞는 듯 들린다 　　　↑ 수식 　　　주어 ( ) 심장마비가 온 사람

immediately, but (lying down) can make it more difficult to breathe.

즉시, 당장 　　　　　　눕는 것 이것(it 가목적어)을 더 어렵게 한다 (it = to breathe 숨쉬는 것)　breath n. 숨, 호흡 breathe v. 숨쉬다
: 누우면 숨 쉬기를 더 어렵게 한다 = Lying down can make breathing more difficult.

⑨ When having a heart attack, ⟨sitting with your knees bent⟩ is better than ⟨lying down⟩
= When you have a heart attack   동명사 주어 sitting 동사 is - sitting is better than lying
불특정 주어 you 일치, 생략   sit with one's knees bent 무릎을 굽힌 채 앉다 lie down 눕다

before going to the hospital.
= before you go to the hospital 불특정 주어 you 일치, 생략

⑩ One more thing : quite a few parents still warn their kids not to swallow
                    = many + 복수명사 parents   warn ( ) to 동사 : ( )에게 …하라고 경고하다
                                                        to부정사의 부정은 to 앞에 not to swallow 삼키지 말라고

chewing gums.
chew 씹다

⑪ They believe those gums will stick to the intestines, but that's a myth.
= parents   …에 들러붙다 stick v. 들러붙다, 찌르다, (끼어) 꼼짝 못하다 n. 나뭇가지, 막대기

⑫ It is true that the gum base remains indigestible,
                                        소화되지 않은 채 남다
                                        digest v. 소화하다 digestive a. 소화의 (digestive system 소화기관)
                                        indigestion n. 소화불량 indigestible a. 소화가 안 되는 (indigest라고는 쓰지 않는다.)

but it passes out of the digestive system harmlessly.
    = gum base   harm 해 + less 없는 + ly = 해가 없이, 해롭지 않게

코피가 날 때 머리를 뒤로 젖히면 안 된다는 거 아세요?

① 알아두면 좋은 몇 가지 의학적 낭설이 있습니다.

② 코피가 날 때 머리를 뒤로 젖히는 건 좋은 생각이 아닙니다.

③ 많은 사람들이 그러면 출혈이 멎는데 도움이 된다고 믿지만, 그건 낭설인데 그럼 피가 목구멍으로 들어가 구역질과 구토가 생길 수 있기 때문입니다.

④ 코피를 멈추게 하는 올바른 방법은 머리를 앞으로 숙이고 손가락으로 콧구멍을 단단히 집는 것입니다.

⑤ 사람들은 아플 때 누워야 한다고 생각합니다.

⑥ 일반적으로 맞는 말입니다.

⑦ 하지만 가끔은, 특히 심장 마비의 경우에는 낭설이 될 수도 있습니다.

⑧ 심장마비가 온 사람은 당장 누워야 한다는 게 맞는 소리 같지만, 누우면 숨쉬기가 더 힘들어질 수 있습니다.

⑨ 심장마비가 오면 병원에 가기 전에 눕기 보다는 무릎을 굽히고 앉아 있는 게 더 낫습니다.

⑩ 한 가지 더. 꽤 많은 부모들이 아이들에게 츄잉껌을 삼키지 말라고 주의를 줍니다.

⑪ 그들은 껌이 장에 늘러 붙으리라 생각하는데 그건 낭설입니다.

⑫ 껌 베이스가 소화되지 않고 남는 건 사실이지만, 소화 기관을 거쳐 아무 해 없이 배출됩니다.

Many people think a peanut allergy is the most common food allergy among children. That's not true. Although it is easy to find people who are allergic to peanuts, and allergic reactions to peanuts are highly threatening, the most common food allergy among children is a cow's milk allergy.

There's another myth about allergies. Some people say, 'I'm allergic to cat (or other furry animals) fur.' In many cases, they are allergic not to the fur but to a certain protein in the animal's saliva or in the flakes of its skin.

Additionally, 'being too clean can be the cause of an allergy' might not be a myth since there is something called the hygiene hypothesis. The hygiene hypothesis suggests that super-clean modern lifestyles may be responsible for an increase in allergies among young children. Thanks to germ-free lifestyles, human bodies don't need to fight germs as much as they did in the past. As a result, the immune system, which hasn't been exposed to various bacteria and fungi, tends to overreact or respond sensitively to not-so-harmful substances such as pollen or mites. In fact, children who are frequently exposed to bacteria and viruses tend to have fewer allergies than children who aren't.

Words & Expressions

the most common food allergy 가장 흔한 음식 알러지 be allergic to ...에 알러지가 있다 allergic reaction 알러지 반응 threatening 위협적인 fur (동물의) 털 protein 단백질 saliva 침 flake (떨어져 나온 얇은)조각 hygiene hypothesis 위생 가설 germ-free 세균이 없는 immune system 면역 체계 fungi 곰팡이 (fungus의 복수형) overreact 과잉반응을 보이다 sensitively 민감하게 pollen 꽃가루 mite 진드기

Understanding Checkpoint

1. What is the main idea of the story?

a. People who are allergic to cat fur must avoid all kinds of furry animals.

b. There are several false myths about allergies.

c. An extremely-clean lifestyle is the main cause of a peanut allergy.

d. Human's immune system must be exposed to various bacteria.

2. According to the passage, which sentence is <u>wrong</u>?

a. The most common food allergy among children is a cow's milk allergy.

b. There is no such thing as the hygiene hypothesis, although some people think there is.

c. Allergic reactions to peanuts could be very dangerous and serious.

d. People who claim they are allergic to cat fur are likely to be allergic to a protein in its saliva.

3. Choose the correct words for each sentence.

a. Thanks to <u>you helped us</u> / <u>your help</u> / <u>help us</u>, we have tickets to the concert.

b. What part of the brain is responsible <u>to</u> / <u>for</u> / <u>of</u> memory?

c. I wonder, does Jack <u>hate</u> / <u>dislikes</u> / <u>cursed</u> me as much as he says he does?

Answer **1.** b **2.** b **3.** your help ┃ for ┃ hate

Listening Drill – Dictation

Many people think a peanut allergy is _____ _____ among children. That's not true. Although it is easy to find people who are allergic to peanuts, and _____ peanuts are _____, the most common food allergy among children is a cow's milk allergy.

There's another myth about allergies. Some people say, 'I'm allergic to cat (or other furry animals) fur.' In many cases, they are allergic not to the fur but to a certain protein in the animal's saliva or in the flakes of its skin.

Additionally, 'being too clean can be the cause of an allergy' _____ since there is something called the _____. The hygiene hypothesis suggests that super-clean modern lifestyles may _____ an increase in allergies among young children. Thanks to germ-free lifestyles, human bodies don't need to _____ as much as they did in the past. As a result, _____, which hasn't been exposed to various bacteria and fungi, tends to overreact or _____ to not-so-harmful substances such as pollen or mites. In fact, children who _____ bacteria and viruses tend to have fewer allergies than children who aren't.

255

Did You Know What The Most Common Food Allergy In Children Is?

1 Many people think a peanut **allergy** is the most common food allergy among children.

알레르기   긴 음절의 최상급 the most common 가장 흔한

둘 사이 between / 둘 이상 among

2 That's not true.

3 Although it is easy to find people (who **are allergic to** peanuts), and

가주어 it, 진주어 to find   ↑ 수식   ( )인 사람들 – 땅콩에 알레르기가 있는 사람들
: 찾는 것은 쉽다

(**allergic reactions to** peanuts) are highly **threatening**,

주어 ( ) peanuts가 아니라 reactions 땅콩에 대한 알레르기 반응들 + 동사 are highly ad. 매우, 대단히

threat n. 협박, 위협 threaten v. 위협하다 threatening a. 위협적인

(the most common food allergy among children) is a cow's milk allergy.

주어 ( ) children이 아니라 allergy 아이들 사이에 가장 흔한 음식 알레르기 + is 동사

4 There's another myth about allergies.

There is (단수 동사) + another + myth (단수 명사)

5 Some people say, 'I'm allergic to cat (or other furry animals) **fur**.'

be allergic to ( ) : ( )에 알레르기가 있다 (to + 명사)   fur n. 동물의 털 furry a. 털이 있는

6 In many cases, they are allergic not to the fur but

not A but B : A가 아니고 B 털이 아니라 특정 단백질에 알레르기가 있다

to a certain **protein** (in the animal's saliva or in the **flakes** of its skin).

↑ 수식   1) 동물 침 saliva에 있는 단백질 또는 2) 동물 피부에서 나온 조각 flakes에 있는 단백질
flake n. 어딘가에서 떨어져 나온 얇고 납작한 작은 조각
(corn flake 콘플레이크 – 옥수수를 얇고 납작하게 만든 시리얼)

7 Additionally, 'being too clean can be the cause of an allergy' might not be a myth

동명사 주어 – 너무 깨끗한 것   n. '원인'   낭설이 아닐 수도 있다 (might 부정 – might not)

since there is something (called the **hygiene hypothesis**).

↑ 수식   hygiene 위생 + hypothesis 가설
something that is called ( ) : ( )라 불리는 것

8 The hygiene hypothesis suggests that (super-clean modern lifestyles)

엄청 깨끗한 현대 생활 방식

may **be responsible for** an increase in allergies among young children.

책임이 있다 (for + 명사)   increase v. 증가하다 n. 증가 (여기서는 명사 증가 – 알레르기 증가에 책임이 있다)
an increase in population 인구 증가

⑨ Thanks to **germ-free** lifestyles, human bodies don't need to fight **germs**
세균 없는 생활 방식 덕분에   – free 없는 (fat-free 무지방 wrinkle-free 주름없는)   germ 세균, 미생물

as much as they did in the past.
…만큼 많이   = fought germs 과거에 그랬던 (세균과 싸웠던) 거 만큼

⑩ As a result, the **immune system**, (which hasn't **been exposed to various**
the immune system 수식하는 ( ) – (다양한 박테리아와 곰팡이에 노출되지 않은) 면역체계
주어 the immune system (3인칭 단수 현재) + 동사 tends to   various 다양한 + 복수 명사

bacteria and **fungi**), tends to [1] **overreact** or [2] **respond sensitively** to
bacterium 단수 – bacteria 복수   tends to overreact or (tends to) respond
   fungus 단수 – fungi 복수   overreact 과잉반응하다 respond sensitively to ( ) : ( )에 민감하게 반응하다

(not-so-harmful substances) such as **pollen** or **mites**.
그다지 해롭지 않은 물질의 예 such as pollen or mites (꽃가루, 진드기)

⑪ In fact, (children who are **frequently** exposed to bacteria and viruses)
        ↑___수식___| 자주, 흔히
   주어 ( ) children 박테리아와 바이러스에 자주 노출된 아이들 + 동사 tend to

tend to have fewer allergies than children (who aren't).
   fewer than 더 적은 (비교급)   ↑___수식___|
   children aren't frequently exposed to bacteria and viruses
   박테리아와 바이러스에 자주 노출되지 않은 아이들보다 (…더 적다)

⟨ 어린이들에게 가장 흔한 음식 알레르기 무엇인지 아세요? ⟩

① 많은 사람들이 어린이들에게 가장 흔한 음식 알레르기는 땅콩이라고 생각합니다.

② 그건 사실이 아닙니다.

③ 땅콩 알레르기가 있는 사람들이 많고 땅콩 알레르기 반응이 대단히 위험하긴 하지만, 어린이들 사이에 가장 흔한 음식 알레르기는 우유 알레르기입니다.

④ 알레르기에 관한 또 다른 낭설이 있습니다.

⑤ '나는 고양이 (또는 털을 가진 다른 동물들) 털에 알레르기가 있어,'라고 말하는 사람들이 있습니다.

⑥ 대부분의 경우, 이들은 고양이의 털이 아니라 고양이 침 혹은 고양이 피부 조각 내의 단백질에 알레르기가 있는 겁니다.

⑦ 또 '너무 깨끗한 게 알레르기의 원인이 될 수도 있다'는 건 낭설이 아닐 지도 모르는데 위생가설이라는 게 있기 때문입니다.

⑧ 위생가설은 너무 깨끗한 현대 생활방식이 어린이들 사이에 알레르기가 증가하는 데 일조했을 수도 있다고 말합니다.

⑨ 세균이 없는 생활방식 덕분에, 인간의 몸은 과거만큼 세균과 싸울 필요가 없어졌습니다.

⑩ 그 결과, 다양한 박테리아와 곰팡이에 노출되지 않은 면역체계는 꽃가루, 진드기처럼 그다지 해롭지 않은 물질에 과민반응을 보이거나 민감하게 반응하는 경향이 생겼습니다.

⑪ 실제로 박테리아와 바이러스에 자주 노출된 어린이들은 그렇지 않은 어린이들보다 알레르기가 더 적게 나타나는 경향이 있습니다.

Parents tell their children 'cut down on sweets because they contain lots of sugar.' That's true. Many sweets contain too much sugar - that's why they are called 'sweets.' But at the same time, that's a myth. If you want to cut down on sugar, you have to stop drinking sodas and drinks like sports beverages. Those sweetened drinks are the major offenders. Most schools in the US haven't gotten rid of all soda vending machines in schools for nothing.

Furthermore, many adults believe that sugar makes their kids severely active. But, according to many studies, that's a myth. Kids are prone to go a bit crazy, bouncing on the sofa and yelling loudly during their birthday parties. That's not because they eat lots of sugary sweets such as cakes, cookies and candies, but because kids just want to have fun. It has been officially proven that sugar doesn't make kids hyperactive.

However, several other rumors about sugar are true. For instance, sugar does cause heart diseases, raise your cancer risk, and even make you look old. So it's a good idea for your health not to eat too much sugar.

Words & Expressions

cut down on ...를 줄이다 contain 함유하다 sweets 단 것, 단 음식들 at the same time 동시에 sports beverage 스포츠 음료 sweetened 단 맛이 가미된 offender 범죄자 get rid of 없애다 vending machine 자동판매기 be prone to ...하는 경향이 있다 bounce 뛰다 officially 공식적으로 hyperactive 활동 과잉의

Understanding Checkpoint

1. What is the main idea of the story?

   a. Sugar is evil because it makes kids crazy.

   b. The best way to cut down on sugar is to stop eating cookies and candies

   c. You had better watch out for sugar you consume and sodas you drink.

   d. If you want to look old, steer clear of sugar.

2. Many schools in the US get rid of soda vending machines in schools since _____ .

   a. students are poor and sodas are expensive

   b. sodas turn students into fools and idiots

   c. sweet sodas make students hyperactive

   d. sodas contain an excessive amount of sugar

3. Choose the correct words for each sentence.

   a. You are building a house <u>for nothing</u> / <u>for something</u> / <u>for free</u> since nobody wants to live in.

   b. Before taking pictures, check how <u>many</u> / <u>much</u> / <u>few</u> light is there.

   c. Anyone who wants to raise chickens has to <u>rise</u> / <u>raise</u> / <u>rose</u> money to buy eggs and to build a hen house.

   Answer **1.** c **2.** d **3.** for nothing ǀ much ǀ raise

Listening Drill - Dictation

Parents tell their children '   sweets because they contain lots of sugar.' That's true. Many sweets contain too much sugar - that's why they are called 'sweets.' But at the same time, that's a myth. If you want to cut down on sugar, you have to
sodas and drinks like sports beverages. Those sweetened drinks are   .
Most schools in the US   all soda vending machines in schools for nothing.

            , many adults believe that sugar makes their kids severely active. But, according to many studies, that's a myth. Kids   go a bit crazy, bouncing on the sofa and yelling loudly during their birthday parties. That's not because they eat lots of sugary sweets such as cakes, cookies and candies, but because kids just want to have fun.   that sugar doesn't   .
However, several other rumors about sugar are true. For instance, sugar   cause heart diseases,   , and even make you look old. So it's a good idea for your health not to eat too much sugar.

259

Did You Know The Majority Of The Sugar We Consume Is Not From Sweets?

1 Parents tell their children 'cut down on sweets because they contain lots of sugar.'

줄이다 (cut back on)　　　　　　　　　　　　　= sweets
sweet a. 단, 사랑스러운 sweeten v. 달콤하게 만들다, 더 유쾌하게(좋게) 만들다 sweets n. 단 것들
sweetened a. 단 성분이 들어간 sweetie 자기, 예쁜이 (애칭)

2 That's true.

3 Many sweets contain too much sugar - that's why they are called 'sweets.'

불가산명사 much - much sugar 많은 설탕　　이것이 '달달한 것들'이라 불리는 이유이다
가산명사는 many - many candies 많은 사탕들

4 But at the same time, that's a myth.

동시에

5 If you want to cut down on sugar,

설탕을 줄이고 싶다면

you have to stop drinking [1] sodas and [2] (drinks like sports beverages).

stop drinking 마시기를 멈추다　마시기를 멈추어야 할 것 [1] 소다 [2] (스포츠 음료 같은) 음료
stop to drink 마시기 위해 하던 걸 멈추다

6 Those sweetened drinks are the major offenders.

앞서 나온 soda and drinks　　　　　　major 주요한 + offenders 범인 = 주범
　　　　　　　　　　　　　　　　offend v. 기분을 상하게 하다, 죄를 저지르다 offense n. 위법, 공격
　　　　　　　　　　　　　　　　offence n. 위법행위, 모욕, 무례 offensive a. 모욕적인, 불쾌한, 공격적인

7 (Most schools in the US) haven't gotten rid of all soda vending machines

주어 ( ) the US가 아니라 schools (복수)　　　get rid of 없애다　　　모든 소다 자동판매기 (vend v. 팔다)
주어 + 동사 not (부정) … for nothing - 주어가 괜히(이유 없이) …한 게 아니다
People don't call me Mr. Fix-it for nothing. 사람들이 괜히 나를 해결사라 부르는 게 아니다.

in schools for nothing.

8 Furthermore, many adults believe that sugar makes their kids severely active.

make ( ) 형용사 : ( )를 …하게 만들다　　　　　　　몹시, 심하게

9 But, according to many studies, that's a myth.

10 Kids are prone to go a bit crazy, [1] bouncing on the sofa and [2] yelling loudly

…하는 경향이 있다　　　　　　go crazy 날뛰다 (go a bit crazy 약간 미친 듯 날뛰다)
be prone to + tend to　　　　(go bad 나빠지다, 썩다 go bankrupt 파산하다)

during their birthday parties.

생일 파티 중에

260

⑪ That's not because they eat lots of sugary sweets (such as cakes, cookies

sugary sweets 설탕이 들어간 단 것들의 예 ( )
not because A(주어+동사), but because B(주어+동사) A 때문이 아니라 B 때문

and candies), but because kids just want to have fun.

⑫ It has been **officially** proven that sugar doesn't make kids hyperactive.

현재완료 has been 부사 pp (부사 위치 주의)   make ( ) 형용사
officially 공식적으로

⑬ However, several other rumors about sugar are true.

several 몇몇 + other + 복수 명사 rumors + 복수 동사 are

⑭ For instance, sugar does [1] cause heart diseases, [2] raise your **cancer** risk,

= for example 예를 들어   조동사 does에 걸리는 본동사 (동사원형) cause, raise, make   암
강조의 조동사 do (주어sugar가 3인칭 단수 현재라서 does)

and even [3] make you look old.

sugar가 하는 일 [1] 심장병을 야기하다 [2] 암 위험을 올리다 [3] 늙어 보이게 하다

⑮ So it's a good idea for your health not to eat too much sugar.

가주어 it 진주어 not to eat 먹지 않는 것

우리가 섭취하는 설탕 대부분이 단 과자에서 나오는 게 아니라는 거 아세요?

❶ 부모님들은 자녀들에게 '설탕이 많이 들어있으니까 단 과자를 줄여라'고 말합니다.   ❷ 맞는 말입니다.

❸ 많은 단 과자에는 과도한 설탕이 들어있고, 그래서 '단 과자'라고 불립니다.

❹ 하지만 동시에 낭설이라고 할 수 있습니다.

❺ 설탕을 줄이려면 탄산음료와 스포츠 음료를 포함한 음료수를 끊어야 합니다.

❻ 이런 단 음료들이 진짜 범인입니다.

❼ 미국의 대부분 학교가 교내의 음료수 자판기를 괜히 없앤 게 아닙니다.

❽ 또 많은 어른들은 설탕이 아이들을 심하게 활동적으로 만든다고 믿습니다.

❾ 하지만 많은 연구에 의하면, 그건 낭설입니다.

❿ 생일 파티 때 아이들은 좀 정신 없이 행동해서 소파에서 뛰고 큰 소리를 지르는 경향이 있습니다.

⑪ 그건 케이크, 쿠키, 사탕 같은 설탕이 든 과자를 많이 먹어서가 아니라, 아이들은 그냥 재미있게 놀고 싶어서 그런 겁니다.

⑫ 설탕이 아이들을 과도하게 활동적으로 만들지 않는다는 건 공식적으로 증명되었습니다.

⑬ 하지만 설탕에 관한 다른 몇 가지 소문은 사실입니다.

⑭ 예를 들어 설탕은 정말로 심장병을 유발하고 암 위험을 높이며 심지어 늙어 보이게 만듭니다.

⑮ 그러니 건강을 위해 너무 많은 설탕을 먹지 않는 게 좋겠습니다.

There is a myth that if you die in your dreams, you'll die in real life. Fortunately, that's just a myth. We often wake up suddenly while falling off a cliff, or everything abruptly stops at the moment of being hit by a bullet while dreaming. Those kinds of dreams are also included in dreams about dying. Given the fact that there are many dreams that we cannot remember, it's safe to say that almost every person has dreamed about dying. But, it's hard to find people who actually died after having a dream in which they died. So, if you have never dreamed those kinds of scary dreams yet, it's nothing to worry about.

By the way, there's an interesting myth about dreams. Some people say we can't control our dreams, but that's another false myth because some people can. And it is called "lucid dreaming." Amazingly, approximately 10% of people can control their dreams or realize they are dreaming when they are dreaming. These people actually manage to control what they want to dream about or change an existing dream into a different one.

Words & Expressions

in real life 실제 현실(삶)에서   **wake up** 잠에서 깨다   **cliff** 절벽   **abruptly** 갑자기, 불쑥   **at the moment of** ...순간에   **bullet** 총알   **control** 통제,관리하다   **false** 잘못된, 틀린   **lucid** 명쾌한, 의식이 명확한

Understanding Checkpoint

1. What can be the best title of this story?

    a. No Need To Worry About Dreams About Death

    b. The Truth About Lucid Dreaming Finally Revealed

    c. Control Your Dream? It's Like A Dream Comes True!

    d. How To Control Your Dream

2. According to the passage, which sentence is right?

    a. Almost every person has dreamed about dying.

    b. If you train hard, you will control your dreams just as you wish.

    c. It is impossible to change an existing dream into a different one.

    d. The experts of lucid dreaming don't have a scary dream.

3. Choose the correct words for each sentence.

    a. Sorry for being late. I just overslept and <u>waken</u> / <u>woke</u> / <u>wake</u> up late.

    b. I am so depressed and exhausted that I can't do <u>which</u> / <u>what</u> / <u>when</u> I'm supposed to do.

    c. About a couple of days ago, Nancy <u>dream</u> / <u>dreaming</u> / <u>dreamt</u> she was being attacked by her own brother.

Answer **1.** a **2.** a **3.** woke | what | dreamt

Listening Drill – Dictation

There is a myth that if you die in your dreams, you'll die   . Fortunately, that's just a myth. We often   while falling off a cliff, or everything abruptly stops   being hit by a bullet while dreaming. Those kinds of dreams   dreams about dying.   there are many dreams that we cannot remember, it's safe to say that   has dreamed about dying. But, it's hard to find people who actually died after having a dream in which they died. So, if you   those kinds of scary dreams yet, it's nothing to worry about.

By the way, there's an interesting myth about dreams. Some people say we can't control our dreams, but that's another false myth because some people can. And it is called "   ." Amazingly,   10% of people can control their dreams or realize they are dreaming when they are dreaming. These people actually   what they want to dream about or change an existing dream into a different one.

Did You Know No Need To Worry When You Die In Your Dreams?

❶ There is a myth that if you die in your dreams, you'll die in real life.

There + is (단수 동사) + a myth (단수 명사)　　　　　　　　　in real life 실제 상황에서, 현실에서

가정법 현재 if 주어 you + 동사 현재 die, 주어 you + will + 동사원형 die

❷ **Fortunately**, that's just a myth.

다행스럽게도

❸ ¹⁾ We often wake up suddenly while falling off a cliff, or ²⁾ everything **abruptly** stops

while we fall off a cliff (주어 일치, 생략)　　　　　　갑자기 suddenly

everything, everyone + 단수동사 (지문에서는 3인칭, 단수 현재 stop + s)

at the moment of being hit by a **bullet** while dreaming.

…의 순간에 (of + 명사, 동명사)　　　　n. 총알　　while we dream (주어 일치, 생략)

being hit by (수동태) …에 치다

❹ Those kinds of dreams are also included in dreams about dying.

those (복수) + kinds of (복수) + dreams (복수) + are

그런 종류의 꿈들　　　　　　　　　be included 수동태 포함되다

❺ **Given** the fact that there are many dreams (that we cannot remember),

= Considering that (또는 Considering the fact that)　↑　수식　│ (우리가 기억하지 못하는) 많은 꿈들

that 이하를 감안할 때

there + are 복수 동사 + dreams 복수명사

it's safe to say that almost every person has dreamed about dying.

that…라고 말해도 된다　　　　　3인칭 단수 주어, 현재 시제 every person = everyone + has

가주어 it 진주어 to say (말하는 건 안전하다, 괜찮다)　　dream about + 명사, 동명사 (about 전치사)

❻ But, it's hard to find people who (actually died after having

가주어 it 진주어 to find　↑　수식　│ people에 대한 추가설명 who 이하

(어떤 사람들을) 찾는 것은 힘들다

a dream in which they died).

after they had a dream (주어 일치, 생략)

a dream in which (그 꿈 안에서) they died

❼ So, if you have never dreamed those kinds of **scary** dreams yet,

have 부정어 never pp　　　　　　scare v. 겁을 주다 scary a. 무서운 scared a. 겁먹은

it's nothing to worry about.

가주어 it 진주어 to worry 걱정할 건 없다(nothing)

❽ **By the way**, there's an interesting myth about dreams.

그런데, 그건 그렇고 (화제를 바꿀 때)

⑨ Some people say we can't control our dreams, but that's another **false** myth

that 주어 + is 동사 (단수 동사) + another + myth (단수 명사)

because some people can.

can control their dreams

⑩ And it is called "**lucid** dreaming."

lucid 의식이 있는 + dreaming 꿈꾸기 = 자각몽

⑪ **Amazingly**, (**approximately** 10% of people) can [1] control their dreams or [2] realize

놀랍게도   주어 ( ) + 동사 can [1] control 또는 [2] realize

they are dreaming when they are dreaming.

⑫ These people actually **manage to** [1] control (what they want to dream about)

쉽지 않지만 어떻게든 …하다   선행사를 포함한 관계 대명사 what (그들이 꿈꾸길 원하는 것)을 통제하다
manage to 동사원형 [1] control 또는 [2] change

or [2] change an existing dream into a different one.

기존의 꿈에서 다른 꿈(one=dream)으로 바꾸다

꿈에서 죽어도 걱정할 필요 없다는 거 아세요?

❶ 꿈에서 죽으면 현실에서도 죽는다는 낭설이 있습니다.

❷ 다행히 그건 낭설일 뿐입니다.

❸ 낭떠러지에서 떨어지는데 갑자기 잠에서 깨거나, 꿈꾸다 총알에 맞는 순간 모든 게 느닷없이 멈춰버리기도 합니다.

❹ 이런 종류의 꿈 역시 죽는 꿈에 포함됩니다.

❺ 우리가 기억하지 못하는 꿈이 많다는 사실을 감안할 때 거의 모든 사람들이 죽는 꿈을 꾼다고 할 수 있습니다.

❻ 하지만 죽는 꿈을 꾼 뒤 죽었다는 사람을 찾기는 쉽지 않습니다.

❼ 그래서 아직 그런 무서운 꿈을 꾼 적이 없다면, 걱정할 필요는 없습니다.

❽ 그런데 꿈에 관한 재미있는 낭설이 있습니다.

❾ 어떤 사람들은 꿈은 통제할 수 없다고 말하지만, 그건 잘못된 낭설인데 어떤 사람들은 할 수 있기 때문입니다.

❿ 그걸 '자각몽'이라고 합니다.

⓫ 놀랍게도 사람들 중 10% 정도는 꿈을 통제할 수 있거나, 자신이 꿈을 꿀 때 꿈이라는 걸 인지할 수 있습니다.

⓬ 이들은 실제 꾸고 싶은 꿈을 통제할 수 있고 현재 꾸는 꿈에서 다른 꿈으로 바꿀 수도 있습니다.

Chapter 07

The Supernatural

MP3

61 Did You Know There Is Palm Reading In Western Culture?

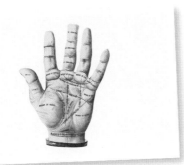

Do westerners believe in palm reading? Many people think western culture is scientific and reasonable, far from being superstitious. But palm reading, also known as palmistry or chiromancy, has been practiced among western countries for a long time. Its root can be found in Indian astrology and gypsy fortune-telling.

Some think they see people's characters and futures by reading their palms. No one knows who started to study and read the lines on palms for the first time, but people around the world, including westerners, noticed there were lots of lines on palms and the lines were different from person to person. They thought these lines must have meant something and could reveal something.

Believe it or not, there are hundreds of books about palm reading in the US, Canada, UK, Germany, and others. It is easy to find some websites about palm reading on the internet. Of course, you can also find palm readers in those western countries.

According to these sources, the four major lines are the heart line, the head line, the life line and the fate line. (Not everyone has the fate line.)

Words & Expressions

palm 손바닥 palm reading 손금 읽기 (pamistry, chiromancy) westerner 서구 사람들 scientific 과학적인 reasonable 논리적인, 합리적인 superstitious 미신적인 (n. superstition) astrology 점성술 fortune-telling 점 be different from person to person 사람마다 다르다 reveal (비밀)드러나다 source 원천, 자료 fate 운명

1. What can be the best title of this story?

    a. To Read Or Not To Read : Everything About Palm Reading

    b. Palm Readers : The messenger From Hell

    c. Palm Readers In Custody

    d. Palm Reading In Western Culture

2. Palm readers claim that they see a person's character by _____ .

    a. reading some lines on their palms

    b. searching hidden lines on their palms

    c. making several lines on their palms

    d. examining facial expressions

3. Choose the correct words for each sentence.

    a. How much do I have to pay to place an ad <u>in</u> / <u>on</u> / <u>at</u> the newspaper?

    b. Not everybody <u>have</u> / <u>has</u> / <u>having</u> a slim body like you.

    c. Even though they believed <u>of</u> / <u>in</u> / <u>to</u> the broken mirror superstition, they pretended not to care about it.

Answer   **1.** d   **2.** a   **3.** in ∣ has ∣ in

Listening Drill – Dictation

Do westerners _____ palm reading? Many people think western culture is scientific and reasonable, _____ . But palm reading, also known as palmistry or chiromancy, _____ among western countries for a long time. Its root can be found in Indian astrology and gypsy fortune-telling.

Some think they __ people's characters and futures _____ . No one knows who started to study and read the lines on palms for the first time, but people around the world, including westerners, noticed there were lots of lines on palms and the lines were different _____ . They thought these lines _____ something and could reveal something.

Believe it or not, there are hundreds of books about palm reading in the US, Canada, UK, Germany, and others. _____ some websites about palm reading _____ .
Of course, you can also find palm readers in those western countries.

According to these sources, the four major lines are the heart line, the head line, the life line and the fate line. (_____ the fate line.)

Did You Know There Is Palm Reading In Western Culture?

① Do westerners believe in palm reading?
믿다, 추종하다   palm 손바닥 + reading 읽기 = 손바닥 읽기, 손금 보기

② Many people think western culture is **scientific** and **reasonable**, far from
과학적인   합리적인   …와는 거리가 먼 + 명사, 동명사
I am far from being a racist. 나는 인종차별주의자와 거리가 멀다.
This is far from a perfect solution. 이건 완벽한 해결책과 거리가 멀다.

being **superstitious**.
superstition n. 미신 superstitious a. 미신의

③ But palm reading, (also known as palmistry or chiromancy), has been practiced
└── = 동격 ──┘   현재 완료 수동태 : 주어 palm reading이라는 관습이 시행되어 왔다

among western countries for a long time.
서구/서양 국가 western country 서양인 westerner

④ Its root can be found in ¹⁾ Indian **astrology** and ²⁾ gypsy **fortune-telling**.
주어 its root (= the root of palm reading) + 동사 can + 수동태 be found   fortune (운) + telling (말하기) 점
astrology 별 점성술 astronomy 천문학   fortune teller 점쟁이
astronaut 우주비행사 asterisk 별*표

⑤ Some think they see people's ¹⁾ **characters** and ²⁾ futures by reading their palms.
see ( ) by reading …읽어서 ( )를 보다   n. 성격, 기질

⑥ No one knows who started to ¹⁾ study and ²⁾ read the lines on palms
아무도 모른다   누가 손바닥의 선을 연구하고 읽기 시작했는지를

for the first time, but (people around the world, including westerners), noticed
처음으로   ↑ 수식   ↑ 수식
주어 ( ) people 서양인을 포함하여 전세계 사람들 + 동사 noticed

¹⁾ there were lots of lines on palms and ²⁾ the lines were different from
be different 다르다 + from person to person 사람마다
개인에 따라 = depending on the individual

person to person.

⑦ They thought these lines ¹⁾ must have meant something and ²⁾ could **reveal** something.
must have pp …임에 틀림없다   reveal v. 드러내다, 폭로하다 revelation n. 폭로, (신의) 계시
mean something 무언가 의미하다 mean nothing 아무 의미 없다

⑧ Believe it or not, there are hundreds of books about palm reading in the US,
믿거나 말거나   there + 복수 동사 are + hundreds of (수백의) + 복수 명사 books

Canada, UK, Germany, and others.

⑨ It is easy to find some websites about palm reading on the internet.

가주어 it + 진주어 to find : 찾는 것은 쉽다   in the internet으로 쓰지 않도록 주의
(= To find some websites about palm reading is easy.)

⑩ Of course, you can also find palm readers in those western countries.

palm reading 손금보기 palm reader 손금 보는 사람
psychic 심령술사 medium 영매 fortune teller, diviner 점쟁이

⑪ According to these sources, the four major lines are (the heart line, the head line,

books and websites about palm reading

the life line and the **fate** line).

n. 운명

⑫ (Not everyone has the fate line.)

not everyone 모두가 다 …인 건 아니다 – 부분 부정은 부정어 not 다음에 오는 주어에 동사를 맞춘다.
Not everyone + 단수 동사 has / Not all people + 복수 동사 have

서구 문화에서도 손금을 읽는다는 거 아세요?

❶ 서구인들도 손금을 믿을까요?

❷ 많은 이들이 서구 문화는 과학적이고 합리적이며 미신과 거리가 멀다고 생각합니다.

❸ 하지만 수상술이라고도 하는 손금은 오랫동안 여러 서구 나라에서 행해져 왔습니다.

❹ 그 근원은 인디언의 점성술과 집시의 점술에서 찾을 수 있습니다.

❺ 어떤 이들은 손금을 읽으면 사람의 성격과 미래를 알 수 있다고 생각합니다.

❻ 누가 제일 처음 손바닥의 선을 연구하고 읽기 시작했는지는 아무도 모르지만, 서구인들을 포함해 전 세계 사람들은 손바닥에 선이 많이 나 있으며 그 선이 사람마다 다르다는 걸 알아챘습니다.

❼ 그들은 그 선이 무언가를 의미하는 게 분명하고 무언가를 밝힐 수 있다고 생각했습니다.

❽ 믿거나 말거나지만, 미국, 캐나다, 영국, 독일 등에서 손금에 관한 책이 수 백 권이나 됩니다.

❾ 인터넷에서 손금에 관한 웹사이트도 쉽게 찾을 수 있습니다.

❿ 물론 이 서구 국가들에서 손금 읽는 사람들도 만날 수 있습니다.

⑪ 이들 자료에 의하면, 주요 네 가지 선은 심장선, 머리선, 생명선, 운명선입니다.

⑫ (운명선은 모두가 갖고 있는 건 아닙니다.)

The Statue of Liberty did disappear in 1983. This magic show aired live on CBS and was performed by David Copperfield. When he made the Statue disappear in front of the audience, viewers were amazed despite already being used to his awesome tricks such as the levitation of a car. How did he do that?

The audience sat in front of two pillars, and the statue was seen in the distance between the two pillars. First, he lowered the curtain hung on the two pillars to make the audience unable to see the statue. When he raised the curtain, the people could no longer see the statue between the two pillars. It was absolutely shocking. Some claimed that the platform the audience was sitting on was a secretly moving platform like a turntable. They said it must have rotated very slowly while Copperfield had lowered the curtain. The audience and the TV viewers couldn't see the giant statue, but the fact would have been, they were looking at a duplicate of another stage.

Or Copperfield might have used the very bright light to make the audience temporarily become night blind for a few seconds.

Either way, the statue did not disappear after all. It was just not seen.

the Statue of Liberty 자유의 여신상　disappear 사라지다　air 방송하다 (on air 방송 중)　audience 관중
viewer 시청자　levitation 공중부양　pillar 기둥　rotate 회전하다　lower 낮추다 내리다　duplicate 사본의, 똑
같은　temporarily 일시적으로, 임시로 (momentarily 잠깐, 순간)　become night blind 야맹증이 되다

Understanding Checkpoint

1. What is the main idea of the story?

    a. Thanks to Copperfield, the Statue of Liberty should be rebuilt again.

    b. Copperfield made the Statue of Liberty disappear by his trick.

    c. The magician was under arrest for deceiving people around the world.

    d. Copperfield was supposed to make the Statute disappear, but he couldn't.

2. According to the passage, which sentence is right?

    a. The Statue of Liberty disappeared in 1983 and never reappeared.

    b. David Copperfield is famous but not popular due to his looks.

    c. Some said Copperfield secretly used the moving platform to trick people.

    d. Unlike the audience, the TV viewers weren't shocked when the statue disappeared.

3. Choose the correct words for each sentence.

    a. The funeral for the president who died last weekend in London will be <u>broadcasting at</u> / <u>aired on</u> / <u>airing through</u> TV.

    b. When I sat <u>between</u> / <u>among</u> / <u>next to</u> Jack and Jill, I totally felt like a third wheel.

    c. Zack wanted to sue the chair manufacturer because the chair he <u>sat on</u> / <u>sat</u> / <u>sitting in</u> collapsed and he got injured.

Answer 1. b   2. c   3. aired on ǀ between ǀ sat on

Listening Drill – Dictation

The Statue of Liberty _____ in 1983. This magic show _____ CBS and was performed by David Copperfield. When he made the Statue disappear in front of the audience, viewers were amazed _____ his awesome tricks such as the levitation of a car. How did he do that?

The audience sat in front of two pillars, and the statue was seen in the distance between the two pillars. First, he _____ the curtain hung on the two pillars to make the audience unable to see the statue. When he _____ the curtain, the people _____ the statue between the two pillars. It was absolutely shocking. Some claimed that the platform the audience was sitting _____ was a secretly moving platform like a turntable. They said it must have rotated very slowly while Copperfield had lowered the curtain. The audience and the TV viewers couldn't see the giant statue, but the fact would have been, they were looking at _____ another stage.

Or Copperfield might have used the very bright light to make the audience _____ for a few seconds.

_____, the statue did not disappear after all. It was just not seen.

273

Did You Know How Copperfield Made The Statue Of Liberty Disappear?

① The **Statue** of Liberty did **disappear** in 1983.

자유의 여신상 　　　　　　　　강조의 조동사 did + 동사원형 disappear (시제는 조동사에 표현되므로 did)

② This magic shown ¹⁾ **aired** live on CBS and ²⁾ was **performed by** David Copperfield.

air 방송하다 (air live 생방송하다)　　be performed by…의해 공연되다 (수동태)
perform 공연하다, 행하다

③ When he made the Statue disappear in front of the **audience**, viewers were **amazed**

사역동사 made ( ) disappeared　　　　　　n. 청중, 관객　사람 주어 be amazed 주어가 놀라다
( )를 사라지게 만들었다　　　　　　　　　사람 아닌 주어 be amazing 주어는 놀랍다

despite already being used to his **awesome** tricks (such as the levitation of a car).

despite + 동명사, 명사 (절이 올 수 없다)　　a. 경탄할 만한, 굉장한　　levitate v. (마술, 정신력으로) 공중에 뜨게 하다
despite being used to …에 익숙함에도 불구하고　(↔ awful 끔찍한, 지독한)　levitation n. 공중부양
= despite the fact that they were used to …
be used to 명사/동명사 : 익숙하다　I am used to the cold weather. 추운 날씨에 익숙하다.
　　　　　　　　　　　　　　I am used to walking home. 집에 걸어오는 게 익숙하다

④ How did he do that?

⑤ The audience sat in front of two **pillars**, and the statue was seen in the distance

앞에　　　　　　pillar n. 기둥　　　　보여지다 (수동태)　먼 거리에서, 멀리서

between the two pillars.

기둥이 두 개라서 between (기둥이 두 개 이상이라면 among the pillars)

⑥ First, he **lowered** the curtain (hung on the two pillars) to make the audience

low a. 낮은 lower v. 낮추다　　수식　걸려 있던 커튼　make ( ) unable to see ( )가 볼 수 없게 만들다
　　　　　curtain (that was hung)　　　　　사역동사는 동사원형 또는 형용사가 올 수 있다.

unable to see the statue.

⑦ When he **raised** the curtain, the people could no longer see the statue between

raise 올리다, 기르다 / rise 올라가다　　더 이상 볼 수 없었다
The sun rises. 태양이 뜬다.
raise money 돈을 모금하다 raise a hand 손을 들다 / raise eyebrows 눈썹을 치켜뜨다 / raise chickens 닭을 키우다

the two pillars.

⑧ It was **absolutely** shocking.

사람 주어 be shocked 주어가 놀라다 / 사람 아닌 주어 be shocking 주어는 놀랍다
it = 여신상이 사라지는 마술쇼 (사람이 아닌 주어)

⑨ Some **claimed** that (the platform the audience was sitting on) was

수식　주어 ( ) the platform 관객이 앉아 있던 플랫폼, 동사 was

a secretly moving platform like a turntable.

⑩ They said it must have rotated very slowly while Copperfield had lowered the curtain.

회전했음에 틀림없다 must have pp   raise the curtain – lower the curtain
it = platform   while 절의 주어는 Copperfield
(주어가 다르기 때문에 while lowering 으로 주어를 생략한 분사구문을 쓸 수 없다.)

⑪ (The audience and the TV viewers) couldn't see the giant statue

, but the fact would have been, they were looking at a **duplicate** of another stage.

콤마로 삽입된 절 – 사실은 …일지도 모른다   look at 보다   복사본의 duplicate v. 복사하다 a. 똑같은 n. 사본
                               look up 올려다 보다, (정보) 찾아보다   another + 단수 명사 stage (other + 복수명사)

⑫ Or Copperfield might have used the very bright light

사용했을지도 모른다

to make the audience **temporarily** become night blind for a few seconds.

사역동사 make 목적어 the audience 부사 temporarily 동사원형 become   for 기간 – 몇 초 동안
become blind 눈이 멀다 / become night blind 야맹 상태가 되다
               temporary a. 일시적인 temporarily ad. 일시적으로

⑬ Either way, the statue did not disappear after all.

둘 중 어느 쪽이든   결국

⑭ It was just not seen.

be not seen 보이지 않다 (수동태)

〔 카퍼필드가 자유의 여신상을 어떻게 사라지게 했는지 아세요? 〕

① 1983년 자유의 여신상이 정말 사라졌습니다.

② CBS에서 생방송으로 방영된 이 마술 쇼는 데이비드 카퍼필드가 진행했습니다.

③ 그가 여신상을 관객들 앞에서 사라지게 했을 때, 자동차 공중 부양 같은 그의 멋진 마술에 이미 익숙해졌음에도 불구하고 시청자들은 놀라지 않을 수 없었습니다.

④ 그는 이를 어떻게 한 것일까요?

⑤ 두 기둥 사이에 관객들이 앉아 있었고, 두 기둥 사이로 멀리 여신상이 보였습니다.

⑥ 먼저 그는 두 기둥에 달린 커튼을 내려 관객들이 여신상을 볼 수 없도록 했습니다.

⑦ 그가 커튼을 올렸을 때 사람들은 두 기둥 사이의 여신상을 볼 수 없었습니다.   **⑧** 참으로 놀랄 일이었습니다.

⑨ 그러나 어떤 이들은 관객들이 앉아 있던 단상이 턴테이블처럼 몰래 움직이는 단이었다고 주장했습니다.

⑩ 카퍼필드가 커튼을 내릴 때 단이 아주 천천히 움직였다는 것입니다.

⑪ 관객과 TV 시청자들은 거대한 여신상을 볼 수 없었지만, 사실상 이들은 똑같이 만든 다른 무대를 보고 있었다는 것입니다.

⑫ 아니면 카퍼필드가 대단히 밝은 조명을 이용해서 관객들을 몇 초 동안 일시적인 야맹 상태가 되게 했을 수도 있습니다.

⑬ 어느 쪽이든 여신상은 결국 사라진 게 아니었습니다.   **⑭** 그냥 안 보인 것 뿐이었습니다.

275

63 Did You Know **How American Psychic Readers Put An AD?**

There are psychic readers, or we can say, fortune-tellers in USA, Canada, UK, and others. It's not hard to find their ads appearing on the internet, in newspapers or in magazines. Here is a sample of one such ad, to show how they promote their fortune-telling business.

Dora Charmcaster : Real Spiritual Psychic Reader, 35 years of experience.

Call today for a better tomorrow. Dora is here for you 24/7.

My services are 200% accurate, even other psychics consult me for advice.

- I offer many kinds of various love spells, such as stay-faithful spells, make-someone-grow-feelings-for-me spell, prevent-my lover-from-lying-to-me spells, and many more. You can also buy love potions for a reasonable price.

- I can help in all matters of life such as marriages, careers, law suits, health and even hair loss problems. I also do tarot card readings, aura cleansing, chakra balancing, and tea leaf readings. My specialty is past life readings.

* One free question for the first time callers. Feel free to call me anytime. *

Words & Expressions

psychic 초자연적인, 심령의 **psychic reader** 점 보는 사람, 심령술사 (= fortune-teller) **it is not hard to ...** 하는 건 어렵지 않다 **ad** 광고 (advertisement) **magazine** 잡지 **put an ad** 광고를 내다(싣다) **spiritual** 영적인 **experience** 경험 **24/7** 하루 24시간 일주일 7일 - 언제나, 항상 **accurate** 정확한 **consult** 상담하다 **offer** 제공하다 **spell** 주문 **love spell** 사랑의 주문 **such as** 이를 테면, ...와 같은 **stay faithful** (상대가) 바람을 피우지 않다 **grow feelings for** ...에 대해 좋아하는 마음이 커지다 **and many more** 이 외에 더 많다 **potion** (한 번 마실 분량의) 물약, 묘약 **reasonable** 합리적인, 저렴한 **all matters of life** 모든 인생 문제 **career** 직업, 직장생활 **law suit** 법적 소송 **hair loss** 탈모 **aura** (독특한) 분위기, 기운, 아우라 **cleansing** 정화, 깨끗하게 하기 **chakra** 차크라, 기 에너지 **tea leaf** 찻잎 **specialty** 전문, 전공 **life** 전생 **free to** ... 부담 없이 ...(to) 하다

276

Understanding Checkpoint

1. What can be the best title of this story?

    a. How Western Psychic Readers Place Ads On The Internet.

    b. Dora Charmcaster : A Psychic Reader or A Psycho?

    c. Call Dora Now For Your Better Future

    d. Magical Love Potions For Sale

2. Other psychics seek Dora's advice because _____ .

    a. she is an accurate fortune teller

    b. her love potions are cheap

    c. the first time callers don't have to pay

    d. Dora forces them to do that

3. Choose the correct words for each sentence.

    a. After the storm clouds disappeared, the stars <u>appearing</u> / <u>appeared</u> / <u>were appeared</u> in the sky.

    b. We need to do various <u>experiments</u> / <u>experiment</u> / <u>an experiment</u> to prove our theory.

    c. Your <u>advise</u> / <u>advice</u> / <u>advised</u> for newlyweds is 'do not marry?'

Answer 1. a 2. a 3. appeared ⏐ experiments ⏐ advice

Listening Drill - Dictation

There are _____ , or we can say, fortune-tellers in USA, Canada, UK, and others. _____ their ads appearing on the internet, in newspapers or in magazines. Here is a sample of one such ad, to show how they promote their fortune-telling business.

Dora Charmcaster : Real Spiritual Psychic Reader, 35 years of experience.

Call today for a better tomorrow. Dora is here for you 24/7.

My services are 200% accurate, even other psychics consult me _____ .

- I _____ various love spells, such as stay-faithful spells, make-someone-grow-feelings-for-me spell, prevent-my lover-from-lying-to-me spells, and many more. You can also buy love potions _____ .

- I can help in _____ such as marriages, careers, _____ , health and even _____ problems. I also do tarot card readings, aura cleansing, chakra balancing, and tea leaf readings. My _____ is past life readings.

* One free question for the first time callers. _____ call me anytime. *

277

Did You Know How American Psychic Readers Put An AD?

1 There are **psychic** readers, (or we can say, **fortune-tellers**) in USA, Canada, UK,

= 동격

there are 복수 동사 + psychic readers 복수 명사
psychic readers = fortune-tellers
psychic a. 초자연적인, 심령의 n. 영매, 점쟁이

and others.

2 It's not hard to find their **ads** appearing on the internet, in newspapers or

가주어 it 진주어 to find   ad 광고(advertisement의 줄임말)   각종 매체 앞에 쓰이는 전치사 주의 (on / in / in)
ads appeared on the internet – 과거 특정 시점에 인터넷에 등장한 광고
ads appearing on the internet – 현재에도 지속적으로 인터넷에 등장하는 광고

in magazines.

3 Here is a sample of one such ad, to show (how they **promote**

그런 광고 하나의 예시   ( )를 보여주기 위해 ( )는 how 의문문이 아니라 명사절 how+주어+동사
promote v. 홍보하다, 광고하다

their fortune-telling business).

4 Dora Charmcaster : Real Spiritual Psychic Reader, 35 years of **experience**.

spiritual 영적인 psychic 심령의 reader 읽는 사람   경력, 경험

5 Call today for a better tomorrow.

더 나은 내일을 위해

6 Dora is here for you 24/7.

24 hours 7 days – 일주일 내내 24시간

7 My services are 200% **accurate**, even other psychics **consult** me for **advice**.

정확한   other + 복수명사 psychics   v. 상담하다   advice n. 조언
psychic reader = psychic   advise v. 조언하다

8 - I offer many kinds of various love **spells**, such as [1] stay-faithful spells,

many많은 kinds of 종류들의 various 다양한 love spells 사랑의 주문들   stay faithful 바람을 피우지 않다
– 모두 복수   하이픈(-)으로 된 형용사 stay-faithful (a) + spells (n)

[2] make-someone-grow-feelings-for-me spells, [3] **prevent**-my lover-**from**-lying-to-me

사역동사 make ( ) 동사원형 grow   prevent ( ) from –ing ( )이 …하지 못하게 방지하다
grow feeling for me 나에 대한 좋은 감정이 자라다   lie to me 나에게 거짓말을 하다

spells, and many more.

9 You can also buy love potions for a **reasonable** price.

potion n. 물약, 마법의 묘약   합리적인(저렴한) 가격으로
portion n. 1인분, 몫   reasonable a. 합리적인, 저렴한

⑩ - I can help in all matters of life such as (marriages, careers, law suits, health and
help in …분야에서 돕다   인생의 모든 문제 – 이를 테면 such as ( )   law suit 소송

even hair loss problems).
탈모 alopecia (원형탈모 pattern baldness)

⑪ I also do ¹⁾ tarot card readings, ²⁾ aura cleansing, ³⁾ chakra balancing, and ⁴⁾ tea leaf
내가 하는(do) 것들 ¹⁾ 타로 카드 읽기 ²⁾ 영기/아우라 정화   ³⁾ 기(차크라氣) 균형 잡기 ⁴⁾ 찻잎 점(읽기)
aura (독특한) 분위기, 기운, 아우라

readings.

⑫ My specialty is past life readings.
special a. 특별한   specialize in v. 전공하다 (major in)   specialty n. 전공   speciality n. 전문, 특산물, 전문 음식
past 과거 + life 인생 = 전생

⑬ * One free question for the first time callers.
공짜의, 무료의   처음 전화하는 분들에게

⑭ Feel free to call me anytime. *
feel free to 동사 원형 : 자유롭게/부담 없이 …하다

미국인 점술사들은 어떻게 광고하는지 아세요?

① 미국, 캐나다, 영국 등에도 점술사 또는 점쟁이가 있습니다.

② 인터넷, 신문, 잡지에 나온 이들의 광고도 어렵지 않게 찾을 수 있습니다.

③ 여기 그들이 점쟁이 사업을 어떻게 홍보하는지 보여주는 그런 광고 중 한 예가 있습니다.

④ 도라 참캐스터 : 진짜 심령술사, 35년 경력

⑤ 더 나은 미래를 위해 오늘 전화하세요.   ⑥ 도라는 항상 여러분 곁에 있습니다.

⑦ 제 점술은 200% 정확해서 심지어 다른 점술사들도 조언을 들으려고 저를 찾아옵니다.

⑧ - 온갖 종류의 다양한 사랑의 주문을 제공하는데 이를 테면, 상대가 바람을 피우지 않게 할 주문, 누군가 자신을 좋아하게
만들 주문, 연인의 거짓말을 방지하는 주문 등 많습니다.

⑨ 또 저렴한 가격에 사랑의 묘약도 구매하실 수 있습니다.

⑩ - 여러 가지 삶의 문제, 예를 들어 결혼, 직장, 소송, 건강, 심지어 탈모 문제까지 도와드립니다.

⑪ 또 저는 타로 카드 읽기, 영기 정화, 차크라 균형 맞추기, 찻잎 점도 봅니다.

⑫ 제 전문은 전생 봐주기 입니다.

⑬ * 처음 전화하신 분은 질문 1회 무료입니다.   ⑭ 언제든 부담 없이 전화하세요. *

64 Did You Know The Tarot Was Originally Used To Play A Card Game?

The tarot is a pack of cards and now widely used in divination. But originally, the tarot was first used in games such as Triumphs and Italian tarocchini. Quite a few Europeans enjoyed these games during the 15th century. At that time, tarot cards were not used by occultists since they thought tarot cards did not have anything to do with magic or mysticism.

But from the late 18th century, people started to use tarot cards as a tool to gain insight into life issues or to read the future. It was said that a Swiss studied religious symbolism in the late 1700s. He thought the Tarot might be associated with Isis, a goddess in ancient Egypt, and Thoth, another of the ancient Egyptian deities. He claimed that the name "tarot" came from the Egyptian word meaning a "royal road." According to his claim, the tarot contained a royal road to secrets and hidden wisdom. Later, other scholars discovered that there was no foundation to prove his claim. Despite this, many people still firmly believe that the tarot is connected to the Egyptian Book of Thoth, and the tarot has been popularized by occult societies.

Words & Expressions

originally 원래 **a pack of cards** 카드 한 팩(꾸러미) **be widely used in** ...에 널리 사용되다 **divination** 점 (fortunetelling) **occultist** 비술(신비한 마술) 하는 사람 **don't have anything to do with** ...와 전혀 관련이 없 다 **mysticism** 신비주의 **tool** 도구 **gain** 얻다 **insight** 통찰력 **issues in life** 삶의 문제들 **a Swiss** 스위스 사람 **religious** 종교적인 **symbolism** 상징주의 **goddess** 여신 **deity** 신 **ancient Egyptian deities** 고대 이집트 신 들 **royal** 왕족의 (loyal 충성스러운) **royal road to** ...로 가는 왕도 **scholar** 학자 **foundation** 근거, 기초 **there is no foundation to** ...할 근거가 없다 **firmly** 굳게, 확고하게 **be connected to** ...와 관련이 있다 **popularize** 대중화하다, 많은 사람들에게 알리다 **occult society** 주술인 모임/사회

280

Understanding Checkpoint

1. What can be the best title of this story?

    a. The Tarot : From the Simple Game to the Tool for Divination

    b. Tarot, A Royal Road To The Secret Hidden Wisdom

    c. A Messenger From Thoth Meets The Tarot

    d. The Secret Of The Tarot Revealed!

2. According to the passage, which sentence is right?

    a. Generally, fortune-tellers and occultists use the tarot in divination.

    b. The tarot has been used in both divination and games in all ages.

    c. It was not until the early 18th century that people started to use the tarot to read the future.

    d. Scholars finally figured out the relation between the tarot and the Egyptian Book of Thoth.

3. Choose the correct words for each sentence.

    a. To my surprise, face transplants <u>now widely are accepted</u> / <u>are now widely accepted</u> / <u>are accepted now widely</u>.

    b. <u>During the early 1900s</u> / <u>In the early 1900</u> / <u>While early 1900s</u>, women's clothing was very much stylish and glamorous.

    c. I thought his novel was <u>connected</u> / <u>connection</u> / <u>connect</u> to his personal experience but it had nothing to do with his experience.

                             Answer **1.** a **2.** a **3.** are now widely accepted I During the early 1900s I connected

Listening Drill – Dictation

The tarot is a pack of cards and now widely used in divination. But   , the tarot   games such as Triumphs and Italian tarocchini. Quite a few Europeans enjoyed these games during the 15th century. At that time, tarot cards were not used by occultists since they thought tarot cards   magic or mysticism.

But from the late 18th century, people started to use tarot cards as a tool to   life issues or to read the future. It was said that a Swiss studied religious symbolism in the late 1700s. He thought the Tarot   Isis, a goddess in ancient Egypt, and Thoth, another of the   . He claimed that the name "tarot" came from the Egyptian word meaning a "royal road." According to his claim, the tarot contained a royal road to secrets and hidden wisdom. Later, other scholars discovered that   prove his claim.   this, many people   the tarot is connected to the Egyptian Book of Thoth, and the tarot   occult societies.

Did You Know The Tarot Was Originally Used To Play A Card Game?

1 The tarot is ¹⁾ a pack of cards and (now widely ²⁾ used in divination).

The tarot is ¹⁾ and ²⁾ used (수동태)　　↑　수식　｜　수동태에서 부사 위치 is now widely used (be동사와 pp사이)
　　　　a pack of 한 팩의　　　　　　　　　　　　　divination n. 점(을 침)
　　　　a pack of cards - 단수 (여러 장의 카드가 모인 하나의 꾸러미)　　divine a. 신의, 신성한　divinity n. 신성, 신학

2 But **originally**, the tarot was first used in games (such as Triumphs and

　　　　　　　수동태에서 부사 위치 : was 부사 pp　　games의 예 ( )
　　　　the tartot 타로라는 카드 (단수)　tarot cards 타로 카드 세트에 들어 있는 개개의 카드들 (복수)

Italian tarocchini).

3 Quite a few Europeans enjoyed these games during the 15th century.

= many + 복수명사

4 At that time, tarot cards were not used by occultists since they thought tarot cards

당시에　　　　　　　　　수동태 부정 be not pp by

did not have anything to do with magic or mysticism.

…와 관련이 없다 = have nothing to do with (관련이 있다 have something to do with)
　　　　　mystic n. 신비주의자　mystical a. 신비주의의　mystique n. 신비로움, 비밀스러움　mysticism n. 신비주의
　　　　　mysterious a. 이해하기 힘든, 신비한　mystery n. 수수께끼, 신비

5 But from the late 18th century, people started to use tarot cards as a tool

　　　18세기 후반부터 (후반 late, 초반 early)　　　　　use tartot cards ¹⁾ to gain insight… or ²⁾ to read the future

¹⁾ to gain **insight** into life issues or ²⁾ to read the future.

통찰력을 얻다

6 It was said that a Swiss studied **religious** symbolism in the late 1700s.

　　　어느 스위스인 한 명　　　　a. 종교적인　　　　　1700년대 후반에

7 He thought the Tarot might **be associated with** Isis, (a goddess in **ancient** Egypt),

　　　　　　…와 관련되어 있을지 모른다 (추측)　　　= 동격　　　고대의
　　　　　　　　　　　　　　　Isis 고대 이집트 풍요의 여신, 이시스
　　　　　　　　　　　　　　　ISIS 아이시스 (Islamic State of Iraq and Syria 이슬람 국가)

and Thoth, (another of the ancient Egyptian **deities**).

　　= 동격　　　　　　　deity n. 신(god), 하느님
another 다음에 deities복수 명사가 온 게 아니라, another god of the ancient Egyptian deities 고대 이집트 신들 중 또 다른 하나의 신

8 He claimed that (the name "tarot") **came from** the Egyptian word (meaning

　　　　that 이하 주어 ( ) tarot가 아니라 the name + 동사 came from　　↑　수식　｜　word which means
　　　　　　come from …에서 나오다, …출신이다 (derive from 유래하다, 비롯되다)

a "royal road.")

⑨ According to his claim, the tarot contained a royal road to (secrets and hidden wisdom).

a royal road to 명사 : …로 가는 왕도 (최고의 길/방법)
wisdom which is hidden = hidden wisdom 감추어진 지혜

⑩ Later, other **scholars** discovered that there was no **foundation** to prove his **claim**.

other 복수명사 scholars   근거가 없다 found 1. find (찾다)의 과거형 2. 설립하다 3. 기반을 두다   주장
foundation n. 기초, 토대, 근거, 재단

⑪ Despite this, ¹⁾ many people still **firmly** believe that the tarot is connected to (the

despite / in spite of 명사/동명사   굳건하게 믿다   …와 관련이 있다
…에도 불구하 (this(앞 문장)에도 불구하고 = despite the fact that the tarot has nothing to do with the Egyptian books or deities

Egyptian Book of Thoth), and ²⁾ the tarot has been **popularized** by occult societies.

현재완료 has been + 수동태 been popularized by
popular a. 인기가 있는   occult 주술적인, 초자연적인
popularization n. 대중화   society 사회, 집단, 단체
popularize v. (많은 이들에게)알리다, 대중화하다

타로가 원래 카드 게임으로 사용되었다는 거 아세요?

① 타로는 한 세트의 카드로 현재 점치는데 널리 사용되고 있습니다.

② 하지만 원래 타로는 트라이엄프스, 이탈리아 타로치니 같은 게임에 사용되었습니다.

③ 15세기에 꽤 많은 유럽인들이 이 게임을 즐겼습니다.

④ 당시 주술사들은 타로 카드가 마법, 신비주의와 아무 관련이 없다고 생각했기 때문에 타로 카드를 받아들이지 않았습니다.

⑤ 하지만 18세기 후반부터 사람들은 인생 문제에 관한 통찰력을 얻기 위한 도구로, 또는 미래를 알기 위한 도구로 타로 카드를 사용하기 시작했습니다.

⑥ 어느 스위스 사람이 1700년대 후반에 종교적 상징주의를 연구했다고 합니다.

⑦ 그는 타로가 고대 이집트 여신 이시스와 고대 이집트 신 중 하나인 토트와 관련이 있을 수 있다고 생각했습니다.

⑧ 그는 '타로'라는 이름이 이집트어에서 온 것이며 '왕의 길'을 뜻한다고 주장했습니다.

⑨ 그의 주장에 따르면 타로는 비밀과 숨겨진 지혜로 가는 왕도를 담고 있다는 것입니다.

⑩ 후에 다른 학자들이 그의 주장을 증명할 근거가 없다는 걸 밝혀냈습니다.

⑪ 그럼에도 불구하고 많은 사람들은 타로가 이집트 토트의 서와 밀접한 관련이 있다고 아직도 굳게 믿고 있으며, 타로는 여전히 주술인들 사이에 대중화되어 있습니다.

There Was A Film In Which The Ghost Of A Dog Appeared?

In October 2011, some investigators claimed that they found the spirit of a dog, Nigger, once owned by Guy Gibson, a heroic English pilot during the Second World War.

The Dam Busters, filmed in 1954, was a war movie about the raid led by Wing Commander Guy Gibson. After this film was released, some people claimed that they could see a black dog running around behind the actors at the end of the film. People thought that the dog might be Nigger's ghost because there was no dog present during filming.

Before the film, there had been rumors that the black dog was seen near the burial place of Gibson, which is now part of the RAF Scampton Historical Museum. Furthermore, Gibson's old office, which hasn't been used for about 50 years, is said to be haunted by Gibson's ghost.

In 2011, the ghost hunters hit the road to find the spirit of Gibson's dog. Their search team, called Paranormal lincs, investigated around the museum with equipment such as infra-red lights and video cameras in an attempt to catch a glimpse of the spirit of Gibson's dog. One of the investigators said that they felt 'the spectre of the dog's spirit' which tried to speak to them as they ran their electronic detection equipment.

Words & Expressions

spirit 영, 귀신 (ghost) nigger 흑인을 비하해 부르는 표현, 검둥이 (지문에서는 개의 이름으로 쓰였다.) own 소유하다 heroic 영웅적인 (hero 남자 영웅 heroine 여자 영웅) during the Second World War 2차 세계 대전 중에 dam 댐 buster 폭파/파괴시키는 것 (destroyer) film 영화, 영화를 찍다 raid 공습 wing commander (영국) 공군중령 release 출시되다 burial place 매장지 haunt 귀신이 출몰하다 ghost hunter 유령 사냥꾼 hit the road 출발하다, 길을 떠나다 search team 수색대 investigate 조사하다 (investigator 조사원) equipment 장비 infra-red lights 적외선 in an attempt to ...하기 위한 시도로 catch a glimpse of 잠깐/힐끗 보다 spectre 유령 electronic detection equipment 전기 추적 장비

1. What is the main idea of the story?

a. There is no such thing as the ghost of a dog or a haunted house.

b. There has been a rumor about the dog's ghost and some people claimed they felt it.

c. It is okay to go near the burial place of Gibson since nothing's there.

d. The Dam Busters was a war movie starred by Guy Gibson and Nigger.

2. When The Dam Buster was released, some people were surprised because _____ .

a. the movie was filmed in the RAF Scampton Historical Museum, the haunted house

b. Nigger appeared on the movie with his owner Guy Gibson

c. the leading actor looked nothing like Guy Gibson

d. they saw the black dog in the movie although there was no dog during filming

3. Choose the correct words for each sentence.

a. I stayed up late last night to <u>make</u> / <u>do</u> / <u>catch</u> a glimpse of Helly's Commet.

b. It took me hours to set up <u>lots of complicated equipments</u> / <u>complicated many equipment</u> / <u>lots of complicated equipment</u>.

c. After the party pooper suddenly yelled 'the party is over!', people went home one by one and there was no one left <u>at the end of the day</u> / <u>in the end that day</u> / <u>the end of the day</u>.

d. In Jacksville, there was a magic pear tree, owned <u>to</u> / <u>by</u> / <u>from</u> a greedy old farmer.

Answer   **1.** b   **2.** d   **3.** catch ⏐ lots of complicated equipment ⏐ at the end of the day ⏐ by

In October 2011, some investigators claimed that they found the spirit of a dog, Nigger, _____ Guy Gibson, a heroic English pilot during the Second World War.

The Dam Busters, _____ 1954, was a war movie about _____ Wing Commander Guy Gibson. After this _____ , some people claimed that they could see a black dog running around behind the actors at the end of the film. People thought that the dog might be Nigger's ghost because _____ during filming.

Before the film, _____ the black dog was seen near the burial place of Gibson, which is now part of the RAF Scampton Historical Museum. Furthermore, Gibson's old office, which _____ for about 50 years, is said to be haunted by Gibson's ghost.

In 2011, the ghost hunters _____ to find the spirit of Gibson's dog. Their search team, called Paranormal lincs, investigated around the museum with equipment such as infra-red lights and video cameras in an attempt to _____ the spirit of Gibson's dog. One of the investigators said that they felt 'the spectre of the dog's spirit' which tried to speak to them as they _____ their electronic detection equipment.

Did You Know There Was A Film In Which The Ghost Of A Dog Appeared?

① In October 2011, some **investigators** claimed that they had found the **spirit** of
n. 조사원, 수사관 investigation 조사, 수사   유령, 영혼, 정신

a dog, Nigger, once owned by Guy Gibson, a heroic English pilot
= 동격   수식   = 동격
a dog = Nigger(개의 이름) = 깁슨에 의해 한 때 소유된 (깁슨이 주인인)
조사원들이 주장한 시점 – 과거 claimed, 조사원들이 개의 혼을 발견한 시점 – 그 이전 과거 had found (과거 완료)
이 지문에서는 개의 이름이라서 그대로 나왔으나 Nigger는 영어권 문화에서는 N****로 표기할 정도로 거부감이 강한 표현으로 N-word는 폭압, 인종차별을 상징한다.

(during the Second World War).

② The Dam Busters, (filmed in 1954), was a war movie about the **raid** (led by
수식   The Dam Busters which was filmed in 1954   수식
주어 The Dam Busters, 동사 was   raid which was led by
…에 의해 지휘된 공습 (…가 이끈 공습)

Wing **Commander** Guy Gibson).
공군 중령

③ After this **film** was **released**, some people claimed that
release v. (책, 영화) 출시/출간/개봉하다
after 절의 주어는 this film, 주절의 주어는 people– 주어가 일치하지 않기 때문에 생략할 수 없다

they could see a black dog running around behind the actors at the end of the film.
dog which ran / was running 달리는 개   영화 후반부에

④ People thought that the dog might be Nigger's ghost because
…일지도 모르다 (조동사) + 동사원형

there was no dog **present** during filming.
(촬영 현장에 참석한) 개는 없었다.   during + 명사, 동명사 during filming 촬영하는 중에 (동명사)
present a. 현재의, 참석/출석한, …에 있는 n. 선물

⑤ Before the film, there had been rumors that the black dog was seen near
that 이하 소문이 있었다   검정개가 보이다 (수동)

the **burial** place of Gibson, which is now part of the RAF Scampton Historical Museum.
매장된 곳   콤마 + which (계속 용법) (which를 받는 선행사는 Gibson이 아니라 place)
깁슨의 매장지 근처인데, 이곳은 현재 … 박물관 일부이다. (계속 용법은 단어 순서대로 해석)

⑥ Furthermore, Gibson's old office, (which hasn't been used for about 50 years), is
주어 Gibson's old office = ( ) 약 50년간 사용된 적 없는 그의 옛 사무실 + 동사 is said to 라고 한다
콤마 + which (계속 용법) 깁슨의 옛 사무실은 약 50년간 사용된 바 없는데, 깁슨의 유령이 출몰한다고 한다

said to **be haunted by** Gibson's **ghost**.
수동태 be haunted by   ghost 귀신, 유령 = specter, phantom, spirit
haunt v. 귀신이 출몰하다 (haunted house 유령 나오는 집)

7 In 2011, the ghost hunters hit the road to find (the spirit of Gibson's dog).

길을 나서다 (이 문장에서는 과거 시제 hit-hit-hit) ( )를 찾기 위해 길을 나서다
hit the book 공부를 시작하다 hit the hay(sack) 잠을 자다 hit the ceiling (분노) 길길이 날뛰다

8 Their search team, (called Paranormal lincs), investigated around the museum

= 동격   파라노말 링스라 불리는 수색팀

with **equipment** (such as infra-red lights and video cameras) in an **attempt** to

장비가 여럿이라도 equipment에 −s가 붙지 않음(불가산명사)   ···하려는 시도로 (to + 동사원형)
equipment의 예 ( )

infra-red light 적외선 / ultraviolet light 자외선

catch a glimpse of the spirit of Gibson's dog.

잠깐 힐끗 보다 (of + 명사)
glimpse n. 잠깐 봄

9 One of the investigators said that they felt 'the **spectre** of the dog's spirit' (which

one of the 복수명사   유령 (영국 spectre 미국 specter)   = 동격
여럿 중 하나(한 명)   spirit 정신, 영혼, 기백, 기분, 유령, 태도, 증류주

tried to speak to them as they **ran** their **electronic** detection equipment).

run 기계를 작동하다   electronic 전자의 + detection 감지, 탐지 + equipment 장비
electric 전기의 electricity 전기
electronic 전자의 electronics 전자공학, 전자장치

개 유령이 나타난 영화가 있다는 거 아세요?

1 2011년 10월, 어떤 사람들이 니거라는 개의 유령을 찾았다고 주장했는데,
니거는 세계 2차 대전 당시 영국인 파일럿 영웅 가이 깁슨이 기르던 개였습니다.

2 1954년에 촬영된 영화 <댐 버스터>는 공군 중령 가이 깁슨이 이끈 공습에 관한 전쟁 영화였습니다.

3 이 영화가 개봉된 후 어떤 사람들이 영화 후반부에 배우들 뒤로 검정개가 뛰어다니는 걸 보았다고 주장했습니다.

4 촬영 때 개는 없었기 때문에 사람들은 그 개가 니거의 유령일지도 모른다고 생각했습니다.

5 영화 이전에도, 누군가 깁슨의 매장지 부근에서 검정개를 본 적이 있다는 소문이 돌았는데,
그 중 일부 지역에 현재 RAF 스캠톤 역사박물관이 위치해있습니다.

6 게다가 약 50년간 아무도 사용하지 않은 깁슨의 예전 사무실은 깁슨의 유령이 출몰한다고 합니다.

7 2011년에 유령 사냥꾼들이 깁슨의 개 유령을 찾고자 길을 나섰습니다.

8 파라노말 링스라는 이 조사단은 적외선 전등, 비디오카메라 같은 장비를 갖고
깁슨의 개 유령을 잠깐이라도 보겠다는 바람으로 박물관 주변을 조사했습니다.

9 조사원 중 한 사람은 그들이 전기 추적 장치를 작동시킬 때 개 혼령의 유령이 자신들에게 말을 시키려는 것 같은 느낌을
받았다고 말했습니다.

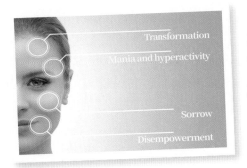

Transformation
Mania and hyperactivity
Sorrow
Disempowerment

"Personology" or "physiognomy" believers think you can and should judge a book by its cover. These face readers believe they can know and judge you by your facial features since the features on your face reveal what kind of person you are.

For example, they can figure out a person's character by his or her eyebrows. People with dark black or bow-looking eyebrows are likely to have a good character. Flat and fat eyebrows mean 'cold-blooded' while soft and narrow eyebrows mean 'a daydreamer.' People with thin eyebrows are said to be arrogant, while people with thick and scattered eyebrows are thought to be aggressive.

Additionally, face readers claim that they can uncover your health condition since they believe internal organs are related to facial parts. They think, for example, that the nose is related to the heart, the lower lip is related to the intestines. So if your lower lip bulges, face readers may say you have constipation or tend to have loose bowels.

But face reading is not always accurate. There are generous and kind people with flat, thick eyebrows, and others with bulging lower lips who can digest enormous amounts of food effortlessly.

Words & Expressions

reveal 드러내다, 밝히다 personality 성격, 개성 personology 관상학 (physiognomy) believer 믿는 사람, 신자, 신봉자 judge a book by its cover 책 표지만 보고 책을 판단하다 (겉모습으로 사람을 판단하다) face reader 관상 보는 사람 facial feature 얼굴의 특징 eyebrows 눈썹 (eyelash 속눈썹) bow-looking 화살처럼 생긴 have a good character 성격이 좋다 flat 납작한 cold-blooded 냉정한, 냉혈한의 daydreamer 공상가 arrogant 거만한 scattered 흩어진 aggressive 공격적인 be related to ..와 연관이 있다 bulge 부풀다, 튀어나오다 constipation 변비 loose bowels 설사 generous 관대한, 너그러운 digest 소화하다 enormous 엄청난, 많은 enormous amounts of 엄청난 양의 effortlessly 노력을 기울이지 않고, 수월하게

Understanding Checkpoint

1. What can be the best title of this story?
   a. The Relation Between Faces and Eye Brows
   b. Watch Out the Deceitful Face Readers
   c. Danger Of A Bulging Lower Lip
   d. Your Face Reveals A Lot

2. According to the passage, which sentence is <u>wrong</u>?
   a. Face readers guess your character and future simply by looking your face.
   b. Face readers think people with black, bow-looking eyebrows are kind and nice.
   c. Cold-blooded people always have flat and fat eyebrows. No exceptions.
   d. Not everybody with thin eyebrows is arrogant and haughty.

3. Choose the correct words for each sentence.
   a. I thought the poverty must be related <u>for</u> / <u>to</u> / <u>with</u> homelessness.
   b. Reptiles are called '<u>cold-blood</u> / <u>cold-blooded</u> / <u>cold bloody</u> animals because the temperature of all reptiles' blood is cold.
   c. The way he teaches is telling what kind of teacher <u>is he</u> / <u>he is</u> / <u>was he</u>.

Answer **1.** d **2.** c **3.** to ǀ cold-blooded ǀ he is

Listening Drill – Dictation

"Personology" or "physiognomy" believers think you can and should   . These face readers believe they can know and judge you by your facial features since the features on your face reveal   .

For example, they can   a person's character by his or her eyebrows. People with dark black or bow-looking eyebrows are likely to have a good character. Flat and fat eyebrows mean 'cold-blooded' while soft and narrow eyebrows mean 'a daydreamer.' People with thin eyebrows are said to be   , while people with thick and scattered eyebrows are thought to be   .

Additionally, face readers claim that they can   since they believe internal organs   parts. They think, for example, that the nose is related to the heart, the lower lip is related to the intestines. So if your lower lip bulges, face readers may say you   or tend to have   .

But face reading is not always accurate. There are generous and kind people with flat, thick eyebrows, and others with bulging lower lips   enormous amounts of food effortlessly.

289

Did You Know Your Face Reveals Your Personality?

1 "**Personology**" or "**physiognomy**" believers think you ¹⁾ can and ²⁾ should
관상학   관상학을 믿는 사람들은 ¹⁾ (판단)할 수 있고 ²⁾ (판단)해야 한다고 생각한다

judge a book by its cover.
표지로 책을 판단하다
(Don't judge a book by its cover. 표지로 책을 판단하지 말라. 외모/겉모습만으로 판단하지 말라 – 속담)

2 These face readers believe they can ¹⁾ know and ²⁾ judge you by your **facial features**
관상 보는 사람들은 ¹⁾ 알 수 있고 ²⁾ 판단할 수 있다고 믿는다   얼굴의 특징으로 (수단 by)

since (the features on your face) **reveal** what kind of person you are.
since 이하 절 주어 ( ) face가 아니라 features + 동사 reveal   what 의문문이 아니고 목적어 구실의 명사절
당신이 어떤 종류의 사람인지를 – 의문문이 아니라서 주어 동사 위치가 도치되지 않음

3 For example, they can **figure out** a person's character by his or her eyebrows.
알아내다   수단 by (눈썹으로)

4 (People with dark black or bow-looking eyebrows) are likely to have a good character.
수식 │ 주어 ( ) eyebrows가 아니라 people + 동사 are   …할 가능성이 있다   성격이 좋다

5 (Flat and fat eyebrows) mean 'cold-blooded' while (soft and **narrow** eyebrows) mean
while 반면 (flat and fat eyebrows vs. soft and narrow eyebrows) – 대조
narrow 좁은

'a daydreamer.'
day 낮 + dreamer 꿈꾸는 사람 = 몽상가 daydreaming 몽상

6 (People with **thin** eyebrows) are said to be **arrogant**,
수식 │ 주어 ( ) eyebrows가 아니라 people + 동사 are   거만한
be said to 동사원형 …라고 한다 (= be thought to)

while (people with **thick** and **scattered** eyebrows) are thought to be **aggressive**.
수식 │ thick 술이 많은 (↔ thin)   aggressive a. 공격적인 aggression n. 공격(성)
반면 (thin eyebrow vs. thick eyebrows) – 대조   scattered 흩어진

7 Additionally, face readers claim that they can **uncover** your health condition
cover v. 덮다 discover v. 발견하다
uncover v. 비밀을 알아내다, 뚜껑을 열다 recover v. 회복하다

since they believe **internal organs** are related to facial parts.
because   신체 내 장기   관련이 있다 (be related to + 명사)

8 They think, for example, that the nose is related to the heart,

290

the lower lip is related to the **intestines**.

low 낮은 lower a. 더 낮은, 더 아래의 (low + er비교) v. 낮추다
the lower lip 아랫입술
the upper lip 윗입술
창자, 장 (항상 복수형)
(large intestine 대장 small intestine 소장)

⑨ So if your lower lip **bulges**, face readers may say you ¹⁾ have constipation or

가정법 현재 if 주어 your lower lip (3인칭 단수) 동사의 현재형 bulges, 주어 may 동사원형
bulge 부풀다, 튀어나오다

²⁾ tend to have loose bowels.

…경향이 있다 have constipation 변비가 있다 / have loose bowels. 설사가 있다 (have diarrhea)

⑩ But face reading is not always accurate.

부분 부정 항상… 인 건 아니다

⑪ There are (**generous** and kind) people (with flat, thick eyebrows), and

there are 복수 동사 + people 복수 명사   수식 ↑ ↑ 수식   (관대하고 친절한) 사람 (납작하고 두터운 눈썹을 가진)

others (with bulging lower lips who can **digest enormous** amounts of

↑ 수식 ┃ others ⇒ there are other people ( )   an enormous amount of (단수형)
people with bulging lower lips 부은 아랫입술을 가진 사람들   enormous amounts of (복수형)

food effortlessly).

effort 노력 + less 없는 + ly

당신의 얼굴이 당신의 성격을 드러낸다는 거 아세요?

❶ "관상학" 또는 "관상"을 믿는 사람들은 책 표지만으로 책을 판단할 수 있고 또 판단해야 한다고 생각합니다.

❷ 관상을 보는 사람들은 얼굴의 특징으로 사람을 알 수 있고 판단할 수 있다고 믿는데, 얼굴의 특징이 어떤 사람인지 드러내기 때문이라고 합니다.

❸ 예를 들어 그들은 상대의 눈썹만 보고도 성격을 알아냅니다.

❹ 진한 검정색 눈썹이나 활 모양의 눈썹을 가진 사람은 성격이 좋을 가능성이 있습니다.

❺ 두툼한 눈썹이 납작하게 났다는 건 "냉정"하다는 뜻이고, 부드러운 눈썹이 듬성듬성 났다는 건 "몽상가"라는 뜻입니다.

❻ 눈썹 숱이 적은 사람은 거만하고, 두꺼운 눈썹이 넓게 퍼져 있으면 공격적인 사람이라고 합니다.

❼ 또 관상 보는 사람들은 건강 상태도 알 수 있다고 주장하는데, 내장 기관이 얼굴 부위와 관련이 있다고 믿기 때문입니다.

❽ 예를 들면, 코는 심장, 아랫입술은 장기와 관련이 있다고 생각합니다.

❾ 그래서 당신의 아랫입술이 부어 있다면, 관상 보는 사람들은 당신이 변비가 있거나 설사를 하는 경향이 있다고 말할 수도 있습니다.

❿ 관상이 항상 정확한 건 아닙니다.

⓫ 납작하고 두꺼운 눈썹을 가진 관대하고 친절한 사람들이 있고, 다른 사람들은 아랫입술이 부었는데 엄청난 양의 음식을 수월하게 소화시킬 수 있습니다.

Some believe it's bad luck to let milk boil over. It could be true, but no one knows for sure because it is just one of the many superstitions about luck. As a matter of fact, there are so many superstitions about luck in the western culture. Superstitions bringing bad luck are as follows:

- Seeing an ambulance is highly unlucky. If you see an ambulance, you must pinch your nose or hold your breath until you see a black or a brown dog.

- It's bad luck to place a hat on a bed. It is also bad luck to walk under a ladder, or see an owl in the sunlight.

- If a robin or a white moth flies into a room through an open window, someone close to you will die soon.

- Don't say the word "pig" while fishing at sea because it brings misfortune.

- To break a mirror means 7 years of bad luck.

- A knife from a lover is not a nice gift since it suggests that the love will end sooner or later.

- Don't forget to cover your mouth when yawning. Your soul may leave your body when you open your mouth wide to yawn.

Words & Expressions

bad luck 불운 boil 끓다 boil over 끓어 넘치다 superstition 미신 be as follows ...는 다음과 같다 purely 순전히 pinch 꼬집다 hole one's breath 숨을 참다 ladder 사다리 sunlight 태양 빛, 햇볕 robin 울새 (새 종류) moth 나방 at sea 바다에서 while fishing at sea 바다에서 물고기를 잡을 때 misfortune 불운, 불행 knife 칼 sooner or later 조만간 yawn 하품하다 open one's mouth wide 입을 크게 벌리다

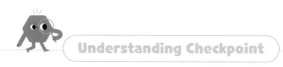

1. What is the main idea of the story?

    a. All superstitions about luck are absolutely true and accurate.

    b. There are many superstitions about luck in western culture.

    c. Believing superstitions about luck is a stupid thing to do.

    d. Never say words like 'pig' or 'broken mirror' since they bring misfortune.

2. If you see an ambulance, you may want to _____ .

    a. pinch your cheeks as hard as you can

    b. cry because that means somebody is dying

    c. hold your breath until you see a black dog

    d. break mirrors and walk under a ladder

3. Choose the correct words for each sentence.

    a. I wonder, why do I have a stomachache while <u>to eat</u> / <u>eating</u> / <u>I ate</u>?

    b. Don't give up now. <u>For the time being</u> / <u>Sooner or later</u> / <u>From time to time</u> things will get better.

    c. We have no choice but to stay in her house <u>when</u> / <u>until</u> / <u>where</u> we find a place to live.

    d. Every morning, my husband never fails to say 'don't forget <u>locking</u> / <u>to lock</u> / <u>locked</u> the front door before you go out.'

Answer **1.** b **2.** c **3.** eating ∣ Sooner or later ∣ until ∣ to lock

Some believe it's bad luck to _____ . It could be true, but no one knows for sure because it is just one of the many superstitions about luck. As a matter of fact, there are so many superstitions about luck in the western culture. Superstitions bringing bad luck are _____ :

- Seeing an ambulance _____ . If you see an ambulance, you must pinch your nose or hold your breath until you see a black or a brown dog.

- It's bad luck to _____ on a bed. It is also bad luck to walk under a ladder, or see an owl in the sunlight.

- If a robin or a white moth flies into a room through an open window, _____ will die soon.

- Don't say the word "pig" _____ because it _____ .

- To break a mirror means 7 years of bad luck.

- A knife from a lover is not a nice gift since _____ the love will end sooner or later.

- Don't forget to cover your mouth when yawning. Your soul _____ when you _____ to yawn.

Did You Know It's Bad Luck To Let Milk Boil Over?

① Some believe it's bad luck to let milk boil over.

가주어 it 진주어 to let   사역동사 let + 목적어 milk + 동사원형   boil boil over 끓어 넘치다

② It could be true, but no one knows for sure because

…일 수도 있다(가능성)   아무도 확실히 모른다

it is just one of the many **superstitions** about luck.

it is 단수동사 + one of the 복수 명사 (여럿 중 하나–단수)   superstition n. 미신 superstitious a. 미신적인

③ As a matter of fact, there are so many superstitions about luck in the western culture.

= in fact   there are 복수 동사 + (so many 매우 많은) 복수 명사 superstitions

④ (Superstitions bringing bad luck) are as follows:

↑ 수식   be as follows 다음과 같다

주어 ( ) luck이 아니라 superstitions + 동사 are

불운을 가져오는 미신 superstitions that bring bad luck

⑤ - (Seeing an ambulance) is **highly** unlucky.

( ) 동명사 주어 – 구급차를 보는 것 (단수)   ad. 매우, 대단히

⑥ If you see an ambulance, you must 1) pinch your nose or 2) hold your breath

가정법 현재 if 주어 you 동사의 현재형 see, 주어 you + must + 동사원형 pinch, hold

pinch one's nose 코를 쥐다   hold one's breath 숨을 참다

until you see (a black or a brown) dog.

개를 볼 때까지 숨을 참다 see a black dog or see a brown dog

⑦ - It's bad luck to place a hat on a bed.

가주어 it 진주어 to place (…에 두는 건 불운이다)

place v. 놓다, 두다 n. 장소 place ( ) on … : …에 ( )를 두다/놓다

⑧ It is also bad luck to 1) walk under a ladder, or 2) see an owl in the sunlight.

가주어 it 진주어 to walk or to see (걷거나 보는 건 불운이다)   해가 비칠 때 (in broad daylight 백주대낮에)

⑨ - If (a robin or a white moth) **flies** into a room through an open window,

울새 또는 나방 중 한 마리 (단수 주어) + flies (fly의 3인칭 단수 현재 시제)   열린 창을 통해

fly v. 날다, 비행하다 (fly-flew-flown . flyng, flies) n. 파리, 바지 지퍼 (복수형 flies)

(someone close to you) will die soon.

↑ 수식   주어 ( ) you가 아니라 someone 너와 친한 누군가 + will die   someone who is close to you

⑩ - Don't say the word "pig" while fishing at sea because it brings **misfortune**.

명령문 주어 you   while you fish (주절의 주어와 일치, 생략)   = bring bad luck 불운을 가져오다

at sea 바다에서 on land 육지에서

⑪ - (To break a mirror) means 7 years of bad luck.
to부정사 주어 ( ) 거울을 깨는 것 – 단수 + 단수 동사 means
동명사 주어 Seeing an ambulance is / to부정사 주어 To break a mirror means (둘 다 단수 주어)

⑫ - (A knife from a lover) is not a nice gift since it suggests that the love will
주어 ( ) lover가 아니라 knife (연인에게서 온 칼) + 동사 is

end sooner or later.
조만간
before long 머지 않은 미래에, 곧 – sooner or later보다 시간상 더 가까운 미래

⑬ - Don't forget to cover your mouth when yawning.
(이후에) 하품할 때 입 가리는 거 잊지 말고 (입을 가려라) 명령문의 주어 you와 일치, 생략 – when you yawn
don't forget to 동사원형 : 나중에 할 일을 잊지 마라
don't forget -ing : 과거에 이미 있던 일을 잊지 마라

⑭ Your soul may leave your body when you open your mouth wide to **yawn**.
leave 1. 남기다 2. 떠나다 (여기는 '떠나다')   open a. 열린 v. 열다, 벌리다 (여기는 '열다')
open wide 넓게 벌리다 (open 동사) wide open 넓게 벌린 (open 형용사)
when 앞 문장의 주어 your soul, when 절의 주어는 you
– 주어가 일치하지 않으므로 when opening으로 쓸 수 없다.

우유를 끓어 넘치게 하면 불운이라는 거 아세요?

① 어떤 사람들은 우유를 끓어 넘치게 하면 불운이라고 믿습니다.

② 그럴 수도 있지만, 확실한 건 아무도 모르는데, 그건 운에 관한 수많은 미신 중 하나이기 때문입니다.

③ 사실 서양 문화에서 운에 관해 미신이 굉장히 많습니다.

④ 불운을 가져오는 미시는 다음과 같습니다.

⑤ - 구급차를 보는 건 엄청난 불운입니다.

⑥ 구급차가 보인다면 코를 꼬집거나 검정, 또는 갈색 개를 볼 때까지 숨을 참아야 합니다.

⑦ - 침대에 모자를 올려놓는 건 불운입니다.

⑧ - 사다리 밑을 걸어가거나, 또는 해가 비칠 때 올빼미를 보는 것 역시 불운입니다.

⑨ - 울새나 흰 나방이 열린 창문을 통해 방에 날아 들어오면 당신과 가까운 누군가가 곧 죽게 됩니다.

⑩ - 바다에서 낚시할 때 "돼지"라는 말을 하면 안 되는데 불행을 가져오기 때문입니다.

⑪ - 거울을 깨뜨리는 건 7년간 불운을 뜻합니다.

⑫ - 연인으로 부터 받은 칼은 좋은 선물이 아닌데, 이유는 사랑이 조만간 끝날 수 있기 때문입니다.

⑬ - 하품할 때 입 가리는 걸 잊지 마십시오.

⑭ 하품 하려고 입을 크게 벌릴 때 영혼이 몸을 떠날 수도 있습니다.

day	Wednesday	Thursday	Friday	Saturday
	4	5	6	7
)	11	12	(13)	14
7	18	19	20	

There are lots of superstitions about Friday and many of them are negative such as 'If you sleep in a different bed on Friday, you will have nightmares.'

People can find many reasons why they have no choice but to hate Fridays in the Bible. Some believe a number of biblical incidents, like the collapse of the Tower of Babel, the death of Jesus Christ and Noah's Great Flood, all took place on Friday.

There are also lots of stories about the unlucky number 13. Judas, who betrayed Jesus, was the 13th guest to the Last Supper. In ancient Rome, 12 witches used to gather together and they considered the 13th as the devil.

In addition, in western culture, 12 is a perfect and complete number. That's why there are 12 months in a year, 12 signs of the zodiac, 12 gods of Olympus. Meanwhile, the number 13 has been connected with bad luck since it breaks the completeness of 12 with a surplus of 1. So, many cities don't have a 13th Street or a 13th Avenue and you won't find a room number 13 in hotels and hospitals.

It's only natural Friday the 13th represents the worst because it is the combination of the worst day and the worst number.

Understanding Checkpoint

1. What is the main idea of the story?

    a. Both the Last Supper and Noah's Great Flood took place on Friday

    b. 12 signs of zodiac have been connected with bad luck for a long time.

    c. Friday the 13th is the combination of the worst day and the worst number.

    d. 12 is a perfect and complete number and 13 is an evil and stupid number.

2. According to the passage, which sentence is right?

    a. Many westerners have negative feelings towards Friday and the number 13.

    b. People around the world believe that Noah's Great Flood happened on Friday the 13th.

    c. Judas, who betrayed Jesus 13 times, did not attend the Last Supper.

    d. It is not hard to find the room number 13 in hospitals in the US.

3. Choose the correct words for each sentence.

    a. The rest of them had no choice but <u>return</u> / <u>to return</u> / <u>returning</u> home because the supervisor kicked them out.

    b. The exact number of victims is not yet revealed, but the rumor says that a number of people <u>is</u> / <u>are</u> / <u>was</u> missing.

    c. Considering the situation, I think you should have <u>considered</u> / <u>consideration</u> / <u>considerate</u> other options before spending a considerable amount of money on this.

Answer **1.** c **2.** a **3.** to return | are | considered

Listening Drill – Dictation

There are   about Friday and many of them are negative such as 'If you sleep in a different bed   , you will have nightmares.'

People can find many reasons why they have no choice but to hate Fridays in the Bible. Some believe   biblical incidents, like the collapse of the Tower of Babel, the death of Jesus Christ and Noah's Great Flood, all took place on Friday.

There are also lots of stories about the unlucky number 13. Judas, who betrayed Jesus, was the 13th guest   . In ancient Rome, 12 witches used to gather together and they considered the 13th as the devil.

In addition, in western culture, 12 is a perfect and complete number. That's why there are 12 months in a year, 12 signs of the zodiac, 12 gods of Olympus. Meanwhile, the number 13   bad luck since it breaks the completeness of 12   1. So, many cities don't have a 13th Street or a 13th Avenue and you won't find   in hotels and hospitals.

        Friday the 13th   because it is   the worst day and the worst number.

Did You Know How Friday The 13th Became The Worst Day?

1 There are lots of superstitions about Friday and many of them are **negative**

there are 복수 동사 + lots of 많은 + superstitions 복수 명사 　　　　　　　　　　　　　　　　부정적인 (↔ positive 긍정적인)

such as 'If you sleep in a different bed on Friday, you will have **nightmares**.'

부정적인 금요일 미신의 예　　　　　　　　　　　　on 요일　　　　　　　　악몽을 꾸다 (get nightmares)

2 People can find many reasons why they have no choice but to hate Fridays

　　　　　　　　　　　　…의 이유　　　　　　(to동사) 할 수밖에 없다
　　　　　　　　　　　　　　　　　　　　= they cannot help hating Fridays

in the Bible.

　　　　bible 성경 biblical 성경의

3 Some believe a number of biblical **incidents**, (like [1] the **collapse**

　　　　a number of (많은) = many + 복수 동사　　성경의 사건들 3가지 예 ( )　　　n. 붕괴 v. 무너지다, 폭락하다
　　　　the number of (…의 수) + 단수 동사　　incident n. 사건
　　　　　　　　　　　　　　　　　　incidents (like…) took place on Friday 이런 사건들이 금요일에 일어났다

of the Tower of Babel, [2] the death of Jesus Christ and [3] Noah's Great **Flood**),

　　　　　　　　　　　　　　　　　　　　　　flood v. 홍수가 나다 n. 홍수
　　　　　　　　　　　　　　　　　　　Great Flood (구약성서에 나오는 노아의 대홍수)

all **took place** on Friday.

　　　　take place = happen, occur

4 There are also lots of stories (about the unlucky number 13).

　　　　　　　　　　　　　　↑　　수식

5 Judas, (who betrayed Jesus), was the 13th guest to the Last **Supper**.

(예수를 배반한) 유다 + was　　　　　　　　　최후 last의 만찬 supper (supper 저녁 식사)
　　　　　　　　　　　　　　　　　예수가 죽기 전 제자들과의 마지막 식사 – 대문자 the Last Supper

6 In ancient Rome, 12 witches used to gather together and they considered

　　　　　　　　　조동사 …하곤 했다 + 동사 원형　　　consider ( ) as 〈 〉: ( )를 〈 〉로 여기다, 간주하다
　　　　　　　consideration n. 사려 깊음, 배려, 숙고 considerate a. 사려 깊은 considerable a. 상당한, 많은

the 13th as the devil.

7 In addition, in western culture, 12 is a (perfect and **complete**) number.

= additionally 게다가　　　　　　　　a perfect number 완벽한 수 / a complete number 완전한 수

8 That's why there are 12 months in a year, 12 signs of the zodiac, 12 gods of Olympus.

　　　　　　　　　　　　　　　　황도대 (12개 별자리)

9 Meanwhile, (the number 13) has been connected with bad luck

한편　　　주어 ( ) 13이 아니라 the number + 단수 동사 has　　현재완료 수동태 has been + been connected

298

since it breaks the completeness of 12 with a **surplus** of 1.

= the number 13   13이라는 수가 12의 완전함 the completeness of 12을 깨다

surplus 잉여, 과잉

⑩ So, many cities don't have a 13th Street or a 13th **Avenue** and

13th 서수 앞이지만, 특정 13번째 거리가 아니라 일반적인 13번가의 의미라서 the가 아닌 a

avenue (도서의) 거리, 길, ~가

you won't find a room number 13 in (hotels and hospitals).

우리말은 13(숫자) + 호실 room, 영어는 a room + number 13

⑪ It's only natural (Friday the 13th) **represents** the worst

당연하다 (that 생략)   represent v. 나타내다   최악을 나타내다 (bad – worse – worst)

because it is (the **combination** of the worst day and the worst number).

Friday the 13th   combination of A and B : A와 B의 조합

combine v. 결합하다 combination n. 조합, 결합

13일의 금요일이 어떻게 최악의 날이 되었는지 아세요?

① 금요일에 관한 미신이 많은데 대부분이 "금요일에 침대를 바꾸면 악몽을 꾼다," 처럼 부정적입니다.

② 금요일을 싫어할 수밖에 없는 이유를 성경에서 찾는 사람들이 있습니다.

③ 어떤 이들은 바벨탑 붕괴, 예수 그리스도의 사망, 그리고 노아의 대홍수 등 수많은 성경의 사건이 금요일에 일어났다고 믿습니다.

④ 또 불운의 숫자 13에 관한 이야기도 많습니다.

⑤ 예수를 배반한 유다는 그리스도 최후의 만찬 때 13번째 손님이었습니다.

⑥ 고대 로마시대에 12명의 마녀들이 모이곤 했는데, 이들은 13번째 온 사람은 악마로 여겼습니다.

⑦ 게다가 서양 문화에서 12는 완전하고 완벽한 숫자입니다.

⑧ 그래서 일 년은 12달이고, 황도대에 12궁도가 있고 올림포스 신도 12명입니다.

⑨ 반면 숫자 13은 불운과 관련지었는데, 1이라는 잉여분으로 인해 12의 완전함이 깨지기 때문입니다.

⑩ 그래서 13번지 거리나 13번가가 없는 도시가 많고, 호텔과 병원에서 13호실은 찾을 수 없습니다.

⑪ 최악의 요일과 최악의 숫자가 만났으니 13일의 금요일이 당연히 최악을 대표하게 되었습니다.

These horrific incidents were initiated not by ignorant poor people but by judges and doctors who were supposed to be intelligent, reasonable and fair. William Griggs, a village doctor, played an important role during the time of the Salem Witch Trials. He diagnosed some villagers as witches, and sent them to be tried. Once they were found guilty of witchcraft, they couldn't avoid being put to death. Under British law in the 17th century, those who were accused of being close to the devil or being witches were considered as felons. They were regarded as criminals having committed a serious crime against the government.

One of the most famous Salem witch trials took place in 1692. About 180 people were arrested on a charge of witchcraft by the authorities. Among them, 29 people were convicted of the felony of witchcraft by the court. Most of them lost their lives by hanging. One man, named Giles Corey, who refused to cooperate with the court, was pressed to death under heavy stones. At least seven other people reportedly died in prison.

Words & Expressions

horrific 끔찍한 initiate 시작하다 ignorant 무지한 intelligent 지적인 fair 공정한 play an important role 중요한 역할을 하다 witch trial 마녀 재판 try 재판하다, 시도하다 be found guilty of (...라는 죄로) 유죄를 선고받다 witchcraft 마술 avoid 피하다 put to death 죽이다 be accused of ...로 비난 받다 felon 중죄인, 흉악범 (felony 중죄, 흉악 범죄) commit a crime 범죄를 저지르다 arrest 체포하다 on a charge of ...의 혐의로 authority 권한, 당국, 권위자 convict 유죄를 선고하다 (be convicted of ...로 유죄선고를 받다) lose one's life 생명을 잃다 by hanging 교수형으로 cooperate 협동하다, 협력하다 be pressed to death 압사당하다

Understanding Checkpoint

1. What can be the best title of this story?

    a. William Griggs, Assaulted by Ignorant Farmers

    b. The Salem Witch Trials : Trials? Or Slaughter?

    c. Witchcraft : The Most Serious Felony Against The Government

    d. The Secret of Salem Witch Trials Finally Revealed

2. During the 17th century, people could be found guilty of _____ .

    a. doing something related to witchcraft

    b. being close to the authorities

    c. trying to cooperate with the court

    d. being ignorant and poor

3. Choose the correct words for each sentence.

    a. The guy who <u>made</u> / <u>committed</u> / <u>did</u> a crime must be thrown into jail.

    b. When I hung up my coat on the hanger, saying 'hang on a minute', she said her brother was sentenced to death by <u>hanging</u> / <u>hung</u> / <u>hanged</u>, which meant he was going to be hanged.

    c. Those who are accused <u>by</u> / <u>of</u> / <u>with</u> racism, or we can say 'racists,' are banned from entering our shop.

Answer **1.** b **2.** a **3.** committed ǀ hanging ǀ of

Listening Drill – Dictation

These ＿＿＿ incidents ＿＿＿＿＿ not by ignorant poor people but by judges and doctors who were supposed to be intelligent, reasonable and fair. William Griggs, a village doctor, ＿＿＿＿＿＿＿＿ during the time of the Salem Witch Trials. He ＿＿＿＿ some villagers as witches, and ＿＿＿＿＿＿＿＿ . Once they ＿＿＿＿＿＿＿ witchcraft, they couldn't ＿＿＿＿＿＿＿＿ . Under British law in the 17th century, those who were accused of being close to the devil or being witches were considered as felons. They were regarded as criminals having committed a serious crime ＿＿＿ the government.

One of the most famous Salem witch trials took place in 1692. About 180 people were arrested on a charge of witchcraft by the authorities. Among them, 29 people ＿＿＿＿ ＿＿＿＿＿＿＿＿ witchcraft by the court. Most of them lost their lives by hanging. One man, named Giles Corey, who refused to cooperate with the court, was pressed to death under heavy stones. At least ＿＿＿＿＿＿＿ reportedly died in prison.

Did You Know How Many People Died Because Of The Salem Witch Trials?

1 These **horrific incidents** were **initiated** not by (**ignorant** poor people) but by

horrific 끔찍한, 무시무시한　　　　　　수동태 시작되었다 not by ( ) but by 〈 〉 : ( )가 아니라 〈 〉에 의해 시작되다
(↔ terrific a. 멋진, 근사한)　　　　　　initiate 시작하다　　　　ignore v. 무시하다 ignorant a. 무식한
　　　　　　　　　　　　　　　　　　　　　　　　　　　　ignorance n. 무지, 무식 ignoble a. 비열한, 야비한
　　　　incident – 단순한 사건/사고/일은 incident (cf. 서류 잘못 작성, 밖에서 이상한 소리 남)
　　　　accident – incident 중에서 예상치 못했고 손상, 부상 등을 야기한 incident (cf. 자동차 사고, 커피 쏟아짐)

(**judges** and doctors) who **were supposed to** be (**intelligent**, **reasonable** and **fair**).

judge 판사　　　　　↑ 　수식　 　　　who의 선행사 – judges and doctors　　지적인　　　이성적인　　공정한
　　　　　　　　　　　　　　　　　　　( )이어야 할 be supposed to 판사들과 의사들

2 William Griggs, (a village doctor), played an important role

　　　　　　　　= 동격　　　　　　　중요한 역할을 하다 = play a key role

during the time of the Salem Witch Trials.

살렘 마녀 재판 당시에　　　　　　　　try v. 시도하다, 노력하다, (법) 심리하다
　　　　　　　　　　　　　　　　　　　trial n. 시도, 재판, 공판, 시련

3 He [1] **diagnosed** some villagers as witches, and [2] sent them to be **tried**.

　　diagnose v. 진단하다 diagnosis n. 진단　　　　　　　sent 보냈다 them 그들을 to be tried 재판 받도록

4 Once they **were found guilty of** witchcraft, they couldn't **avoid** being put to death.

　　　　　　be found guilty of …의 죄로 유죄가 되다　　avoid + ing 피하다　　　be put to death 사형당하다
　　　　　　　　　　　　　　　　　　　　couldn't avoid 피할 수 없다 + being put to death 사형에 처해지다

5 Under British law in the 17th century, those who **were accused of** (being close to

영국 법에 의해　　　　　　　　　　　　　　　　　↑ 수식　　be accused of + 동명사/명사 …로 고발당하다
　　　　　　　　　　those who…인 사람들(주어) – [1] 악마와 친하다고 고발당한 사람들　be close to ..와 가깝다, 친하다
　　　　　　　　　　　　　　　　　　　　[2] 마녀라고 고발당한 사람들

the devil or being witches) were considered as **felons**.

　　　　　　those who ( ) were considered as ( )인 사람들은 …로 간주되었다.
　　　　　　　　　　　　　　felon 중죄인, 흉악범 felony 중죄, 흉악 범죄

6 They were regarded as **criminals** (having **committed** a serious crime against

　　　　　　　　　↑ 　수식　　　　　　　　　　　　　…에 대항(반대)하는 범죄
앞 문장의 those who ( )　be regarded as …로 간주되다 (be considered as)
　　　　　　criminals who had committed = criminals having committed…

the government).

7 One of the most famous Salem witch trials **took place** in 1692.

one of the 복수 명사 + 복수 동사　　　　　　　　= happened

8 About 180 people were **arrested on a charge of** witchcraft by the **authorities**.

　　　　　　　　체포되다 (수동태) …라는 죄목으로　　witch 마녀 witchcraft 마술　authority 권한, 당국, 권위자

⑨ Among them, (29 people) **were convicted of** the felony of witchcraft by the court.

be convicted of 범죄 by …에 의해 어떤 죄로 유죄판결을 받다　　felony (serious crime) 중범죄 (felon 중범죄인)
misdemeanor, light offense 경범죄

⑩ Most of them lost their lives by hanging.

lose one's life/lives 생명을 잃다 = die　by hanging 교수형에 의해
hang　1. 매달다, 걸다 (hang-hung-hung)
2. 교수형에 처하다 (hang-hanged-hanged)

⑪ One man, (named Giles Corey, who refused to **cooperate with** the court),

↑ 수식

One man에 대한 추가 설명 ( ) : 가일즈 코레이라는 이름의, 법정에 협력하기를 거절한 가일즈 코레이 + 동사 was

was pressed to death under heavy stones.

be pressed to death 압사당하다　be beaten to death 맞아 죽다　be put to death 사형당하다

⑫ At least seven other people reportedly died in prison.

앞서 나온 사람들 외 일곱 명　　보도된 바에 의하면, 전해진 바에 따르면 (allegedly 알려진 바에 의하면)

(살렘 마녀 재판 때문에 몇 명이 사망했는지 아세요?)

❶ 이 끔찍한 사건은 무지하고 가난한 사람들이 아니라, 지적이고 이성적이고 공정해야 할 판사와 의사에 의해 시작되었습니다.

❷ 동네 의사였던 윌리엄 그리그스는 살렘 마녀 재판 당시 중요한 역할을 맡았습니다.

❸ 그는 일부 동네 사람들을 마녀로 진단하고 재판에 넘겼습니다.

❹ 일단 마녀행위(마술)로 유죄를 선고 받으면 죽음을 피할 수 없었습니다.

❺ 17세기 영국 법에 따라, 악마와 친하거나 마녀로 고소당한 사람들은 범죄자로 여겨졌습니다.

❻ 그들은 정부에 반한 중대한 범죄를 저지른 죄인으로 취급 받았습니다.

❼ 살렘 마녀 재판에서 가장 유명한 재판 중 하나는 1962년에 열렸습니다.

❽ 약 180여명이 당국에 의해 마녀 행위(마술) 혐의로 체포되었습니다.

❾ 그 중 29명이 법원에 의해 마술이라는 중대 범죄로 유죄선고를 받았습니다.

❿ 이들 대부분이 교수형으로 목숨을 잃었습니다.

⑪ 가일스 코레이라는 남성은 법정에 협조하기를 거부해 무거운 돌에 깔려 압사 당했습니다.

⑫ 최소한 7명의 또 다른 사람들이 감옥에서 사망했다고 합니다.

Sarah Winchester built a "Mystery House" because she was a super-rich widow and a huge believer in supernatural powers. After the death of her only baby daughter, she became mentally unstable. As worse came to worst, her dear husband and father-in-law passed away too. This made her the heiress to the Winchester Repeating Arms Company. Thanks to that, she could get $1,000 a day. (This amount of money is equivalent to about $30,000 a day in 2024.)

She was a moneybag, however, she was too sad to do anything. A psychic told her that the spirits who had died from Winchester rifles were starting to take revenge, and that she should build a house. Sarah believed that if she finished building her house, those spirits would kill her. From then on, she spent her fortune and time only on her house, which became known as the Winchester Mystery House. This house has many staircases and doors leading to nowhere. There are about 160 rooms and lots of maze-like corridors. She built her house like this to make the spirits confused. The construction of this house came to an end with her death. Sarah Winchester died in her sleep at the age of 83.

Words & Expressions

mystery 수수께끼, 미스터리 super-rich 굉장히 부유한 widow 과부 huge 막대한 supernatural 초자연적인 only daughter 무남독녀 become mentally unstable 정신적으로 불안정해지다 worse comes to worst 설상가상으로 farther-in-law 시아버지 pass away 세상을 떠나다 heiress 상속녀 repeating 반복하는, (총) 연발의 arms 무기 make a vast fortune 엄청난 돈을 벌다 manufacture 제조하다 rifle 소총 the Civil War 미국 남북전쟁 thanks to …덕분에 equivalent (의미, 가치) 동등한, …에 상응하는 moneybag 돈주머니, 부자 psychic 영매, 점쟁이 revenge 복수 from then on 그 때부터 staircase 계단 maze-like 미로 같은 corridor 복도 construction 건축 come to an end 끝나다 die in one's sleep 자다가 사망하다

1. What is the main idea of the story?

    a. Although Winchester was not very rich, she was forced to build the huge house.

    b. Spirits loved the Mystery House since there were many rooms.

    c. Winchester had built the weird and absurd house to make ghosts confused

    d. The Mystery House has been famous for being haunted.

2. According to the passage, which sentence is <u>wrong</u>?

    a. The founder of the Winchester Repeating Arms Company was Sarah Winchester.

    b. Sarah was rich but she couldn't do anything because she was sad.

    c. Sarah believed that the cause of her family's tragedy was the revenge of the ghosts.

    d. It was not that Sarah became strange until her daughter passed away.

3. Choose the correct words for each sentence.

    a. If you want to talk softly and politely, use the expression like '<u>pass away</u>' / '<u>pass by</u>' / '<u>pass out</u>' rather than 'kick the bucket.'

    c. David is too excited <u>sitting</u> / <u>to sit</u> / <u>sat</u> down on his chair.

    d. The news about his death made me <u>surprised</u> / <u>to surprise</u> / <u>surprising</u>.

Answer   **1.** c   **2.** a   **3.** pass away ǀ to sit ǀ surprised

Listening Drill ~ Dictation

Sarah Winchester built a "Mystery House" because she was a super-rich   and a huge believer in supernatural powers. After the death of her only baby daughter, she became mentally unstable.   , her dear husband and father-in-law   too. This made her the heiress to the Winchester Repeating Arms Company. Thanks to that, she could get $1,000 a day. (This amount of money   about $30,000 a day in 2024.)

She was a moneybag, however, she was too sad to do anything. A psychic told her that the spirits who had died from Winchester rifles were starting to   , and that she should build a house. Sarah believed that if she   her house, those spirits would kill her. From then on, she spent her fortune and time only on her house,   the Winchester Mystery House. This house has many staircases and doors   . There are about 160 rooms and lots of   .

She built her house like this to make the spirits confused. The construction of this house   with her death. Sarah Winchester died in her sleep at the age of 83.

Did You Know The Mystery 'GHOST' House?

1 Sarah Winchester built a "Mystery House" because she was [1] a super-rich **widow**

그녀가 [1] 엄청 부유한 과부이고 [2] …의 열렬한 신자
widow 과부 widower 홀아비 window 창문

and [2] a **huge** believer in **supernatural** powers.

막대한   …를 믿는 사람, 신도   super초 + natural 자연적인 (paranormal 과학적으로 설명할 수 없는)

2 After the death of her only baby daughter, she became **mentally unstable**.

하나 뿐인, 외동의   정신적으로   불안정한
only son 외동 아들 only daughter 외동 딸

3 As worse came to worst, (her dear husband and father-in-law) **passed away** too.

설상가상으로   남편   시아버지   pass away = die
worse(더 나쁜)가 worst(가장 나쁜)가 되어

4 This made her the **heiress** to the Winchester Repeating **Arms** Company.

이것(남편, 시아버지의 사망) + 만들었다 made + her 그녀를 + the heiress 상속녀로   arms 무기 armory 무기고
heir 상속인 / heiress 상속녀 + to …의

5 Thanks to that, she could get $1,000 a day.

that (상기의 사건들) 덕분에   = per day 하루에 1천달러 = 매일 1천 달러

6 (This amount of money **is equivalent to** about $30,000 a day in 2024.)

…와 가치가 동등한 (to)

7 She was a moneybag, however, she was too sad to do anything.

money돈 + bag 주머니 = 부자   too 형용사 to 동사 : 너무 (형용사)해서 (동사)할 수 없다
not이 없지만 부정문이라서 anything이 쓰였다.

8 A **psychic** told her [1] that the **spirits** (who had died from Winchester rifles) were

영매 (점쟁이)가 그녀에게 한 말 [1], [2]   ↑ 수식
the spirits ( ) were starting to take revenge ( )인 영혼들이 복수를 시작했다

starting to take **revenge**, and [2] that she should build a house.

복수하다 (avenge v. 복수하다 revenge / vengeance n. 복수)

9 Sarah believed that if she finished building her house, those spirits would kill her.

finish -ing …하는 것을 끝내다

10 From then on, she spent (her fortune and time) only on her house, which

그 때부터   spend (돈, 시간) 쓰다 + on + 명사, 동명사   콤마 + which (계속 용법)
그녀는 ( )를 오직 집에만(only on her house) 썼는데, 이 집이 (, which) …로 알려졌다 (known as)

became known as the Winchester Mystery House.

306

⑪ This house has many (staircases and doors) leading to nowhere.

↑ 수식 | 아무데도 이어지지 않는 (어디와도 연결되지 않은)

⑫ There are about ¹⁾ 160 rooms and ²⁾ lots of **maze**-like corridors.

방이 160개 정도 + 미로 같은 많은 복도   maze 미로 = labyrinth

⑬ She built her house like this to make the spirits **confused**.

이런 식으로   make ( ) confused : ( )를 혼란스럽게 만들다

⑭ (The construction of this house) **came to an end** with her death.

끝이 나다   그녀의 사망으로

⑮ Sarah Winchester died in her sleep at the age of 83.

(die in sleep 자다 사망하다) 자면서, 자는 중   …의 나이에

미스테리 '유령의'집을 아세요?

❶ 사라 윈체스터가 미스테리 하우스를 지은 건 그녀가 엄청난 부자 과부인데다 초자연적인 힘의 광팬이기 때문이었습니다.

❷ 하나 뿐인 아기 딸이 사망한 후 그녀는 정신적으로 불안해졌습니다.

❸ 설상가상으로 사랑하는 남편과 시아버지까지 세상을 떠나고 말았습니다.

❹ 그래서 그녀는 윈체스터 리피팅 암스 컴퍼니의 상속녀가 되었습니다.

❺ 덕분에 그녀는 하루에 약 1000 달러를 받았습니다.

❻ (이 금액은 2024년 기준으로 하루에 약 30,000달러를 받는 것과 비슷한 액수입니다.)

❼ 그녀는 거부였지만 너무 슬퍼서 아무것도 할 수 없었습니다.

❽ 영매(점쟁이)는 그녀에게 윈체스터 총에 사망한 혼령들이 복수를 시작했다면서 그녀가 집을 지어야 한다고 했습니다.

❾ 사라는 만약 집 건축이 끝나면 혼령들이 그녀를 죽이리라 믿었습니다.

❿ 그 때부터 사라는 재산과 시간을 윈체스터 미스테리 하우스로 알려진 이 집에 쏟아 부었습니다.

⑪ 이 집에는 아무 쓸모도 없는 계단과 문이 아주 많습니다.   ⑫ 방이 약 160개이고 미로 같은 복도도 많습니다.

⑬ 그녀가 이런 식으로 집을 지은 건 혼령을 혼란스럽게 만들기 위해서라고 합니다.

⑭ 그녀의 죽음과 함께 이 집 건축도 끝이 났습니다.   ⑮ 사라 윈체스터는 83세의 나이로 잠을 자던 중 사망했습니다.

Chapter 08

Interesting
Stories

MP3

This animal really does have 3 heart, 9 brains, and blue blood. It is not a monster but a sea creature. We don't know if it is smart thanks to its 9 brains, but it is thought to be smarter than other sea creatures.

Its 9 brains are nothing compared to its muscle because 90% of its body is muscle. So it has got the brains and the muscles. There is something amazing about its muscle. It can move even after being cut off. You can check it out for yourself. Chop up this muscly smart guy and put him in a pan with seasoning. You can see his arms continue to move for several minutes while being cooked.

So... it has got the brains, the muscles, and the moves. But unfortunately, it hasn't got the looks. It has no legs, no face, just many arms. However, it has a special talent in its arms. When it gets attacked by a predator and loses one of its arms, it doesn't worry about it since its arms grow back. This guy is even scary and merciless enough to eat its own kind. Moreover, it produces venom that is delivered through a bite.

Could you guess what it is? This amazing sea creature is the blue-ringed octopus.

Words & Expressions

heart 심장 brain 뇌 monster 괴물 sea creature 바다생물 compared to ...에 비하면, ..와 비교하면 muscle 근육 got the brains 뇌가 있다, 즉 똑똑하다 got the muscles 근육이 있다, 즉 근육질이다 cut off 잘라내다 chop 썰다, 자르다 muscly 근육질의 seasoning 양념 got the moves 멋진 동작(움직임, 춤, 무술 등)을 할 줄 안다 got the looks 외모가 된다, 멋지다 talent 재능, 능력 get attacked 공격을 당하다 predator 포식자 grow back 다시 자라다 merciless 무자비한 venom 독

Understanding Checkpoint

1. What can be the best title of this story?

   a. The Reason Why The Blue-Ringed Octopus Is Amazing

   b. Warning! A Sea Monster Attack

   c. The Blue-Ringed Octopus VS. Other Sea Creatures

   d. Here Comes The Scary Creature : He Got The Muscles

2. We can say the Blue-Ringed octopus hasn't got the looks since _____ .

   a. its face is all muscly and moving continuously

   b. it has too many faces

   c. its face is unbearably ugly

   d. it doesn't have face at all

3. Choose the correct words for each sentence.

   a. I wonder how this paint got <u>its</u> / <u>it's</u> / <u>it is</u> color?

   b. We can do anything together since you've got <u>brains</u> / <u>the brains</u> / <u>a brain</u> and I've got the muscles.

   c. The robber appeared out of nowhere and he <u>got robbed</u> / <u>robbed</u> / <u>was robbed</u> me of my money.

Answer **1.** a **2.** d **3.** its ⏐ the brains ⏐ robbed

Listening Drill - Dictation

This animal _____ 3 heart, 9 brains, and blue blood. It is not a monster but a sea creature. We don't know if it is smart _____ its 9 brains, but _____ be smarter than other sea creatures.

Its 9 brains are nothing _____ its muscle because 90% of its body is muscle. So it _____ the brains and the muscles. There is something amazing about its muscle. It can move even _____ . You can check it out for yourself. Chop up this muscly smart guy and put him in a pan with seasoning. You can see his arms _____ for several minutes while being cooked.

So... it has got the brains, the muscles, and the moves. But unfortunately, it _____ the looks. It has no legs, no face, just many arms. However, it has a special talent in its arms. When _____ by a predator and loses one of its arms, it doesn't worry about it since its arms grow back. This guy is even scary and merciless enough to eat its own kind. Moreover, it produces venom that is delivered through a bite.

Could you guess _____ ? This amazing sea creature is the blue-ringed octopus.

311

Did You Know What Animal Has 3 Hears, 9 Brains And Blue Blood?

❶ This animal really does have (3 heart, 9 brains, and blue blood).

강조의 조동사 do = 주어 this animal이 3인칭, 단수이고 시제가 현재라서 does + 동사원형 have

❷ It is not a monster but a sea **creature**.

괴물이 아니라 not 바다 생물 but   n. 생물

❸ We don't know if it is smart thanks to its 9 brains,

여기서 if는 wheather (···인지 아닌지)   덕분에 - 9개 뇌 덕분에 똑똑한지 여부는 모른다

but it is thought to be **smarter** than other sea creatures.

be thought to ~라고 한다   더 똑똑한 (비교)

❹ Its 9 brains are nothing compared to its muscle because (90% of its body) is **muscle**.

( ) be nothing compared to ··· : ···에 비하면 ( )는 아무것도 아니다   n. 근육

❺ So it has got (the brains and the muscles).

get the brains 머리가 좋다 / get the muscles 근육질이다

❻ There is something amazing about its muscle.

something, someone + 형용사 : something amazing 무언가 굉장한 것 someone important 중요한 사람

❼ It can move even after being cut off.

주절의 주어 it과 일치, 생략 after it is cut off. ('잘리는' 즉 수동의 의미라서 be동사의 -ing인 being)

❽ You can check it out for yourself.

check out for oneself 스스로/직접 확인하다

❾ ¹⁾ Chop up this muscly smart guy and ²⁾ put him in a pan with **seasoning**.

잘게 썰다   명령문 ¹⁾ chop up and ²⁾ put   양념과 함께   season n. 계절 v. 양념을 하다
seasoning n. 양념   seasoned a. 양념이 된, 노련한, 경험이 많은

❿ You can see his **arms** continue to move for several minutes while being cooked.

arm n. 팔   arms n. 무기, 팔들(arm의 복수형)   주절의 주어 his arms와 일치, 생략 while his arms are cooked

⓫ So... it has got the brains, the muscles, and the moves.

get the moves 자세가 좋다, 멋진 동작을 할 줄 안다 (스포츠, 춤, 격투기 등)

⓬ But **unfortunately**, it hasn't got the looks.

ad. 불행하게도   get the looks 외모가 좋다, 매력적이다
get the brains, get the muscles, get the moves, get the looks - 모두 the가 와야 하고 복수형(-s)이 쓰인다.
She got the looks in her family. 그녀는 가족들 중 외모가 좋다. (주어가 단수라도 the looks 복수형)

⓭ It has ¹⁾ no legs, ²⁾ no face, just ³⁾ many arms.

다리, 얼굴은 없고 팔만 많다

⑭ However, it has a special **talent** in its arms.

                               n. 재능

⑮ When it ¹⁾ gets attacked by a **predator** and ²⁾ loses one of its arms,

          수동태 get attacked by   포식자 (↔ prey 먹이)

it doesn't worry about it since its arms grow back.

                      because   다시 자라다 (regrow its arms)

⑯ This guy is even (**scary** and **merciless**) enough to eat its own kind.

                                형용사 enough to 동사 …할 만큼 …한   kind a. 친절한 n. 종류 (여기서는 '종류')

                scary enough to eat 잡아먹을 만큼 무서운   eat its own kind 자기 동족을 잡아 먹다

                    mercy 자비 + less 없는 : merciless 무자비한 (merciful a. 자비로운)

⑰ Moreover, it produces **venom** that is delivered through a **bite**.

                            = 동격   무는 것(bite)을 통해 전달되다 (수동)   v. 물다 n. 무는 행위

            뱀, 벌, 전갈, 문어 등의 독 venom (다른 생물을 물거나 쏘아서 독을 퍼트리는 경우)

            toxin – 살아있는 유기체에 의해 만들어지는 독, poison – 자연적으로 혹은 인공적으로 만들어진 독

            모든 toxin은 poison이지만, 모든 poison이 다 toxin은 아니다. (보톡스의 독은 toxin, 비소나 수은 등은 poison)

⑱ Could you guess (what it is)?

                what 의문문이 아니라 목적어 역할의 명사절이라 주어 동사가 도치되지 않음

                What is it? (의문문) 이것은 무엇인가? / Tell me what it is. (평서문) 이것이 무엇인지 나에게 말해주시오.

⑲ This amazing sea creature is the blue-ringed **octopus**.

                        blue-ringed 푸른 고리가 있는 – 푸른 고리 문어

어떤 동물이 3개의 심장, 9개의 뇌, 그리고 파란 피를 가졌는지 아세요?

① 이 동물은 정말 세 개의 심장, 아홉 개의 뇌, 그리고 파란 피를 갖고 있습니다.   ② 이 동물은 괴물이 아니라 바다 생물입니다.   ③ 아홉 개의 뇌 덕분에 똑똑한지는 모르겠지만, 다른 바다 동물보다 더 똑똑하다고 합니다.

④ 아홉 개의 뇌는 이것의 근육에 비하면 놀랄 일도 아닌데, 이유인즉 이것은 몸의 90%가 근육이기 때문입니다.   ⑤ 그러니까 이것은 똑똑한 머리와 근육질 몸을 가진 것입니다.   ⑥ 이것의 근육에 놀라운 점이 있습니다.   ⑦ 이것은 잘린 후에도 움직일 수 있습니다.   ⑧ 여러분이 직접 확인할 수도 있습니다.   ⑨ 근육질의 똑똑한 이 녀석을 잘라서 양념과 함께 팬에 넣어보세요.   ⑩ 요리되는 몇 분 동안 팔이 계속 움직이는 걸 볼 수 있습니다.

⑪ 그러니까... 이것은 똑똑한 머리에 근육질 몸매, 거기다 움직임(멋진 자세)까지 갖춘 셈입니다.   ⑫ 그러나 불행히도 이것은 멋진 얼굴은 갖추지 못했습니다.   ⑬ 다리도 없고 얼굴도 없고 팔만 많습니다.   ⑭ 하지만 이것의 팔은 특별한 능력이 갖고 있습니다.   ⑮ 포식자의 공격을 받아 팔 중 하나를 잃어도 팔이 다시 자라기 때문에 이것은 걱정하지 않습니다. ⑯ 그리고 이 녀석은 무섭고 무자비해서 자기 종족도 먹습니다.   ⑰ 게다가 이것은 독을 만들어내는데 물어서 독이 전달됩니다.

⑱ 이게 무엇인지 알 수 있나요?   ⑲ 놀라운 이 바다 동물은 푸른 고리 문어입니다.

Experts acknowledged that Elizabeth Tower, which houses Big Ben, is leaning slightly to one side, similar to the Leaning Tower of Pisa. They said Elizabeth Tower, the most famous landmark of London, leans 0.26 degrees to the north-west. That means the 315-feet-high tower is sinking into the banks of the river Thames. Although its tilt is visible to the naked eye, experts don't think they need to do anything right now. They say it would take around 4,000 years to reach the same angle as the Leaning Tower of Pisa. Mike McCann, the keeper of the tower, agreed with them.

The problem is that no one knows what causes it. Some claim that the London clay on which the tower was built might be the cause. It is thought that its clay foundation made the tower tilt while drying out. Or, it might be caused by work on the Underground near the tower, in spite of the fact that surveyors found no evidence of that.

Either way, people around the world hope that the future of Big Ben is not at risk of sinking into the river Thames.

Words & Expressions

acknowledge 인정하다, (수신을) 확인하다 St. Stephen's clock tower 성 스테판 시계탑 (영국 런던에 위치한 시계 탑. 거대한 시계 빅 벤 (Big Ben)이 위치해 있어서 '빅벤'으로 불리기도 한다.) lean 기울다 landmark 주요 지형물 tilt v 기울다. n. 기울어짐 visible 눈으로 보이는 naked 벌거벗은 naked eye 육안, 맨눈 unstable 불안정한 collapse 무너지다 keeper 관리인 clay foundation 진흙 토대(기초) either way 어느 쪽이든 be at risk 위험에 처하다

Understanding Checkpoint

1. What is the main idea of the story?

   a. Elizabeth Tower is sinking into the Han river.

   b. The fate of Elizabeth Tower is safe for now.

   c. The Big Ben is the largest clock in the world.

   d. Mike McCann is the keeper of the Leaning Tower of Pisa.

2. According to the passage, which sentence is <u>wrong</u>?

   a. The Big Ben is leaning to the side, but there is nothing we can do about it for now.

   b. The height of Elizabeth Tower is 315 feet.

   c. Although the tilt of the tower is so obvious, only experts can notice that.

   d. Elizabeth Tower was built on the London clay.

3. Choose the correct words for each sentence.

   a. There <u>is</u> / <u>are</u> / <u>were</u> no evidence for your theory. Just give me some information to prove it.

   b. I saw Nedd, a tall and <u>leaning</u> / <u>lean</u> / <u>leaned</u> guy in my office, leaning against the wall.

   c. We <u>surveied</u> / <u>surveyed</u> / <u>surveyied</u> 100 teachers last week and got the shocking result you might want to know.

Answer 1. b 2. c 3. is | lean | surveyed

Listening Drill – Dictation

Experts acknowledged that Elizabeth Tower, which houses Big Ben, _____ one side, similar to the Leaning Tower of Pisa. They said Elizabeth Tower, the most famous landmark of London, leans 0.26 degrees to the north-west. That means the 315-feet-high tower is sinking into the _____ of the river Thames. Although its tilt is _____, experts don't think they need to do anything right now. They say it would _____ around 4,000 years to reach the same angle as the Leaning Tower of Pisa. Mike McCann, the keeper of the tower, _____ them.

The problem is that no one knows what causes it. Some claim that the London clay _____ the tower was built might be the cause. It is thought that its clay foundation _____ while drying out. Or, it might be caused by work on the Underground near the tower, _____ the fact that surveyors _____ of that.

Either way, people around the world hope that the future of Big Ben _____ sinking into the river Thames.

> # Did You Know Elizabeth Tower Is Leaning To One Side Just Like The Leaning Tower Of Pisa?

1 Experts **acknowledged** that Elizabeth Tower, which houses Big Ben,

인정하다, (그렇다고) 확인해주다   빅벤이 위치한 엘리자베스 타워   house v. 보관/수용하다, 거처를 제공하다

is **lean**ing slightly to one side, similar to the Leaning Tower of Pisa.

…와 비슷한/유사한
lean v. 기울다, 기대다, 의지하다 (on) a. (지방, 군살) 없이 마른, (고기)기름기 없는
lean to the 방향 : (어느 쪽으로 to) 기울다 lean to one side 한쪽으로 기울다

2 They said Elizabeth Tower, (the most famous **landmark** of London),

└──── = 동격 ────┘   주어 Elizabeth Tower = ( ) 동사 leans

leans 0.26 **degrees** to the north-west.

degree 각도, 도

3 That means the 315-feet-high tower is **sink**ing into the **banks** of the river Thames.

하이픈(-)으로 연결된 형용사 315미터 높이의   bank 1. 은행 2. (강)둑
sink v. 가라앉다, 침몰시키다 (sink-sank-sunken) n. 개수대, 싱크대 (여기서는 '가라앉다')

4 Although its **tilt** is **visible** to the naked eye,

타워의 기울기   보이다/볼 수 있다   맨눈으로, 육안으로 (eyes로 쓰지 않는다.)
tilt v. 기울다 n. 기울어짐
visible 눈에 보이는 / invisible 보이지 않는

experts don't think they need to do **anything** right now.

do something 무언가 하다 / don't do anything 아무것도 하지 않다 (부정문 anything)

5 They say it would take around 4,000 years to reach the same angle as

시간이 걸리다 it takes 시간 (지문은 조동사 would + 동사원형)   같은 각도에 도달하다 reach
it would take 시간이 걸릴 것이다 (추측)

the Leaning Tower of Pisa.

6 Mike McCann, (the keeper of the tower), agreed with them.

└── = 동격 ──┘

7 The problem is that no one knows (what **causes** it).

선행사를 포함한 관계대명사 what, 의문문이 아니라 명사절
– 무엇이 이를 초래하는지를
causes v. …을 야기하다

8 Some claim that (the London clay on which the tower was built) might be the **cause**.

타워가 지어진 on 런던 진흙   that 절 주어 ( ) the London clay + 동사 might be   n. 원인, 이유
= the London clay might be the cause because the tower was built on that clay

316

⑨ It is thought that (its **clay foundation**) made the tower tilt while drying out.

(타워의 진흙 토대) 사역동사　　　make + 동사원형 tilt

주절의 주어 ( )와 일치, 생략 while its clay foundation dried out

⑩ Or, it might be caused by work on the Underground near the tower,

…에 의해 야기되었을 수도 있다 (수동, 추측)　　　영국 지하철 (미국 subway)

in spite of the fact that **surveyors** found no evidence of that.

= despite the fact that 절 (주어+동사)　　　찾은 증거가 없다 evidence 불가산명사 (복수형으로 쓰지 않는다)

survey v. 조사하다 (surveyed / surveying)

surveyor n. 조사원

⑪ Either way, (people around the world) hope that the future of Big Ben is

둘 중 어느 쪽이든　　　that 이하 주어 Big Ben이 아니라 the future + 동사 is

not at risk of sinking into the river Thames.

be at risk of –ing …의 위험에 처하다

> 엘리자베스 타워가 피사의 사탑처럼 한쪽으로 기울어지고 있다는 거 아세요?

❶ 전문가들은 빅벤이 위치한 엘리자베스 타워가 피사의 사탑과 비슷하게 한 쪽으로 약간 기울었다는 걸 확인했습니다.

❷ 그들은 영국에서 가장 유명한 주요 지형물인 엘리자베스 타워가 북서쪽으로 0.26도 기울었다고 말했습니다.

❸ 그 말은 315피트 높이의 탑이 템스 강 강둑으로 가라앉고 있다는 뜻입니다.

❹ 기울었다는 게 육안으로 알 수 있을 정도지만, 전문가들은 당장 무언가를 할 필요는 없다고 생각합니다.

❺ 그들은 피사의 사탑과 동일한 각도가 되려면 대략 4천년은 지나야 한다고 말합니다.

❻ 탑 관리인인 마이크 맥캔 역시 이에 동의했습니다.

❼ 문제는 그 원인을 아무도 확실히 모른다는 것입니다.

❽ 일부는 탑이 세워진 런던 진흙이 원인일 수도 있다고 주장합니다.

❾ 진흙 기초가 마르면서 탑을 움직이게 했다는 것입니다.

❿ 또는, 증거는 없지만 탑 근처 지하철에서의 작업이 원인일 수도 있습니다.

⑪ 어느 쪽이든 전 세계 사람들은 빅벤의 미래가 템스 강에 가라앉는 위험은 없기를 바라고 있습니다.

After his second wife Mumtaz Mahal passed away after giving birth to their 14th child in 1631, Shah Jahan, the fifth Mughal emperor, was devastated. Although she was one of his many wives and not a beauty queen at all, he loved her the most.

Six months later, he started to build the most magnificent tomb for her, the Taj Mahal. He didn't spare anything when it came to the Taj. He brought the building materials from not only India but also several countries of central Asia. In order to transport the enormous amount of the material to the construction site, all available methods were used, including elephants. Over 20,000 people worked laboriously morning to night for 22 years on the tomb of their emperor's dead wife.

They did a wonderful job. The beauty of the Taj was perfect enough for it to become a UNESCO World Heritage Site in 1983. Additionally, the symmetry of this huge marble structure was so perfect that it was chosen as one of the New Seven Wonders of the World in 2007. Shah Jahan knew it was the best tomb ever and he didn't want anyone to build that kind of beautiful structure again.

So on his order, the hands of the master craftsmen were amputated.

Words & Expressions

pass away 사망하다 **emperor** 황제(남) (여황제 empress) **devastate** 완전히 파괴하다, 비탄에 빠지다
beauty queen 미인 대회 우승자, 예쁜 여자 **tomb** 무덤(grave) **magnificent** 멋진, 웅장한 **spare** 아끼다
when it comes to ...에 관해서라면 **building material** 건축자재 **construction site** 건축 현장 **all available
methods** 모든 가능한 방법(수단) **laboriously** 힘들게, 어렵게 **do the job** 일을 하다, 해내다 **heritage** 유산
balance 균형 **huge marble structure** 거대한 대리석 건축물 **mysterious** 신비한 **Seven Wonders of the
World** 세계 7대 불가사의 **amputate** 손발을 자르다 **craftsman** 장인, 수공예가

Understanding Checkpoint

1. What can be the best title of this story?

　　a. Mumtaz Mahal's Bizzare Love for Tombs

　　b. Shah Jahan : The Cruel Emperor Killed His Wife

　　c. The Taj Mahal, The Most Beautiful and Perfect Tomb Ever

　　d. The Miracle Of Love

2. Shah Jahan cut the workers' hands off because _____ .

　　a. the master craftsmen were lazy and dishonest

　　b. he didn't want anyone to build a beautiful tomb as the Taj

　　c. UNESCO didn't choose the Taj as one of the New Seven Wonders of the World

　　d. he was the most horrible and brutal emperor ever

3. Choose the correct words for each sentence.

　　a. It's hard to understand how the storm <u>ruined</u> / <u>spared</u> / <u>ruptured</u> my house while nearby houses were totally destroyed.

　　b. You must keep a fire extinguisher <u>available</u> / <u>to no avail</u> / <u>being available</u> at all times.

　　c. The volcano eruption literally devastated my hometown. It was the most <u>devastating</u> / <u>devastated</u> / <u>devastate</u> disaster ever.

Answer 1. c　2. b　3. spared ┃ available ┃ devastating

Listening Drill – Dictation

After his second wife Mumtaz Mahal passed away after 　　　　　　their 14th child in 1631, Shah Jahan, the fifth Mughal emperor, was devastated. Although she was 　　　his many wives and not a beauty queen at all, he 　　　　　.

Six months later, he started to build the most magnificent tomb for her, the Taj Mahal. He 　　　　　　　　　　when it came to the Taj. He brought the building materials from not only India but also several countries of central Asia. In order to transport 　　　　　　　　　the material to the construction site, 　　　　　　　were used, including elephants. Over 20,000 people 　　　　　　　morning to night for 22 years on the tomb of their emperor's dead wife.

They did a wonderful job. The beauty of the Taj was perfect enough for it to become a UNESCO World Heritage Site in 1983. Additionally, the 　　　　　of this huge marble structure was so perfect that it was chosen as one of the New Seven Wonders of the World in 2007. Shah Jahan knew it was the best tomb ever and he didn't want anyone to build that kind of beautiful structure again.

So 　　　　　, the hands of the master craftsmen 　　　　　　.

Did You Know Why The Emperor Who Built The Taj Mahal Cut His Workers' Hands Off?

1 After his second wife (Mumtaz Mahal) passed away after giving birth to their

= 동격

종속절 주어 his second wife (Mumtaz Mahal)

pass away = die

after 절의 주어와 일치, 생략
= after she gave birth to

14th child in 1631 Shah Jahan, (the fifth Mughal emperor), was **devastated**.

= 동격

주어 Shah Jahan = ( ) + 동사 was
after절의 주어와 주절의 주어가 다름
사람 주어 be devastated : 주어가 비탄에 빠지다
사람이 아닌 주어 be devastating : 주어는 파괴적이다

devastate 완전히 파괴하다
비탄에 빠지다

2 Although she was $^{1)}$ one of his many wives and $^{2)}$ not a beauty queen at all,

one of the 복수명사

미인대회 우승자, 미인

he loved her the most.

가장, 제일 – love ( ) the most ( )를 가장 사랑하다 trust ( ) the most 가장 신뢰하다

3 Six months later, he started to build

(the most **magnificent** tomb) for her, the Taj Mahal.

magnificent 멋진, 웅장한
(↔ maleficent 해로운)

= 동격

b 묵음 : tomb, climb, thumb, bomb, lamb, dumb, comb, limb, plumber, doubt

4 He didn't **spare** anything when it came to the Taj.

spare v. 아끼다 a. 남는, 여분의
not spare anything 아무것도 아끼지 않다 (Spare me. 좀 봐주세요, (안 좋은 것에서) 나를 빼주세요.)

when it comes to ( ) : ( )에 관해서라면 (시제가 과거라서 came)

5 He brought the building materials from (not only India but also several countries

건축자재

인도 뿐 아니라 중앙 아시아의 다른 나라들에서도

of central Asia).

6 In order to **transport** (the **enormous** amount of the material) to

in order to transport ( ) to the site 현장에 ( )를 운반하기 위해
transport v. 수송하다 enormous a. 엄청난

the construction site, all **available** methods were used, including elephants.

건설 현장 (site 장소)   모든 가능한 수단/방법들   이 문장의 주어 methods, 동사 were

7 (Over 20,000 people) worked **laboriously** morning to night for 22 years on

…에서 on 일하다 (work on the tomb 무덤에서 일하다)   아침부터 밤까지 + 22년 동안 (for)
laboriously ad. 힘들게 laborious a. 힘든, 고된 labor n. 노동, (분만)산통 v. 노동하다, 애쓰다

the tomb of their **emperor**'s dead wife.

emperor 황제

8 They did a wonderful job.

do a good/wonderful job 일을 잘하다 do a terrible job 일을 잘 못하다
You can do a good job on this project. 너는 이 프로젝트를 잘 할 수 있다.
He did a terrible job fixing the car. 그는 자동차 고치는 걸 엄청 망쳤다.

9 (The beauty of the Taj) was perfect enough for it to become

주어 ( ) the Taj가 아니라 the beauty + 동사 was

perfect enough (for it) to become 이것(the Taj)이 …될 정도로 충분히 완벽한

a UNESCO World Heritage Site in 1983.

유네스코 세계 유적지

10 Additionally, (the **symmetry** of this **huge marble** structure) was so perfect that

수식

주어 ( ) structure가 아니라 the symmetry

so 형용사 that 절
너무 (형용사)해서 that… 이다

it was chosen as one of the New Seven Wonders of the World in 2007.

…로 선정되다   이해할 수 없는 것, 불가사의

11 Shah Jahan knew it was the best tomb ever and he didn't want anyone to build

최고의 무덤

that kind of beautiful structure again.

저 정도의, 저런

12 So on his order, (the hands of the master craftsmen) were amputated.

그의 명령으로   주어 ( ) craftsmen이 아니라 the hands + 동사 were   수동태 be amputated 절단되다

타지마할을 건축한 황제가 일꾼들의 손을 자른 이유를 아세요?

1 그의 두 번째 아내 뭄타즈 마할이 1631년 14번째 아기를 출산한 후 세상을 떠났을 때, 무굴의 5번째 황제 샤 자한은 크게 상심했습니다. **2** 그녀는 수많은 아내들 중 하나였고 그다지 예쁘지는 않았지만 그는 그녀를 가장 사랑했습니다.

3 6개월 후, 그는 그녀를 위해 가장 웅장한 무덤, 타지마할을 건축하기 시작했습니다. **4** 그는 타지마할에 관해서라면 무엇이든 아끼시 않았습니다. **5** 그는 건축 사재를 인노 뿐 아니라 숭앙아시아의 여러 나라에서 늘여왔습니다. **6** 엄청난 양의 건축자재를 건축 현장으로 운반하기 위해 모든 가능한 수단이 동원되었는데 그 중에는 코끼리도 포함되어 있었습니다. **7** 2만 명 이상의 사람들이 황제의 죽은 아내의 무덤을 위해 22년 동안 아침부터 저녁까지 고되게 일했습니다.

8 이들은 일을 멋지게 해냈습니다. **9** 타지마할의 아름다움은 완벽해서 1983년 유네스코 세계 유산으로 지정될 정도였습니다. **10** 그 뿐만 아니라 거대한 대리석 구조물의 균형은 너무나 완벽해서 2007년 신 세계의 7대 불가사의 중 하나로 선정되기도 했습니다. **11** 샤 자한도 최고의 무덤이라는 걸 알았고, 그렇게 아름다운 건축물을 누군가 또 다시 만드는 걸 원치 않았습니다.

12 그래서 그의 명령으로 장인들의 손이 잘리게 되었습니다.

Two Indonesians tied the knot in 2006 after getting approval from the High Court. Their marriage knocked everyone's socks off because of their age difference. Sudar, the bridegroom, was 105 years old and Ely, the bride, was 22. At the time, Sudar was still married to Fatemah, who was 69 and very much ill. Fatemah was said to welcome her husband's second wife, for she couldn't carry out her responsibilities as a wife, although she added that if she were not ill, she would never allow her husband's second marriage.

Ely allegedly felt sorry for Sudar since he had to take care of his ailing wife in spite of being very old and weak himself. She could help them as a friend or a maid, but she decided to marry him anyway.

It is hard to understand this whole situation, but you know what they say: nothing matters when it comes to true love. Ms. 22 must have loved Mr. 105 very much.

Words & Expressions

tie the knot 결혼하다 (marry) approval 승인, 허락 High Court 고등법원 knock someone's socks off
깜짝 놀라게 하다 age difference 나이 차이 bridegroom 신랑 bride 신부 welcome 환영하다 carry out
one's responsibility 책임을 다하다, 수행하다 ailing wife 병든 아내 maid 하녀 when it comes to ...에 관
해서라면

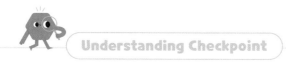

1. What can be the best title of this story?

    a. The Oldest Man Finally Married

    b. Ailing Wife Dumped By Vicious Husband

    c. The Beauty And The Old Man : True and Touching Love Story

    d. Mr. 105 Married Ms. 22 : Nothing Matters But Love

2. According to the passage, which sentence is right?

    a. Sudar married Fatemah in 2006 although he has already been married to Ely.

    b. Sudar's second marriage was illegal because the court didn't permit his marriage to Ely.

    c. It seemed that Fatemah didn't welcome her husband's second wife wholeheartedly.

    d. The age difference between the bridegroom and the bride was over 90.

3. Choose the correct words for each sentence.

    a. I'm going to confess that I did something that <u>matters</u> / <u>matter</u> / <u>mattered</u> to you.

    b. If it <u>was</u> / <u>were</u> / <u>is</u> not for him, she would fail the test.

    c. When I asked John when he is going to tie the knot, he avoided answering my question, <u>tying the knot</u> / <u>tieing a knot</u> / <u>tying a knot</u> in a rope.

Answer **1.** d **2.** c **3.** mattered | were | tying a knot

Two Indonesians   in 2006 after   the High Court. Their marriage   because of their age difference. Sudar, the bridegroom, was 105 years old and Ely, the bride, was 22. At the time, Sudar   Fatemah, who was 69 and very much ill. Fatemah was said to welcome her husband's second wife, for she couldn't   as a wife, although she   , she   allow her husband's second marriage. Ely allegedly felt sorry for Sudar since he had to take care of his ailing wife in spite of   and weak himself. She could help them as a friend or a maid, but she decided to marry him anyway.

It is hard to understand this whole situation, but you know what they say: when it comes to true love. Ms. 22   Mr. 105 very much.

Did You Know Why Fatemah Allowed Her Husband's Second Marriage?

1 Two Indonesians **tied the knot** in 2006 after getting **approval** from

= marry 결혼하다   주절의 주어 일치, 생략 (after they got)
tie the know 결혼하다 tie a knot 매듭 묶다   get approval 허락을 얻다
pop the question 프러포즈를 하다 pop a question 질문 하나를 하다
                                                      approval 승인, 허락 approve 승인하다

the High Court.

2 Their marriage knocked everyone's socks off because of their age difference.

knock one's socks off 누구를 놀라게 하다   나이 차이
knock my socks off 나를 놀라게 하다

3 Sudar, (the **bridegroom**), was 105 years old and Ely, (the **bride**), was 22.

= 동격 | (bride)groom 신랑   = 동격 | bride 신부

4 At the time, Sudar was still **married** to Fatemah, who was 69 and very much ill.

be married to 사람 : 누구와 결혼한 상태이다   who = Fatemah   be ill = be sick
marry 결혼하다 (with를 쓰지 않는다)
Will you marry me? (O) Will you marry with me? (X)

5 Fatemah was said to welcome her husband's second wife,

환영했다고 한다 (be thought to)

for she couldn't **carry out** her **responsibilities** as a wife, although she added that

because   carry out 수행하다 + responsibilities 의무, 책임 – 책임을 다하다
                    responsibility 의무, 책임

if she were not ill, she would never allow her husband's second marriage.

가정법 과거 (현재사실의 반대) if 주어she + 동사 과거 (be동사의 경우 were), 주어 would 동사원형
= She was ill, so she allowed her husband's second marriage. 그녀가 아파서 남편의 두 번째 결혼을 허락했다.
주어에 상관없이 be동사인 경우 were를 써야 한다.
If I were you, I would buy that book. 내가 너라면 저 책을 샀을 텐데. (네가 아니라서 저 책을 사지 않는다.)

6 Ely **allegedly** felt sorry for Sudar since he had to **take care of** his **ailing** wife

알려진 바에 의하면   because   돌보다   병을 앓는
                                              ail v. 아프게 하다 ailment n. 질병 ailing a. 병든

in spite of being very (old and weak) himself.

in spite of + 명사, 동명사

7 She could help them as (a friend or a **maid**), but she decided to marry him anyway.

n. 하녀

❽ It is hard to understand this whole situation, but you know what they say:
가주어 it 진주어 to understand   이런 말도 있다
it's hard to understand 이해하기 어렵다 (To understand this situation is hard.)

nothing matters when it comes to true love.
아무것도 문제되지 않는다   진정한 사랑에 관해서라면 (to 다음에 동사가 오지 않고 명사가 온다.)

❾ Ms. 22 must have loved Mr. 105 very much.
           …임에 틀림없다 (must have pp) - 강한 추측

페이트마가 남편의 두 번째 결혼을 허락한 이유를 아세요?

❶ 두 명의 인도네시아인들이 2006년 고등법원의 허락을 받아 결혼했습니다.

❷ 이들의 결혼은 나이 차이 때문에 다들 놀라 자빠질 뻔 했습니다.

❸ 신랑 수다는 105살, 신부 엘라이는 22살이었습니다.

❹ 당시 수다는 69살에 굉장히 몸이 아픈 페이트마와 여전히 결혼한 상태였습니다.

❺ 페이트마는 자신이 아내의 책임을 감당할 수 없어서 남편의 두 번째 부인을 환영했다는데, 자신이 아프지 않았다면 남편의 두 번째 결혼을 절대 허락하지 않았을 거라는 말을 덧붙였다고 합니다.

❻ 엘라이는 자신도 늙고 연약한데 병든 아내를 돌봐야 하는 수다에게 연민의 정을 느꼈다고 합니다.

❼ 그녀는 친구나 하녀로 이들을 도울 수도 있었지만 어쨌든 그와 결혼하기로 결정했습니다.

❽ 이 상황을 이해하기 힘들지만, 진정한 사랑에 관해서라면 아무것도 문제될 게 없다는 말도 있지 않습니까.

❾ 22살 아가씨는 105살 남자를 대단히 사랑했던 게 틀림없습니다.

Mosquitoes are kind of picky eaters, so they do not suck just anybody's blood. They select their victims carefully before sticking in their long and thin mouths.

If you want to be the mosquitoes' favorite target and you are a brunette, consider dyeing your hair blonde or red since mosquitoes prefer blondes and redheads to brunettes. Furthermore, mosquitoes usually prefer to bite women over men. So, it's safe to say that blondies are mosquitoes' favorite.

If you don't want to dye your hair and you are not female, but still want to be their favorites, no need to worry. There is more than one way to be the chosen one.

Mosquitoes are attracted by smells, specifically, foul smells. So if you sweat a lot and keep your feet unwashed and stinky, you will have a much better chance at donating blood to hungry mosquitoes than who don't. There are two more things that attract mosquitoes : carbon dioxide and lactic acid. The more you produce these things, the more likely you can lure them to you. How? Simple, be obese or jittery, because overweight or fidgety people are said to produce more carbon dioxide and lactic acid than people who aren't.

Words & Expressions

mosquito 모기 picky 까다로운 (picky eater 식성이 까다로운 사람) suck 빨다 stick (뾰족한 것으로) 찌르다, 붙이다 brunette 흑갈색 머리를 가진 백인 여자, 흑갈색 머리의 prefer 더 좋아하다, 선호하다 redhead 빨강 머리(를 가진 사람) bite 물다 blondie 금발 머리 여자 favorite 총애하는, 좋아하는 것(사람) the chosen one 선택 받은 자 attract 끌다 specifically 구체적으로 smelly 악취가 나는 sweat 땀이 나다 unwashed 닦지 않은 stinky 냄새 나는 have a chance to ...할 기회가 있다 donate 기부하다 (donate blood 헌혈하다) carbon dioxide 이산화탄소 lactic acid 젖산 lure 유혹하다 obese 비만한 overweight 과체중의 fidgety 가만히 있지 못하는

Understanding Checkpoint

1. What can be the best title of this story?

    a. The Hidden Secret About Mosquitos Revealed

    b. The Best Way To Expel Mosquitoes

    c. Tips For People Who Want To Be Mosquitoes' Favorites

    d. Watch Out For Fidgety People

2. Mosquitoes tend to bite people who are _____ .

    a. blond or redhead and male

    b. tall, thin and brunette

    c. black-haired and female

    d. blond and female

3. Choose the correct words for each sentence.

    a. My wife prefers sports to reading, but I prefer to read books <u>to</u> / <u>rather than</u> / <u>not to</u> play sports outside.

    b. When I saw two <u>mosquitos</u> / <u>mosquitoes</u> / <u>mosquito</u> on my arm, I slapped them.

    c. Have you ever considered <u>to move</u> / <u>moving</u> / <u>move</u> to another country?

        Answer **1.** c **2.** d **3.** rather than ❘ mosquitoes ❘ moving

Listening Drill – Dictation

Mosquitoes are _____ picky eaters, so they do not suck just anybody's blood. They _____ before sticking in their long and thin mouths.

If you want to be the mosquitoes' favorite target and you are a brunette, _____ your hair blonde or red since mosquitoes prefer blondes and redheads to brunettes. Furthermore, mosquitoes usually prefer to bite women over men. So, _____ that blondies are mosquitoes' favorite.

If you don't want to dye your hair and you are not female, but still want to be their favorites, no need to worry. _____ be the chosen one.

Mosquitoes are attracted by smells, _____ , foul smells. So if you _____ and keep your feet unwashed and stinky, you will _____ donating blood to hungry mosquitoes than who don't. There are two more things that attract mosquitoes : carbon dioxide and lactic acid. The more you produce these things, _____ you can lure them to you. How? Simple, be obese or jittery, because overweight or fidgety people _____ more carbon dioxide and lactic acid than people who aren't.

327

Did You Know Who Can Be Mosquitoes' Favorites?

1 Mosquitoes are kind of picky eaters, so they do not **suck** just anybody's blood.

약간   입맛이 까다로운 사람   부정어 not + anybody 아무나
suck 1. 빨다 2. 엉망이다

2 They select their **victims** carefully before sticking in their (long and thin) mouths.

victim n. 희생자, 피해자   주절의 주어 they (mosquitoes)와 일치, 생략 before they stick in (찔러 넣다)

3 If [1] you want to be the mosquitoes' **favorite** target and [2] you are a brunette,

a. 좋아하는 n. 좋아하는 것(사람)   머리카락이 흑갈색인 여성, 흑갈색

consider dyeing your hair (blonde or red) since mosquitoes

consider -ing …하는 것을 고려하라   blonde a. 금발인 n. 금발 여성 (첫번째 blonde는 형용사 '금발인' 두번째 blondes 금발 여성들
dye hair blonde 머리카락을 금발로 염색하다 (dye - dyed - dyed, dyeing)

prefer (blondes and redheads) to **brunettes**.

prefer A to B : B보다 A를 더 좋아하다 (+ 명사, 동명사)   blonde, brunette 여성 redhead 사람(남성/여성)
prefer (금발 여성들과 빨강머리인 사람들) to (흑갈색 머리 여성들)

4 Furthermore, mosquitoes usually prefer to bite women over men.

prefer (더 좋아하다) + to 동사 (…하기를) + over (…보다 더)
prefer to read books over watching movies 영화보기 보다 책 읽기를 더 좋아하다

5 So, it's safe to say that **blondies** are mosquitoes' **favorite**.

…라고 말해도 된다, 라고 할 수 있다   blond(e) a. 금발인 blondie n. 금발 여성   a. 좋아하는 n. 좋아하는 사람/물건

6 If you don't want to **dye** your hair and you are not **female**,

주어 you 당신이 [1] 염색하기 싫고 [2] 여자도 아니지만 [3] 모기의 총애를 받고 싶다면   female 여성 (↔ male 남성)
dye 염색하다

but still want to be their favorites, no need to worry.

There is no need to worry. = Nothing to worry about. 걱정할 거 없다

7 There is more than one way to be the chosen one.

There is more than one way to skin a cat. 속담을 변형 인용
고양이 가죽 벗기는 방법은 하나 이상이다, 무언가를 할 때 다양한 방법이 있다.

8 Mosquitoes are **attracted** by smells, **specifically**, **foul** smells.

(수동) 끌리다   specific a. 구체적인   a. 더러운, 악취 나는, 안 좋은 n. 반칙, 파울
specifically ad. 구체적으로

9 So if you [1] **sweat** a lot and [2] keep your feet (unwashed and **stinky**), you will

땀을 흘리다   keep 목적어 feet ( ) : 발을 ( ) 상태로 유지하다   악취가 나는

have a much better chance at donating blood to hungry mosquitoes than who don't.

have a chance at -ing a much 훨씬 better 더 많은 chance 기회/가능성 than ⋯보다 (비교급)
⋯할 가능성/기회가 있다   donate blood 헌혈하다 (to ..에게)
you will have a better chance ⋯ than who don't sweat a lot or keep their feet unwashed and stinky

⑩ There are two more things that attract mosquitoes : carbon dioxide and lactic acid.

things 복수 + attract (모기를) 유인하는 것들   이산화탄소   젖산

⑪ The more you produce these things, the more likely you can lure them to you.

the 비교급, the 비교급   carbon dioxide and lactic acid   ⋯할 가능성이 높은   v. 유혹하다
: ⋯할수록 더 ⋯하다 (만들어낼수록 가능성이 더 높아진다)

⑫ How?

⑬ Simple. be obese or jittery, because (overweight or fidgety people) are

be obese 과체중이 되라 obese a. 비만인   a. 과체중인   a. 가만히 못 있는
be jittery 초조해하라 jittery a. 초조해하는

said to produce more (carbon dioxide and lactic acid) than people who aren't.

people who are not overweight or fidgety

모기의 총애를 받는 사람이 누구인지 아세요?

❶ 모기는 나름 입맛이 까다로워서 아무 피나 빨아 먹지 않습니다.

❷ 모기는 길고 얇은 주둥이를 찔러 넣기 전에 먹잇감을 신중하게 선별합니다.

❸ 모기의 총애를 받고 싶은데 머리카락이 암갈색이라면, 모기는 암갈색 머리보다 금발이나 빨강 머리를 더 좋아하니까 금발이나 빨강으로 염색하는 걸 고려해보세요.

❹ 그리고 모기는 일반적으로 남자보다 여자를 무는 걸 더 좋아합니다.

❺ 그러니까 금발 여성이 모기의 총애를 받는다고 말할 수 있습니다.

❻ 머리카락을 염색하기도 싫고 여성도 아니지만 그래도 모기의 총애를 받고 싶다 해도 걱정할 건 없습니다.

❼ 선택받은 자가 되는 방법이 단 한 가지인 건 아닙니다.   ❽ 모기는 냄새, 특히 지독한 냄새에 끌립니다.

❾ 그래서 땀을 많이 흘리고 발을 닦지 않아 악취가 풍기도록 유지하면 그렇지 않은 사람보다 배고픈 모기에게 헌혈할 가능성이 훨씬 높아집니다.   ❿ 모기를 끌어들이는 게 두 가지 더 있는데, 바로 이산화탄소와 젖산입니다.

⑪ 이것들을 많이 배출할수록 모기를 더 많이 유혹할 수 있습니다.   ⑫ 하지만 어떻게 할까요?

⑬ 간단한데, 비만해지거나 많이 움직이세요. 비만하거나 가만히 있지 못하는 사람들이 그렇지 않은 사람들보다 더 많은 이산화탄소와 젖산을 만들어내기 때문입니다.

When two Russians posted their alien video on the YouTube in April 2011, people around the world were taken aback.

Timur Hilall, 18, and Kirill Vlasov, 19, thought their alien video was fun so they expected to get some interesting comments on the internet comment section. They did their job well enough to draw attention from around the world, including alien experts and the police. Although alien experts suspected the whole thing would be just another alien hoax, they thought it might be worth looking into because the alien in the video looked like the real deal. But the fact was that the "alien" was homemade bread. When the police visited their house, Timur and Kirill had to show them the alien made from flour, eggs and milk. The secret of its skin was also revealed: It was chicken skin. The teenagers had covered the oven-baked alien's body with chicken skin to look mysteriously biological. Brilliant.

UFO communities, which are already used to this kind of hoax, published a statement saying 'we don't know how to take this incredibly strange and perhaps enviably creative hoax.'

Understanding Checkpoint

1. What is the main idea of the story?

   a. The stupid UFO communities were tricked by Russian teenagers.

   b. Alien experts complimented two Russians on their alien made from flour and milk.

   c. Two Russians' so-called alien was turned out to be a fake.

   d. Russian teenagers were enviably creative.

2. According to the passage, which sentence is right?

   a. Two Russian teenagers were under arrest after making a fake alien.

   b. Timur and Kirill just wanted to bake bread because they were hungry.

   c. It seems that there are many other alien hoaxes in the world.

   d. Alien experts tricked by these Russian teenagers hated chicken skin.

3. Choose the correct words for each sentence.

   a. These are all wooden handicrafts. I guarantee that they are all <u>ready-made</u> / <u>homemade</u> / <u>handmade</u>.

   b. I think there's no reason to make a fuss about Cathy's necklace. I know it's a <u>real deal</u> / <u>really deal</u> / <u>real dealing</u> but not a big deal.

   c. I think this movie is worthwhile to watch, but that movie is not worth <u>watching</u> / <u>to watch</u> / <u>watch</u>.

Answer **1.** c **2.** c **3.** handmade ǀ real deal ǀ watching

When two Russians _____ their alien video on the YouTube in April 2011, people around the world _____ .

Timur Hilall, 18, and Kirill Vlasov, 19, thought their alien video was fun so they expected to get some interesting comments _____ . They did their job well enough to _____ from around the world, including alien experts and the police. Although alien experts _____ would be just another alien hoax, they thought it might _____ because the alien in the video looked like the real deal. _____ the "alien" was homemade bread. When the police visited their house, Timur and Kirill had to show them the alien _____ flour, eggs and milk. The secret of its skin was also revealed: It was chicken skin. The teenagers had covered the oven-baked alien's body with chicken skin to look _____ . Brilliant.

UFO communities, which are already used to this kind of hoax, _____ saying 'we don't know how to take this incredibly strange and perhaps enviably creative hoax.'

Did You Know How Two Russians Made An Amazing Alien?

1 When two Russians **posted** their **alien** video on the YouTube in April 2011,

post … on ( ) …를 ( )에 올리다, 게재하다
alien 외계인

(people around the world) were taken aback.

주어 ( ) world가 아니라 people + 동사 were　　사람주어 be taken aback : 주어가 깜짝 놀라다

2 (Timur Hilall, 18, and Kirill Vlasov, 19), thought their alien video was fun so

( ) was fun so that they 주어 동사 : ( )이 재미있어서 that… 이다

they expected to get some interesting comments on the internet comment section.

expect to 동사 : …할 것을 기대하다 (expectant a. 기대하는, (출산을) 기대하는) expectant mother 임산부
get comments on the comment section 댓글창에 댓글이 올라오다 (the internet comment section 인터넷 댓글창)

3 They did their job well enough to draw **attention** from around the world,

do one's job 일을 하다　관심을 끌기에 충분한 정도로 잘　　　n. 주목, 관심

including 1) alien experts and 2) the police.

4 Although alien experts **suspected** (the whole thing) would be just another

( ) 이 모든 일　　　　　　　　(이전의 장난들 외) 또 다른 장난 another + 단수명사
suspect v. 의심하다 n. 용의자 (usual suspect) suspicion n. 혐의, 의심　suspicious a. 의심쩍은, 수상한

alien hoax, they thought it might be worth looking into

be worth -ing …할 가치가 있다 + look into 조사하다

because (the alien in the video) looked like the real deal.

진짜처럼 보이다

5 But the fact was that the "alien" was **homemade** bread.

사실은 that …이다　　　　　　　homemade 집에서 만든 handmade 손으로 만든
↔ ready-made 기성의, 이미 만들어진

6 When the police visited their house, (Timur and Kirill) had to show them

the alien made from (flour, eggs and milk).

the alien which was made from
be made from ( ) : ( )로 만들어지다
made of 원재료를 알아볼 수 있을 때 (This table was made of wood. 이 탁자는 나무로 만들어졌다.)
made from 원재료를 알아볼 수 없을 때 (Paper is made from wood. 종이는 나무로 만들어진다.)

7 (The secret of its skin) was also **revealed**: It was chicken skin.

주어 ( ) the secret + 동사 was　　be revealed (수동) 밝혀지다　　　　닭 껍질
reveal 밝히다, 드러내다

⑧ The teenagers had covered the oven-baked alien's body with chicken skin

cover ( ) with… : ( )를 …로 덮다, 감싸다

to look mysteriously biological.

…처럼 보이게 하기 위해   look biological 생물체처럼 보이다

⑨ Brilliant.

It is brilliant. (It's 생략 – Excellent! Marvelous! 대단하다! 멋지다!)

⑩ UFO communities, (which are already used to this kind of **hoax**),

수식   콤마 which (계속) – UFO모임들은 이런 종류의 장난에 이미 익숙한데

주어 UFO communities + 동사 published   be (부사) used to 명사/동명사 …에 익숙하다 (부사는 be동사와 pp사이)

hoax 장난, 거짓말

published a **statement** saying 'we don't know how to take this [1] incredibly strange

성명서를 발표하다 = release a statement   어떻게 받아들일지   수식

and perhaps [2] **enviably creative** hoax.'

수식

이들의 장난질 hoax [1] 믿을 수 없게 이상하고 [2] 부러울 정도로 창의적인

두 명의 러시아인들이 놀라운 외계인을 어떻게 만들었는지 아세요?

❶ 두 러시아인들이 2011년 4월 유튜브에 외계인 비디오를 올렸을 때, 전 세계 사람들은 놀라 자빠질 뻔 했습니다.

❷ 18살의 티머 히랄과 19살의 키릴 브라소프는 자신들의 외계인 비디오가 재미있어서 인터넷 게시판에
흥미로운 댓글이 올라오리라 예상했습니다.

❸ 그들이 얼마나 잘 만들었는지 외계인 전문가들과 경찰을 포함해 세계적인 관심까지 끌었습니다.

❹ 외계인 전문가들은 또 다른 외계인 장난으로 의심하면서도 비디오 속의 외계인이 진짜 같아서 한 번 살펴볼 만 하다고
생각했습니다.

❺ 하지만 사실 "외계인"은 집에서 구운 빵이었습니다.

❻ 경찰이 이들의 집을 찾아갔을 때, 티머와 키릴은 밀가루, 계란, 우유로 만든 외계인을 보여주어야 했습니다.

❼ 그리고 피부의 비밀도 밝혀졌는데, 바로 닭 껍질이었습니다.

❽ 이 두 십대들은 진짜 생물체처럼 신비하게 보이도록 오븐에 구운 외계인 몸을 닭 껍질로 감쌌던 것입니다.

❾ 대단합니다.

❿ 이미 이런 장난에 익숙해진 UFO 모임에서는 '믿을 수 없을 만큼 이상하고 부러울 정도로 창의적인 이번 사건을
어떻게 받아들여야 할지 모르겠다'는 성명을 발표했습니다.

In 2010, two American-born pandas, Mei Lan from Zoo Atlanta and Tai Shan from the Washington Zoo, were sent to China. Shortly after arriving in China, the super cuddly pandas were given a grand welcome. They even appeared on several TV programs just like they did in the United States.

Both of them had been loved so much by the American people ever since they were born in the US, and they served as goodwill ambassadors for China in the US. Then, why were they sent to China? It's because China has ownership of them. Ten years ago, China lent several giant pandas to the United States in exchange for ten million dollars. That's a very expensive price for borrowing something. Under the agreement between the US and China, China would retain ownership of the pandas and their future babies. So, Mei Lan and Tai Shan were destined to return to China although they were born in the US through artificial insemination.

Then again, why did the US spend millions of dollars on borrowing (not buying) giant pandas? That's because so many people wanted to see these endangered animals, and the only way to come by them is through China.

Words & Expressions

shortly after ...직후 cuddly 안아주고 싶은, 사랑스러운 give a grand welcome 크게 환영하다 appear 출연하다(on) goodwill ambassador 친선대사 ownership 소유권 lend 빌려주다 (lend-lent-lent) (borrow 빌리다) in exchange for ..와 교환하여 under the agreement between ... and ... ...(둘) 사이의 동의 하에 retain 보유하다 rented (임대료를 내고) 빌린 be destined to ...할 운명이다 artificial insemination 인공수정 endangered animal 멸종 위기 동물 come by 얻다, 획득하다

1. What can be the best title of the story?

a. The Giant Panda : The Super Cutest Animal Ever

b. China's Unfair Trade Practices

c. The US Spent Exorbitant Money On Mei Lan

d. Two Giant Pandas Go Back To Their Homeland

2. Two America-born giant pandas were sent to China because _____ .

a. they wanted to go back to their homeland

b. bamboo shoots in the US were not delicious

c. China had ownership of them

d. greedy China insisted all giant panda cubs belong to China

3. Choose the correct words for each sentence.

a. They are willing to <u>borrow</u> / <u>lend</u> / <u>rent</u> their support to noble and worthy causes.

b. If I have a library card and ask a librarian to lend me some books with my card, I can <u>borrow</u> / <u>lend</u> / <u>rent</u> them for free.

c. <u>Ever since</u> / <u>During</u> / <u>While</u> his wife was ill in bed, he has had a hard time.

Answer **1.** d **2.** c **3.** lend ǀ borrow ǀ Ever since

Listening Drill – Dictation

In 2010, two American-born pandas, Mei Lan from Zoo Atlanta and Tai Shan from the Washington Zoo, _____ China. Shortly after arriving in China, the super cuddly pandas _____ . They even _____ several TV programs just like they did in the United States.

Both of them had been loved so much by the American people _____ in the US, and they _____ goodwill ambassadors for China in the US. Then, why were they sent to China? It's because China has ownership of them. Ten years ago, China lent several giant pandas to the United States _____ ten million dollars. That's a very expensive price for borrowing something. _____ between the US and China, China would retain ownership of the pandas and their future babies. So, Mei Lan and Tai Shan were destined to return to China although they were born in the US through _____ .

Then again, why did the US spend millions of dollars on borrowing (not buying) giant pandas? That's because so many people wanted to see these endangered animals, and the only way to _____ is through China.

Did You Know Why American-born Giant Pandas Were Sent Back To China?

1 In 2010, two American-born pandas, (Mei Lan from Zoo Atlanta) and
미국에서 태어난 　　　　　　　= 동격

(Tai Shan from the Washington Zoo), were sent to China.
send 보내다 be sent to …로 보내지다 (수동)

2 Shortly after arriving in China, the super cuddly pandas were given a grand welcome.
주절의 주어 pandas 일치, 생략 　　　　　　　　　　　　　　　　　 성대한 환영을 받다 (be given 수동태)
Shortly after they arrived

3 They even **appeared on** several TV programs just like they did in the United States.
appear on TV 텔레비전에 나타나다 (출연하다) 　　　　　　　 = appeared

4 Both of them had been loved so much by the American people
완료 + since + 단순 과거 동사
과거완료 had been loved + ever since they were born 태어난 이래로 사랑받았다

ever since they were born in the US, and they served as goodwill **ambassadors**
…이래로 　　　　　　　　　　　　　　 …로 일하다, 봉사하다 　　　 친선대사

for China in the US.
미국에서 중국을 위한

5 Then, why were they sent to China?

6 It's because China has ownership of them.
have ownership of ( ) : ( )의 소유권을 갖다
retain ownership of ( ) : 원래 갖고 있던 ( )의 소유권을 잃지 않고 유지하다/계속 보유하다

7 Ten years ago, China **lent** several giant pandas to the United States
빌려주다 lend – lent – lent : China lent ( ) to US : 중국은 미국에 ( )를 빌려주었다
빌리다 borrow – borrowed : US borrowed ( ) from China. 미국은 중국으로부터 ( )를 빌렸다.

in exchange for ten million dollars.
…와 교환하여 　　　 ten 10 + million 1,000,000 = ten million 10,000,000 천만 (1천만 달러 – 약 143억원)

8 That's a very **expensive** price for borrowing something.
비싼 (↔ inexpensive 비싸지 않은) 　 …하는데 드는(for) 비용/값 + 동명사
price n. 값 pricey a. 비싼

9 Under the agreement between the US and China,
둘 사이 between의 동의 하에

China would **retain** ownership of (the pandas and their future babies).
( )의 소유권을 유지하다

⑩ So, Mei Lan and Tai Shan were destined to return to China although
…할 운명이다 (수동태) destiny 운명 destination 목적지, 도착지

they were born in the US through **artificial insemination**.
인공 artificial + 수정 insemination (in vitro fertilization 체외 수정)

⑪ Then again, why did the US spend millions of dollars on borrowing
spend 돈 on -ing 얼마를 …하는데 쓰다 / spend 시간 -ing
spend 100 dollars on pants 바지에 100달러 쓰다 / spend two hours cooking 요리하는데 2시간 쓰다

(not buying) giant pandas?

⑫ That's because so many people wanted to see these **endangered** animals,
endangered a. 멸종 위기의 extinct a. 멸종된

and (the only way to come by them) is through China.
주어 ( ) way + 동사 is

미국에서 태어난 자이언트 판다들이 왜 중국으로 돌려보내졌는지 아세요?

❶ 2010년, 미국 태생의 판다 두 마리, 애틀란타 동물원의 메이 란과 워싱턴 동물원의 타이 샨이 중국으로 보내졌습니다.

❷ 중국에 도착한 직후, 너무나 안아주고 싶은 판다들은 큰 환영을 받았습니다.

❸ 또 미국에서 그랬던 것처럼 몇몇 TV 프로그램에도 출연했습니다.

❹ 두 마리 모두 미국에서 태어난 이후 미국인들에게 많은 사랑을 받았고, 미국에서 중국의 친선대사와 같은 존재였습니다.

❺ 그런데 왜 이들이 왜 중국에 돌려보내졌을까요?

❻ 그것은, 중국이 이들의 소유권을 갖고 있기 때문입니다.

❼ 10년 전, 중국은 천만 달러를 받고 미국에 자이언트 판다 몇 마리를 빌려주었습니다.

❽ 무언가를 빌리는 돈으로 상당히 비싼 금액입니다.

❾ 미국과 중국의 합의 하에, 중국은 빌려준 판다들과 미래의 새끼들에 대한 소유권을 보유하게 되었습니다.

❿ 그래서 메이 란과 타이 샨은 인공 수정에 의해 미국에서 태어났음에도 불구하고 중국으로 돌아갈 운명이었습니다.

⓫ 다시 한 번, 왜 미국은 자이언트 판다를 (구매하는 게 아닌) 빌리는데 수천만 달러를 썼는지 궁금해집니다.

⓬ 그건 멸종 위기의 이 동물을 보길 원하는 사람들은 아주 많은데, 판다를 얻을 수 있는 유일한 길이 중국뿐이기 때문입니다.

337

The Kennedy Curse is an expression used to describe tragic accidents which have happened to the Kennedy family. No one knows whether those unfortunate events have resulted from the curse or from sheer bad luck, but it is true that there have been many repeated and continual instances of misfortune in the Kennedy family.

Here are some of this family's tragic accidents.

In 1963, then U.S. President John F. Kennedy was assassinated by Lee H. Oswald. And his older son John F. Kennedy, Jr. died of a plane accident in 1999. His aircraft crashed into the Atlantic Ocean while he was in the cockpit. At that time he was only 39. Rober F. Kennedy, the younger brother of JFK, was also assassinated in 1968. He was shot by Sirhan Sirhan.

In 1984, David Anthony Kennedy died of a cocaine overdose and Michael Kenneedy died in a skiing accident in 1997. Kara Kennedy Allen died of a heart attack while exercising in a health club in 2011. In 2012, Mary Richardson Kennedy, a wife of RFK Jr. (the son of the former U.S. senator Robert Kennedy) committed suicide.

Words & Expressions

curse 저주 expression 표현 describe 묘사하다, 서술하다 tragic 비극적인 unfortunate 불운한 repeated 반복된 continual 연속적인 misfortune 불운, 불행 assassinate 암살하다 sheer bad luck 순수한 불운 plane crash 비행기 사고 cockpit 조종석 respectively 각각 die of a heart attack 심장마비로 사망하다 cocaine overdose 코카인 과량 복용

Understanding Checkpoint

1. What is the main idea of the story?

   a. It is true there have been lots of tragic accidents in the Kennedy family.

   b. The Kennedy curse is a mere superstition.

   c. Many members of the Kennedy family were politicians.

   d. John F. Kennedy Jr. and Kara Kennedy died because of the curse.

2. According to the passage, which sentence is right?

   a. All family members in the Kennedy family are meant to die.

   b. Nothing happened to the Kennedy family so the Kennedy Curse is not true.

   c. Both John F. Kennedy and his older son were killed by the same assassin.

   d. It seemed that David Anthony Kennedy was a cocaine user.

3. Choose the correct words for each sentence.

   a. An <u>assassin</u> / <u>assassinate</u> / <u>assassinators</u> is a person who murders someone prominent or important.

   b. Judy was accused of fraud in 2023 by <u>than</u> / <u>then</u> / <u>their</u> her assistance and her close friend Maria.

   c. A toddler fell to the floor while <u>stomping</u> / <u>he stomped</u> / <u>to stomp</u> her feet.

   d. Michael, the <u>late</u> / <u>former</u> /<u>early</u> president of the World Trade from 2022 to 2024, was my father's friend.

Answer **1.** a **2.** d **3.** assassin ǀ then ǀ stomping ǀ former

Listening Drill – Dictation

The Kennedy Curse is an expression used to describe tragic accidents which have   the Kennedy family. No one knows whether those unfortunate events have   the curse or from   , but it is true that there have been many repeated and continual instances of misfortune in the Kennedy family.

Here are some of this family's tragic accidents.

In 1963,   U.S. President John F. Kennedy   Lee H. Oswald. And his older son John F. Kennedy, Jr. died of a plane accident in 1999. His aircraft crashed into the Atlantic Ocean while he   . At that time he was only 39. Rober F. Kennedy, the younger brother of JFK, was also assassinated in 1968. He   Sirhan Sirhan.

In 1984, David Anthony Kennedy   cocaine overdose and Michael Kenneedy died in a skiing accident in 1997. Kara Kennedy Allen died of   while exercising in a health club in 2011. In 2012, Mary Richardson Kennedy, a wife of RFK Jr. (the son of the former U.S. senator Robert Kennedy)   .

Did You Know What The Kennedy Curse Is?

1 The Kennedy **Curse** is an expression used to **describe tragic** accidents (which

n. 저주, 욕   accidents – 케네디 가문에 일어난 사건들 ↑ 수식
expression which is used to describe 묘사하기 위해 사용되는 표현

have happened to the Kennedy family).

2 No one knows whether those **unfortunate events** have **resulted** (from

아무도 모른다   whether 비극적 사건들이 (저주에서인지) or (순전히 운이 나빠서인지)   result from …의 결과이다, …에서 기인하다
unfortunate a. 불운한   event n. 사건   accident 사고

the curse) or (from **sheer** bad luck), but it is true that there have been

sheer 순수한 bad luck 불운   현재완료–불운한 사례들이 있어왔다

many (repeated and **continual**) instances of **misfortune** in the Kennedy family.

(반복적이고 지속적인) 사례들 | 수식 ↑ ↑ 수식 | instances of misfortune 불운한 사례들

3 Here are some of this family's tragic accidents.

Here 복수동사 are + 복수 명사 accidents (Here is + 단수 명사)

4 In 1963, then U.S. President John F. Kennedy was **assassinated** by Lee H. Oswald.

암살당하다 (수동태)
assassinate v. 암살하다 assassination n. 암살
assassin / assassinator n. 암살범

5 And his older son (John F. Kennedy), Jr. died of a **plane** accident in 1999.

| = 동격 | 비행기 사고로 사망하다
plane / airplane 비행기

6 His **aircraft crashed** into the Atlantic Ocean while he was in the cockpit.

주절의 주어 his aircraft, while절 주어 he (일치하지 않아서 생략 불가)   be in the cockpit 조종석에 있다, 조종하다

7 At that time he was only 39.

당시   = he was only 39 years old.

8 Robert F. Kennedy, (the younger brother of JFK), was also assassinated in 1968.

| = 동격 | 암살당하다 (수동태에서 be와 pp사이 부사)

9 He was shot by Sirhan Sirhan.

…에 의해 총살당하다 (수동)
shoot v. (총, 활) 쏘다 (shoot-shot-shot)

⑩ In 1984, David Anthony Kennedy died of a cocaine **overdose** and

코카인 과다복용 over 과도한 + dose (약) 1회분 복용양

Michael Kenneedy died in a skiing accident in 1997.

⑪ Kara Kennedy Allen died of **a heart attack** while exercising in a health club in 2011.

die of 사망 원인 (심장마비)   주절의 주어와 일치, 생략 while she exercised

⑫ In 2012, Mary Richardson Kennedy, (a wife of RFK Jr.) (the son of the former

RFK Jr.의 부인   = 동격   = 동격   Robert Kennedy의 아들
(* Mary의 시아버지 – Robert Kennedy)

U.S. senator Robert Kennedy) committed suicide.

자살하다 = kill oneself, take one's own life (안 좋은 일을 저지를 때 commit)
commit a crime 범죄를 저지르다 commit a sin 죄를 짓다 commit an offense 불법을 저지르다

케네디가의 저주가 무엇인지 아세요?

❶ 케네디가의 저주는 케네디 가문에 일어난 비극적 사건을 표현할 때 사용되는 표현입니다.

❷ 그런 불행한 사건들이 저주인지 아니면 순전히 불운인지 아무도 모르지만, 반복적이고 지속적인 불운한 사례들이 케네디 가문에 있었왔던 건 사실입니다.

❸ 이 가문의 비극적 사건 중 일부는 이렇습니다.

❹ 1963년, 당시 미국 대통령이었던 존 F. 케네디가 리 H. 오스왈드에 의해 암살되었습니다.

❺ 그리고 그의 큰 아들 존 F. 케네디 2세는 1999년에 비행기 사고로 사망했습니다.

❻ 그가 조종석에 있을 때 그의 비행기가 대서양으로 추락했습니다.

❼ 당시 그의 나이는 겨우 39세였습니다.

❽ JFK의 남동생 로버트 K. 케네디 역시 1968년에 암살당했습니다.

❾ 그는 시르한 시르한이 쏜 총에 맞았습니다.

❿ 1984에 데이비드 앤터니 케네디는 코카인 과량 복용으로 사망했고, 마이클 케네디는 1997년에 스키 사고로 사망했습니다.

⑪ 카라 케네디 알렌은 2011년 헬스클럽에서 운동하던 중 심장 마비로 사망했습니다.

⑫ 2012년에는 RFK 2세 (전 미국 상원의원 로버트 케네디의 아들)의 아내인 메리 리처드슨 케네디가 자살했습니다.

79 Mount Rushmore Was Carved With The Help Of Dynamite?

Mount Rushmore National Memorial, located in South Dakota, is a monumental super-giant granite sculpture of the heads of former U.S. presidents, George Washington, Thomas Jefferson, Theodore Roosevelt and Abraham Lincoln. Its length from the top of the heads to the chins is a whopping 18m and you can see it from 90 km away.

The man who designed the heads was Gutzon Borglum. He, and 400 people mustered for the most enormous carving project ever, had painstakingly worked for years. The carving started in 1927 and ended in 1941. At that time, there was no road to the mountain, so the workers had to ride horses, walk, or even climb to get to the top of the mountain.

Interestingly, they didn't chip away the stone. To carve the huge heads into the face of Mount Rushmore, Borglum used dynamite. After blasting away large portions of rock with dynamite, Borglum and his workers carved the heads with drills, hammers and chisels. The memorial is notable for not only its size but also the fact that no one died during the carving, although that was a very dangerous job.

Understanding Checkpoint

1. What is the main idea of the story?

   a. Mount Rushmore is famous for its height and beautiful scenery.

   b. While carving giant faces on Mount Rushmore, workers used dynamite.

   c. Explosives like dynamite must not be used under any circumstances.

   d. Borglum forced workers to use only hammers and chisels.

2. To carve four huge heads on Mount Rushmore, Borglum and workers _____ .

   a. rode cars or wagons to get to the top of the mountain

   b. blasted large portions of rock away with the help of dynamites

   c. used only their hands and sticks for safety

   d. had chipped away the stone for over 10 years

3. Choose the correct words for each sentence.

   a. I need a proper <u>carve</u> / <u>carving</u> / <u>carved</u> knife to cut this big chunk of meat in half.

   b. Spleen <u>is located in</u> / <u>locates in</u> / <u>located in</u> the left upper part of the abdomen.

   c. All workers should start working <u>at</u> / <u>in</u> / <u>on</u> September 1 and finish their work during December.

Answer 1. b 2. b 3. carving ┃ is located in ┃ on

Mount Rushmore National Memorial,   South Dakota, is a   super-giant granite sculpture of the heads of former U.S. presidents, George Washington, Thomas Jefferson, Theodore Roosevelt and Abraham Lincoln. Its length from the top of the heads to the chins is   18m and you can see it from 90 km away.

The   designed the heads was Gutzon Borglum. He, and 400 people   for the most enormous carving project ever,   for years. The carving started in 1927 and ended in 1941. At that time,   the mountain, so the workers had to ride horses, walk, or even climb to get to the top of the mountain. Interestingly, they didn't   the stone. To carve the huge heads into the face of Mount Rushmore, Borglum used dynamite. After blasting away   rock with dynamite, Borglum and his workers carved the heads with drills, hammers and chisels. The memorial is notable for not only its size but also   no one died during the carving, although that was a very dangerous job.

343

Did You Know Mount Rushmore Was Carved With The Help Of Dynamite?

1 Mount Rushmore National Memorial, (located in South Dakota), is a monumental

Mount Rushmore National Memorial 주어 + is 동사　　　… Memorial which is located in …에 위치한　　a. 기념비적인

super-giant granite sculpture of the heads of former U.S. presidents, (George

기념비적인 + 엄청 큰 + 화강암 + 조각상　　　미국 전 대통령들의 머리 – 대통령들 ( )　　= 동격

　　　　　sculpture 조각　　　　　former 전의

Washington, Thomas Jefferson, Theodore Roosevelt and Abraham Lincoln).

2 (Its length from the top of the heads to the chins) is a whopping 18m and you

주어 ( ) the chins가 아니고 its length 머리 꼭대기에서 턱까지 길이 + 동사 is　　자그마치 18미터　a + 수를 수식하는 형용사 + 수

　　　　　　　　　　　　　　　　　　　He weighs a staggering 100 kg. 그는 체중이 무려 100kg이다.

can see it from 90km away.

90km 멀리 (떨어진) 거리에서 (away 시간이나 공간이 얼마 떨어진/먼)

Your birthday is a year away. 네 생일은 1년 이후이다. The test is only two days away. 겨우 이틀 후에 시험이다.

3 (The man who designed the heads) was Gutzon Borglum.

주어 ( ) the heads가 아니고 the man 머리를 디자인한 남자 + 동사 was

4 He, (and 400 people mustered for the most enormous carving project ever),

　　　　　↑ㅡㅡ수식ㅡㅡㅣ muster 모으다, 소집/동원하다　a. 거대한　carve v. 조각하다 carving n. 조각

주어 He 동사 had　people who were mustered 소집된 400명의 사람들 + 가장 거대한 조각 프로젝트를 위해

had painstakingly worked for years.

과거 완료 had + 부사 + pp + for 기간　　수년 간

painstakingly ad. 공들여서, 힘들여서

5 The carving started in 1927 and ended in 1941.

년도 앞에 in　on March 29, 2025 – 2025년 3월 29일 하루 (기간의 범위가 좁은 경우)

in March 2025 – 2025년 3월 한 달 (기간의 범위가 넓은 경우)

6 At that time, there was no road to the mountain, so the workers had to [1] ride

…로 향하는 (to) 길이 없다　　산 정상에 오르기 위해 일꾼들은 [1] 말을 타거나 [2] 걷거나 [3] 등반

horses, [2] walk, or even [3] climb to get to the top of the mountain.

산 꼭대기에 오르다

7 Interestingly, they didn't chip away the stone.

chip 작은 조각 (chip away 작은 조각으로 쪼다, 깎아내다 / chip in 돈을 조금씩 거두어 모으다)

8 To carve the huge heads into the face of Mount Rushmore, Borglum used dynamite.

산 표면에 거대한 머리들을 조각하기 위해　　러쉬모어 산의 표면

face n. 얼굴, 측면, 표면 v. 마주보다, 향하다, 직면하다

⑨ After blasting away (large **portions** of rock) with dynamite, (Borglum and

portion 일부분 / potion 물약, 마법 독약
after they blasted away ( ) with dynamite 다이너마이트로 ( )를 날려버린 후
주절의 주어 Borglum and his workers와 일치, 생략

his workers) carved the heads with (drills, hammers and chisels).

( )로 머리들을 조각하다 드릴, 망치, 끌

⑩ The memorial **is notable for** not only its size but also the fact that

= be famous for   크기 뿐 아니라 that…라는 사실 또한 (not only ~ but also ~)

no one died during the carving, although that was a very dangerous job.

아무도 조각하는 중 사망하지 않았다

마운트 러슈모어가 다이너마이트의 도움으로 조각되었다는 거 아세요?

❶ 사우스 다코타에 위치한 마운트 러슈모어 국립 기념비는 엄청나게 큰 기념비적인 화강암 조각으로 미국의 전 대통령 네 사람, 조지 워싱턴, 토마스 제퍼슨, 테오도르 루즈벨트, 그리고 아브라함 링컨의 머리 조각상입니다.

❷ 머리 꼭대기에서 턱까지의 길이가 무려 18미터로 90km 멀리에서도 볼 수 있습니다.

❸ 머리 상을 디자인한 사람은 거츤 보글럼입니다.

❹ 보글럼과 가장 거대한 조각 프로젝트를 위해 소집된 400명의 사람들은 수 년 동안 땀을 흘리며 일을 했습니다.

❺ 조각은 1927년에 시작되어 1941년에 끝났습니다.

❻ 당시에는 산까지 가는 길이 없었기 때문에 일꾼들은 산꼭대기까지 가기 위해 말을 타거나 걷거나 심지어 등산까지 해야 했습니다.

❼ 재미있게도 이들은 돌 조각을 조금씩 깨는 식으로 일하지 않았습니다.

❽ 러슈모어 산 표면에 거대한 얼굴을 조각하기 위해 보글럼은 다이너마이트를 이용했습니다.

❾ 다이너마이트로 상당한 분량의 바위를 폭파시킨 후, 보글럼과 일꾼들은 드릴, 망치, 끌로 얼굴을 조각했습니다.

❿ 이 기념비는 그 크기로도 유명하지만 매우 위험한 일이었음에도 불구하고 조각 작업 중 사상자가 한 명도 없었다는 사실로도 유명합니다.

Many Kayan people, a minority tribe of Burma, fled from Burma due to the brutal military regime. They had no choice but to live in the Thai border area as illegal immigrants. But, the authorities have let them live there since the giraffe-looking Kayan women attract tourists, and allow them to pocket some money.

Kayan women are famous for 'giraffe women' since their necks are much longer than normal. They actually make their necks longer on purpose. Traditionally, as far as their women's necks are concerned, the longer, the better. So in order to have longer necks, most Kayan women start wearing brass (or silver) neck rings when they are young.

They gradually add rings to their necks over the years. The heavy weight of rings pushes down their shoulders, making their necks look longer.

The village where they live is an artificial village built by Thai businessmen. Most tourists visit there only to see the long-necked, exotic-looking Kayan women, and often refer to this village as a human zoo.

Understanding Checkpoint

1. What can be the best title of this story?

    a. Thai Businessmen, The Archenemy of Kayan Women

    b. Illegal Immigrants Found Unconscious In The Thai Border

    c. Kayan Women : Why Are They Called "Giraffe Women?"

    d. Burma Military Regime Forced Kayan To Be Giraffes.

2. According to the passage, which sentence is <u>wrong</u>?

    a. The population of the Kayan tribe seems to be less than other tribes.

    b. Kayan people living in the Thai border area are illegal immigrants.

    c. Kayan women made their necks long to earn money.

    d. The reason Thai authorities allow Kayan people to live in their territory is money.

3. Choose the correct words for each sentence.

    a. My parents are <u>migration</u> / <u>immigrants</u> / <u>emigrants</u>. They left South Korea 10 years ago to start a new life in here, North America.

    b. Many people think, as far as Hollywood starlets are <u>concern</u> / <u>concerns</u> / <u>concerned</u>, the thinner, the better.

    c. Water is often referred <u>to</u> / <u>with</u> / <u>for</u> as the beginning of life.

                                         Answer 1. c   2. c   3. immigrants ∣ concerned ∣ to

Listening Drill – Dictation

Many Kayan people,   Burma, fled from Burma due to the brutal military regime. They   live in the Thai border area as   . But, the authorities have let them live there since the giraffe-looking Kayan women attract tourists, and allow them to   .

Kayan women are famous for 'giraffe women' since their necks are much longer than normal. They actually make their necks longer   . Traditionally, as far as their women's necks are concerned, the longer, the better. So in order to have longer necks, most Kayan women   brass (or silver) neck rings when they are young.

They   add rings to their necks over the years. The heavy weight of rings pushes down their shoulders, making their necks look longer.

The   is an artificial village built by Thai businessmen. Most tourists visit there   see the long-necked, exotic-looking Kayan women, and often   a human zoo.

Did You Know There Are Giraffe-looking Women?

① Many Kayan people, (a minority tribe of Burma), fled from Burma

= 동격

주어 Many Kayan people = ( ) 버마의 소수 민족인 카얀인들 + 동사 fled

flee 도망치다 (flee-fled-fled / fleeing)

Burma 버마: Myanmar미얀마의 옛 이름

due to the **brutal** military **regime**.

때문에　　　잔혹한　　군사　　regime 정권, 제도 regimen 식이요법 regiment (군)연대, 다수

due to = because of 때문에 / thanks to 덕분에

② They had no choice but to live in the Thai **border** area as **illegal immigrants**.

…하는 거 외에 다른 선택이 없다 (to + 동사원형)　　　n. 국경, 경계　　불법 이민자로　immigrant 타국에서 온 이민자

emigrant 타국으로 간 이민자

③ But, **the authorities** have let them live there since (the giraffe-looking

현재완료 have pp

사역동사 let + 목적어 them + 동사원형 live

그들이 살도록 놔두다 (let-let-let)

주어 ( ) + 동사 1) attract 2) allow

Kayan women) 1) **attract** tourists, and 2) **allow** them to **pocket** some money.

attract tourists 관광객들을 끌어들이다

attraction 관광명소

v. 주머니에 넣다, 챙기다 n. 주머니

④ Kayan women **are famous for** 'giraffe women' since their necks are

유명하다 (be well known for 잘 알려져 있다)

much longer than normal.

정상보다 훨씬 더 긴

⑤ They actually make their necks longer **on purpose**.

make ( ) longer : ( )를 더 길게 만들다　　고의로, 일부러 = purposedly

⑥ Traditionally, as far as their women's necks are concerned, the longer, the better.

as far as ( ) be concerned : ( )에 관해서라면　　　the 비교급, the 비교급 – 길수록 좋다

⑦ So in order to have longer necks, most Kayan women start wearing brass

더 긴 목을 갖기 위해　　　start wearing rings 고리를 걸기 시작하다

(or silver) neck rings when they are young.

⑧ They **gradually** add rings to their necks over the years.

서서히 gradually 추가하다 add　　　수 년에 걸쳐 (for years 수년 동안)

⑨ (The heavy weight of rings) pushes down their shoulders,

주어 ( ) rings가 아니라 weight (3인칭, 단수) + 동사 pushes　　push down shoulders 어깨를 아래로 밀다

making their necks **look** longer.

사역동사 make + 목적어 necks + 동사원형 look

⑩ (The village where they live) is an **artificial** village built by Thai businessmen.

↑ 수식 | 그들이 사는 마을   a. 인공적인   village which was built by …의해 지어진 마을

⑪ Most tourists [1] visit there only to see the (long-necked, **exotic**-looking)

오직 보기/구경하기 위해   목이 길고 이국적인 외모의   이국적인, 외국의

Kayan women, and often [2] **refer to** this village **as** a human zoo.

refer to A as B : A를 B라고 부르다
refer 조회하다, 지시하다, 참조하다, 언급하다, …라 부르다

기린처럼 보이는 여성들이 있다는 거 아세요?

❶ 버마의 소수 종족인 많은 카얀인들은 무서운 군사 정부 때문에 버마에서 도망 나왔습니다.

❷ 이들은 불법 체류자로 타이 국경 지역에서 살 수 밖에 없었습니다.

❸ 하지만 당국은 이들이 그곳에 살게 놔두는데, 기린처럼 보이는 카얀 여성들이 관광객들을 끌어들여 돈을 챙길 수 있게 해주기 때문입니다.

❹ 카얀 여성들은 기린 여성으로 유명한데, 이들의 목이 보통보다 훨씬 길기 때문입니다.

❺ 사실 이들이 일부러 목을 길게 만든 겁니다.

❻ 전통적으로 카얀 여성의 목에 관해서라면 길수록 좋다고 합니다.

❼ 그래서 긴 목을 만들기 위해 대부분의 카얀 여성들은 놋 (또는 은) 고리를 어려서부터 목에 걸고 삽니다.

❽ 수년에 걸쳐 서서히 목에 고리를 늘입니다.

❾ 무거운 고리 무게가 어깨를 아래로 밀어 목이 길어 보이는 겁니다.

❿ 이들 사는 동네는 타이 사업가들이 지은 인공 동네입니다.

⓫ 대부분의 관광객들은 오직 목이 길어서 이색적인 볼거리가 되는 카얀 여성을 보기 위해 그 곳을 방문하는데, 종종 그 마을을 인간 동물원이라 부르기도 합니다.

Chapter 09

The Amazing Records

MP3

Sultan Kosen, a Turk, is the tallest living person in the world. When he was listed in Guinness World Records as the tallest person in 2009, he was 247cm tall. When Guinness measured his height again in his home town in 2011, his height was measured 251cm.

His unusual growth is caused by a pituitary tumor affecting his growth hormone. Recently, he underwent treatments for his tumor and is taking medicine to control his excessive levels of growth hormone. Now, his hormone levels are said to be almost normal. But he has already grown too much, so he must use crutches when walking.

He couldn't complete his schooling because of his uncontrollably ever-growing height. He couldn't go inside the school building due to the ceiling being too low for him. He also always has a hard time finding his clothes and shoes that fit him, as well as fitting himself into a car. In spite of this, he says he enjoys a normal life, like playing computer games with his friends and helping his mom change light bulbs.

Words & Expressions

measure 측정하다 height 신장, 키 hold the record 기록을 보유하다 unusual growth 이상한 성장 pituitary 뇌하수체 tumor 종양 affect 영향을 미치다 growth hormone 성장 호르몬 hormone level 호르몬 수치 crutches 목발 complete one's schooling 학업을 마치다 uncontrollably 통제할 수 없게 ceiling 천장 light bulb 전구

1. What is the main idea of the story?

    a. The tallest person has to use crutches all the time.

    b. Sultan Kosen became the tallest person because of his disease.

    c. A Turk named Sultan Kosen has the current biggest feet in the world.

    d. Tallest or not, Kosen should have completed his schooling.

2. According to the article, a pituitary tumor _____ .

    a. was measured 251cm

    b. was caused by his abnormal growth hormone

    c. was a kind of incurable cancer

    d. affected Kosen's height

3. Choose the correct words for each sentence.

    a. My job is to watch the rate of economic <u>growth</u> / <u>grow</u> / <u>growing</u> closely.

    b. The construction workers <u>have already received</u> / <u>already have received</u> / <u>have received already</u> their payment from their office.

    c. We measure his height once a week but his weight <u>measure</u> / <u>is measured</u> / <u>measuring</u> on a daily basis.

Answer **1.** b **2.** d **3.** growth ǀ have already received ǀ is measured

Listening Drill – Dictation

Sultan Kosen , a   , is the tallest living person in the world. When he was listed in Guinness World Records as the tallest person in 2009, he was 247cm tall. When Guinness   his height again in his home town in 2011, his height was measured 251cm. His unusual growth   a pituitary tumor affecting his growth hormone. Recently, he   his tumor and is   to control his excessive levels of growth hormone. Now, his hormone levels are said to be almost normal. But he   too much, so he must use crutches when walking. He couldn't complete his schooling because of his   . He couldn't go inside the school building   being too low for him. He also always has a hard time finding his clothes and shoes that fit him, as well as   . In spite of this, he says he enjoys a normal life, like playing computer games with his friends and helping his mom   .

Did You Know Who The Tallest Person In The World Is?

1 Sultan Kosen , (a Turk), is the tallest living person in the world.

　　　　└─ = 동격 ─┘　　터키인 술탄 코센　　키가 제일 큰 + 생존하는 + 사람

2 When he was listed in Guinness World Records as the tallest person in 2009,

　　　be listed in ( ) as … : ( )에 …로 오르다 (목록에 올라가다)

he was 247cm tall.

3 When Guinness **measured** his height again in his home town in 2011,

　　　키를 측정하다/재다 (능동- 측정하는 주체가 기네스)

his height was **measured** 251cm.

　　　키가 측정되다 (수동-기네스가 그의 키를 측정하고 그의 키는 측정되는 것)

4 (His unusual growth) is caused by a pituitary **tumor** (**affecting** his growth hormone).

　　　　　　　　　　　　　　↑　수식　　　그의 성장 호르몬에 영향을 미치는 종양
　　　　　　　　현재 분사 … tumor that affects his growth hormone

5 Recently, he [1] **underwent treatments** for his tumor and

　　　치료를 받다 (undergo는 자체에 수동의 의미가 있어서 수동태로 쓰지 않는다.)
　　　undergo - underwent - undergone　그는 [1] underwent (과거에 치료 받았고) [2] is taking (현재 약 복용하다)

[2] is **taking medicine** to control (his **excessive** levels of growth hormone).

　　약을 복용하다 take　　　　　　　　과도한 성장 호르몬 정도 - control levels
　　take - take medicine/pills/medication 약 먹다　excessive 과도한
　　take photos 사진찍다 take precautions 예방조치 하다

6 Now, his hormone levels are said to be almost normal.

7 But he has already grown too much, so he must use crutches when walking.

　　현재완료의 부사 has + 부사 + pp　　　　　　　use crutches 목발 짚다　when he walks (주어 일치, 생략)
　　　　　　　　　　　wear a cast 깁스하다 get an IV 링거주사 맞다

8 He couldn't complete his schooling because of his uncontrollably ever-growing height.

　　complete schooling 학교를 마치다 (졸업하다)　　　수식　↑　　수식　↑
　　　　　　　because of + 명사 : 통제 불능으로 계속 자라는 키

9 He couldn't go inside the school building **due to** the ceiling (being too low for him).

　　　　　　천장 때문에 (due to + 명사, 동명사)　그에게 너무 낮은 천장 때문에
　　　　　　= because the ceiling was too low for him

⑩ He also always has a hard time ¹⁾ finding (his clothes and shoes) that fit him,

have a hard time -ing …하는데 어려움을 겪다   수식   그에게 맞는 ( )

as well as ²⁾ fitting himself into a car.

뿐만 아니라   fit oneself into a car 자동차에 들어가게 자신을 맞추다

⑪ In spite of this, he says he enjoys a **normal** life, like ¹⁾ playing computer games

a normal life의 예 ¹⁾ 놀기 ²⁾ 도와주기

with his friends and ²⁾ helping his mom change light bulbs.

help + 목적어 mom + 동사원형 change   change 갈다, 교환하다 light bulbs 전구

(세상에서 가장 큰 사람이 누구인지 아세요?)

❶ 술탄 코센이라는 터키인이 세상에서 생존한 가장 큰 사람입니다.

❷ 2009년에 가장 큰 사람으로 기네스 세계 기록에 오를 당시 그의 키는 247cm였습니다.

❸ 그리고 2011년에 그의 고향에서 기네스가 다시 키를 측정했는데, 251cm로 측정되었습니다.

❹ 그의 키가 이상하게 커진 원인은 건 뇌하수체 종양이 성장 호르몬에 영향을 미쳤기 때문입니다.

❺ 그는 종양 치료를 받았고 성장 호르몬의 과도한 수준을 조절하기 위한 약도 복용하고 있습니다.

❻ 현재 그의 호르몬 수치는 거의 정상이라고 합니다.

❼ 하지만 그는 이미 너무 많이 커버렸기 때문에 걸을 때 목발을 사용해야만 합니다.

❽ 통제할 수 없이 계속 자라는 키 때문에 그는 학교도 마칠 수 없었습니다.

❾ 천장이 너무 낮아 학교 건물 안에 들어갈 수 없었던 겁니다.

❿ 또 옷과 신발을 구하거나 자동차 안에 들어가는데 항상 어려움을 겪습니다.

⑪ 그럼에도 불구하고 그는 친구들과 컴퓨터 게임을 하거나 엄마가 전구 갈아 끼우는 걸 도와드리는 등
평범한 생활을 한다고 말합니다.

werewolf syndrome

This 11-year-old girl wants to become a doctor so she can help people. Maybe she said she wants to help patients with rare diseases like her. Supatra Sasuphan, known as Wolf Girl, was born with hypertrichosis, which causes an excessive amount of hair growth on her face and body. This syndrome is often called 'werewolf syndrome' and that's how she got the nickname Wolf Girl.

Her appearance is very extraordinary thanks to thick hair growing all over her face and body except on her two eyes and her mouth. The hair on her face and body is thick enough to make her hold the world record as the "Hairiest Girl in the World."

She said she was happy to be in the Guinness World Records. However, being the hairiest girl in the world is not easy or fun. She has undergone laser treatments to remove the hair, but after a short while it grows back. Also, she has been teased many times and called 'monkey face.'

Fortunately, she has gradually been accepted by friends and neighbors since setting the world's record. Although she enjoys being a record holder, her parents still want their little daughter to be cured. But, for now, there is no known cure for her condition.

1. What is the main idea of the story?

   a. The real name of Wolf girl shouldn't be revealed to protect her privacy.
   b. The body of Supatra is pretty much covered with thick hair.
   c. Supatra's neighbors must avoid her because werewolf syndrome is contagious.
   d. Being the hairiest girl in the world is easy and fun.

2. According to the passage, which sentence is right?

   a. Supatra has more than one nick name and one of them is 'wolf face.'
   b. Supatra's appearance is abnormal but her friends have never made a fun of her.
   c. Supatra can not afford to get treatments to remove her bushy hair.
   d. Supatra's entire body is covered with thick hair, but her eyes and mouth are an exception.

3. Choose the correct words for each sentence.

   a. You are safe <u>forever</u> / <u>for instance</u> / <u>for now</u>. But no one knows what will happen next.
   b. This robot was programmed to attack everyone <u>only</u> / <u>toward</u> / <u>except</u> the person who programmed it.
   c. We can say <u>a 15 year old girl</u> / <u>a 15-year-old girl</u> / <u>a 15-years-old girl</u> is on the brink of womanhood.
   d. These days, the number of patients <u>of</u> / <u>with</u> / <u>for</u> constipation is increasing day by day.

Answer **1.** b **2.** d **3.** for now ⏐ except ⏐ a 15-year-old girl ⏐ with

This 11-year-old girl wants to become a doctor so she can help people. Maybe she said she wants to help   like her. Supatra Sasuphan,   Wolf Girl, was born with hypertrichosis, which causes   hair growth on her face and body. This syndrome is often called 'werewolf syndrome' and that's how she   Wolf Girl.

Her appearance is very   thanks to thick hair growing all over her face and body   her two eyes and her mouth. The hair on her face and body is thick enough to make her hold the world record as the "Hairiest Girl in the World."

She said she was happy to be   the Guinness World Records. However, being the hairiest girl in the world is not easy or fun. She has undergone laser treatments to remove the hair, but after a short while it grows back. Also, she   many times and called 'monkey face.'

Fortunately, she   by friends and neighbors since setting the world's record. Although she enjoys being a record holder, her parents still want their little daughter to be cured. But, for now,   for her condition.

Did You Know What Wolf Girl Wants To Be In The Future?

1 This 11-year-old girl wants to become a doctor so she can help people.

11살짜리 (형용사) (11-years-old X)
= She is 11 years old. 그녀는 11살이다. = She is an 11-year-old girl. 그녀는 11살인 소녀이다

2 Maybe she said she wants to help **patients** with **rare** diseases like her.

patient a. 참을성 있는 n. 환자 (patience 인내심)   a. 드문, 희귀한, 거의 없는, (고기) 덜 익힌
patient with 병명 : 어떤 병을 가진 환자 be born with 병명 : 어떤 병을 갖고 태어나다 die of 병명/사망 원인 : ..로 죽다

3 Supatra Sasuphan, (known as Wolf Girl), was born with hypertrichosis, which causes

= 동격

be born with 병명 : 어떤 병을 갖고 태어나다
다모증 (선행사) 콤마 which 동사 (계속) …다모증을 갖고 태어났는데, 이(다모증)는 …를 야기한다
선행사가 3인칭 단수이고 현재 시제 – cause + s

an excessive amount of hair growth on her face and body.

과도한 양의 모발 성장   (피부 표면) 위에 on
a large/huge/enormous amount of 많은 양의 an excessive amount of (적정수준 보다 많아서) 과도한 양의 (부정적 어감)

4 This **syndrome** is often called '**werewolf** syndrome'

syndrome 증후군 / symptom 증상, 징후   늑대인간

and that's (how she got the nickname Wolf Girl).

어떻게 해서 소녀가 늑대소녀라는 별명을 얻었는지 – how절은 의문문 X : how 주어 + 동사 (순서가 바뀌지 않음)

5 Her **appearance** is very **extraordinary** (thanks to **thick** hair growing

appear v. 나타나다   a. 평범하지 않은 (↔ ordinary a. 평범한)   수식
appearance n. 외모   thick hair which grows all over her face and body
                                                       얼굴과 몸 전체에 자라는 두터운 털 덕분에 (thanks to)

all over her face and body) except on (her two eyes and her mouth).

( )위만 빼고   (표면) 위에 on

6 (The hair on her face and body) is thick enough to make her hold the world record

수식   그녀가 (세계 기록을) 보유하게 만들 정도로 충분히 두터운
주어 ( ) body가 아니라 the hair + 동사 is

as the "**Hairiest** Girl in the World."

hair 머리카락, 털 hairy a. 털이 많은, 털이 난 (비교급 hairier 최상급 hairiest)

7 She said she was happy to be in the Guinness World Records.

8 However, (being the hairiest girl in the world) is not easy or fun.

동명사 주어 ( ) 세계에서 가장 털이 많은 소녀라는 것 + 동사 is

9 She has **undergone** laser treatments to remove the hair, but after a short while

(치료, 수술) 받다 (수동태로 사용하지 않음)   얼마 후
undergo – underwent – undergone

it grows back.
= the hair (집합명사-단수)

⑩ Also, she has been ¹⁾ **teased** many times and ²⁾ called 'monkey face.'
현재완료 수동태 has been teased 놀림당했다 / has been called …라 불려졌다

⑪ Fortunately, she has **gradually** been accepted by friends and neighbors
현재 완료 수동태 has + 부사 gradually + pp been / be동사 been + pp accepted + by

since setting the world's record.
= since she set the world's record (주어 일치, 생략 – setting 동명사 형태로 단순화)
set the record 기록을 세우다 break the record 기록을 깨다 hold the record 기록을 보유하다

⑫ Although she enjoys being a record holder, her parents still want
enjoy -ing …인 것을 즐기다   주어 want ( ) to 동사원형
being a record holder 기록보유자라는 것   주어는 ( )이 …하기를 원하다

their little daughter to be **cured**.
be cured 치료되다

⑬ But, for now, there is no known **cure** for her **condition**.
당장은, 현재는   …에 대한(for) 알려진 치료법은 없다
known cure 알려진 치료법   condition n. 질환, 병, 상태, 조건

늑대 소녀가 나중에 무엇이 되고 싶은지 아세요?

❶ 11살 이 소녀는 의사가 되어 사람들을 도와주고 치료해주고 싶다고 합니다.

❷ 아마도 소녀는 자기처럼 희귀병을 앓는 환자를 돕고 싶은지도 모르겠습니다.

❸ 늑대 소녀로 알려진 수파트라 사수판은 다모증을 가지고 태어났는데, 덕분에 얼굴과 몸에 엄청난 양의 털이 자랍니다.

❹ 이 증후는 종종 '늑대인간 증후군'으로 불리는데, 소녀가 늑대 소녀라는 별명을 갖게 된 것도 이 때문입니다.

❺ 소녀의 외모가 대단히 눈에 띄는 이유는 두 눈과 입을 제외한 얼굴 전체에 자란 두터운 털 때문입니다.

❻ 얼굴과 몸의 털이 꽤나 두터워서 소녀는 세계에서 가장 털이 많은 소녀로 세계 기록을 보유하게 되었습니다.

❼ 소녀는 기네스 세계 기록에 올라 행복하다고 말했습니다.

❽ 하지만 세계에서 가장 털이 많은 소녀라는 건 쉽지도, 재미있지도 않습니다.

❾ 소녀는 털을 제거하기 위해 레이저 치료를 받고 있지만, 얼마 못 가 털이 다시 자랍니다.

❿ 또 놀림도 많이 당했고 '원숭이 얼굴'이라고 불리기도 했습니다.

⓫ 다행히 세계 기록을 보유한 이후 친구들과 이웃들이 점차 소녀를 받아들이고 있습니다.

⓬ 기록 보유자라는 걸 소녀가 즐기고 있긴 하지만, 그래도 부모는 어린 딸이 치료받게 되기를 원합니다.

⓭ 그러나 현재까지 소녀의 상태를 치료할 방법은 알려진 바 없습니다.

WARNING!
MANCHINEEL TREE

THE LEAVES BARK, AND FRUITS OF THESE TREES CONTAIN A CAUSTIC SAP WHICH MAY BE INJURIOUS IF TOUCHED. COLUMBUS DESCRIBED THE SMALL GREEN FRUITS AS DEATH APPLES. THE TREES ARE COMMON ALONG CARIBBEAN SHORES. AVOID CONTACT WITH ANY PART OF THIS TREE!

The most dangerous tree in the world is the Poison Guava, also called the manchineel. This tree is found in the Florida Everglades and sandy beaches of the Caribbean coast. So if you visit there, be careful not to touch it or sit under this tree when it's raining. You should even hold your breath and cover your eyes when it is burned. Of course, don't even think of eating one of its sweet-smelling apple-like fruits. The best way to deal with it is to steer clear of it.

If the poisonous sap exuded from its trunk contacts your skin, it will cause serious blisters. If it touches your eyes, you may go blind, because of its highly acidic poison. Due to the same reason, it should never be your shelter from the rain. Raindrops containing its sap can be as dangerous as its sap itself. When this tree is burned, just run away from that area, because the smoke can irritate your eyes and even cause blindness. Although its fruits look good and smell good, they are fatal. Its leaves, bark, sap - anything you name - is purely dangerous. That's how the Poison Guava ascended the throne as the most dangerous tree in the world.

1. What can be the best title of this story?

    a. The Manchineel, The Deadliest Tree

    b. The Poison Guava : Just Taste Its Ultimate Sweetness

    c. Stand Aside, Apples! Make Way For The Poison Guava!

    d. The Manchineel, Smells Good & Tastes Good

2. You must get away from the Poison Guava when it rains because _____ .

    a. its poisonous sap make you go bold

    b. its fruits are big and heavy

    c. you will get wet because its leaves are small and thin

    d. raindrops may contain its dangerous sap

3. Choose the correct words for each sentence.

    a. A couple of days ago, I had a <u>blister</u> / <u>cut</u> / <u>contusion</u> on my hand from tennis and I popped it.

    b. Two boys scratched their backs <u>itself</u> / <u>themselves</u> / <u>himself</u> although they could easily scratch each other's backs.

    c. The best and easiest way to learn about their cultural heritages <u>is</u> / <u>are</u> / <u>be</u> to read books about them.

    d. There are several factors that lead to bad <u>breathe</u> / <u>breath</u> / <u>breathing</u>.

Answer **1.** a   **2.** d   **3.** blister ∣ themselves ∣ is ∣ breath

Listening Drill – Dictation

The most dangerous tree in the world is the Poison Guava, also called the manchineel. This tree _____ the Florida Everglades and sandy beaches of the Caribbean coast. So if you visit there, be careful not to touch it or sit under this tree when it's raining. You should even _____ and cover your eyes when it is burned. Of course, _____ _____ eating one of its sweet-smelling apple-like fruits. _____ deal with it is to steer clear of it.

If the poisonous sap _____ its trunk contacts your skin, it will cause serious blisters. If it touches your eyes, you may go blind, because of its _____ . Due to the same reason, it should never be your shelter from the rain. Raindrops containing its sap can be _____ its sap itself. When this tree is burned, just run away from that area, because the smoke can _____ and even cause blindness. Although its fruits _____ , they are fatal. Its leaves, bark, sap - anything you name - is purely dangerous. That's how the Poison Guava _____ as the most dangerous tree in the world.

Did You Know What The Most Dangerous Tree In The World Is?

1 (The most dangerous tree in the world) is the **Poison** Guava, (also called
주어 ( ) world가 아니라 tree + 동사 is   독, 독약   = 동격
the tree is also called the manchineel
also called …라고 불리는 / also known as ..로 알려진

the manchineel).

2 This tree is found in ¹⁾ the Florida Everglades and ²⁾ sandy **beaches**
be found in 지역 …에서 발견되다   ¹⁾ 플로리다 대습지 ²⁾ sandy모래의 + beaches 해변

of the Caribbean **coast**.
coast 해안(지방)
beach 모래가 있는 바닷가

3 So if you visit there, be careful not to ¹⁾ touch it or ²⁾ sit under this tree
be careful to 동사원형 : (동사) 하도록 주의하라
be careful not to 동사원형 : (동사)하지 않도록 주의하라 – 만지지 않도록, 앉지 않도록 주의하라

when it's raining.
비올 때 (날씨를 말할 때 it)

4 You should even ¹⁾ hold your breath and ²⁾ cover your eyes when it is burned.
심지어 ¹⁾ and ²⁾ 해야 한다   숨을 참다   눈을 가리다   이것이 불에 딸 때 (수동태)

5 Of course, don't even think of eating one of its (sweet-smelling apple-like) fruits.
…할 생각조차 하지 마라 (of + –ing)   냄새가 달콤하고 사과 같은

6 (The best way to deal with it) is to **steer clear of** it.
주어 ( ) it이 아니라 way + 동사 is   피하다

7 If (the poisonous **sap exuded** from its **trunk**) **contacts** your skin,
if 절 주어 ( ) trunk가 아니라 sap + 동사 contacts   나무 몸통   contact v. 접촉하다 n. 접촉, 연락
가정법 현재 주어 + 동사의 현재형 contracts, 주어 + will + 동사원형 cause
sap which is exuded from …에서 흘러나온 수액 = sap being exuded from

it will cause serious blisters.
수포가 생기게 하다

8 If it touches your eyes, you may go blind, because of its highly **acidic** poison.
가정법 현재   눈이 멀다   because of + 명사(구) highly 심한 acidic 산성의 poison 독

9 Due to the same reason, it should never be your **shelter** from the rain.
같은 이유로   it = the Poison Guava 너의 피난처가 되어서는 안 된다 (조동사 should + 부정어 never + 동사원형)

⑩ (Raindrops containing its sap) can be as dangerous as its sap itself.

주어 ( ) sap이 아니라 raindrops + 동사 can　　　　　　　…만큼이나 위험한

⑪ When this tree is burned, just run away from that area,

…에서 도망치다 (steer clear of …를 피하다)

because the smoke can [1] **irritate** your eyes and even [2] cause blindness.

눈이 따가워지다　　　　　　　　　　　실명을 유발하다 go blind 눈이 멀다
irritate v. 따갑게 하다, 자극하다, 짜증나게 하다

⑫ Although its fruits look good and smell good, they are **fatal**.

보기에 좋고 냄새도 좋다　　　　　　　fatal a. 죽음을 초래하는, 치명적인
fatality n. 사망자, 치사율

⑬ Its leaves, bark, sap - anything you name - is **purely** dangerous.

leaves = leaf잎의 복수형　　　name v. 이름을 대다 - 당신이 이름을 대는 것 무엇이든
bark 나무 껍질 sap 수액　　　pure a. 순수한 purely ad. 순전히 (utterly, completely)

⑭ That's how the Poison Guava **ascended** the **throne** as (the most dangerous tree

…라는 (as) 왕좌에 오르다

in the world).

〔 세상에서 가장 위험한 나무가 무엇인지 아세요? 〕

❶ 세계에서 가장 위험한 나무는 포이즌 구아바 또는 맨치닐이라는 나무입니다.

❷ 이 나무는 플로리다 에버글레이즈와 캐리비안의 모래 해안에서 발견됩니다.

❸ 그러니 그 곳에 갈 때는 이 나무를 만지지도 말고, 비가 올 때 나무 밑에 앉지 않도록 주의하세요.

❹ 심지어 이 나무가 불에 탈 때는 숨을 참고 눈을 가려야 합니다.

❺ 물론 달콤한 향기가 풍기는 사과와 비슷한 나무의 과일을 먹을 생각은 하지도 말아야 합니다.

❻ 이 나무를 상대하는 최선의 방법은 나무를 멀리하는 것입니다.

❼ 나무 기둥에서 새어나오는 독성 수액은 대단히 위험한데 수액이 피부에 닿으면 엄청난 물집이 생기게 됩니다.

❽ 만약 수액이 눈에 들어가면 강한 산성 독액으로 인해 눈이 멀 수도 있습니다.

❾ 같은 이유로 비가 올 때 나무로 피신하면 안 됩니다.　❿ 수액이 함유된 빗방울은 수액 자체만큼이나 위험할 수 있습니다.

⑪ 이 나무가 불에 탈 때는 가능한 한 빨리 그 곳에서 달아나야 하는데, 나무에서 나온 연기로 눈이 따갑거나 심지어 눈이 멀 수도 있기 때문입니다.

⑫ 이 나무의 열매는 보기도 좋고 향기도 좋지만 치명적입니다.

⑬ 나뭇잎, 나무껍질, 수액, (이 나무에 관한 건 무엇이든) 절대적으로 위험합니다.

⑭ 이렇게 해서 포이즌 구아바는 세계에서 가장 위험한 나무라는 왕좌에 등극하게 되었습니다.

84 Did You Know **How Long The Longest Tongue In The World Is?**

This comedian seems normal, but his tongue is anything but ordinary. Recognized by the Guinness World Records for its incredible length, his tongue is truly extraordinary. Measuring 10.1cm - just over the length of a standard 10cm ruler - it's more "unbelievable" than simply "amazing." To put it into perspective, it's twice as long as the average tongue. When he sticks it out, he almost looks like a lizard.

Nick, an artist and comedian, first realized his tongue was unusually long when he noticed it in photos where he was sticking it out. After earning a spot in the Guinness World Records for having the world's longest tongue, he embraced the attention it brought. "Not only can I lick my nose," he jokes, "but I can also lick my elbow!"

People often wonder what it's like to have such a long tongue. Unsurprisingly, it's the question he gets asked most frequently. While many assume it must be uncomfortable, Nick says the only real downside is, "I have to spend more time brushing my tongue in the morning."

He broke the record previously held by Brit Stephen Taylor, whose 9.8 cm tongue had claimed the title since 2002.

Words & Expressions

normal 평범한 anything but 결코 ...아닌 ordinary 평범한, 일반적인 extraordinary 평범하지 않은, 비범한 incredible 믿기 힘든 length 길이 unbelievable 믿을 수 없는 measure 재다, (길이, 크기) ...이다 ruler 자 average 평균의 stick out 내밀다 lizard 도마뱀 be listed 등록되다 attention 관심 lick 핥다 elbow 팔꿈치 unsurprisingly 놀랍지 않게도 frequently 자주 assume 추정하다 downside 단점 break the record 기록을 깨다 hold the title 타이틀을 보유하다

364

Understanding Checkpoint

1. What can be the best title of this story?

   a. The Shocking Secret About Nick's Freaky Tongue

   b. A Normal Guy Who Has The Abnormal Tongue

   c. A Lizard Named Brit Stephen Taylor Broke The World's Record

   d. 10 Ways To Lengthen Your Tongue

2. According to the passage, which sentence is right?

   a. When sticking his tongue out, Nick looks like a comedian, not an artist.

   b. When brushing his teeth, he knew he had an extra large tongue.

   c. Not many people can lick their noses with their tongues, but licking elbows is easy.

   d. Before him, Taylor held the record for the longest tongue in the world.

3. Choose the correct words for each sentence.

   a. Her tongue was so <u>amazing</u> / <u>amazed</u> / <u>amaze</u> that she was listed in the Guinness World Records.

   b. This recipe is not only easy to make <u>since</u> / <u>but also</u> / <u>because</u> healthy and delicious.

   c. Did you know the window <u>got</u> / <u>took</u> / <u>let</u> broken during the storm?

   d. She's <u>nothing but</u> / <u>everything but</u> / <u>anything but</u> shy when it comes to public speaking. She is so bold.

Answer **1.** b **2.** d **3.** amazing | but also | got | anything but

Listening Drill – Dictation

This comedian seems normal, but his tongue is   .
the Guinness World Records   , his tongue is truly extraordinary.
Measuring 10.1cm - just   a standard 10cm ruler - it's more
"unbelievable" than simply "amazing."   , it's twice as long as the
average tongue. When he sticks it out, he almost looks like a lizard.
Nick, an artist and comedian, first realized his tongue was unusually long when he
noticed it in photos where he was sticking it out. After   in the Guinness
World Records for having the world's longest tongue, he   it
brought. "   can I lick my nose," he jokes, "but I can also lick my elbow!"
People often wonder what it's like to have such a long tongue. Unsurprisingly, it's the
question he   most frequently. While many assume it must be uncomfortable,
Nick says the only real downside is, "I have to spend more time brushing my tongue in
the morning."
He   previously held by Brit Stephen Taylor, whose 9.8 cm tongue had
claimed the title since 2002.

Did You Know How Long The Longest Tongue In The World Is?

① This comedian seems **normal**, but his tongue is **anything but ordinary**.
평범해 보이다   결코 아닌 (절대 일반적이지 않다)   평범한, 일반적인
                                                nothing but 그저, 단지

② Recognized by (the Guinness World Records) for its **incredible length**,
…의 인정을 받은 (수동)   혀의 믿을 수 없는 길이 때문에

his tongue is truly **extraordinary**.
extra 추가의 + ordinary 평범한 : 보기 드문, 비범한, 기이한, 놀라운

③ **Measuring** 10.1cm - just over the length of a standard 10cm **ruler** -
…의 길이를 넘는 + a standard 10 cm ruler 표준 10cm 자   자

it's more "**unbelievable**" than simply "amazing."
it's more A than B : B보다 A가 더 맞다/적당하다
unbelievable 믿을 수 없는

④ To put it into perspective, it's twice as long as the **average** tongue.
넓게 보자면, 구체적으로 설명해보자면   길이가 두 배   평균의
put it 언급하다, 설명하다 (Let me put it this way. 이런 식으로 설명해보겠다.)

⑤ When he **sticks** it **out**, he almost looks like a **lizard**.
stick v. 찌르다, 들러붙다 n. 막대기   도마뱀
stick out 내밀다 stick to 고수하다, 굳게 지키다

⑥ Nick, (an artist and comedian), first realized his tongue was unusually long
┌─── = 동격 ───┐   처음 인식하다/깨닫다   대단히/특이하게 긴

when he noticed it in photos where he was sticking it out.
사진에서 – 그가 혀를 내밀고 찍은 사진

⑦ After earning a spot in the Guinness World Records (for having the world's
한 자리 얻다 – 기네스 세계 기록에서 (가장 긴 혀를 가진 기록 보유자라는) 자리를 얻다
주절의 주어 he 일치, 생략 After he earned a spot

longest tongue), he embraced the **attention** it brought.
세간의 관심을 받아들이다 (즐기다)   = 기네스 세계 기록에 오른 것
embrace v. 받아들이다, 안다   …the attention that it brought : it이 가져온 관심

⑧ "Not only can I **lick** my nose," he jokes, "but I can also lick my **elbow**!"
not only가 문장 맨 앞에 올 경우, 주어와 동사 자리가 바뀐다. Not only 동사 + 주어   팔꿈치
= I can lick not only my nose, but also my elbow.
lick 핥다

⑨ People often wonder (what it's like to have such a long tongue).

주어 wonder ( ) : 주어는 ( )를 궁금해하다
what it's like to 동사 : …가 어떤 것인지
Tell me what it's like to live in a big city. 대도시에 사는 게 어떤지 말해줘.

⑩ **Unsurprisingly**, it's the question he gets asked most **frequently**.

놀랍지 않게도

be대신 get이 쓰인 수동태 　　　가장 빈번하게
get 수동태 : get injured 부상당하다 get fired 해고당하다 get paid 돈을 받다

⑪ While many **assume** it must be uncomfortable, Nick says the only real **downside** is,

many 많은 사람들 + assume 추측하다　　불편할 게 분명하다 (강한 추측 must)　　　단점
while …이겠지만 (although의 의미)

"I have to spend more time brushing my tongue in the morning."

spend 시간 -ing …하는데 시간을 보내다
spend 값 on… 어디에 돈 얼마를 쓰다

⑫ He **broke the record** (previously held by Brit Stephen Taylor),

기록을 깨다/경신하다
the record which previously was held by 이전에 테일러에 의해 보유되던 기록

whose 9.8cm tongue had claimed the title since 2002.

Taylor's　　　　　타이틀(여기서는 기록 보유자라는 타이틀)이 자기 것이라 주장하다, 타이틀을 차지하다

세상에서 가장 긴 혀가 얼마나 긴지 아세요?

❶ 이 코미디언은 평범해 보이지만 그의 혀는 전혀 평범하지 않습니다.

❷ 믿을 수 없는 길이 덕분에 기네스 세계 기록의 인정을 받은 그의 혀는 진짜 놀랍습니다.

❸ 일반적인 10센티미터 자의 길이를 넘는 10.1센티미터로 측정되었는데, 이건 단지 '놀랍다'기보다 '믿기 힘들다'고 해야 합니다.

❹ 구체적으로 설명해보자면, 평균 혀보다 2배 더 깁니다.

❺ 그가 혀를 내밀면 거의 도마뱀처럼 보입니다.

❻ 예술가이지 코미디언인 닉은 혀를 내밀고 찍은 사진에서 혀를 알아보고 자기 혀가 대단히 길다는 걸 처음 깨달았습니다.

❼ 기네스 세계 기록에서 세계에서 가장 긴 혀를 가진 것으로 등재된 후 그는 이것이 가져온 관심을 받아들였습니다.

❽ "나는 코를 핥을 수 있을 뿐만 아니라 팔꿈치도 핥을 수 있습니다"라며 농담을 합니다.

❾ 사람들은 그렇게 긴 혀를 가졌다는 게 어떤지 종종 궁금해합니다.

❿ 놀랍지 않게도 이는 그가 가장 빈번하게 받는 질문이기도 합니다.

⓫ 많은 이들이 불편할 게 분명하다고 추측하지만 닉은 유일한 진짜 단점이라면 '아침에 혀를 칫솔질하는 시간이 더 들어야 한다'는 것 뿐이라고 말합니다.

⓬ 브릿 스테판 테일러가 보유했던 이전 기록을 그가 깬 것인데, 테일러의 혀는 9.8 센티미터로 2002년부터 (가장 긴 혀 기록) 보유자였습니다.

So the period of their engagement was 67 years.

If you want to hold a world record in the field of marriage, you may have to register with your local gym right away.

Octavio Guillien and Adrian Martinez set the record for the longest engagement. When they were 15 years old, they got engaged. It was not until they hit 82 that they married. Their engagement happened in 1902 and their marriage took place in 1969. So the period of their engagement was 67 years.

And, when our next couple married in June 2011, US President Obama sent a congratulatory card. Why? That's because the wedding ceremony took place on the 100th birthday of the bridegroom. The happy old groom, Forrest Lunsway, and his newly-wed, 90-year-old bride, Rose Lunsway officially became husband and wife after 30 years of living together. But amazingly, Forrest Lunsway was not the oldest bridegroom. In 1984, Harry Steven set the record for the oldest bridegroom ever, and his record hasn't been broken yet. He married when he was 103 years old.

As you may have already noticed, if you want to set or break a record in the field of marriage, do not die early.

Words & Expressions

marriage 결혼 (marry 결혼하다) register 등록하다 gym 체육관 engagement 약혼 get engaged 약혼하다 period 기간 elementary school 초등학교 send a congratulatory card 축하 카드를 보내다 wedding ceremony 결혼식 newly-wed 신혼의, 막 결혼한

Understanding Checkpoint

1. What can be the best title of this story?

a. When To Engage & How To Marry

b. Barak Obama Sent A Card To Whom?

c. The Lunsways Broke The World Record

d. A Useful Tip To Set A World's Record In The Field Of Marriage

2. If you want to set or break a record in the field of marriage, you _____ .

a. have to engage during elementary school

b. must be healthy and live long

c. will have to send a congratulatory card to Mr. President

d. must die early along with your partner

3. Choose the correct words for each sentence.

a. Until 2024 that / It was not until 2024 that / It was 2024 until my sister returned home and started to go to school.

b. He said he sent me a letter two weeks ago, but I haven't received it still / yet / until.

c. Which historical events took over / took part in / took place during the Baroque period?

Answer 1. d 2. b 3. It was not until 2024 that ǀ yet ǀ took place

If you want to hold a world record in the field of marriage, you may have to ~~~~~~~~ ~~~~~~~~ right away.

Octavio Guillien and Adrian Martinez set the record for the longest engagement. When they were 15 years old, they ~~~~~~~~. It was not until they ~~~~~ that they married. Their engagement happened in 1902 and their marriage took place in 1969. So ~~~~~~~~ their engagement was 67 years.

And, when our next couple married in June 2011, US President Obama ~~~~~~~~ ~~~~~~~~. Why? That's because the wedding ceremony ~~~~~~~~ 100th birthday of the bridegroom. The happy old groom, Forrest Lunsway, and his ~~~~~~~~, 90-year-old bride, Rose Lunsway ~~~~~~~~ husband and wife after 30 years of living together. But amazingly, Forrest Lunsway was not the oldest bridegroom. In 1984, Harry Steven set the record for the oldest bridegroom ever, and his ~~~~~~~~ ~~~~~~~~. He married when he was 103 years old.

~~~~~~~~, if you want to set or break a record in the field of marriage, do not die early.

Did You Know How To Hold A World Record In The Field Of Marriage?

1 If you want to hold a world record in the **field** of marriage,

hold a record 기록을 보유하다   결혼 분야에서
                                field 들판, 분야, 지역, 현장

you may have to **register** with your local **gym** right away.

동네 체육관에 등록하다   체육관
register 신고하다, 등록하다

2 (Octavio Guillien and Adrian Martinez) set the record for the longest **engagement**.

주어 ( ) + 동사 set   기록을 세우다   n. 약혼

3 When they were 15 years old, they **got engaged**.

= when they were 15-year-old teenagers   약혼하다

4 It was not until they hit 82 that they married.

It was not until A (that) B   82살이 되다   marry 결혼하다 (with를 쓰지 않는다.)
A하고 나서야 B했다 – 82살이 되어서야 결혼했다   get married to 결혼 상대 / in 결혼한 장소
                                                be married 결혼한 상태이다
                         I am married to Kate. 나는 케이트와 결혼한 상태이다 (유부남이다)
                         I married Kate 10 years ago. 나는 케이트와 10년 전 결혼했다.
                         I got married to Kate. 나는 케이트와 결혼(식)을 했다. (현재도 부부인지 알 수 없다.)
                         I am married to Kate and we got married in NY. 나는 케이트와 부부인데 우리는 뉴욕에서 결혼했다.

5 Their engagement happened in 1902 and their marriage **took place** in 1969.

일어나다, 발생하다   (사건, 행사) 개최하다, 발생하다

6 So (the **period** of their engagement) was 67 years.

주어 ( ) engagement가 아니라 the period + 동사 was (기간은 67년이다)
        period 기간, 시기

7 And, when our next couple married in June 2011,

7월까지 나오고 일/날짜가 나오지 않았으므로 in (날짜도 나오면 on)

US President Obama sent a **congratulatory** card.

축하 카드를 보내다 (get-well card 병 회복을 기원하는 카드, thank you card 감사 카드)
congratulatory a. 축하의 congratulation n. 축하

8 Why?

9 That's because the wedding **ceremony** took place on the 100th birthday of

결혼식 (예식)   100번째 생일에 (on)

the **bridegroom**.

신랑 (= groom) ↔ 신부 (bride)

⑩ (The happy old **groom**, Forrest Lunsway), and (his **newly-wed**, 90-year-old bride,

　　신랑 ┃ = 동격 ┃　　　　　　　　　　　　　　　　┃ = 동격 ┃
　　　　　　　　　　　　　　　　　　　　　　　　　　　　newly-wed 막 결혼한 newly-wed couple 신혼부부

Rose Lunsway) **officially** became husband and wife after 30 years of living together.

공식적으로 남편과 아내가 되었다　　　　　　　　　　　　　　　　　　　　　　동거

⑪ But **amazingly**, Forrest Lunsway was not the oldest bridegroom.

놀랍게도

⑫ In 1984, Harry Steven set the record for the oldest bridegroom ever,

and his record hasn't been broken yet.

(기록이) 아직 깨지지 않았다
현재완료 수동태 has 부정어 not + been + pp

⑬ He married when he was 103 years old.

⑭ As you may have already noticed, if you want to set or break a record in the field

may have pp (추측) – 아마도 이미 눈치챘을 텐데　　　　　　set a record or break a record

of marriage, do not die early.

결혼 분야에서 세계 기록을 보유하려면 어떻게 해야 하는지 아세요?

① 결혼 분야에서 세계 기록을 보유하고 싶다면 당장 동네 체육관에 등록해야 할 겁니다.

② 옥타비오 길리엔과 에이드리안 마티네즈는 가장 오랜 약혼 기간이라는 기록을 보유하고 있습니다.

③ 이들은 15살 때 약혼했습니다.　　　④ 그리고 82살이 되서야 결혼했습니다.

⑤ 약혼은 1902년에 했고 결혼은 1969년에 했습니다.　　　⑥ 그래서 약혼 기간이 67년입니다.

⑦ 다음 커플이 2011년 6월에 결혼했을 때 미국 대통령 오바마가 축하 카드를 보냈습니다.

⑧ 왜냐고요?

⑨ 결혼식이 신랑의 100번째 생일에 이루어졌기 때문입니다.

⑩ 행복한 늙은 새신랑 포레스트 런즈웨이와 90살의 새 신부 로즈 런즈웨이는 30년간의 동거 후 공식적인 남편과 아내 사이가 되었습니다.

⑪ 그런데 놀랍게도 포레스트 런즈웨이는 가장 나이 든 신랑이 아닙니다.

⑫ 1984년 해리 스티븐이 가장 늙은 신랑 기록을 세웠는데 지금까지 기록이 깨지지 않고 있습니다.

⑬ 그는 103살에 결혼했습니다.

⑭ 이미 눈치 채셨겠지만, 결혼 분야에서 기록을 세우거나 기록을 깨려면 빨리 죽지 마십시오.

Darrell Best was listed in the Guinness Book of World Records as the reverend who has presided over weddings in the fastest and easiest way, with the help of his wedding chapel on wheels called "The Best Man." His ceremony doesn't take much time, and needs only two witnesses other than the bride and groom.

Rolf Iven, a young German, set the record for walking the longest distance over hot plates. Of course those hot plates were on while he walked on them. He set the world record by walking 22.90m on 'very hot' hot plates in Milan, Italy, on 18 April 2009.

Walking on hot plates must be very dangerous and scary, but not as dangerous and scary as this next challenge. Kanchana Ketkaew, a Thai woman, entered the Guinness Book of World Records as a person who lived in a glass room with 5,320 scorpions for 33 days and nights. From 22 December 2008 to 24 January 2009, she was stung thirteen times, although those particular scorpions were not deadly or harmful to humans.

Words & Expressions

reverend 목사 preside 사회를 보다, 주례 서다 (over) convert 바꾸다, 전환하다 on the road 거리에서 a Thai 타이 사람 한 명 sting 쏘다 (be stung 쏘이다, 물리다)

Understanding Checkpoint

1. What is the main idea of the story?

    a. The longest distance walking over hot plates was the hardest.

    b. To live in a glass room with scorpions, you have to fast at least 33 days.

    c. The most foolish thing to do is to live with scorpions in a glass room.

    d. Many people try to set the record in various ways.

2. According to the passage, which sentence is right?

    a. The Best Man of the rev. Best is a vehicle which can be used as a wedding chapel.

    b. When Rolf Iven was trying to set the record in 2009, hot plates were off.

    c. A Thai woman was listed as the most-stung-by-scorpions person in the world.

    d. Darrell Best is a German, so are Rolf Iven and Kanchana Ketkaew.

3. Choose the correct words for each sentence.

    a. This horror movie was supposed to be horrific but not as <u>scared</u> / <u>scary</u> / <u>scare</u> as I thought.

    b. Please turn <u>off</u> / <u>on</u> / <u>into</u> the lights. It's too dark to read my book.

    c. The principal of my school stepped forward to <u>preside over</u> / <u>president for</u> / <u>preside at</u> the opening ceremony.

Answer **1.** d **2.** a **3.** scary | on | preside at

Listening Drill – Dictation

Darrell Best   the Guinness Book of World Records as the reverend who has presided over weddings in the fastest and easiest way, with the help of his   called "The Best Man." His ceremony doesn't   , and needs only two witnesses   the bride and groom.

Rolf Iven, a young German, set the record for walking the longest distance over hot plates. Of course those hot plates   while he walked on them. He set the world record by walking 22.90m on 'very hot' hot plates in Milan, Italy, on 18 April 2009.

Walking on hot plates   and scary, but not as dangerous and scary as this next challenge. Kanchana Ketkaew, a Thai woman,   the Guinness Book of World Records as a person who lived in a glass room with 5,320 scorpions   . From 22 December 2008 to 24 January 2009, she   , although those particular scorpions were not   to humans.

Did You Know These Guinness Trivias?

① Darrell Best was listed in the Guinness Book of World Records as the reverend who

이 문장의 주어 Darrell Best + 동사 was

who …한 목사로 (등재되다)

be listed 등재되다 as …로

reverend (rev.), pastor 목사 father 신부 preacher 설교자

has **presided** over weddings in the fastest and easiest way, with the help of

가장 빠르고 가장 쉬운 방식으로   …의 도움으로

preside over weddings 결혼식을 주례하다   a library on wheel 이동 도서관

preside over a ceremony 예식을 주재하다 (사회를 보다)   a hospital on wheel 이동 병원

his wedding **chapel** on wheels (called "The Best Man.")

= 동격

'The Best Man'이라 불리는 (앞서 나온 바퀴 달린 결혼식용 이동 교회)

결혼식 올리는 교회 + 바퀴 달린

결혼식 때 신랑 옆에 서는 친구를 best man, 신부의 친구를 bridemaid라고 하는데, 공교롭게도 주례자의 이름이 Best이다.

그래서 결혼식 용 교회로 개조한 자동차를 'The Best Man'이라 불렀다고 함.

② His **ceremony** [1] doesn't take much **time**, and [2] needs only two **witnesses**

시간이 얼마 걸리다 take – 많은 시간이 걸리지 않는다   증인 (bear / give witness 증언하다, 증인이 되다)

time – 불가산명사라서 '많은 시간'은 much time / lots of time (many time X)

other than (the bride and groom).

(신랑과 신부) 외에 other than

③ Rolf Iven, (a young German), set the record for walking the longest **distance**

= 동격

set – set – set (여기서는 과거 동사)   distance 거리 / long distance 긴/먼 거리

walk over ( ) : ( ) 위를 걷다

over hot **plates**.

walk over ( ) : ( ) 위를 걷다

plate n. 판, 접시

④ Of course those hot plates were on while he walked on them.

on 켠 / off 끈   while walking으로 쓸 수 없다 (주절의 주어와 while 주절이 다름)

⑤ He set the world record by walking 22.90m on 'very hot' hot plates in Milan, Italy,

set the record for walking 걸은 것으로 기록을 세우다 (기록의 내용)

set the record by walking 걸어서 기록을 세우다 (기록에 오른 방식)

on 18 April 2009.

on 날짜, 월, 년도 (날짜 없이 월과 년도만 있으면, in)

⑥ (Walking on hot plates) must be very (dangerous and **scary**),

동명사 주어 ( ) 열판 위를 걷는 것 (단수) + 동사 must   a. 무서운

but not as (dangerous and scary) as this next challenge.

as 형용사 as ( ) : ( ) 만큼 …한   다음 도전만큼이나 ( )하지 않은 (부정 not)

7 Kanchana Ketkaew, (a Thai woman), entered the Guinness Book of World Records

= 동격   = be listed (기네스 세계 기록에 오르다)

as a person (who lived in a glass room with 5,320 **scorpions** for 33 days and nights).

수식
who…한 사람으로 …와(with) 유리방에서 살다   scorpion 전갈   for 기간 - 33일 밤낮 동안

8 From 22 December 2008 to 24 January 2009, she was **stung** thirteen times,

from A to B : A에서 B까지   be stung (벌, 전갈) 쏘이다 (수동태)

although those **particular** scorpions were not (**deadly** or **harmful**) to humans.

그 특정 전갈들 (그녀와 유리 방에 있던 전갈 종류들)   치명적이거나 해로운 to …에게
deadly −ly가 붙었지만 부사가 아니라 형용사이다. − 치명적인

이런 기네스 기록도 있다는 거 아세요?

1 다렐 베스트는 '더 베스트 맨'으로 알려진 그의 바퀴 달린 결혼식장의 도움으로 가장 빠르고 쉽게 40회 이상의 결혼식을 주례한 목사로 기네스북에 기록되었습니다.

2 그의 예식은 오랜 시간이 걸리지 않고 신랑, 신부 외에 두 명의 증인만 필요합니다.

3 젊은 독일인 로프 이벤은 가장 먼 거리의 요리용 열판 걷기 기록을 세웠습니다.

4 물론 그가 걸을 때 열판은 켜져 있었습니다.

5 그는 2009년 4월 18일 이탈리아의 밀라노에서 아주 뜨거운 열판 위를 22.90미터나 걷는 세계 기록을 세웠습니다.

6 열판 걷기는 상당히 위험하고 무서운 일이지만 이 도전만큼 위험하고 무섭지는 않을 겁니다.

7 태국인 칸차나 케카유는 33일 밤낮으로 5,320마리의 전갈과 유리로 된 방에서 생활한 사람으로 기네스 세계 기록에 올랐습니다.

8 이 특정 전갈들이 치명적이거나 사람에게 해로운 건 아니었지만 2008년 12월 22일에서 2009년 1월 24일까지 그녀는 13번을 물렸습니다.

87 Did You Know **What Kind Of Record Dr. Marcel Petiote Held?**

Marcel Petiot was a doctor by day, a serial killer by night.

Nazi-occupied Paris was an absolutely horrible place to be during World War II. Many Jews wanted to escape from France because people were just "disappearing" so often. Dr. Petiot lured many Jews desperate to leave Paris. He got paid by them with the expectation of his helping them to leave for South America. But those poor Jews wouldn't set foot on South America, because they were instead savagely killed by Petiot. Most of the victims were dismembered and burned.

In 1944, neighbors of Petiot called the police and complained about the terrible smell coming from the chimney of his house. When the police entered his house and went down to the basement, they couldn't believe what they saw. Human remains, such as arms and legs, were scattered throughout the basement.

He was accused of murdering 27 people, but authorities suspected he might have killed as many as 150 people. He claimed that he was innocent and he only had killed enemies of France like double agents or German spies. But no judges or jurors believed him. On 25 May, 1946, Petiot was beheaded on the guillotine.

Words & Expressions

by day 낮에는 **serial killer** 연쇄살인범 **by night** 밤에는 **Nazi-occupied** 나치가 지배하던 **Jews** 유대인 **escape** 도망치다 **lure** 유혹하다 **desperate** 필사적인 **leave for** ...향해 떠나다 **savagely** 잔인하게 **dismember** 사지를 자르다 **chimney** 굴뚝 **basement** 지하실 **remains** 남은 부분 **scatter** 흩어지다 **murder** 살인하다 **innocent** 죄가 없는, 결백한 **double agent** 이중 첩자 **juror** 배심원 **behead** 참수하다 **guillotine** 단두대

376

Understanding Checkpoint

1. What is the main idea of the story?

    a. The enemies of France were beheaded on the guillotine.

    b. During World War II, many Jews disappeared.

    c. Marcel Petiot brutally killed many people.

    d. Petiot's basement was his secret laboratory.

2. Many Jews gave Petiot money because they thought _____ .

    a. he would help them escape from Paris to South America.

    b. he was a good doctor who cured people for free

    c. he was a double agent and German spy

    d. he had a nice and spacious basement

3. Choose the correct words for each sentence.

    a. Katie is a normal average mom <u>by</u> / <u>at</u> / <u>in</u> day, a brave crimefighter by night.

    b. She couldn't believe what she <u>heard</u> / <u>saw</u> / <u>smelled</u> even though she was watching it with her own eyes.

    c. When are you going to leave your parents' house <u>for</u> / <u>to</u> / <u>at</u> the dormitory?

    d. When Dean was accused of <u>burglary</u> / <u>he was a thief</u> / <u>he stole something</u>, he claimed that he was falsely accused.

Answer **1.** c **2.** a **3.** by ǀ saw ǀ for ǀ burglary

Listening Drill – Dictation

Marcel Petiot was a doctor by day, a serial killer by night.

Nazi-occupied Paris was an absolutely horrible _____ during World War II. Many Jews wanted to escape from France because people were just "disappearing" so often. Dr. Petiot lured many Jews _____ Paris. He got paid by them _____ his helping them to leave for South America. But those poor Jews wouldn't _____ South America, because they were instead savagely killed by Petiot. Most of the victims were dismembered and burned.

In 1944, neighbors of Petiot called the police and complained about the terrible smell coming from the chimney of his house. When the police entered his house and went down to the basement, they _____ . Human remains, such as arms and legs, were scattered _____ the basement.

He _____ murdering 27 people, but authorities _____ he might have killed _____ 150 people. He claimed that he was innocent and he only had killed enemies of France like double agents or German spies. But no judges or jurors believed him. On 25 May, 1946, Petiot was beheaded _____ .

Did You Know What Kind Of Record Dr. Marcel Petiote Held?

1 Marcel Petiot was a doctor by day, a **serial killer** by night.
낮에는   연쇄 살인범   밤에는
serial 같은 일을 여러 번 반복한 – serial cheater 사기를 반복적으로 치는 사람

2 (Nazi-**occupied** Paris) was an **absolutely horrible** place to be during World War II.
나치가 점령한 파리 | 수식 ↑ | be a horrible place to be 있기에 끔찍한 곳이다   2차대전 중
be a nice place to stay 머무르기 좋은 곳이다

3 Many **Jews** wanted to escape from France because people were just "**disappearing**"
유대인, 유대교도   에서 (from) 도망치다   appear 나타나다 ↔ disappear 사라지다

so often.

4 Dr. Petiot **lured** many Jews (**desperate** to leave Paris).
lure 유혹하다, 꾀다   ↑| 수식 | Jews (who were) desperate …파리를 떠나기를 절실히 원하는 유대인들

5 He got paid by them with the expectation of his helping them to leave for
get 수동태 : 돈을 받다   …의 기대감으로   그의 도움 + 그들이 남아메리카를 향해 떠날 수 있게
help는 동사원형, to부정사 모두 올 수 있는데, 이 문장에서는 to leave가 왔다. leave로 써도 맞다.

South America.

6 But those poor Jews wouldn't set foot on South America,
가난한, 불쌍한 (이 문장은 '불쌍한')   …에 발을 들이다, 들어가다 (set a foot on으로 쓰지 않는다.)

because they were instead **savagely** killed by Petiot.
instead 남아프리카에 들어가는 대신 + savagely 잔인하게 + were killed by …에 의해 살해되다
수동태에서 부사 위치 be동사와 pp 사이

7 (Most of the **victims**) were [1] **dismembered** and [2] burned.
주어 ( ) 동사 were   수동태 were dismembered 사지가 잘리고 were burned 태워졌다
victim 희생자   dismember (이미 사망한 사람, 동물) 사지를 자르다 amputate (수술로) 팔다리(사지)를 절단하다

8 In 1944, (neighbors of Petiot) [1] called the police and [2] **complained** about
complain v. 불평하다 complaint n. 불평

the **terrible** smell (coming from the **chimney** of his house).
↑| 수식 | … smell which came from …에서 나오는 냄새

9 When the police [1] entered his house and [2] went down to the **basement**,
지하실

they couldn't believe what they saw.
= the police   선행사를 포함한 관계대명사 what – 그들이 본 것 what을 믿지 못하다

⑩ Human **remains**, ⟨such as arms and legs⟩, were **scattered** throughout the basement.

Human remains = ( ) 팔, 다리 같은 인간의 유해 + 동사 were　　　　scatter 흩다, 퍼트리다 (be scattered 흩어져있다)
remain v. 남다. 여전히 ..이다 remains n. 유적, 남은 것, (죽은 생물) 유해　　　throughout 도처에,

⑪ He **was accused of** murdering 27 people, but **authorities suspected**

be accused of 명사/동명사　　　　　　당국　　　　의심하다
기소당하다 (수동)

he might have killed as many as 150 people.

might have pp 했을지 모른다　많게는 (people이 가산 명사이기 때문에 many)

⑫ He claimed that ¹⁾ he was **innocent** and ²⁾ he only had killed enemies of France

순진한, 죄가 없는 (이 문장은 죄가 없는)　　　　　　　　프랑스의 적 예 ( ) 이중첩자나 독일 스파이
play innocent (죄가 있지만) 결백한 척 하다

⟨like double agents or German spies⟩.

= such as 이를 테면

⑬ But no **judges** or **jurors** believed him.

부정문 Judges and jurors didn't believed him.

⑭ On 25 May, 1946, Petiot was **beheaded** on the guillotine.

behead 참수하다 be beheaded 참소되다 (수동)

마르셀 프티오 의사가 어떤 기록을 보유했는지 아세요?

❶ 마르셀 프티오는 낮에는 의사, 밤에는 연쇄 살인범이었습니다.

❷ 2차 세계대전 중 나치가 점령한 파리는 대단히 끔찍한 곳이었습니다. ❸ 많은 유태인들은 파리를 떠나길 원했는데 사람들이 그냥 사라지는 경우가 잦았기 때문이었습니다. ❹ 프티오 의사는 파리를 떠나길 간절히 원하는 많은 유태인들을 꾀어냈습니다. ❺ 그는 그가 남아메리카로 이주하도록 도와주리라 기대한 이들에게서 돈을 받았습니다. ❻ 하지만 그 불쌍한 유태인들은 남아메리카 땅을 밟을 수 없었는데, 프티오에게 잔인하게 살해당했기 때문이었습니다. ❼ 희생자들 대부분은 사지가 잘려 불에 태워졌습니다.

❽ 1944년, 프티오의 이웃들이 경찰에 전화를 걸어 그의 집 굴뚝에서 고약한 냄새가 난다며 불평했습니다. ❾ 경찰이 그의 집을 찾아가 지하실로 들어갔을 때 그들은 눈앞에 펼쳐진 광경을 믿을 수 없었습니다. ❿ 지하실에는 팔, 다리 같은 시신 유해들이 나뒹굴고 있었습니다.

⑪ 그는 27명을 살해한 혐의로 기소당했지만 당국에서는 그가 많게는 150명까지 살해했으리라 추측했습니다. ⑫ 그는 자신은 죄가 없으며, 이중 첩자나 독일 스파이처럼 프랑스의 적들만 살해했다고 주장했습니다. ⑬ 하지만 판사나 배심원 어느 누구도 그의 말을 믿지 않았습니다. ⑭ 1946년 5월 25일, 프티오는 기요틴에서 참수 당했습니다.

As far as a war is concerned, shorter is better. Then, how short did the shortest war last? The war between Zanzibar and England in 1896 was the shortest war in recorded history. It was called the 'Anglo-Zanzibar War.'

After the Sultan of Zanzibar died on 25 August 1896, his nephew Bargash rose to the throne, but the British Empire had another person in mind. The British thought this person would be much easier to manipulate. So, the British ordered Bargash to step down from the throne. Bargash refused.

The British sent the Royal Navy to the front of the palace where Bargash had just moved in. Despite the fact that Bargash made efforts to negotiate for a peaceful ending, the British Navy opened fire. The palace started to crumble and people, civilians and soldiers alike, started to die right in front of him. He knew he couldn't win this battle, so he made a hasty retreat to the German consulate. After that, the British stopped firing and Zanzibar surrendered. This battle started at 9 am and lasted for just 38 to 45 minutes.

Even though the British had won the battle pretty easily and got what they had wanted, they demanded Zansibar to pay for the shells fired on Zanzibar.

1. What is the main idea of the story?

    a. The shortest war is the best war.

    b. Anglo-Zanzibar War, the shortest war, lasted for about 38 minutes.

    c. The British opened fire first so the British army was to blame for Anglo-Zanzibar War.

    d. The cause of Anglo-Zanzibar War was Bargash.

2. According to the passage, which sentence is right?

    a. Bargash was too scared to make efforts to negotiate for peace.

    b. Anglo-Zanzibar War was the best war in recorded history.

    c. The British Empire wanted Bargash to rise to the throne.

    d. Bargash, a member of the royal family, stepped up and became a sultan.

3. Choose the correct words for each sentence.

    a. <u>Even though</u> / <u>During</u> / <u>When</u> I have met him several times, I still can't remember his name.

    b. Pack up your belongings and go to the place <u>where</u> / <u>when</u> / <u>who</u> you belong.

    c. One man savagely killed the victim and the other just stood beside him. But both of them were guilty <u>like</u> / <u>alike</u> / <u>likely</u>.

Answer   **1.** b   **2.** d   **3.** Even though ⏐ where ⏐ alike

Listening Drill – Dictation

As far as _____ , shorter is better. Then, how short did the shortest war last? The war between Zanzibar and England in 1896 was the shortest war in recorded history. It was called the 'Anglo-Zanzibar War.'

After the Sultan of Zanzibar died on 25 August 1896, his nephew Bargash _____ , but the British Empire _____ . The British thought this person would be _____ . So, the British ordered Bargash to step down from the throne. Bargash refused.

The British sent the Royal Navy to the front of the palace where Bargash had just moved in. _____ Bargash _____ negotiate for a peaceful ending, the British Navy opened fire. The palace started to crumble and people, _____ , started to die right in front of him. He knew he couldn't win this battle, so he _____ to the German consulate. After that, the British stopped firing and Zanzibar surrendered. This battle _____ 9 am and lasted for just 38 to 45 minutes.

Even though the British had won the battle pretty easily and got _____ , they demanded Zansibar to pay for the shells fired on Zanzibar.

381

Did You Know The Shortest War Lasted Only 38 Minutes?

1 As far as a war is concerned, shorter is better.

전쟁에 관해서라면   비교급, 비교급 – 짧을수록 더 좋다

2 Then, how short did the shortest war **last**?

얼마나 짧은   last v. 지속하다 a. 마지막에, 가장 최근의

3 (The war between Zanzibar and England in 1896) was the shortest war

↑ 수식 | 주어 ( ) the war + 동사 was

in recorded history.

기록으로 남은 역사 상

4 It was called the 'Anglo-Zanzibar War.'

5 After the Sultan of Zanzibar died on 25 August 1896, his nephew Bargash

After 절과 주절의 주어가 다르기 때문에 After dying 으로 쓸 수 없다

rose to the **throne**, but the British Empire **had** another person **in mind**.

왕위에 오르다   have ( ) in mind : ( )를 마음에 두다

another + 단수 명사 person 다른 한 명

6 The British thought this person would be much easier to **manipulate**.

다루기(조종하기) 더 쉽다 (much easier to manipulate than Bargash)

7 So, the British **ordered** Bargash to **step down** from the throne.

order ( ) to step down 내려오라고 ( )에게 명령하다   왕좌에서 내려오다/물러나다

8 Bargash refused.

9 The British sent the Royal Navy to the front of the **palace** (where Bargash had

where의 선행사 palace – 바가시가 막 이사 들어온 궁전 (장소 where) ↑ 수식

just **moved in**).

이사오다

10 Despite the fact that Bargash **made efforts to negotiate** for a peaceful ending,

despite + 명사, 동명사   to 동사 하려고 노력하다   협상하다 + 평화로운 결말을 위해

despite the fact that 주어 + 동사

the British Navy opened fire.

사격을 시작하다 fire 불, 발사, 총격

11 [1] The palace started to **crumble** and [2] people, (civilians and soldiers alike),

궁전은 무너지기 시작했고   ( ) 사람들은 죽기 시작했다 (민간인 군인 할 거 없이 alike)

started to die right in front of him.
바로 코앞에서

⑫ He knew he couldn't win this battle, so he made a hasty **retreat** to
make a (hasty) retreat to …로 (황급하게) 후퇴하다

the German **consulate**.
consulate 영사관 embassy 대사관

⑬ After that, the British stopped firing and Zanzibar **surrendered**.
stop -ing …를 중지하다   항복하다
open fire 발포하다 / stop firing 포격을 중지하다

⑭ This battle started at 9 am and lasted for just 38 to 45 minutes.
(for 기간) 얼마 동안 지속하다

⑮ Even though the British had won the battle **pretty** easily and got what they
꽤나 쉽게   got the thing that they had wanted
pretty a. 예쁜 ad. 꽤, 몹시   선행사를 포함한 관계 대명사 what

had wanted, they **demanded** Zansibar to pay for the shells (fired on Zanzibar).
demand ( ) to pay ( )에게 돈을 내라고 요구하다   pay for …에 대한 돈을 내다, 지불하다   수식
the shells <u>that were</u> fired on …에 발사된 포탄들
shell 조개껍데기, 포탄

가장 짧은 전쟁이 단 38분간 지속되었다는 거 아세요?

❶ 전쟁에 관해서라면 짧을수록 좋습니다.   ❷ 그렇다면 가장 짧은 전쟁은 얼마나 짧은 시간 지속되었을까요?   ❸ 1896년 잔지바르와 영국 간의 전쟁이 기록된 역사상 가장 짧은 전쟁이었습니다.   ❹ 이는 '앵글로-잔지바르 전쟁'이라 불립니다.

❺ 잔지바르의 술탄(지배자)이 1896년 8월 25일에 사망한 후, 그의 조카 바가쉬가 왕위에 올랐지만 대영제국에서는 다른 사람을 마음에 두고 있었습니다.   ❻ 영국은 이 사람이 다루기 훨씬 쉽다고 생각했던 것입니다.   ❼ 그래서 영국은 바가쉬에게 왕위에서 물러날 것을 명령했습니다.   ❽ 바가쉬는 이를 거부했습니다.

❾ 영국은 바가쉬가 막 이사 온 궁궐 앞에 해군을 보냈습니다.   ❿ 바가쉬가 평화로운 결말을 위해 노력했지만 영국 해군은 공격을 시작했습니다.   ⓫ 궁궐은 무너지기 시작했고 민간인 군인 할 것 없이 사람들이 그의 눈앞에서 죽어가기 시작했습니다.   ⓬ 그는 이번 전투를 이길 수 없음을 알았고 독일 영사관으로 황급히 도피했습니다.   ⓭ 이후 영국은 공격을 중단했고 잔지바르는 항복했습니다.   ⓮ 이 전투는 오전 9시에 시작해 38분에서 45분 정도 지속되었습니다.

⓯ 영국은 꽤 수월하게 전투에서 승리하고 원하는 걸 얻었지만, 잔지바르에 발사한 포탄 비용을 물어내라고 잔지바르에 요구했다고 합니다.

Giving birth to 69 children? Sounds impossible. Actually it would have been almost impossible had she not given birth to twins or triplets... or quadruplets.

This super mom did give birth to a whopping 69 children with the help of multiple births. She had 16 pairs of twins, 7 sets of triplets, and 4 sets of quadruplets. It's no wonder that her name, Mrs. Feodor Vassilyev, was listed in the 2004 edition of the Guinness Book of World Records as the most prolific mom ever, although this unbelievable story happened in the 1700s. Her shocking record has not been broken yet.

The Guinness Book acknowledged her improbable feat, but giving birth to 69 children... isn't that a little too much to believe?

Some people doubt it. They think the story is a mere rumor or a made-up story. But what kind of people would have made this kind of story? And why on earth would they do such a thing?

Well, some people do make up this kind of story for various reasons. In 1983, a Chilean woman claimed that she had given birth to 58 children. But, after she died, police discovered that this prolific woman had lied in order to get government-provided food assistance. She had had only 16 children.

1. What can be the best title of this story?

    a. The Biggest Scam Ever : A Mom of 69 Children

    b. Who Are To Blame For Giving Birth To 69 Children?

    c. Believe It Or Not : The Unbelievably Prolific Mom

    d. The Government Takes Action To Feed 69 Children

2. Although Mrs. Vassilyev gave birth to 69 children in the 1700s, _____ .

    a. a Chilean mom is acknowledged as the most living prolific mom ever

    b. the Guinness Book of World Records refused to acknowledge her record

    c. her story was introduced in the 2004 edition of the Guinness Book of World Records

    d. nobody has acknowledged her awesome feat for decades

3. Choose the correct words for each sentence.

    a. <u>You have tried</u> / <u>Had you tried</u> / <u>Had tried you</u> this diet, you could have lost some weight.

    b. All of my friends said nothing's going on between John and Kate, but I said, "I <u>doubt</u> / <u>am doubt</u> / <u>take doubt</u> it."

    c. What <u>in the earth</u> / <u>on earth</u> / <u>at earth</u> am I here for? And why in the world am I doing this thing?

Answer **1.** c   **2.** c   **3.** Had you tried | doubt | on earth

Listening Drill – Dictation

Giving birth to 69 children?   . Actually it would have been almost impossible   birth to twins or triplets... or quadruplets.

This super mom did give birth to a whopping 69 children   .

She had 16 pairs of twins, 7 sets of triplets, and 4 sets of quadruplets. It's no wonder that her name, Mrs. Feodor Vassilyev, was listed in the 2004 edition of the Guinness Book of World Records as   , although this unbelievable story happened in the 1700s. Her shocking record has not been broken yet.

The Guinness Book   , but giving birth to 69 children... isn't that   ?

Some people doubt it. They think the story is a mere rumor   . But what kind of people would have made this kind of story? And why on earth would they   ?

Well, some people do make up this kind of story   . In 1983, a Chilean woman claimed that she had given birth to 58 children. But, after she died, police discovered that this prolific woman had lied in order to get government-provided   . She had had only 16 children.

385

Did You Know There Was A Mother Of 69 Children?

① **Giving birth to** 69 children?

누구를 낳다 give birth to a son 아들을 낳다

② Sounds **impossible**.

= It sounds impossible. 불가능한 일로 들린다.

③ Actually it would have been almost impossible had she not given birth

가정법 과거완료 – if 주어 had pp, 주어 would have pp 또는 if를 생략하고 Had 주어 pp, 주어 would have pp
지문에서는 if 절이 뒤에 위치했고 if가 생략되고 had 주어 pp 형태로 왔다.
= If she had not given birth to twins or triplets, it would have been almost impossible.

to **twins** or **triplets**... or **quadruplets**.

쌍둥이   세 쌍둥이   네 쌍둥이

④ This super mom did give birth to a whopping 69 children

강조의 조동사 do (과거시제 did)   무려 69명의 아이들
69 children은 복수지만 숫자를 수식하는 whopping과 함께 쓰이면 a가 온다.
There are a whopping 4,000 people. 자그마치 4천명의 사람들이 있다.

with the help of **multiple** births.

다둥이 출산의 도움으로

⑤ She had (16 pairs of twins), (7 sets of triplets), and (4 sets of quadruplets).

쌍둥이는 pairs, 그 이상은 sets – 쌍둥이 16쌍 (32명), 세 쌍둥이 7세트 (21명), 네 쌍둥이 4세트 (16명)

⑥ It's no wonder that her name, (Mrs. Feodor Vassilyev), was listed

that이하가 놀랍지 않다, 당연하다   = 동격

in the 2004 edition of the Guinness Book of World Records as the most **prolific**

2004년판   (작가) 다작의, (여성) 다산의, 열매를 많이 맺는

mom ever, although this **unbelievable** story happened in the 1700s.

믿을 수 없는 이야기   1700년대에

⑦ Her shocking record has not been broken yet.

주어 record 기록   현재완료 수동태 (아직 깨지지 않았다)

⑧ The Guinness Book **acknowledged** her **improbable** feat,

(사실임을) 인정하다   probable 있을 거 같은, 개연성 있는 improbable 개연성 없는
feat 위업, 업적

but giving birth to 69 children... isn't that a little too much to believe?

too ( ) to 동사 : 너무 ( )해서 …하기 어려운 (부정 의미) – 믿기에는 너무 심한, 너무 나가서 믿기 힘든

⑨ Some people **doubt** it.

v. 의심하다 n. 의심

⑩ They think the story is (a **mere** rumor) or (a **made-up** story).

그저 소문   지어낸 이야기

⑪ But what kind of people would have made this kind of story?

어떤 종류의 사람들   이런 종류의 이야기

⑫ And why on earth would they do such a thing?

도대체 ⇒ why would they do such a thing? 그런 일을 왜 하는 것인가?
Why (on earth) did you do that? (도대체) 왜 그렇게 한 건데?

⑬ Well, some people do **make up** this kind of story for **various** reasons.

강조 조동사 do + 동사원형   다양한 이유로 (various 다양한 + 복수 명사)

⑭ In 1983, a Chilean woman claimed that she had given birth to 58 children.

주장하다 (과거시제)   낳다 (주장한 시점보다 더 과거) (과거완료)

⑮ But, after she died, police discovered that this prolific woman had lied

경찰 -집합명사 (a, the를 쓰지 않는다.)   = a Chilean woman   그녀가 죽은 시점보다 더 과거에 거짓말

in order to get government-provided food **assistance**.

…하기 위해   수식   ↑ 정부 + 제공하는 + 식품 보조/지원

⑯ She had had only 16 children.

과거완료 had + pp (have only 16 children-have의 pp인 had)   자녀가 겨우 16명이었다

69명의 자녀를 낳은 어머니가 있다는 거 마세요?

❶ 69명의 아이들을 낳았다?   ❷ 불가능한 것처럼 들립니다.   ❸ 사실 쌍둥이, 세 쌍둥이... 또는 네 쌍둥이를 낳지 않는다면 거의 불가능합니다.

❹ 이 수퍼맘은 다생아 출산의 도움으로 무려 69명의 아이들을 낳았습니다.   ❺ 그녀는 쌍둥이 16번, 세 쌍둥이 7번, 네 쌍둥이 4번을 낳았습니다.   ❻ 대단한 이 이야기가 1700년대 일어나긴 했지만 피오도르 바실레프 여사라는 그녀의 이름이 2004년 판 기네스 세계 기록 책에 세상에서 가장 출산을 많이 한 어머니로 기록될 만합니다.   ❼ 그리고 그녀의 놀라운 기록은 아직까지 깨지지 않고 있습니다.

❽ 기네스 세계 기록이 믿기 힘든 그녀의 업적을 인정하긴 했지만 69명의 자녀 출산이라니... 믿기에는 너무 심한 것 같지 않나요?

❾ 어떤 이들은 이를 의심합니다.   ❿ 이들은 이 이야기가 그저 소문 혹은 지어낸 이야기라고 생각합니다.   ⑪ 하지만 누가 이런 이야기를 만들어 내겠습니까?   ⑫ 그리고 도대체 왜 이런 걸 지어내겠습니까?

⑬ 글쎄, 다양한 이유로 이런 이야기를 만들어내는 사람들이 실제 있습니다.   ⑭ 1983년 한 칠레 여성이 58명의 자녀를 낳았다고 주장했습니다.   ⑮ 하지만 그녀가 사망한 후 한 경찰은 이 출산의 여왕이 정부 보조 음식 지원을 받기 위해 거짓말했다는 사실을 밝혀냈습니다.   ⑯ 그녀는 겨우 16명의 자녀만 두었습니다.

90 Did You Know **How Fast Bruce Lee's Kicks Were?**

Bruce Lee, born in 1940 and died in 1973, was a martial artist, actor, martial arts instructor, director, and film producer, and was able to move with jaw-dropping speed. Literally, his speed was fast enough to make your jaw drop. How fast? His kicks were so fast that his films had to be slowed down because people couldn't see his moves. The same goes for his punches.

Since his kicks and punches were extremely fast, some people tried to measure their speed. When Lee demonstrated a kick with his left leg in front of a video camera, his kick only took about a fifth of a second. The people who watched his demonstration on the spot were left speechless when they learned that it was Lee's right leg that was dominant.

Most action films, especially martial art films, are sped up to make their fighting scenes look faster and more active. However, Lee's cases were the opposite. Film screeners had to run his films a little bit slower so audiences could see his kicks and punches.

Words & Expressions

martial artist 무술인 **instructor** 지도자 **director** 감독 **film producer** 영화 제작자 **jaw-dropping** 턱이 아래로 빠질 정도의, 놀라운 **slow down** 느리게 하다 **punch** 주먹으로 치다, 펀치 **extremely** 대단히 **demonstrate** 입증하다 **a fifth of** 1/5 의 **on the spot** 현장에서 **speechless** (너무 놀라) 말을 못 하는 **fighting scene** 격투 장면

1. What is the main idea of the story?

  a. Many marshal artists are right-handed.

  b. Action films must be sped up to make them more active.

  c. Bruce Lee could kick and punch extremely fast.

  d. Bruce Lee was an excellent martial artist but not a good actor.

2. According to the passage, which sentence is <u>wrong</u>?

  a. Lee was an actor, director and a film producer as well.

  b. Lee demonstrated his kick with his left leg in front of people.

  c. Film makers ran Lee's films a little bit slower by mistake.

  d. Generally, action films are sped up in order to make their scenes look more exciting.

3. Choose the correct words for each sentence.

  a. It <u>took</u> / <u>made</u> / <u>had</u> him a week to solve this puzzle.

  b. When I saw her room, I <u>left</u> / <u>was left</u> / <u>leave</u> speechless because it looked like a bomb hit it.

  c. What I want to know is how to make my brother <u>do</u> / <u>to do</u> / <u>doing</u> what I want.

Answer **1.** c **2.** c **3.** took ǀ was left ǀ do

Listening Drill - Dictation

Bruce Lee, born in 1940 and died in 1973, was a _____ , actor, martial arts instructor, director, and film producer, and was able to _____ . Literally, his speed was _____ make your jaw drop. How fast? His kicks were so fast that his films had to be slowed down because people couldn't see his moves. _____ his punches.

Since his kicks and punches were extremely fast, some people tried to measure their speed. When Lee demonstrated a kick with his left leg in front of a video camera, his kick only took about _____ . The people who watched his demonstration _____ were _____ when they learned that it was Lee's right leg that was _____ .

Most action films, especially martial art films, _____ make their fighting scenes look faster and more active. However, Lee's cases were _____ . Film screeners had to run his films a little bit slower so audiences could see his kicks and punches.

389

Did You Know How Fast Bruce Lee's Kicks Were?

1 Bruce Lee, (born in 1940 and died in 1973), [1] was (a martial artist, actor,

　　　　수식　　　　　Lee who was born in… 언제 태어나고 언제 사망한 브루스 리 + (동사) was + [1] ( ) 였고 [2] 빨리 움직일 수 있었다.

martial arts **instructor**, director, and film producer), and [2] was able to move

무술의　　　　　강사, 지도자　　　　　　　　　　　　　　　　be able to = can

with **jaw**-dropping speed.

with + jaw-dropping 놀라운 + 속도로
놀라운, 대단한 - jaw-dropping 놀라 턱 빠질 정도의 eye-popping 눈 튀어 나올 정도의

2 **Literally**, his speed was fast enough to make your jaw drop.

말 그대로　　　　　　　　　　(to 동사)할 만큼 충분히 빠른　　사역동사 make + 목적어 your jaw + 동사원형 drop

3 How fast?

4 His kicks were so fast that his films had to be slowed down

　　　　　　　　so 형용사 that : 너무 빨라서 that…했다　　　주어는 리, 스크린 등이 아니라 '영화 film'이므로
　　　　　　　　　　　　　　　　　　　　　　　　　　'영화/화면을 느리게 해야 했다' 수동태 (be slowed down)

because people couldn't see his moves.

5 The same goes for his punches.

for…에도 똑같이 적용된다, …도 마찬가지이다

6 Since (his kicks and punches) were **extremely** fast, some people tried to

because　　　　　　　　　　　　　　　　몹시, 매우

measure their speed.

v. 측정하다, 재다 n. 조치, 양, ,정도
주어가 his hicks and punches라서 their (복수)

7 When Lee **demonstrated** a kick with his left leg in front of a video camera,

　　　　　　시연해보이다, 증명하다, 데모하다 (왼발로 발차기를 시연하다)　　　앞에서 (코앞에서 right under my nose)

(his kick) only took about a fifth of a second.

　　　take 시간이 얼마 걸리다　　　a fifth (1/5) of a second (1초) : 1초의 1/5

8 (The people who watched his **demonstration** on the spot) were left speechless

　　　　수식　　　　주어 ( ) spot이 아니라 the people + 동사 were　　　말문이 막힌 상태가 되어지다 (수동) 할 말을 잃다
즉석에서(현장에서 on the spot) 그의 실연(demonstration 증명, 데모)을 지켜본 사람들

when they learned that it was Lee's right leg that was **dominant**.

그것은 리의 오른다리였다 + 우세한 것이 : 그는 오른발잡이였다 (it is ( ) that 강조)
Are you right leg dominant? 너는 오른발잡이니? I am right handed. 나는 오른손잡이이다.
dominant 우세한

⑨ Most action films, (especially martial art films),

대부분의 액션 영화들은 (특히 무술 영화들)　　　martial art 무술 + films 영화

are sped up to make their fighting scenes look (faster and more active).

속도가 높여지다　　사역동사 make + 목적어 scenes + 동사원형 look　　look faster and look more active
　　　　　　　　빨라지게 하다 (수동태)　　　　　　　　　　　더 빠르고 더 활기차게 보이다
　　　　　　　　　　　　　　　　　　　　　　　　　　　　속도를 높이지 않은 화면이 비해 (비교)

⑩ However, Lee's cases were the **opposite**.

　　　　　리의 경우는 반대였다　　oppose v. 반대하다, 겨루다 opposition n. 반대, 경쟁사
　　　　　　　　　　　　　　　opposite a. 반대의, 맞은편의 n. 반의어

⑪ Film screeners had to run his films a little bit slower so audiences could see

　　　　　　　　　　　(필름/화면) 더 느리게 돌리다

his kicks and punches.

❶ 1940년에 태어나 1973년에 사망한 브루스 리 (이소룡)는 무술인, 배우, 무술 지도자, 감독, 그리고 영화 제작자였는데, 입이 벌어질 정도의 놀라운 속도로 움직일 수 있었습니다.

❷ 말 그대로 속도가 너무 빨라서 입이 벌어질 정도였습니다.

❸ 얼마나 빨랐을까요?

❹ 그의 발차기는 사람들이 움직임을 볼 수 없을 만큼 너무 빨라서 필름을 천천히 돌려야만 했습니다.

❺ 그의 주먹 날리는 속도 역시 마찬가지였습니다.

❻ 그의 발차기와 주먹 날리기가 어찌나 빨랐던지 그 속도를 측정하려는 사람들이 있었습니다.

❼ 이소룡이 비디오카메라 앞에서 왼발로 발차기 시범을 보였을 때 그의 발차기는 1/5 초밖에 걸리지 않았습니다.

❽ 현장에서 그의 시범을 본 사람들은 그가 오른발잡이라는 사실에 할 말을 잃고 말았습니다.

❾ 대부분의 액션 영화들, 특히 무술 영화는 싸우는 장면이 더 빠르고 박진감 있게 보이게 하려고 속도를 빨리 합니다.

❿ 그러나 이소룡의 경우는 반대였습니다.

⓫ 영화 스크리너들은 관객들이 그의 발차기와 주먹을 볼 수 있도록 필름을 다소 느리게 돌려야 했습니다.

Chapter 10
Proverbs & Idioms

MP3

A leopard cannot change its spots. Also, the tiger cannot change its stripes. A leopard has lots of spots on its fur. No matter how hard it tries to remove them, its spots will never vanish or become faint. Whether taking a bath, scrubbing with brushes, using all kinds of soap... it's "no can do", for it's not a matter you can solve by scrubbing the outside of its skin. Originally, this proverb is from the Bible.

"Can the Ethiopian change his skin, or the leopard his spots? Then may you also do good, that are accustomed to do evil." (Jeremiah 13:23)

It's impossible for a dark-skinned African to change his skin color to be like that of a fair-skinned European ; neither can an evil person change his evil ways easily, because he is accustomed to do evil. Thus, you can use this proverb when you want to describe someone who cannot change his or her essential nature.

For example, there was a lazy guy and he was always late for work. When he arrived at his office, late as usual, he said that he's sorry and won't be late again. But the next day, he was late as everybody expected. Seeing him, his co-workers and boss said, "a leopard cannot change its spots."

Words & Expressions

leopard 표범 spot 점 stripe 줄무늬 proverb 속담 remove 제거하다 vanish 사라지다 become faint 흐려지다 rub 문지르다 brush 솔 no can do 소용없다, 할 수 없다 originally 원래 Jeremiah 예레미야(사람 이름, 구약 성경 예레미야서) do good 좋은 일을 하다, 이롭다 be accustomed to 익숙하다 fair-skinned 피부가 밝은 essential nature 본성 as usual 평소대로 co-worker 동료

1. What is the main idea of the story?

    a. It is not easy to change your essential nature.

    b. A dark-skinned African should not try to change his skin color.

    c. People who do good are likely to have spots on their skin.

    d. Lazy workers must scrub their skin with brushes.

2. According to Jeremiah 13:23, _____ .

    a. The Ethiopians didn't use brushes when taking a bath

    b. The Ethiopians can't change his skin, neither can the leopard

    c. Tigers and leopards are evil animals

    d. The Ethiopians are accustomed to do evil

3. Choose the correct words for each sentence.

    a. Mark, who is <u>fair-skinned</u> / <u>fairy skin</u> / <u>skin of fair</u> and has fair hair, is a fair person.

    b. No matter how <u>often</u> / <u>far</u> / <u>little</u> it is, I will walk there. No cars or bikes, just walking.

    c. He didn't care what was going on there and <u>neither she did</u> / <u>neither did she</u> / <u>she neither did</u>.

Answer 1. a   2. b   3. fair-skinned ∣ far ∣ neither did she

Listening Drill – Dictation

A   cannot change its spots. Also, the tiger cannot change its stripes. A leopard has lots of spots on its fur. No matter how hard it tries to remove them, its spots will never   . Whether taking a bath, scrubbing with brushes, using all kinds of soap... it's "   ", for it's not a matter you can solve by scrubbing the outside of its skin. Originally, this proverb is from the Bible.

"Can the Ethiopian change his skin, or the leopard his spots? Then may you also do good, that are accustomed to do evil." (Jeremiah 13:23)

It's impossible for a dark-skinned African to change his skin color   that of a   European ;   can an evil person change his evil ways easily, because he   do evil. Thus, you can use this proverb when you want to describe someone who cannot change his or her   .

For example, there was a lazy guy and he was always late for work. When he arrived at his office,   , he said that he's sorry and won't be late again. But the next day, he was late as everybody expected.   , his co-workers and boss said, "a leopard cannot change its spots."

Did You Know A Leopard Cannot Change Its Spots?

❶ A leopard cannot change its spots.

spot n. 점, 얼룩, 소량, 장소, 현장 v. 발견하다 (이 문장에서는 '점')

* 속담 – 표범이 자기 점을 바꿀 수 없다. 사람은 쉽게 안 변한다.

❷ Also, the tiger cannot change its stripes.

* 속담 – 호랑이가 무늬 못 바꾼다. 사람은 쉽게 안 변한다.　　줄무늬 (Stars and Stripes (별과 줄무늬) 성조기)

❸ A leopard has lots of spots on its fur.

lots of / a lot of + 가산명사, 불가산 명사

on its fur 털 위에 (on)

❹ No matter how hard it tries to remove them,

아무리 힘들게 노력한다 해도 it = leopard / them = spots

no matter how 형용사 + 주어 + 동사 : 아무리 … 해도

its spots will never (vanish or become faint).

사라지거나 흐려지다　　　　　　a. 희미한 v. 졸도하다 (paint n. 페인트 칠, 물감　v. 칠하다)

vanish = disappear　v. 사라지다 (banish v. 추방하다)

❺ Whether (1) **taking a bath,** 2) **scrubbing with brushes,** 3) **using all kinds of soap...**)

whether ( ) : 1), 2), 3)을 하든 하지 않든　　　scrub 북북 문지르다　　　　　　soap 불가산명사로 –s를 붙이지 않는다.

whether (or not) …하든지 말든 (or not 생략)

it's "no can do", for it's not a matter (you can solve by scrubbing the outside

= 할 수 없다, 안 된다　　　　　　↑　수식　　　　　　…해서(by –ing) 해결할 수 있는 문제가 아니다

solve (문제를) 해결하다　　피부 외부를 문질러서

of its skin).

❻ Originally, this proverb is from the Bible.

원래　　　　　　　proverb, old saying 속담

❼ "Can the Ethiopian change his skin, or the leopard his spots?

에티오피아인이 피부를 바꾸거나　　　　　　　　표범이 점을 바꿀 수 있는가 can the leopard change his spots?

❽ Then may you also do good, that are accustomed to do evil." (Jeremiah 13:23)

do good 선을 행하다 / do evil 악을 행하다 do someone good 누군가를 이롭게 하다

be accustomed to 동사원형 / –ing (두 가지 모두 가능) …에 익숙하다

❾ It's impossible for (a dark-skinned African) to change his skin color to be like

어두운 피부의 아프리카인 + to change his skin color 피부색을 바꾸다 + to be like …처럼 되려고

가주어 it 진주어 to change – it's impossible for ( ) to 동사 : ( )가 …하는 건 불가능하다

that of a fair-skinned European ;

skin color　　흰 피부의 유럽인의 피부처럼 (to be like that of…)

fair-skinned 피부가 흰 fair hair 금발

fair a. 공정한, (피부) 밝은, 금발인, 상당한, 꽤 괜찮은, (날씨) 맑은　n. 박람회, 축제, 품평회

396

neither can (an evil person) change his evil ways easily,

부사 neither가 문두에 올 경우 주어와 동사 위치가 바뀐다.

neither 동사 can + 주어 an evil person (지문은 조동사 can이 주어 앞으로, 주어 다음에 본동사 change가 왔다.)

because he **is accustomed to** do evil.

⋯에 익숙하다 (get used to) + 동사원형(or –ing)

⑩ Thus, you can use this proverb when you want to describe someone (who

(who⋯) 사람을 묘사하고 싶을 때 ↑ ⎸ 수식 ⎸

cannot change his or her essential nature).

essential 필수적인, 핵심적인 + nature 성질, 특성 = 본성

⑪ For example, there was a lazy guy and he was always late for work.

출근이 늦은 (late for school 학교에 늦는)

부사 위치 : be + 부사 + late (I am never late for work. 출근에 절대 늦지 않는다.)

⑫ When he arrived at his office, (late as usual), he said that (he's sorry and

⋯에 도착하다   평소처럼 as usual 늦은   그가 한 말 ( ) – 미안하다, 다시 안 늦겠다

won't be late again).

⑬ But the next day, he was late as everybody expected.

다음날 the following day   모두가 예상한대로

⑭ Seeing him, his co-workers and boss said, "a leopard cannot change its spots."

주어 일치 생략 (his co-workers and boss)

= The moment they saw him / As soon as they saw him 그를 보자마자

(표범이 자신의 점들을 바꿀 수 없다는 거 아세요?)

❶ 표범은 자신의 점을 바꿀 수 없습니다.   ❷ 호랑이 역시 자신의 줄무늬를 바꿀 수 없습니다.   ❸ 표범은 털에 점이 아주 많습니다.   ❹ 그걸 없애기 위해 아무리 열심히 노력한다 해도, 그 점들은 없어지거나 흐려지지 않습니다.   ❺ 목욕하고, 솔로 문질러 보고, 또는 온갖 종류의 비누를 사용해도⋯ 그래도 안 되는 이유는 겉 피부를 문질러 씻어서 해결할 수 있는 문제가 아니기 때문입니다.   ❻ 원래 이 속담은 성경에서 나왔습니다.

❼ "에디오피아인이 그의 피부를 바꿀 수 있으며, 표범이 그의 점들을 바꿀 수 있느냐?   ❽ 그렇다면 악을 행하는데 익숙한 너희도 선을 행할 수 있으리라." (예레미야 13장 23절)

❾ 피부색이 짙은 아프리카인이 밝은 피부의 유럽인처럼 피부색을 바꾸는 건 불가능합니다.   ❿ 사악한 사람이 사악한 행실을 쉽게 바꾸지 못하는 건 사악을 행하는데 익숙해있기 때문입니다.   ⑪ 그래서 이 속담은 자신의 본성을 바꾸지 못하는 누군가를 표현할 때 사용할 수 있습니다.

⑪ 예를 들어 게을러서 항상 직장에 지각하는 사람이 있다고 합시다.   ⑫ 평소처럼 사무실에 늦게 도착한 그는 미안하다며 다시는 늦지 않겠다고 말했습니다.   ⑬ 하지만 다음 날, 그는 모두의 예상대로 지각했습니다.   ⑭ 그를 보며 그의 동료들과 상사는 "표범이 자기 점은 못 바꾸지."라고 말했습니다.

You can 'paint the town red' not with a paintbrush but with lots of alcohol, because this expression has nothing to do with a paint job. It means, "to engage in a wild and riotous spree."

There is more than one suggestion as to the origin of this expression. The most well-known theory is that it was started by a nobleman named Henry. This guy was so mischievous that he ran riot in a Leicestershire town with a group of his friends, painting the town's buildings and bars red in the 1800s.

Some claim that the 'red light district' might be the origin. In the past, the section of a town where bars and saloons were located was called the red light district. Thus they think the word 'red' might have come from 'red light district.' Or, it could have originated in red blood. In fact, some think this expression came from a kind of crazy behavior including shedding blood and painting walls and buildings with blood. Yet, no one knows which is the real origin.

Anyway, when the 2010 Winter Olympics was held in Vancouver, Canadians cheered on their athletes with the slogan 'paint the town red' since it also has the meaning of 'have lots of fun.'

Understanding Checkpoint

1. What is the main idea of the story?

    a. Henry hated to live in the red light district

    b. 'Paint the town red' has nothing to do with a paint job.

    c. If you paint the town red, you will be under arrest by the local police.

    d. 'Paint the town red' means to shed blood.

2. According to the passage, which sentence is <u>wrong</u>?

    a. The expression 'to paint the town red' has something to do with alcohol and parties.

    b. Henry was mischievous enough to paint buildings and bars red.

    c. There were many bars and pubs in the red light district.

    d. Everybody knows the origin of 'to paint the town red.'

3. Choose the correct words for each sentence.

    a. <u>What</u> / <u>Which</u> / <u>That</u> one do you like more, coffee or tea?

    b. The new-comer told me that he came <u>after</u> / <u>from</u> / <u>again</u> the land of the ice and snow.

    c. I went to the church on Friday morning, where Dave's funeral <u>was held</u> / <u>hold</u> / <u>held</u>.

Answer **1.** b   **2.** d   **3.** Which ∣ from ∣ was held

Listening Drill – Dictation

You can 'paint the town red' not with a paintbrush but with lots of alcohol, because this expression has nothing to do with a paint job. It means, "to engage in a wild and

    ."

There is more than one suggestion   the origin of this expression. The most well-known theory is that   a nobleman named Henry. This guy was so   that he   in a Leicestershire town with a group of his friends, painting the town's buildings and bars red in the 1800s.

Some claim that the 'red light district' might be the origin. In the past, the section of a town   bars and saloons   was called the red light district. Thus they think the word 'red' might have come from 'red light district.' Or, it could have   in red blood. In fact, some think this expression came from a kind of crazy behavior including   and painting walls and buildings with blood. Yet, no one knows which is the real origin.

Anyway, when the 2010 Winter Olympics   in Vancouver, Canadians cheered on their athletes with the slogan 'paint the town red' since it also has the meaning of 'have lots of fun.'

399

Did You Know You Can 'Paint The Town Red' Without A Paintbrush?

1 You can 'paint the town red' not (with a paintbrush) but (with lots of **alcohol**),
not A but B 붓이 아니라 술로   알코올, 술

because this expression has nothing to do with a paint job.
= doesn't have anything to do with ···와 상관없다   a paint job 페인트 칠하는 일/작업
a nose job 코 성형 수술, a hair job 미용 일, a car repair job 차 고치는 일

2 It means, "to engage in a (wild and **riotous**) spree."
···에 참여하다   wild 흥분한, 신나는 + riotous 흥청거리는
spree 한바탕 (shopping spree 쇼핑하기 killing spree 대량학살)

3 There is more than one suggestion as to (the **origin** of this expression).
하나 이상의 제안 (단수 명사, 단수 동사)   about ···에 관해   origin 기원, 유래 originate in ···에서 유래하다

4 The most well-known theory is that it was started by (a **nobleman** named Henry).
가장 잘 알려진   시작되다 (수동)   수식   헨리라는 이름의 귀족
a nobleman who was named Henry / a nobleman whose name was Henry

5 This guy was so **mischievous** that he ran **riot** in a Leicestershire town (with a group
so 형용사 that 너무 ···해서 that하다   난동 피우다

of his friends), painting (the town's buildings and bars) red in the 1800s.
and he painted ( ) red : ( )를 붉게 칠하면서(-ing) + in the 1800s 1800년대에
and 생략, 주어 일치 생략, 능동적 행동 - painting

6 Some claim that the 'red light **district**' might be the origin.
red light 홍등/붉은 등 + district 거리, 지역   유래일 수 있다 (조동사 might + 동사원형 be)

7 In the past, (the **section** of a town where bars and saloons were located) was called
수식   where의 선행사 town   be called ( ) ···라 불린다
주어 ( ) the section 술집과 살롱이 위치한 도시의 부분 + 동사 was called (수동태)

(the red light district).

8 Thus they think the word 'red' might have come from 'red light district.'
might have pp ···일지도 모른다 (추측) (come-came-come)

9 Or, it could have **originated** in red blood.
could have pp ···일 수도 있다 (추측)
originate 유래하다

10 In fact, some think this expression came from a kind of crazy behavior
일종의 (kind of 약간)

including ¹⁾ shedding blood and ²⁾ painting (walls and buildings) with blood.
¹⁾ 피를 흘리는 것과　　　　　　　　²⁾ ( )를 피로 칠하는 것

⑪ Yet, no one knows which is the real origin.
　　　　　　　　　　　　앞서 소개한 3가지 유래 설 중

⑫ Anyway, when the 2010 Winter Olympics **was held in** Vancouver,
　　　　　　　　　　　　　　　　올림픽이 개최되다 (수동)

Canadians cheered on their athletes (with the slogan 'paint the town red')
　　　　　　　　( )로 선수들을 응원하다　　　　　슬로건(문구)으로

since it also has the meaning of 'have lots of fun.'
왜냐하면　　　　　　…의 의미를 갖다

> 붓 없이도 '시내를 빨갛게 칠할' 수 있다는 거 아세요?

❶ 붓이 아니라 다량의 술로 '시내를 빨갛게 칠할' 수 있는 이유는 이 표현이 페인트칠과 아무 상관이 없기 때문입니다.

❷ 이 표현의 의미는 "소란스럽고 시끄럽게 한 바탕 마시고 놀다"입니다.

❸ 이 표현의 유래에 관해 여러 가지 의견이 분분합니다.

❹ 가장 잘 알려진 이론은 헨리라는 이름의 귀족에 의해 시작되었다는 것입니다.

❺ 이 남자는 너무 장난이 심해서 1800년대에 일단의 친구들과 함께 레스터셔 도시에서 난동을 부리며 도시의 건물과 술집을 빨갛게 칠했다고 합니다.

❻ 어떤 이들은 '홍등가'가 유래일 수도 있다고 주장합니다.

❼ 과거에 술집과 살롱이 위치한 도시의 특정 지역을 홍등가라고 불렀습니다.

❽ 이들은 '빨강'이라는 단어가 홍등가에서 나왔을 수도 있다고 생각합니다.

❾ 아니면 빨간 피에서 유래했을 지도 모릅니다.

❿ 사실 어떤 이들은 피를 흘리게 하고 피로 벽과 건물을 칠하는 등의 정신 나간 행동에서 이 표현이 유래했다고 생각합니다.

⓫ 하지만 어느 것이 진짜 유래인지는 아무도 모릅니다.

⓬ 어쨌든 밴쿠버에서 2010년 동계 올림픽이 열렸을 때 슬로건이 '시내를 빨갛게 칠하자'였는데, 이 표현이 '신나게 즐기자'라는 뜻으로도 쓰이기 때문입니다.

Cats are said to have nine lives. Then what can kill cats? The answer can be found in the proverb 'curiosity killed the cat.' This means that curiosity or inquisitiveness can lead to dangerous situations. You can use this proverb when trying to stop someone from asking unwanted questions.

Cats are famous for being curious and for having nine lives. Generally, it is supposed to be almost impossible to kill something that has nine lives, but cats can be killed by their own curious natures. Cats are that curious. Maybe that's how this proverb came to be. But originally, what killed the cat was not 'curiosity' but 'care.' In this context, 'care' means 'worry or sorrow.' In fact, 'care killed the cat' was used until the late 1800s.

It is very much difficult to pinpoint exactly when this proverb was started, or how the word 'care' was replaced with 'curiosity.' All we know is that the original form of this proverb changed 'care killed the cat' into 'curiosity killed the cat.'

Maybe we should stop being curious about the origin of this proverb. After all, curiosity killed the cat.

Words & Expressions

curiosity 호기심 inquisitiveness 꼬치꼬치 캐묻기 좋아함 unwanted 원하지 않는 care 돌봄, 보살핌, 걱정 pinpoint 정확히 찾아내다, 콕 짚어내다 replace 대체하다

 **Understanding Checkpoint**

1. What is the main idea of the story?

    a. Don't even think of killing cats although cat meat is delicious.

    b. Cats are curious creatures, so there is a proverb like 'curiosity killed the cat.'

    c. Cats have nine lives so you will have to kill them ten times if you want to eliminate them.

    d. The right expression is 'Care killed the cat', not 'Curiosity killed the cat.'

2. During the 1800s, _____ .

    a. people believed only curious cats had nine lives

    b. curious cats were killed by people

    c. many proverbs about cats were made

    d. people had used the proverb 'care killed the cat'

3. Choose the correct words for each sentence.

    a. It is easy <u>of saying</u> / <u>to say</u> / <u>into say</u> for you, Diane, but unfortunately it's not that easy.

    b. Hundreds of Indian girls shares the same name meaning "<u>wanted</u> / <u>savior</u> / <u>unwanted</u>" in Hindi since their parents wanted boys not girls.

    c. Much to my surprise, even I can change the world <u>from</u> / <u>into</u> / <u>as</u> a better place.

Answer **1.** b   **2.** d   **3.** to say ┃ unwanted ┃ into

Listening Drill – Dictation

Cats _____ have nine lives. Then what can kill cats? The answer can be found in the proverb 'curiosity killed the cat.' This means that curiosity or _____ can lead to dangerous situations. You can use this proverb when trying to stop someone from asking unwanted questions.

Cats are famous for being curious and for having nine lives. Generally, it _____ be almost impossible to kill something that has nine lives, but cats can be killed by their own _____. Cats are that curious. Maybe that's how this proverb came to be. But originally, _____ was not 'curiosity' but 'care.' In this context, 'care' means 'worry or sorrow.' In fact, 'care killed the cat' was used _____ 1800s.

It is very much difficult to _____ this proverb was started, or how the word 'care' _____ 'curiosity.' _____ the original form of this proverb changed 'care killed the cat' into 'curiosity killed the cat.'

Maybe we should _____ about the origin of this proverb. After all, curiosity killed the cat.

403

Did You Know What Can Kill The Cat With Nine Lives?

1 Cats are said to have nine lives.

···라고 한다   lives 1. 동사 live의 3인칭 단수 현재 2. life (생명, 목숨)의 복수형 (여기서는 두번째)

= It is said that cats have nine lives.

2 Then what can kill cats?

3 The answer can be found in the proverb 'curiosity killed the cat.'

속담에서 찾을 수 있다 (수동)   호기심이 고양이를 죽인다 (속담) 과한 호기심이 위험할 수 있다

4 This means that (curiosity or inquisitiveness) can lead to dangerous situations.

inquisitive a. 캐묻기 좋아하는, 호기심 많은   ···로 이어지다, 인도하다

inquisiveness n. 캐묻기 좋아함, 호기심 많음 inquire v. 묻다

5 You can use this proverb when trying to stop someone from asking

주절의 주어 you일치, 생략 when you try   stop ( ) from –ing 누가( ) ···하는 것을 멈추게 하다

unwanted questions.

원치 않는 (uncalled for 부적절한, 불필요한)

6 Cats are famous [1] for being curious and [2] for having nine lives.

be famous [1] 호기심 많은 것으로 [2] 목숨이 9개인 것으로 유명하다   be famous for +명사, 동명사

7 Generally, it is supposed to be almost impossible to kill something (that has

일반적으로   be supposed to···하기로 되어 있다   that 선행사 - something (3인칭, 단수 현재) has ↑ 수식

You were supposed to finish your job on time. 너는 제 시간에 일을 끝내야 했다.

They are not supposed to be here. 저들이 여기 오지 않기로 되어 있다.

nine lives), but cats can be killed by their own curious natures.

호기심 많은 성격/천성

8 Cats are that curious.

that 강조 – 그 정도로 I didn't know he was that stubborn. 그가 이 정도로 고집이 센 줄 몰랐다.

9 Maybe that's how this proverb came to be.

= originated   이렇게 해서 이 속담이 나오게 되었다

10 But originally, (what killed the cat) was not 'curiosity' but 'care.'

주어 ( ) cat이 아니라 what (선행사를 포함한 관계대명사-고양이를 죽이는 것) + 동사 was

11 In this context, 'care' means 'worry or sorrow.'

이 문맥에서   n. 돌봄, 주의, 염려 v. 관심을 가지다, 배려하다

404

⑫ In fact, 'care killed the cat' was used until the late 1800s.

1800년대 후반까지 (the early 1800s 1800년대 초반)

⑬ It is very much difficult to **pinpoint** exactly when this proverb was started,

가주어 it 진주어 to pinpoint · · · 정확히 집어내다 · · · when 의문문이 아니라 명사절이라서 when 주어 + 동사
꼭 짚어내는 건 어렵다 · (이 속담이 언제 시작되었는지를)

or how the word 'care' was **replaced with** 'curiosity.'

how 의문문이 아닌 명사절 how + 주어 + 동사 · · · · · ···으로 교체/대체하다
(어떻게 care가 curiosity로 대체되었는지를)

⑭ (All we know) is that (the original form of this proverb) changed 'care killed

주어 ( ) 단수 + 단수 동사 is · · that절 이하 주어 ( ) proverb가 아니라 form + 동사 changed · · · · change A into B : A가 B로 바뀌다 (변화하다)

the cat' into 'curiosity killed the cat.'

⑮ Maybe we should stop being curious about the origin of this proverb.

stop -ing ···하는 하는 것을 중단하다 (호기심을 갖는 걸 중단하다)
stop eating 먹기를 중단하다 / stop to eat 먹기 위해 (하던 일을) 중단하다

⑯ After all, curiosity killed the cat.

결국

목숨이 9개인 고양이를 죽일 수 있는 게 무엇인지 아세요?

❶ 고양이는 목숨이 9개라고 합니다. ❷ 그럼 무엇이 고양이를 죽일 수 있을까요?

❸ 정답은 '호기심이 고양이를 죽였다'는 속담에서 찾을 수 있습니다.

❹ 그 의미는 호기심 혹은 캐묻기 좋아하는 태도 때문에 위험한 상황에 빠질 수 있다는 뜻입니다.

❺ 누군가 원치 않는 질문을 하는데 이를 멈추게 하고 싶을 때 이 속담을 사용할 수 있습니다.

❻ 고양이는 호기심이 많은 것과 목숨이 9개인 것으로 유명합니다.

❼ 일반적으로 목숨이 9개인 누군가를 죽이는 건 거의 불가능하지만, 고양이는 자신의 천성적인 호기심으로 죽을 수 있습니다.

❽ 그만큼 고양이가 호기심이 많다는 것입니다. ❾ 아마 이 속담은 이렇게 만들어졌을 겁니다.

❿ 하지만 원래 고양이를 죽일 수 있는 건 '호기심'이 아니라 '걱정'이었습니다.

⑪ 이 문맥에서 '걱정'은 '근심거리, 슬픔' 을 뜻합니다.

⑫ 사실 '걱정이 고양이를 죽였다'는 1800년대 후반까지 통용되었습니다.

⑬ 이 속담이 언제 시작되었는지, 어떻게 '걱정'이라는 단어가 '호기심'으로 바뀌었는지 정확히 설명하기는 매우 어렵습니다.

⑭ 우리가 아는 건, 속담의 원래 모습인 '걱정이 고양이를 죽였다'가 '호기심이 고양이를 죽였다'로 바뀌었다는 것뿐입니다.

⑮ 어쩌면 이 속담의 유래에 대한 호기심을 그만 접어야 할지도 모르겠습니다.

⑯ 어쨌든 호기심이 고양이를 죽이니까요. (호기심이 위험할 수 있으니까요.)

You can 'get the axe' or 'give the axe' although there is no actual axe given or taken away. It is possible because the word 'axe' has several different meanings.

An axe is a hand tool used for cutting wood or chopping down trees. It is also used as a verb, and its meaning is 'to chop, cut, or trim with an axe.' Its second meaning is a 'dismissal' especially from employment. So, words like 'discharge, removal, layoff...' are synonyms of an 'axe.' That's how the expression 'to give the axe' got the meaning of 'to fire.' Similarly, 'get the axe' means 'to get fired.'

Speaking of 'getting fired', there is another phrase you might want to know : the sack. 'Sack' is widely known as a kind of bag. But, it also has the meaning of dismissal, just like the word 'axe.' So 'to get the sack' is the same in meaning as 'to get the axe.'

One more thing : If you want to use the words 'sack' or 'axe' with the meaning of dismissal, do not omit the word 'the.' If you say, 'my boss gave me an axe (or a sack)', people will think that you received an actual axe (or sack) from your kind boss.

Words & Expressions

axe 도끼 get the axe 해고당하다 give the axe 해고하다 actual 실제 hand tool 수공구 split 쪼개다
chop 자르다 verb 동사 trim 다듬다 dismissal 해고 discharge 해고 removal 제거, 해고 layoff 일시 해고
synonym 유의어 sack 가방 be widely known as ...로 널리 알려지다

406

Understanding Checkpoint

1. What is the main idea of the story?

a. If someone gives you the axe, you will have to pay for it.

b. "Get the axe" means "get fired."

c. "Get the axe" and "give the sack" have the same meaning.

d. An axe is more expensive than a sack.

2. According to the passage, which sentence is right?

a. If you don't like one of your lazy employees, you can give him an axe.

b. The word 'axe' has at least five different meanings.

c. Synonyms of 'employment' are 'discharge' and 'layoff.'

d. 'Get the axe' is totally different from 'get an axe.'

3. Choose the correct words for each sentence.

a. You have to permit the <u>layoff</u> / <u>dismiss</u> / <u>sack</u> of some staff members due to budget cuts.

b. What religions <u>are commonly practiced</u> / <u>practiced are commonly</u> / <u>commonly are practiced</u> in Africa?

c. No way to play soccer under the scorching sun without you <u>get burned</u> / <u>getting burned</u> / <u>to get burning</u>.

Answer **1.** b **2.** d **3.** layoff ∣ are commonly practiced ∣ getting burned

Listening Drill – Dictation

You can 'get the axe' or 'give the axe' although there is no actual axe   or   .
It is possible because the word 'axe'   .
An axe is a hand tool used for cutting wood or chopping down trees. It is also used as a verb, and its meaning is 'to chop, cut, or trim with an axe.' Its second meaning is a '   ' especially from employment. So, words like 'discharge, removal, layoff...' are synonyms of an 'axe.' That's how the expression 'to give the axe' got the meaning of 'to fire.'   , 'get the axe' means 'to get fired.'
            'getting fired', there is another phrase you might want to know ∶ the sack. 'Sack'   a kind of bag. But, it also has the meaning of dismissal, just like the word 'axe.' So 'to get the sack'   as 'to get the axe.'
One more thing ∶ If you want to use the words 'sack' or 'axe' with the meaning of dismissal, do not   the word 'the.' If you say, 'my boss gave me an axe (or a sack)', people will think that you received an   (or sack) from your kind boss.

Did You Know You Can "Get The Axe" Without Receiving Any Actual Axe?

❶ You can '**get the axe**' or '**give the axe**' although there is no actual
   해고 당하다(= get fired)   해고하다(= fire)

   axe given or taken away.
   실제 도끼가 주어지고 빼앗기는 (수동) ···axe which is given or taken

❷ It is possible because the word 'axe' has several different meanings.
   앞 문장 (실제 도끼 없이도 get the axe, give the axe 할 수 있는 것)

❸ An axe is a hand tool used for [1] cutting wood or [2] chopping down trees.
   tool (which is) used   나무를 자르다   나무를 베어 쓰러뜨리다

❹ It is also used as a verb, and its meaning is 'to **chop**, cut, or **trim** with an axe.'
   이것의 의미   베다/썰다, 자르다, or 다듬다 + 도끼로
   돼지고기 요리 중 '폭찹' porkchop 돼지갈비살 (뼈가 붙은 것)

❺ (Its second meaning) is a '**dismissal**' especially from **employment**.
   dismiss v. 묵살하다, 일축하다, 해고하다   employ v. 고용하다 employer n. 고용자 employee n. 직원
   dismissal n. 묵살, 해고, (소송, 재판) 기각   employment n. 고용

❻ So, (words like '**discharge**, **removal**, **layoff**...') are **synonyms** of an 'axe.'
   주어 ( ) words + 동사 are   synonym 유의어 (↔ antonym 반의어)
   discharge v. 해고하다 n. 해고, 방출 removal n. 해고, 없애기 layoff n. 일시 해고

❼ That's how (the expression 'to give the axe') got the meaning of 'to **fire**.'
   이렇게 해서/그리하여 ···하게 되다   how + 주어 ( ) + 동사 got ...라는 의미를 갖다   n. 불 v. 해고하다

❽ **Similarly**, 'get the axe' means 'to **get fired**.'
   비슷하게, 마찬가지로   해고 당하다 (cf. get injured 부상당하다)

❾ Speaking of 'getting fired', there is another phrase you might want to know :
   말이 나온 김에, 라는 말이 나와서 하는 말인데   당신이 알고 싶어할 수도 있는

   the sack.

❿ 'Sack' is widely known as a kind of bag.
   ...로 (as) 널리 알려지다 (수동태 be + 부사 + knows as)
   be widely known 널리 알려지다 / be well known 잘 알려지다

⓫ But, it also has the meaning of dismissal, just like the word 'axe.'

⑫ So 'to **get the sack**' is the same in meaning as 'to get the axe.'
　　　　　해고 당하다　　　　　　　as와 같은 의미이다

⑬ One more thing :

⑭ If you want to use the words ('sack' or 'axe') with the meaning of dismissal,
　사용하고 싶다면 + ( )라는 단어를 + 해고의 의미로

do not **omit** the word 'the.'
　　　　빼다 omission n. 생략, 누락

⑮ If you say, 'my boss gave me an axe (or a sack)',
　가정법 현재 if 주어 동사의 현재형, 주어 will 동사원형

people will think that you received an actual axe (or sack) from your kind boss.
　　　that … 이라고 생각할 것이다 (people will think that…) - 현재 상태에서 가정

실제 도끼를 받지 않고도 'get the axe' 할 수 있다는 거 아세요?

❶ 받거나 빼앗기는 실제 도끼(axe)가 없어도 'get the axe' 할 수도 있고 'give the axe' 할 수도 있습니다.

❷ 그게 가능한 건 'axe'에 여러 가지 의미가 있기 때문입니다.

❸ axe는 나무를 자를 때 또는 나무를 베어낼 때 사용되는 수공구입니다.

❹ 이는 또한 동사로도 쓰이는 데, 의미는 '도끼로 자르거나 베거나 다듬다'는 뜻입니다.

❺ 두 번째 의미는 특히 직장에서의 '해고'를 뜻합니다.

❻ 그래서 'discharge, removal, layoff…' 등이 'axe'의 유의어입니다.

❼ 이렇게 해서 'give the axe'가 '누구를 해고하다'하는 뜻을 갖게 되었습니다.

❽ 마찬가지로 'get the axe'는 '해고되다'는 뜻입니다.

❾ '해고'라는 말이 나온 김에 알아두면 좋을 또 다른 단어가 있는데 바로 'the sack'입니다.

❿ 'sack'은 일종의 가방으로 널리 알려져 있습니다.　　　⓫ 하지만 'axe'처럼 '해고'라는 뜻도 갖고 있습니다.

⓬ 그래서 'get the sack'은 'get the axe'와 뜻이 똑같습니다.　　⓭ 한 가지 더.

⓮ 'sack' 이나 'axe'를 '해고'의 의미로 사용하고 싶다면, 'the'를 빼면 안 됩니다.

⓯ 만약 'my boss gave me an axe (or sack)'으로 말한다면, 사람들은 당신이 친절한 사장님으로 부터
　　실제 도끼 (또는 자루)를 받았다고 알아들을 것입니다.

95 What Happens To Fish When they Go Belly-up?

If a fish goes belly-up, it's dead. Think about a dead fish. It doesn't swim or move its fins. It just floats upside-down on the water, showing its belly.

The expression 'belly-up' means the same thing, since its origin is the floating position of a dead fish. So to 'go belly-up' means to 'be hopelessly ruined', 'fail' or 'go bankrupt.' Generally, this expression is used in financially difficult situations.

For example, you can say :

"Builders are on the verge of going belly-up because the price of the cement is getting higher and higher."

"He is certain that he won't go belly-up even though his debt problem is getting worse day by day."

"Many fish farmers are about to go belly-up since more and more fish in fish farms are literally going belly-up due to harmful pollutants being emitted from power plants."

But, there is no such thing going 'belly-down.'

Words & Expressions

go belly-up 망하다, 파산하다, 배를 드러내다 **fin** 지느러미 **float** 물에 뜨다 **upside down** 뒤집혀, 위 아래가 바뀌어 **ruin** 파괴하다 **financially** 경제적으로 **builder** 건축업자 **be on the verge of** ...하기 직전이다 **debt** 빚 **fish farmer** 양식어민 **pollutant** 오염물질 **power plant** 발전소

410

1. What is the main idea of the story?

a. You will go belly-up if you eat dead fish.

b. You can use the expression 'go belly-up' when someone suffers from stomach cancer.

c. The expression 'go belly-up' have something to do with fish and it means to 'fail.'

d. Fish farmers and builders are about to go belly-up.

2. The expression 'belly-up' comes from _____ .

a. the builder who has a debt problem

b. the position of fish swimming in the water

c. the floating position of a dead fish

d. the hopeless situation of being ruined

3. Choose the correct words for each sentence.

a. A group of fish is often called a school. So a school of fish <u>meaning</u> / <u>means</u> / <u>mean</u> the same as a group of fish.

b. My grocery bill is getting <u>better and better</u> / <u>higher and higher</u> / <u>larger and larger</u> due to inflation.

c. When the robber threatened to kill her, she called 911 and yelled, 'I'm about <u>to die</u> / <u>die</u> / <u>being dead</u>!'

d. My brother <u>was on the verge of</u> / <u>is about that</u> / <u>was planning to</u> nervous breakdown after failing to win the contest.

Answer 1. c 2. c 3. means ∣ higher and higher ∣ to die ∣ was on the verge of

Listening Drill – Dictation

If a fish _____ , it's dead. Think about a dead fish. It doesn't swim or move its fins.
It just floats _____ on the water, showing its belly.
The expression 'belly-up' _____ , since its origin is the
of a dead fish. So to 'go belly-up' means to 'be hopelessly ruined', 'fail' or '_____.'
Generally, this expression is used in _____ .
For example, you can say :
"Builders _____ going belly-up because the price of the cement is getting
higher and higher."
"He is certain that he won't go belly-up even though his debt problem is getting worse
day by day."
"Many fish farmers _____ go belly-up since more and more fish in fish farms are
literally going belly-up due to harmful pollutants being _____ power plants."
But, _____ going 'belly-down.'

411

Did You Know What Happens To Fish When they Go Belly-up?

❶ If a fish goes **belly-up**, it's dead.

fish '물고기'라는 집합명사로도 쓰이고 a fish '물고기 한 마리'로도 쓰인다.
배가 위를 향하다, 배를 드러내다

❷ Think about a dead fish.

❸ It doesn't ¹⁾ swim or ²⁾ move its **fins**.

fin 지느러미 (shark's fin 샥스핀 요리 dorsal fin 등지느러미)

❹ It just **floats upside-down** on the water, showing its belly.

float v. 물에 뜨다   위아래가 바뀐 채   물 위(on 표면)에서   = while it shows its belly (주어 일치 생략)
n. 찌, 부낭

❺ The expression 'belly-up' means the same thing, since its origin is

같은 것을 의미한다   = because
feel the same way 똑같은 식으로 느끼다
be bitten by the same bug 똑같은 벌레에게 물리다 (same앞에 the 필요)

the floating position of a dead fish.

죽은 물고기의 떠 있는 자세

❻ So to 'go belly-up' means to 'be hopelessly ruined', 'fail' or '**go bankrupt**'.

절망적으로 망하다, 실패하다, 파산하다   파산하다 (= go broke)

❼ Generally, this expression is used in financially difficult situations.

수식 ↑ 수식 ↑
경제적으로 어려운 상황 (부사 + 형용사 + 명사) 부사는 형용사 수식, 형용사는 명사 수식

❽ For example, you can say :

❾ "Builders **are on the verge of** going belly-up because the price of the cement

···하기 직전이다 (of + 명사, 동명사)

is getting higher and higher."

점점 더 높아지는 중이다 (현재 진행) get + 비교급 and 비교급 get worse and worse 점점 더 나빠지다

❿ "He is certain that he won't go belly-up even though his debt problem

that···를 확신하다   ···임에도 불구하고

is getting worse **day by day**."

점점 더 나빠지는 중이다 (현재 진행)   day by day 나날이, 조금씩 week by week 한 주 두 주 지나면서
month by month 다달이 year by year 매년, 해가 갈수록

⑪ "Many fish farmers **are about to** go belly-up since more and more (fish in fish farms)
···하기 직전이다 (to 동사원형) = be on the verge of –ing   점점 더   주어 fish 물고기들 + are
양어장의 물고기들 (복수) fish의 복수형 fish / fishes

are **literally** going belly-up (due to harmful **pollutants** being emitted from
수식
pollutants <u>which are</u> emitted from···에서 나오는 오염물질들

power plants)."

⑫ But, there is no such thing as going 'belly-down.'
as··· 같은 건 없다

물고기가 배를 드러내면 어떻게 되는지 아세요?

❶ 물고기가 배를 드러내면, 죽은 겁니다.

❷ 죽은 물고기를 생각해보세요.

❸ 헤엄치지도 않고 지느러미를 움직이지도 않습니다.

❹ 그냥 배를 드러낸 채 물 위를 뒤집혀 떠다닐 뿐입니다.

❺ 'belly-up'이라는 표현도 같은 의미인데, 죽은 물고기의 떠다니는 자세에서 유래된 표현이기 때문입니다.

❻ 그래서 '배를 드러내다 go belly-up'는 뜻은 '절망적으로 망하다' '실패하다' 또는 '파산하다'는 뜻입니다.

❼ 일반적으로 경제적인 어려움에 빠진 상태일 때 이 표현이 사용됩니다.

❽ 예를 들어 이렇게 말할 수 있습니다.

❾ "건축업자들은 시멘트 가격이 점점 높아지고 있어서 파산하기 직전이다."

❿ "그의 부채 문제가 갈수록 악화되는 데도 그는 파산하지 않으리라 확신한다."

⑪ "많은 양어민들이 망하기 일보직전인데, 이는 발전소에서 방출된 해로운 오염물질로 인해 점점 더 많은 양어장 물고기들이
말 그대로 배를 드러내고 있기 때문이다."

⑫ 하지만 'belly-down' 이라는 건 없습니다.

'Gung ho' comes from Chinese characters. Gung(工) means 'work' and Ho(和) means 'together, in harmony.' So, the literal meaning of 'gung ho' is 'work together.' However, if you look it up in the dictionary, you will read 'extremely enthusiastic, zealous.'

Actually, 'gung ho' has been used in English since 1942. Evans Carlson, the U.S. Marine Corps leader of the World War II, admired the spirit of the Chinese Industrial Cooperative Society during his stay in China. So, when WW II began, he clipped these long Chinese-pronounced phrase to the two words 'gung ho' and took them as a slogan for his battalion. Since then, 'gung ho' has become an unofficial motto of the US Marine Corps as an expression of spirit and "can- do" attitude.

Have you never heard of this expression before? 'Gung ho' has been used more frequently than you think. The title of a 1986 comedy film, directed by Ron Howard, was 'Gung Ho.' You can find a book titled 'Gung Ho' by Ken Blanchard and Sheldon Bowles in a bookstore. And, there is a Japanese video game company named 'GungHo Online Entertainment.' As you can see, quite a few people are gung ho about this expression 'gung ho.'

Words & Expressions

Chinese character 한자 literal meaning 문자 그대로의 의미 look up (참고 도서, 사전 등) 찾아보다
dictionary 사전 enthusiastic 열정적인 zealous 열성적인 U.S. Marine Corps 미해병대 admire 존경하다
industrial 산업의 cooperative 협동의 clip 자르다, 깎다 unofficial 비공식적인 motto 좌우명, 모토 can-do
attitude 할 수 있다는 자세 be gung ho about ...에 열성적이다.

1. What is the main idea of the story?

  a. Chinese characters have been frequently used by North Americans.

  b. Carlson is the person who made the expression 'Gungho' during his stay in Japan.

  c. The expression 'Gung ho' has been the slogan of Chinese Marine Corps since 1942.

  d. The expression 'Gung ho' made of Chinese characters means 'enthusiastic.'

2. According the passage, which sentence is right?

  a. The figurative meaning of 'Gung ho' is 'work together.'

  b. You cannot find the expression 'Gung ho' in the dictionary because it's not English.

  c. 'Gung ho' has been the motto of the US Marine Corps since World War I.

  d. 'Gung ho' is the title of the movie directed by Ron Howard.

3. Choose the correct words for each sentence.

  a. When a robber shouted "freeze!", I had to run to the library to look the word 'freeze' <u>up</u> / <u>out</u> / <u>at</u> in the dictionary because I didn't know its meaning.

  b. Just look at the window. You have no choice but to <u>admirable</u> / <u>admiral</u> / <u>admire</u> the beautiful scenery.

  c. Ron and his brother <u>have enjoying</u> / <u>have enjoyed</u> / <u>enjoyed</u> various sports since they were young.

Answer **1.** d **2.** d **3.** up ǀ admire ǀ have enjoyed

Listening Drill - Dictation

'Gung ho' comes from   . Gung(工) means 'work' and Ho(和) means 'together,   .' So, the literal meaning of 'gung ho' is 'work together.' However, if you   , you will read 'extremely   , zealous.'

Actually, 'gung ho' has been used in English since 1942. Evans Carlson, the U.S. Marine Corps leader of the World War II, admired the spirit of the Chinese Industrial Cooperative Society during his stay in China. So, when WW II began, he   these long Chinese-pronounced phrase to the two words 'gung ho' and took them as a slogan for his battalion. Since then, 'gung ho' has become   the US Marine Corps as an expression of spirit and "can- do" attitude.

               this expression before? 'Gung ho'   than you think. The title of a 1986 comedy film, directed by Ron Howard, was 'Gung Ho.' You can find a book   'Gung Ho' by Ken Blanchard and Sheldon Bowles in a bookstore. And, there is a Japanese video game company named 'GungHo Online Entertainment.' As you can see, quite a few people   this expression 'gung ho.'

Did You Know 'Gung Ho' Are Chinese Characters?

① 'Gung ho' comes from Chinese **characters**.

···에서 오다, ···출신이다   한자 (한글의 경우 Hangul로 쓰기도 하고 Korean character, Korea alphabet으로 쓰기도 한다.
한자는 뜻글자라서 Chinese alphabet으로는 쓰지 않는다.)

② Gung(工) means 'work' and Ho(和) means 'together, in harmony'.

③ So, the **literal meaning** of 'Gung ho' is 'work together.'

(비유나 숨은 뜻이 아닌) 문자 그대로의 의미

④ However, if you **look** it **up** in the dictionary, you will read '**extremely enthusiastic,**

it = gungho   사전에서 이것을 찾아보다   매우 열렬한   열정적인
look up (사전, 도서) 찾아보다 look out 조심하다 look into 조사하다 look at 쳐다보다

zealous.'

zeal n. 열의, 열성

⑤ Actually, 'Gung ho' has been used in English since 1942.

현재완료 since 언제 이래로 ···해오다 (현재완료 수동태 have been used)

⑥ Evans Carlson, (the U.S. Marine **Corps** leader of the World War II), **admired**

= 동격   주어 Evans Carlson + 동사 admired   admire 존경하다
corps 군단 (ps 묵음)

the **spirit** of the Chinese Industrial **Cooperative** Society during his stay in China.

기백, 정신, 마음, 유령, 영혼, 태도, 기분, 증류주   a. 협동의   그가 중국에 머무는 중

⑦ So, when WW II began, he [1] clipped (these long Chinese-pronounced phrase) to

clip 깎다, 자르다, 오리다 (긴 중국어 발음 구절)을 the two words로 오려내다/줄이다
nail clipper 손톱깎이

the two words 'Gung ho' and [2] took them as a **slogan** for his **battalion**.

채택했다 took + 두 단어를 them + 구호로 as a slogan + 그의 부대를 위한 for his battalion

⑧ Since then, 'Gung ho' has become an unofficial **motto** of the US Marine Corps

그 때 이후 + 현재완료   비공식적인 좌우명   미국 해병대 corps 발음 주의 (ps 묵음)
발음 주의- core 핵심, 씨 (corps와 발음이 같다) corpse 시체 corps 군단, 단체

as an expression of (spirit and "can-do" **attitude**).

( )의 표현으로   기백   할 수 있다는 자세

⑨ Have you never heard of this expression before?

들어본 적이 없습니까 (현재완료 경험)

⑩ 'Gung ho' has been used more **frequently** than you think.

당신이 생각하는 것 보다 더 자주

⑪ The title (of a 1986 comedy film), (directed by Ron Howard), was 'Gung Ho.'

수식
주어 the title 동사 was ( ) 부분은 삽입구

수식
(론하워드가 감독한) 영화 제목은 '겅호'이다.

⑫ You can find a book (titled 'Gung Ho') by (Ken Blanchard and Sheldon Bowles)

수식 ··· a book which is titled ···라는 제목의 (제목이 붙여진) 책

in a bookstore.

⑬ And, there is a Japanese video game company (named 'GungHo Online

··· company which is named ···라는 이름의 (이름이 붙여진) 회사   수식
⑪번 문장은 콤마로 directed by Ron Howard 구절이 삽입된 형식인데, 우리말 번역은 비슷하게 나온다.

Entertainment').

⑭ As you can see, quite a few people are gung ho about this expression 'Gung ho.'

보다시피   quite a few많은 + people 사람들(복수 명사) + are (복수동사)

be gung ho about ···에 열광하다, 열정적이다 = be enthusiastic about

'Gung ho'가 한자라는 거 아세요?

❶ Gung ho는 한자입니다.   ❷ gung(工)은 '일하다', ho(和)는 '함께, 조화'라는 뜻입니다.

❸ 그러니까 'Gung ho'의 단어 그대로의 의미는 '함께 일하다' 입니다.

❹ 하지만 사전을 찾아보면 '매우 열정적인, 열심인'이라고 나와 있습니다.

❺ 사실 'Gung ho'가 영어가 된 건 1942년부터 입니다.

❻ 2차 대전 때 미국 해병대 지휘관이었던 에반스 칼슨은 중국에 머물 때 중국 산업 협동조합의 정신에 감탄했습니다.

❼ 그래서 2차 대전에 참전하자 그는 긴 중국어 발음을 'Gung ho' 두 단어로 짧게 줄이고,
이를 자기 군대의 슬로건으로 삼았습니다.

❽ 그 때 이후 'Gung ho'는 열성과 '할 수 있다'는 태도의 표현으로 미 해병대의 비공식적인 모토가 되었습니다.

❾ 이 표현을 들어본 적이 없다고요?   ❿ 'Gung ho'는 생각보다 많이 쓰입니다.

⑪ 론 하워드 감독의 1986년 코미디 영화 제목이 'Gung Ho'였습니다.

⑫ 켄 블랜차드와 셸든 보울즈가 쓴 'Gung Ho'라는 책도 서점에 있습니다.

⑬ 그리고 'GungHo Online Entertainment'라는 일본의 비디오 게임 회사도 있습니다.

⑭ 보시다시피 상당히 많은 사람들이 'Gung ho'라는 표현에 열성적입니다.

Some mice had been living happily in a house for a long time until the owner of the house brought a big fat cat named Cutie. Cutie was misnamed because he was far from being cute. Cutie chased the mice all the time. The mice were so afraid of Cutie that they were having a hard time wandering around the house to find food.

One mouse, named Smartie, raised his hand. He was also misnamed because he was not smart but dumb. So his friends called him Dumb Smartie.

Smartie said, "I've got a great idea. Just put a bell around Cutie's neck so he can't move around without making a ringing sound. If that nasty ugly guy comes near us, we will be able to hear the sound and run away before he catches us."

Then Grandpa Mouse said, "That sounds easy. So when will you put the bell around his neck?"

Startled, Smartie said, "What? Me? No way. I will be surely eaten by Cutie if I try to put a bell around his neck."

"Easier said than done. Your friends don't call you Dumb Smartie for nothing." Grandpa Mouse answered.

Words & Expressions

mice 쥐들(mouse 의 복수형) misname 이름을 잘못 붙이다 be far from ing ...와 거리가 멀다 wander 돌아다니다 dumb 멍청한 ugly 못생긴 nasty 나쁜, 못된 startle 깜짝 놀라다 easier said than done 행동보다 말이 쉽다

1. What is the main idea of the story?

   a. Mice don't stand a chance to defeat cats.

   b. It is easy to say something, but not so easy to do that.

   c. The best way to deal with a big cat is to put a bell around its neck.

   d. Dumb people must not open their mouth to speak.

2. Both Cutie and Smartie were misnamed because _____ .

   a. Cutie was smart and Smartie was cute

   b. they came from China, not the US

   c. Cutie was dumb and Smartie was ugly

   d. Cutie was not cute, Smartie was not smart

3. Choose the correct words for each sentence.

   a. It should be 'Seoul', not 'Soul.' The name of the city is <u>misnamed</u> / <u>misspelled</u> / <u>misplaced</u> on the map.

   b. My brother can do rope skipping without <u>touch</u> / <u>touching</u> / <u>he touches</u> the ground.

   c. The <u>startling</u> / <u>startled</u> / <u>startle</u> students started to scream loudly, and that sound startled their teacher.

Answer **1.** b **2.** d **3.** misspelled ǀ touching ǀ startled

Listening Drill - Dictation

Some mice had been living happily in a house for a long time _____ the owner of the house brought a big fat cat named Cutie. Cutie _____ because he was _____ . Cutie chased the mice all the time. The mice were so afraid of Cutie that they were having a hard time wandering around the house to find food.

One mouse, named Smartie, _____ . He was also misnamed because he was not smart but dumb. So his friends called him Dumb Smartie.

Smartie said, "I've got a great idea. Just put a bell around Cutie's neck so he can't move around without making a ringing sound. If that nasty ugly guy _____ us, we will be able to hear the sound and run away _____."

Then Grandpa Mouse said, "That _____ . So when will you put the bell around his neck?"

_____ , Smartie said, "What? Me? No way. I _____ Cutie if I try to put a bell around his neck."

"Easier said than done. Your friends don't call you Dumb Smartie _____ ." Grandpa Mouse answered.

Did You Know The Meaning Of 'Easier Said Than Done'?

1 Some **mice** had been living happily in a house for a long time

Cutie가 등장한 것(과거 brought)보다 쥐들이 행복하게 살았던 건 그 이전 과거 (과거완료 had been living)
mouse 쥐 - mice 쥐들 (louse 이, 머릿니 - lice 이들)

until the owner of the house brought (a big fat cat named Cutie).

…하기 까지 (그 전까지)　　　　　　　　　　　　　　　　　　수식　　　　　Cutie라는 이름의 크고 뚱뚱한 고양이

2 Cutie was **misnamed** because he was **far from** being cute.

be misnamed 이름이 잘못 지어지다　　　　…와 거리가 멀다 (+ 명사, 동명사) = He was anything but cute.
(주어 입장에서 이름을 부여 받는 것이므로 수동)

3 Cutie **chased** the mice all the time.

뒤쫓다　　　　　　　　　항상 always

4 The mice were so afraid of Cutie that they were having a hard time wandering around

so 형용사 that 주어+동사　　　　　　　　have a hard time -ing …하는데 어려움을 겪다
너무 (형용사)해서 that…하다 - Cutie가 너무 무서워서 that… 했다 wander around 돌아다니다

the house to find food.

5 One mouse, (named Smartie), raised his hand.

＝동격　　　　　손을 들다 raise a hand　돈을 모으다 raise money
눈썹을 치켜 뜨다 raise eyebrows　목소리를 높이다 raise voice

6 He was also **misnamed** because he was not **smart** but **dumb**.

misnomer 잘못 붙여진(지어진) 명칭, 이름, 부적절한 단어　　　똑똑하지 않고 멍청한 (not A but B)
이 지문 내용 상 Smartie, Cutie 모두 misnomer라고 할 수 있다.

7 So his friends called him **Dumb** Smartie.

dumb a. 말을 못 하는, 멍청한 dumbo 멍텅구리 play dumb 멍청한 척(모르는 척)하다 (b 묵음)

8 Smartie said, "I've got a great idea.

9 Just put a bell around Cutie's neck so he can't move around without making

명령문 (주어 생략) + 동사의 현재형　　　　　　　without + 명사, 동명사 (종 울리는 소리를 내지 않고)
put… so… 목에 방울 달아라, 그러면

a ringing sound.

10 If (that **nasty ugly** guy) comes near us, we will be able to [1] hear the sound and

가정법 현재 주어 ( ) 동사의 현재형 comes, 주어 will 동사원형 be　　will be able to [1] hear and [2] run
nasty 못된 ugly 못생긴　　　　　　　　　할 수 있을 것이다 (be able to = can) will can (조동사 2개를 연이어 쓰지 않는다)

[2] run away before he catches us."

시간의 부사절 - 현재형 동사가 미래 시제를 대신 (catches)
'이따가 밥을 못 먹으면, 나는 울 것이다.' 우리말로도 이따가 있을 미래의 일이지만 현재시제 '못 먹으면'으로 표현하듯,
영어에서도 '그가 우리를 잡으면 (he 3인칭 단수 + catches 현재)'으로 표현한다.

⑪ Then Grandpa Mouse said, "That sounds easy.

쉽게 들린다 (That seems easy. 쉬워 보이다)

⑫ So when will you put the bell around his neck?"

⑬ **Startled**, Smartie said, "What? Me? No way.

startle(깜짝 놀라게 하다)의 주체는 Smartie   안 된다
놀란 Smartie가 말했다. (주어 + be startled (수동태 형태로) 주어가 놀라다)

⑭ I will be surely eaten by Cutie if I try to put a bell around his neck."

가정법 현재 (if절이 뒤에 옴) 주어 will 동사원형, if 주어 동사의 현재형
will be + 부사 (surely) + pp (eaten) 분명 잡아먹힐 것이다

⑮ "Easier said than done.

행동보다 말이 더 쉽다
It is easier to say than to do. = Saying is easier than doing. = It's easy to say, but it's hard to do.

⑯ Your friends don't call you Dumb Smartie for nothing." Grandpa Mouse answered.

너를 괜히(이유 없이) 멍청한 똘똘이라 부르는 게 아니다 – 멍청한 똘똘이라 부를 만하다
People don't admire this guy for nothing. He is a hero. 사람들이 그를 괜히 존경하는 게 아니다. 그는 영웅이다.

'Easier said than done'의 의미를 아세요?

❶ 쥐들은 집 주인이 '귀염둥이'라는 이름의 크고 살찐 고양이를 데려오기 전까지 집에서 행복하게 살았습니다.   ❷ 귀염둥이는 전혀 귀엽지 않기 때문에 이름이 잘못 붙여진 겁니다.   ❸ 귀염둥이는 노상 쥐들을 쫓아다녔습니다.   ❹ 쥐들은 귀염둥이가 너무 무서워서 음식을 찾으려 집안을 돌아다니기가 힘들었습니다.

❺ 똘똘이라는 이름의 쥐가 손을 들었습니다.   ❻ 그 쥐 역시 이름이 잘못 지어졌는데 똘똘하지 않고 멍청하기 때문입니다.
❼ 그래서 친구들은 그를 멍청한 똘똘이라고 부릅니다.

❽ 똘똘이가 말하기를 "제게 좋은 생각이 있습니다.   ❾ 귀염둥이 목에 방울을 달면 녀석은 방울 소리를 내지 않고 움직일 수 없게 됩니다.   ❿ 못생기고 끔찍한 그 녀석이 우리 근처에 오면 우리는 소리를 듣고 녀석이 우리를 잡기 전에 도망칠 수 있습니다."

⑪ 그러자 할아버지 쥐가 말하기를 "그거 쉽구먼.   ⑫ 그럼 자네가 언제 고양이 목에 방울을 달 건가?"   ⑬ 똘똘이가 화들짝 놀라며 말하기를 "뭐라고요? 제가요? 그건 안 됩니다.   ⑭ 녀석의 목에 방울을 달려다 귀염둥이에게 잡아먹힐 게 확실하니까요."

⑮ "실천하기보다 말이 쉽지.   ⑯ 자네 친구들이 자네를 괜히 멍청한 똘똘이라고 부르는 게 아니라네," 할아버지 쥐가 대답했습니다.

It was Harry's seventh birthday. Harry was so excited and happy. Then things started to go wrong, but that's not his fault. He just did what he was told to do. He blew out the candles on a chocolate cake because his dad told him to do so. But, his blowing force was a bit strong, so his grandma, sitting on the opposite side, was covered with chocolate cream.

"Sorry, Grandma. I blew it," he apologized.

"Yes, you did," Grandma answered, wiping her face with a paper towel.

Then Harry blew up the balloons because his mom told him to do so. But, his blowing force was kind of strong, so the balloons popped and his little sister cried.

"Sorry, sis. I blew it," he apologized again.

"Yes, you did," his mom replied, comforting his crying sister.

His family should have been careful, then, when telling him to blow the little toy trumpet. Unfortunately Harry blew it hard, although he didn't meant to hurt his mom's ear.

"Sorry mom. I blew it," he apologized.

"Yes, you really did," his dad replied, taking his mom to the hospital.

Words & Expressions

go wrong 잘못되다 fault 잘못, 실수 blow out candles 초를 입으로 불어 끄다 blowing force 후- 부는 힘
apologize 사과하다 paper towel 키친 타올 comfort 달래다, 위로하다 reply 대답하다

Understanding Checkpoint

1. What can be the best title of this story?

    a. Mommy, The Promise Breaker

    b. Daddy, The Trumpet Maker

    c. Harry, The Super-Breath Boy

    d. Granny, The Party Pooper

2. According to the passage, which sentence is <u>wrong</u>?

    a. Harry's grandma attended his birthday party.

    b. The problem was that Harry looked for trouble and didn't do what he was told to do.

    c. It seemed that Harry's birthday party was over earlier than expected.

    d. Harry's grandma was covered with chocolate cream on her face.

3. Choose the correct words for each sentence.

    a. Some people say 'do as I say, not as I do.' But I say, 'do as I <u>was told you to do</u> / <u>tell you not</u> / <u>tell you to do</u>, not as you want to do.'

    b. I am sorry about lying to you. I <u>should let</u> / <u>should have let</u> / <u>shouldn't have let</u> you know the truth.

    c. As soon as I <u>apologize</u> / <u>apology</u> / <u>apologized</u> him about my mistake, he answered, 'your apology is accepted.'

Answer **1.** c **2.** b **3.** tell you to do | should have let | apologized

Listening Drill – Dictation

It was Harry's seventh birthday. Harry was so excited and happy. Then things
    , but that's not his fault. He just did what he was told to do. He
    on a chocolate cake because his dad   . But, his blowing force was a bit strong, so his grandma, sitting   , was covered with chocolate cream.

"Sorry, Grandma. I blew it," he   .

"Yes, you did," Grandma answered, wiping her face with a paper towel.

Then Harry   because his mom told him to do so. But, his blowing force was kind of strong, so the balloons popped and his little sister cried.

"Sorry, sis. I blew it," he apologized again.

"Yes, you did," his mom replied, comforting his crying sister.

His family   , then, when telling him to   .

Unfortunately Harry blew it hard, although he   hurt his mom's ear.

"Sorry mom. I blew it," he apologized.

"Yes, you really did," his dad   , taking his mom to the hospital.

423

Did You Know The Meaning Of 'Blow It'?

1 It was Harry's seventh birthday.

2 Harry was so **excited** and happy.

사람 주어 be excited 주어가 신이 나다　　　He was excited. 그는 신이 났다.
사물 주어 be exciting 주어는 신난다/재미있다　　His book was exciting. 그의 책은 재미있었다.

3 Then things started to go wrong, but that's not his fault.

일이 잘못되다 things go wrong　　start to go wrong 잘못되기 시작하다

4 He just did what he was told to do.

선행사를 포함한 관계 대명사 what - do things that he was told to do 그가 하라고 들은 그것을 하다

5 He blew out the candles on a chocolate cake because his dad told him to do so.

초의 촛불을 숨을 내쉬어 끄다
blow 불다 (blow-blew-blown) - 촛불을 후 불다, 나팔 등 악기를 불다, 풍선을 불다
blow it 일을 망치다 (it이 특정한 무언가를 지칭하는 게 아니라 blew it 관용 표현)

6 But, his blowing force was a bit strong, so his grandma, (sitting

부는 힘　　= a little bit 좀, 약간　　수식
his grandma who was sitting 앉아 있던 할머니 ( ) 삽입구
so 이하 절 his grandma was covered 할머니가 뒤집어 썼다

on the **opposite** side), was covered with chocolate cream.

반대편의　　be covered with …를 뒤집어 쓰다, 뒤덮다 (수동)

7 "Sorry, Grandma. I blew it," he **apologized**.

내가 망쳤다 + 초를 불었다 (2가지 의미 가능)　　apologize v. 사과하다 apology n. 사과

8 "Yes, you did," Grandma answered, wiping her face with a paper towel.

주어 일치, 생략 while she wiped 얼굴을 닦으며　　우리말 키친타올 = paper towel 종이수건

9 Then Harry blew up the balloons because his mom told him to do so.

촛불을 불어서 끄다 blow out / 풍선을 불다 blow up

10 But, his blowing force was kind of strong, so the balloons **popped** and

a bit = kind of 약간, 좀　　터지다 (pop-popped-popped)
pop corn (옥수수 터트린 것) 팝콘 pop-eyed (눈이 터질 듯 커진) 눈이 휘둥그레진

his little sister cried.

11 "Sorry, sis. I **blew it**," he **apologized** again.

sis = sister　　실수하다, 망치다　　apologize v. 사과하다 aprology n. 사과
bro = brother

⑫ "Yes, you did," his mom replied, **comforting** his crying sister.

주어 일치 생략 while she comforted 달래며

⑬ His family should have been careful, then, when telling him to blow

···했어야 했는데 그러지 않았다   주어 일치 생략 when they (his family) told
I shouldn't have lied to you. 너에게 거짓말을 하지 말았어야 했는데 거짓말을 했다.
You should have done it by now. 지금은 네가 이것을 끝냈어야 하는데 그러지 않았다.

the little toy trumpet.

⑭ Unfortunately Harry blew it hard, although he didn't meant to hurt his mom's ear.

나팔/악기 등을 부는 건 전치사 없이 blow   다치게 할 의도는 없었다
blow the trumpet hard 세게/힘차게 나팔을 불다

⑮ "Sorry mom. I blew it," he apologized.

⑯ "Yes, you really did," his dad replied, taking his mom to the hospital.

주어 일치 생략 while he took (엄마를 병원에) 데려가며

'Blow it'의 의미를 아세요?

❶ 해리의 일곱 번째 생일이었습니다.   ❷ 해리는 신이 났고 행복했습니다.   ❸ 그러다 일이 잘못 되기 시작했는데, 그건 그의 잘못이 아니었습니다.   ❹ 해리는 시키는 대로 했을 뿐이었습니다.   ❺ 아빠가 촛불을 불라고 해서 해리는 초콜릿 케이크 위의 초를 불어 껐습니다.   ❻ 문제는 부는 힘이 다소 강해서 맞은편에 앉아 있던 할머니가 초콜릿 크림을 뒤집어 쓰게 되었습니다.

❼ "할머니, 죄송해요. 제가 망쳤어요,(불었어요)" 해리가 사과했습니다.
❽ "그렇구나," 할머니는 키친 타올로 얼굴을 닦으며 대답했습니다.

❾ 해리가 풍선을 분 것도 엄마가 그렇게 하라고 했기 때문이었습니다.   ❿ 하지만 부는 힘이 약간 강해서 풍선이 죄다 터져 버렸고 어린 여동생이 울었습니다.

⓫ "미안하다, 동생아. 내가 망쳤어,(불었어)" 해리가 다시 사과했습니다.
⓬ "그렇구나," 엄마가 우는 동생을 달래며 대답했습니다.

⓭ 가족들은 그에게 작은 장난감 나팔을 불라고 말할 때 조심했어야 했습니다.   ⓮ 불행히도 엄마 귀를 다치게 할 생각은 아니었지만 해리는 나팔을 세게 불었습니다.

⓯ "엄마, 죄송해요. 제가 망쳤어요,(불었어요)" 해리는 사과했습니다.
⓰ "정말 그렇구나," 아빠는 이렇게 대답하며 엄마를 병원에 데려갔습니다.

Chris knew something was wrong but didn't know what was wrong. He was late for work, so he had to run to the subway station. While running, he noticed several people were looking at him. When he hopped on the subway, several people glanced sideways at him again. While he took the elevator in his office building, people standing behind him giggled quietly. Chris was a little upset, but he didn't have time to find out what was going on, so he just rushed to his office.

When he entered the office, everybody simultaneously looked at him. He couldn't stand it anymore. "What is it? Why is everybody looking at me with a weird look?"

But no one would step forward to say what was going on.

"Please, come on, just spill the beans."

Then his co-workers began to open their mouths, one by one.

"Um... Your fly is down."

"And your pants are ripped in the back."

"There is a large chunk of cheese in your hair."

"And... you are wearing mismatched socks."

Understanding Checkpoint

1. What can be the best title of this story?

    a. Never Wear Mismatched Socks

    b. Chris, The Bean Spiller, Finally Arrested!

    c. No Wonder Everybody Was Looking At Him

    d. Chris Fed Up With His Rude Co-workers

2. Everybody looked at him with a weird look because _____ .

    a. he was wearing a Pororo tie

    b. beans he spilled accidently were expensive

    c. he arrived at his office very early

    d. there's something seriously wrong with his appearance

3. Choose the correct words for each sentence.

    a. When I wear this pair of jeans, I look like <u>a chunk of</u> / <u>a pack of</u> / <u>a bowl of</u> meat.

    b. Put all your belongings <u>step by step</u> / <u>from time to time</u> / <u>one by one</u> on your desk. I have to check them carefully.

    c. Yesterday, when my <u>fly</u> / <u>flew</u> / <u>flying</u> was open, a small fly flew into its hole.

Answer **1.** c **2.** d **3.** a chunk of ┃ one by one ┃ fly

Listening Drill – Dictation

Chris knew _____ but didn't know _____ . He was late for work, so he had to run to the subway station. While running, he noticed several people were looking at him. When he _____ the subway, several people _____ him again. While _____ in his office building, people standing behind him _____ quietly. Chris was a little upset, but he didn't have time to find out what was going on, so he just rushed to his office.

When he entered the office, everybody _____ looked at him. He couldn't stand it anymore. "What is it? Why is everybody looking at me with a weird look?"

But no one would _____ say what was going on.

"Please, come on, just spill the beans."

Then his co-workers began to open their mouths, one by one.

"Um... Your _____ ."

"And your pants are ripped in the back."

"There is a large chunk of cheese in your hair."

"And··· you are wearing _____ ."

427

Did You Know The Meaning Of 'Spill The Beans'?

❶ Chris knew something was wrong but didn't know what was wrong.
무언가 잘못되다   무엇이 잘못된 것인지를 (선행사를 포함한 관계대명사)

❷ He was late for work, so he had to run to the subway station.

❸ While running, he noticed several people were looking at him.
while he ran / while he was running 주어 일치 생략

❹ When he **hopped** on the subway, several people **glanced** sideways **at** him again.
폴짝 뛰어서 지하철을 타다   비스듬히 sideways + 곁눈질로 보다 glance + 그를 at him

❺ While he took the elevator in his office building, (people standing behind him)
엘리베이터를 타다   ↑ 수식   (people who stood behind him 그 뒤에 서 있던 사람들) + 조용히 웃었다

giggled quietly.
giggle 피식 웃다, 키득거리다 chuckle 낄낄웃다 smile 미소짓다

❻ Chris was a little **upset**, but he didn't have time to (find out what was going on),
a. 속상한   …할 시간이 있다 (to 동사원형) (무슨 일인지 알아보다)

so he just rushed to his office.
…로 달려가다, 서둘러 가다

❼ When he entered the office, everybody **simultaneously** looked at him.
동시에, 일제히
주절과 종속절의 주어가 다르기 때문에 (he / everybody) when entering으로 쓸 수 없다.

❽ He couldn't **stand** it anymore.
stand 1. 서다 2. (부정문) 견디다, 참다

❾ "What is it? Why is everybody looking at me with a **weird** look?"
이상한 표정으로

❿ But no one would step forward to say (what was going on).
나서서 말하다, 말하려고 앞으로 나서다   (무슨 일인지)

⓫ "Please, come on, just **spill the beans**."
비밀을 털어놓다 (beans 항상 복수) Spill the beans! 또는 그냥 Spill! 이라고도 한다.

⑫ Then his co-workers began to open their mouths, one by one.
입을 열다, 말하다　　　　　　　하나씩, 한 명씩

⑬ "Um... Your **fly** is down."
fly n. 파리, 바지 지퍼　v. 날다 (fly-flew-flown / flying)　　fly is open = fly is down 바지 지퍼 열리다

⑭ "And your **pants** are ripped in the back."
pants 바지, glasses 안경 - 항상 복수
be ripped in the back 엉덩이 부분이 찢어지다 (수동)

⑮ "There is a large **chunk** of cheese in your hair."
cheese는 불가산 명사로 세는 단위에 복수를 표현 two chunks of cheese 치즈 두 덩어리

⑯ "And⋯ you are wearing mismatched socks."
몸에 두르거나 입을 때 wear　　　짝짝이 양말
- wear socks, wear pants, wear glasses, wear a hat, wear a bandage, wear an eye patch

'Spill the beans'의 의미를 아세요?

❶ 크리스는 무언가 잘못되었다는 건 알았지만 뭐가 잘못되었는지는 몰랐습니다.　　　❷ 그는 출근이 늦어서 지하철까지 달려 가야 했습니다.　　　❸ 달려가는 동안 몇몇 사람들이 자신을 쳐다본다는 걸 알았습니다.　　　❹ 지하철에 뛰어 올랐을 때에도 일부 사람들이 다시 자신을 곁눈질했습니다.　　　❺ 사무실 건물의 엘리베이터에 탔더니 그의 뒤에 서있던 사람들이 작은 소리 로 웃었습니다.　　　❻ 크리스는 좀 짜증이 났지만 무슨 일인지 알아볼 시간이 없어서 사무실로 급히 뛰어 들어갔습니다.

❼ 사무실 안에 들어가니 모든 사람들이 일제히 그를 쳐다보았습니다.　　　❽ 그는 더 이상 참을 수 없었습니다.

❾ "뭡니까? 왜 모두들 이상한 표정으로 나를 쳐다보는 겁니까?"

❿ 하지만 아무도 나서서 무슨 일인지 말하려 들지 않았습니다.

⑪ "제발 무슨 일인지 털어 놓아보세요."

⑫ 그러자 동료들이 한 명 씩 입을 열었습니다.

⑬ "어... 당신 바지 지퍼가 내려갔어요."　　　⑭ "그리고 바지 뒤가 뜯어졌어요."　　　⑮ "머리카락에 큰 치즈 덩어리가 묻 어 있고요."　　　⑯ "그리고 짝짝이 양말을 신고 있어요."

There's a little boy who wets his pants quite often inadvertently. He knew that it was embarrassing, but he couldn't help it. One day, this boy's family attended a family reunion.

Before they left home, his dad said to him, "Hey, son. Mind your P's and Q's. Whatever you do, don't forget to behave yourself, OK?"

"Dad, I don't want to go. What if I wet my pants again? Surely all the other cousins will laugh at me." He sounded like he was about to cry.

"Um... First and foremost, don't try to hold your urine in. If you even slightly feel like you need to go for a pee, do not hesitate and rush to the toilet," replied his dad.

"But I can't go to an unfamiliar toilet alone." he said.

"Just cue me. The moment you cue me, I will stop whatever I'm doing and go to the toilet with you."

"So all I have to do is to mind my pee and cue."

"As I told you, mind your P's and Q's."

Understanding Checkpoint

1. What can be the best title of this story?
   a. A Wet Blanket Wet His Pants
   b. Mind Pee And Que Instead of P's And Q's
   c. Oops! The Boy Did It Again
   d. Stop Whatever You Do

2. The boy didn't want to go to the family reunion since _____ .
   a. he couldn't behave himself
   b. his cousins would surely laugh at him
   c. he was worried about wetting his pants in front of his family
   d. he couldn't go to the unfamiliar toilet

3. Choose the correct words for each sentence.
   a. I can see <u>familiar</u> / <u>unfamiliar</u> / <u>similar</u> faces among those people. I think I have never met them before.
   b. I told the police, "He is not dead yet, but he <u>is about to be</u> / <u>is going to dead</u> / <u>must have died</u>. He is dying!"
   c. You can do <u>however</u> / <u>whoever</u> / <u>whatever</u> you want and leave whenever you wish.

   Answer **1.** b **2.** c **3.** unfamiliar ⏐ is about to be ⏐ whatever

Listening Drill – Dictation

There's a little boy who _____ quite often inadvertently. He knew that it was embarrassing, but he _____. One day, this boy's family attended a family reunion.

Before they left home, his dad said to him, "Hey, son. Mind your P's and Q's. Whatever you do, don't forget to _____, OK?"

"Dad, I don't want to go. _____ I wet my pants again? Surely all the other cousins will laugh at me." He sounded like he was about to cry.

"Um… _____, don't try to _____ your urine in. If you even _____ feel like you need to _____, do not hesitate and rush to the toilet," replied his dad.

"But I can't go to an unfamiliar toilet alone." he said.

"Just cue me. The moment you cue me, I will _____ and go to the toilet with you."

"So all I have to do is to mind my pee and cue."

"As I told you, _____."

431

Did You Know The Meaning Of 'Mind One's P's And Q's'?

1 There's a little boy who wets his pants quite often inadvertently.

바지에 오줌 싸다 　　 quite 꽤 + often 자주 + inadvertently 자기도 모르게

2 He knew that it was embarrassing, but he couldn't help it.

사람 주어 be embarrassed 주어가 창피해하다 　 어찌할 수 없다
사람이 아닌 주어 be embarrassing 주어는 창피한 것이다

3 One day, this boy's family attended a family reunion.

가족 모임에 참석하다 (school reunion 동창회)

4 Before they left home, his dad said to him, "Hey, son. Mind your P's and Q's.

leave 떠나다, 뒤에 남기다 (이 문장은 '떠나다'의 과거형 left) 　　 = behave oneself 예의 바르게 행동하다

5 Whatever you do, don't forget to behave yourself, OK?"

무엇을 하든 간에 　　 don't forget to 동사 : (미래에) 할 것을 잊지 마라
whoever you meet 누구를 만나든 간에 whenever you arrive here 언제 여기 도착하든 간에
whichever he chooses 그가 무엇을 선택하든 간에 wherever she lives 그녀가 어디에 살든 간에

6 "Dad, I don't want to go.

7 What if I wet my pants again?

만약 …한다면? What if 주어 + 동사의 현재 (What if she doesn't come home? 만약 그녀가 집에 안 온다면?)

8 Surely all the other cousins will laugh at me."

사촌 　　 laugh 웃다 laugh at 비웃다
He laughs. 그는 웃는다. He laughs at me 그가 나를 비웃다.
He laughs with me. 그가 나와 함께 웃다.

9 He sounded like he was about to cry.

…처럼 들리다 　　 울기 직전이다
(seem like …처럼 보이다)

10 "Um... First and foremost, don't try to hold (your urine) in.

가장 중요한 것은 　　 hold ( ) in ( )를 참다, 안에 담다

11 If you even slightly feel like you need to go for a pee,

심지어 even 조금이라도 slightly …라고 느끼다 feel like 　 소변보러 가다

1) do not hesitate and 2) rush to the toilet," replied his dad.

망설이지 말고 　　 화장실로 달려라

432

⑫ "But I can't go to an unfamiliar toilet alone." he said.

familiar 낯익은, 익숙한 unfamiliar 낯선 (similar 비슷한 – 철자 혼동 주의)

⑬ "Just **cue** me.

cue n. (무언가 하라는) 신호, (연극, 영화에서 배우게 보내는 신호) 큐
v. (무언가 하라고) 신호를 보내다 (이 문장은 동사 '신호를 보내다')

⑭ **The moment you cue me,** I will ¹⁾ stop (whatever I'm doing) and ²⁾ go to the toilet

the moment 주어 동사 …하는 순간   (무엇을 하고 있든) 멈추고
= as soon as you cue me 나에게 신호를 보내자마자

with you."

⑮ "So all I have to do is to **mind** my pee and cue."

mind one's Ps and Qs가 원래 속담이고, 발음이 비슷하게 변형한 표현
mind n. 마음, 정신, 생각 v. 언짢아하다, 조심하다, 신경쓰다
Mind your own business 네 일이나 신경 써라
I don't mind. 나는 신경 쓰지 않는다. (괜찮다, 싫지 않다)

⑯ "As I told you, mind your P's and Q's."

('Mind one's P's and Q's'의 의미를 아세요?)

❶ 자기도 모르게 바지에 오줌을 자주 싸는 어린 소년이 있었습니다.

❷ 창피하다는 건 잘 알고 있었지만 소년도 어쩔 수가 없었습니다.   ❸ 어느 날 소년의 가족은 가족 모임을 갖게 되었습니다.

❹ 집을 출발하기 전, 아버지가 소년에게 말하기를 "아들아, 예의바르게 행동해라.

❺ 무슨 일을 하든 예의 있게 행동하는 거 잊지 말아야 해. 알겠지?"   ❻ "아빠, 저는 가기 싫어요.

❼ 또 바지에 오줌을 싸면 어떻게 해요?   ❽ 분명 다른 사촌들 모두 저를 비웃을 거예요."

❾ 소년의 말은 금방이라도 울 것처럼 들렸다.   ❿ "그럼… 무엇보다 소변을 참으면 안 돼.

⑪ 조금이라도 소변보고 싶은 마음이 들면 주저하지 말고 화장실로 달려가라," 아빠가 대답했습니다.

⑫ "하지만 저는 낯선 화장실은 혼자 못 간다고요," 소년이 말했습니다.   ⑬ "나한테 신호를 보내.

⑭ 네가 신호를 보내자마자 나는 무슨 일이든 하던 일을 멈추고 너랑 화장실을 갈 테니."

⑮ "그럼 제가 할 일은 오줌에 신경 쓰고 신호를 보내는(mind my pee and cue) 거네요."

⑯ "내가 뭐랬니, 예의 바르게 행동하면(mind your P's and Q's) 된다고 했잖니."

MEMO

MEMO